APACHE
SERVER
SURVIVAL GUIDE

Manuel Alberto Ricart

201 West 103rd Street
Indianapolis, Indiana 46290

To Diana, Julisa, and Isabella

COPYRIGHT © 1996 BY SAMS.NET PUBLISHING

PRESIDENT, SAMS.NET PUBLISHING	*Richard K. Swadley*
PUBLISHING TEAM LEADER	*Dean Miller*
MANAGING EDITOR	*Cindy Morrow*
DIRECTOR OF MARKETING	*John Pierce*
ASSISTANT MARKETING MANAGERS	*Kristina Perry, Rachel Wolfe*

ACQUISITIONS EDITOR
Grace Buechlein

DEVELOPMENT EDITOR
Brian-Kent Proffitt

SOFTWARE DEVELOPMENT SPECIALIST
Cari Skaggs

PRODUCTION EDITOR
Colleen Williams

COPY EDITORS
Kim Hannel
Kate Shoup
Kitty Wilson

INDEXER
Tim Griffin
Cheryl Dietsch
Johnna L. VanHoose

TECHNICAL REVIEWER
Randy Terbush
Karl Garrison
Matt Liggett

EDITORIAL COORDINATOR
Bill Whitmer

TECHNICAL EDIT COORDINATOR
Lynette Quinn

EDITORIAL ASSISTANTS
Carol Ackerman
Andi Richter
Rhonda Tinch-Mize

COVER DESIGNER
Jay Corpus

BOOK DESIGNER
Alyssa Yesh

COPY WRITER
Peter Fuller

PRODUCTION TEAM SUPERVISOR
Brad Chinn

PRODUCTION
Stephen Adams, Debra Bolhuis, Jeanne Clark, Jason Hand, Daniel Harris, Sonja Hart, Chris Livengood, Carl Pierce, Casey Price, Lauri Robbins, Bobbi Satterfield, Janet Seib, Mark Walchle

Overview

Contents

10 Apache Modules   185

PART IV   KEEPING UP: WEB SERVER SYSTEM ADMINISTRATION

PART V   SECURITY: OPTIONS AND PROCEDURES

14 Secure Web Servers   317

15 Access Control and User Authentication   337

Acknowledgments

Writing and developing the material in this book was one of my most interesting experiences in recent memory— not that I can remember much else at the moment. This project literally fell into my hands as the result of a press release my software development company, SmartSoft, Inc., published on Usenet in late April 1996. On April 23, 1996 I received an e-mail from Grace Buechlein, acquisitions editor, inquiring as to my interest to contribute to books on Web servers, to which I responded by explaining I also had a Web consulting business (accessLINK, inc.) dedicated to all the ins and outs of Web technology.

Life since then has been nonstop. The monumental task of writing and developing this book while at the same time trying to keep up with daily business was a very interesting experience. These three months probably squeezed a year out of me, but also packed the most joy in a while. Juggling the book, a new baby, a teaching trip to a different part of the world, plus all the work of a small office has provided a very interesting and intense ride indeed.

Writing a book requires support from many people. In order of appearance, I would like to thank Grace for giving me the opportunity to accomplish this and for never losing faith. To Chris Gonderzik who developed many of the CGI examples that you see in this book and provided an always available helping hand for research and discussion, and whom I can never thank enough. Chris is the leading engineer at accessLINK for Web-based technologies. To Jim for always keeping faith. Additional thanks go to Brian Proffitt, Colleen Williams, and the other editors at Sams.net for making sure my words really said what I meant. Special thanks go to Ryan Brooks, who is always available regardless of the network status, especially during those weird hours of the night when router lights blink inexplicably.

And last but not least, to my wife Diana who has gone through the joys and pains of being a mother for a second time while this book was being written, and to whom I have not been able to help as I should have. And to our two beautiful daughters, Julisa and Isabella, whom I didn't get to play with this summer. I promise to make it up to you all. Thank you for letting me do these things.

And to you for buying this book. Have fun setting up your Apache Web server!

About the Authors

Manuel Alberto Ricart is one of the founders of accessLINK, inc., a high-technology firm that provides Internet and Web consulting services worldwide.

Alberto has been involved with computers since the late 70s when he was introduced to programming on a then state-of-the-art IBM system 32, which had a whopping 32KB of RAM and a tiny hard disk. Since then, Alberto has developed software products for Macintosh and NeXTSTEP, as well as provided UNIX and PC system administration support to a wide range of clients since the mid-80s.

In 1992, he founded a software company, SmartSoft, Inc., that develops a wide range of commercial shrink-wrap software for NeXTSTEP/OPENSTEP (UNIX) operating systems. Their products are sold worldwide.

In 1995, he co-founded a second firm dedicated to building Internet solutions that enable companies to harness the Internet for business. Their technologies range from simple static Web publishing to dynamic content-driven Web systems that use database sources for their information infrastructure. AccessLINK also provides a number of hosting products and services.

Alberto specializes in Internet and Web core technologies such as the Apache Web server and all other technologies required to support it, such as UNIX network connectivity, administration, training, and support. Other responsibilities include the invention and design of software products and tools.

Alberto can be reached at `aricart@accessLINK.com` where he can usually be found tinkering with computers and software all day long.

TELL US WHAT YOU THINK!

As a reader, you are the most important critic and commentator of our books. We value your opinion and want to know what we're doing right, what we could do better, what areas you'd like to see us publish in, and any other words of wisdom you're willing to pass our way. You can help us make strong books that meet your needs and give you the computer guidance you require.

Do you have access to CompuServe or the World Wide Web? Then check out our CompuServe forum by typing GO SAMS at any prompt. If you prefer the World Wide Web, check out our site at http://www.mcp.com.

Note

If you have a technical question about this book, call the technical support line at (800) 571-5840, ext. 3668.

As the team leader of the group that created this book, I welcome your comments. You can fax, e-mail, or write me directly to let me know what you did or didn't like about this book—as well as what we can do to make our books stronger. Here's the information:

FAX: 317/581-4669

E-mail: opsys_mgr@sams.mcp.com

Mail: Dean Miller
          Comments Department
          Sams Publishing
          201 W. 103rd Street
          Indianapolis, IN 46290

Introduction

CONVENTIONS USED IN THIS BOOK

The primary highlighting that you will find throughout the book are tips, notes, technical notes, and warnings.

Tip

Identified in text blocks like this are cool or unusual tips and ideas.

Note

Sections like this identify noteworthy features or highlight key points being covered in the text. This draws your attention to something that should not be overlooked.

Technical Note

This note provides you with specific technical information that goes beyond the regular text.

Warning

Here I warn you against making a mistake, either by overlooking an important step or by doing something that you may otherwise try to do. A mistake here could cause problems later.

Any terms that are code or that are used in the process of creating or using code (such as directives, filenames, and so on) appear in a special `computer` font.

Code and other output examples are presented separately from regular paragraphs and appear in a `computer` typeface. Here is an example:

```
<A NAME="accesslink">This is a text hyperlink to <A HREF="http://www.
➥accesslink.com">accessLINK, inc.</A>
<P>
Graphics can be clickable images with a border:
```

The ➥ symbol in the preceding example is a code continuation character. It signifies that the code on the previous line is continued to the next.

A CD-ROM is included with this book. When an item that appears on the CD-ROM is mentioned in the book, you will see an icon next to the paragraph.

The Apache 1.1 icon directs you to features that are unique to Apache 1.1.

This icon points out features special to Apache 1.2.

In several chapters you will encounter special notation for directives. The following is an example:

Syntax: `AllowOverride [All] | [None] | [AuthConfig][FileInfo][Indexes][Limit][Options]`

In this example, `AllowOverride` is the command. Items inside brackets are *options* to the command. If items are separated by a pipe (|), they are exclusive of any other setting, meaning you can only use one of that option and nothing else. In this example, the only legal options are

◆ `AllowOverride All`

◆ `AllowOverride None`

◆ `AllowOverride AuthConfig` or

◆ `AllowOverride AuthConfig FileInfo Indexes Limit Options`

Items that require an argument (data supplied by the user) are typically set in italics.

Now you should be ready to enter the world of Apache.

- Why the Apache Server?

- Installing and Configuring the Apache Server

- Organizing Your Web Site

PART I

Getting Started: Installation and Configuration

CHAPTER 1

Why the Apache Server?

WHAT IS A WEB SERVER?

A Web server is the server software behind the World Wide Web. It listens for requests from a client, such as a browser like Netscape or Microsoft's Internet Explorer. When it gets one, it processes that request and returns some data. This data usually takes the form of a formatted page with text and graphics. The browser then renders this data to the best of its ability and presents it to the user. Web servers are in concept very simple programs. They wait for requests and fulfill them when received.

Web servers communicate with browsers or other clients using the Hypertext Transfer Protocol (HTTP), which is a simple protocol that standardizes the way requests are sent and processed. This allows a variety of clients to communicate with any vendor's server without compatibility problems.

Most of the documents requested are formatted using Hypertext Markup Language (HTML). HTML is a small subset of another markup language called Standard General Markup Language (SGML), which is in wide use by many organizations and the U.S. Government.

HTML is the lifeblood of the Web. It is a simple markup language used for formatting text. Browsers interpret the markup information and render its intent to the best of their abilities. More importantly, HTML allows linking to different documents and resources; this is the hypertext portion of the Web.

Hypertext allows a user to refer to other documents stored in the same computer or in a computer located in a different part of the world. It allows information to be almost tridimensional. Not only can you read sequentially, but you can jump for more elsewhere.

The information retrieval process is completely transparent to the user; it's easy and free-form. Navigation through this sea of information is in an ad hoc way. While the results and implications of this new learning process are yet to be seen, it sure is powerful. It provides a seamless exploration experience of documents and services. This is what the Web is all about. It allows you to gather information easily and presents it in a way that is easy to digest. It's graphic, and it can combine sound and moving pictures.

You can learn more and find related issues that spark your interest; it's interactive. Instead of paging through a book (still a good thing), you can use the computer to remove much of the legwork associated with retrieving related information, and it allows you to explore the material that fits your needs or mood. It's like TV, but you get to choose the programming.

The Web server is responsible for fetching you this information. While Web servers may have been simple at some point, they are not anymore. All Web servers are not created equal.

If all the sudden you were asked to set up a Web site, you would be confronted with a variety of issues that you would need to resolve before you code your first HTML page. The most important issue, and probably the reason why you bought this book, is deciding which server software to use. Given the myriad of Web servers available, the choice is undoubtedly difficult.

The following is a list of issues that you should use to evaluate any piece of software before you commit work to it:

> Commercial versus freeware
> Ease of installation
> Ease of configuration
> Ease of extending or customizing some aspect of the server
> Features
> Size of the installed base
> Ongoing development
> Performance and resource consumption
> Secure transaction support
> Source code availability
> Technical support
> Platform support
> Third-party support

COMMERCIAL VERSUS FREEWARE

Apache is freeware; therefore, you invariably have to confront the issue of free software. Is free software really cheap? After all, who do you go to if you have problems? What are the odds of the product not being supported? Free software usually has sparse documentation and no direct technical support. However, there are a few software packages out there that are superbly documented, supported, and maintained. In my view, Apache belongs to that list.

EASE OF INSTALLATION

If you have a little understanding about UNIX, know how to use an UNIX editor such as vi, pico, or emacs, and are not afraid of the shell, Apache is a great choice. It is easy to install and configure, even for people who are not too savvy on the UNIX ways. The software is available in two types: precompiled and in source form.

Precompiled binaries are available for

- ◆ AUX 3.1
- ◆ BSDI 2.0
- ◆ FreeBSD 2.1
- ◆ HP-UX 9.07
- ◆ IRIX 5.3
- ◆ Linux
- ◆ NetBSD 1.1
- ◆ NeXTSTEP
- ◆ SolarisX86 2.5
- ◆ Solaris 2.4
- ◆ Solaris 2.5
- ◆ SunOS 4.1.3
- ◆ UnixWare 1.1.2

There's also an OS/2 version. Rumor has it that a Windows NT version of Apache is also in the works. Given the growing popularity of both Apache and Windows NT in corporate networks, such a port would help to capture an even bigger segment of the Web server market.

If your OS/hardware is not available precompiled and you have a UNIX compiler such as GNU's GCC, there are configuration directives for almost every UNIX variant imaginable. All you need to do is set up a few options, type make, and your software will be built. The next chapter walks you through the process of compiling and installing your Apache server.

Installing a Web server—be it through a graphical user interface (GUI)-based Netscape product or Apache—is simple. The GUI tools may give more reassurance to people who are afraid of command line interfaces, but in general, configuration and installation are fairly straightforward in either version. If you are not sure what a configuration value is, more than likely you will be stumped in either presentation. This is where documentation, such as this book, will help you. This book doesn't assume that you know much about UNIX or anything else. However, it will give you enough background to get going and will enlighten you about some of the possibilities. I hope your curiosity awakens.

EASE OF CONFIGURATION

Configuring Apache is very easy to do. Apache utilizes three configuration files; all of which are already preset to safe default behaviors. You just need to specify a few file locations, and name your server so that Apache can find its configuration files and the location of the document tree it is serving. To do this, all you need is a good UNIX text editor that you feel comfortable with. Chances are your version of UNIX has some sort of graphical editor you already feel comfortable with. Chapter 2, "Installing and Configuring the Apache Server," explains all the basic configuration steps you need to take to get your Apache server running fast. It's easy to do.

Ease of Extending or Customizing Some Aspect of the Server

If you are customizing some aspect of the server, you'll love Apache. Its source code is clearly written but is a little thin on the documentation side. The Apache server is implemented as a set of software modules. Creating a new module that modifies the behavior of the server in some way will require less to learn on your part. There's a growing list of freely available third-party modules. More than likely you can find a module that implements the functionality you need.

Features

The Apache server implements the same, if not more, features than the equivalent commercial Web server, and basically every aspect of the Apache server's functionality is configurable. This makes it easy to get the server to behave the way you want or need for your site.

Some of the most important features include the following:

◆ It's a plug-and-play replacement for NCSA Web servers.

◆ Fixes bugs and security holes found on NCSA 1.3 and 1.4 servers.

◆ It's very fast, much faster than NCSA servers.

◆ Compiles better with the current HTTP specifications. By the time you read this, Apache should be unconditionally compliant with HTTP/1.1 specifications.

◆ Apache provides several forms of implementing multihomed and virtual servers. A multihomed server serves requests under various names, such as http://www.x.com and http://www.y.com. Both of which are resident on the same computer and are served by the same process. One of these is a non-IP intensive method that works in conjunction with popular browsers.

◆ You can customize the error responses with the use of files or scripts. The server will intercept an error and display the specified file or execute a CGI that could perform an on-the-fly diagnosis of the problem. This enables your server to return more meaningful error messages to visitors or to perform some special action in response to an error condition.

◆ Apache servers can automatically negotiate content retrieval with a browser and can serve the most appropriate out of various sets of equivalent documents. This allows the server to retrieve the document having the best representation that the client is willing to accept. For example, when serving documents in English and Spanish, depending on your browser settings, Apache will automatically retrieve the version most appropriate for you.

◆ Apache includes an automatic index file selection. You can instruct the server to return any of several resources for directory requests (`http://www.company.com/`). The server will search for a matching index file(s) and return the first one found to the client. Should none of the specified files be found, the server can be configured to produce an automatically generated listing of all the resources available in that directory.

◆ Apache provides several user authentication methods ranging from flat-file user databases, to indexed files and relational database support. Third-party modules allow Apache to interface with many popular network authentication systems.

SIZE OF THE INSTALLED BASE

At the time of this writing, Apache was the leader in the Web server installed base. According to the August 1996 Netcraft survey (`http://www.netcraft.co.uk/Survey/Reports/`), Apache brand Web servers comprised 35.68 percent (37.16 percent if you add all the secure versions of the server) of the Web servers in their survey. That doesn't seem like much until you realize that the competition is far behind, and the entire Web server market is dominated by three products:

Server Brand	Market Share
Apache	35.68%
NCSA	18.25%
Netscape Communications	7.25%
Netscape Commerce	6.83%
CERN	6.22%
Microsoft Internet Information Server	5.49%
WebSite	3.40%
WebSTAR	1.95%
BESTWWWD	1.68%
Apache SSL US	1.43%
Purveyor	1.38%
WebSitePro	1.07%

The other remaining 424 server brands didn't even get one percent of the market share! The Netcraft survey currently includes 342,081 servers. Check the details of the survey for yourself on Netcraft's Web site because this information changes monthly.

ONGOING DEVELOPMENT

The Apache server was originally based on the NCSA code. Its development was started because of some security problems associated with the NSCA server and concerns for having a UNIX Web server that implemented some special features. Also driving the effort was a concern to somehow guarantee that a free UNIX server would always be available to the UNIX community. The Apache group was then formed, which developed a series of patches for the NCSA server—hence the name, Apache, from A PAtCHy server.

The Apache server has undergone several releases since its initial inception. There have been 32 different releases including five beta releases for version 1.1.0—the current version at the time of this writing is 1.1.1. However, by the time this book is printed, version 1.2 should be available. The Apache team develops new revisions faster than I can document. Bug fixes are addressed almost immediately. More importantly, advisories from the Computer Emergency Response Team (CERT) Coordination Center and other parties are corrected immediately to ensure that no security problems are present in the server.

In terms of total code lines, the server has more than doubled from approximately 10,000 lines in its initial NCSA-fixed version, to over 25,000 in its current released incarnation (these counts include comment lines). In its current form, it bears little resemblance to the NCSA server; it's a whole new animal.

While all this performance is not an indication of anything but past performance, the development patterns are there. The main reason for the existence of Apache is to ensure that a freely available UNIX Web server is always available to the UNIX community. Apache was created so that there would be an HTTP server that functioned the way some WWW providers thought it ought to work. After all, many of the Apache programmers have real jobs involved with providing WWW services or Internet connectivity.

PERFORMANCE AND RESOURCE CONSUMPTION

The Apache server offers superior performance over the NCSA server. It has a pre-forking model that manages a configurable amount of child processes. A preforking model is one where server processes are waiting to answer requests. Many servers start a process only when they receive a request. Once the request is fulfilled, the server process dies, requiring this cycle to start all over with the next request.

Under UNIX, forking (launching) a process can be very expensive. It takes time that a busy server doesn't have and creates an impact on the system that further aggravates performance. By preallocating a number of servers to wait for requests, Apache can respond quickly and more efficiently. By reusing already available servers to respond to new requests, Apache is able to gain additional performance because it spends more time serving requests than setting up and cleaning after itself.

Using a conservative approach, the number of children processes changes dynamically. As server demands change, the number of processes is adjusted accordingly. Children processes are reused for a certain number of connections after which the parent server process kills them and recycles those resources with a new process.

Apache also implements a new HTTP 1.1 draft feature: Keep-Alive persistent connections. (Apache 1.2 is fully HTTP/1.1 compliant.) Keep-Alive allows a single TCP connection to serve several requests from a client. The original model instigated a new connection for each request, requiring the overhead of starting and closing a Transmission Control Protocol (TCP) connection with the server for each element in a page. If an HTML page referenced five images, a total of six different requests would be generated. Under the new persistent connection scheme, the six elements are transmitted through the same TCP connection. This approach increases performance on pages that contain multiple images by as much as 50 percent. However, this feature only works with supporting browsers (currently Netscape Navigator, Spyglass, and Microsoft's Internet Explorer). Also, Keep-Alive connections only work if the size of a file is known beforehand, meaning that output from a CGI program doesn't benefit from the new connection model.

SECURE TRANSACTION SUPPORT

The standard Apache release does not provide secure transaction support. However, there are products based on the Apache source code that do (Apache-SSL and Apache-SSL-US). Both of these servers are fully compatible with Netscape's encryption mechanism, and rumor has it that these two products are the reason why the Netscape product offerings were drastically reduced in price.

SOURCE CODE AVAILABILITY

Following UNIX's tradition of source code availability, Apache's source code is distributed with every copy at no extra charge, making it possible to compile your own customized version easily. This allows you to compile a version of Apache for a nonpopular UNIX box. Source code availability invariably plays an important role in UNIX software acceptance. On sites where stringent security is important, system administrators have the ability to examine the source code line by line, thus ensuring no undesirable effects or hidden security risks are present.

TECHNICAL SUPPORT

Great technical support for Apache is available from Usenet at `comp.infosystems.www.servers.unix`. Many members of the Apache team answer questions there regularly.

To search for questions that may have already been asked, surf to `http://www.dejanews.com`. Dejanews is a useful Usenet database. It archives all Usenet newsgroups and has a fast search engine that allows you to find the information you need in seconds. If your question has been asked before, it will be there.

Commercial support for Apache is available through a number of third-party organizations. One of the most popular is available from `http://www.ukweb.com`. However, it is expensive (around $1,500 per year).

THIRD-PARTY SUPPORT

Because of Apache's modular design, many third-party developers have programmed modules to meet their specific needs, such as custom authentication modules, embedded Perl interpreters, SSI scripting extensions, and so on. Chapter 7, "Third-Party Modules," covers many of the more important ones. Chances are good that something you need has already been developed by someone else. If the module you need was not included with the Apache release, you can probably find what you need at

`http://www.zyzzyva.com/erver/module_registry/`

Some of the extensions and modules you'll find there include support for the following:

> Cookie-based authentication
> Support for setting the UID and GID of executing CGI scripts
> User authentication using UNIX system account databases
> Enhanced Server Side Includes (SSI) modules
> Embedded Perl interpreter
> Kerberos-based authentication
> Character set translators
> Postgres95 and mSQL database user authentication modules
> Web page counters
> Extended log formats
> NIS authentication
> URI/URL rewriting modules

Tcl scripting processor
CGI module alternatives

SUMMARY

The most important reason to use Apache should be subjective. It should be based on how Apache fits *you*. Software evaluation is like test-driving a car. You wouldn't buy a car just by looking at the brochure. To feel how you like the server, you need to test-drive it.

Luckily, most of the Web servers out there have some sort of demo version available. Unless you are going to customize some portion of the Apache server, such as writing a custom module, your commitment is small. Should a better product for UNIX appear, your HTML documents would migrate effortlessly. So your risk is minimal. To avoid a crapshoot, test-drive the software and deploy on the basis of your experiences with it. Experience is your best guide.

While it is impossible to determine in a few hours if a solution will be the right one for you, the Internet is a close knit community of software junkies. Make use of the collective knowledge. Ask questions on Usenet and read the frequently asked questions (FAQ).

Apache is the choice for a server at accessLINK, Inc. They were NCSA users in the beginning, but a few features won them over and they have liked Apache ever since. To gain credibility, I don't have any association with the Apache group, save that I use their software and like it very much. The reasons why I use Apache are the subject of this book. Apache provides many features that make it a very powerful Web server. Its continued development has put pressure on even the high-powered brands that are currently available, which were complacent until recently.

CHAPTER 2

Installing and Configuring
the Apache Server

This chapter guides you through the installation and configuration of Apache using a basic setup. You will find the latest stable server software, as well as the latest beta releases of the Apache source distribution, on the Apache group's Web server (http://www.apache.org). (See Figure 2.1.) A copy of the latest release available at the time this book was written (Apache 1.1.1) is included on the CD-ROM that accompanies this book.

If you don't have access to a compiler, you can still install Apache provided that you can find a precompiled version of the server that works with your hardware and operating system. I have included the precompiled servers I found at the Apache group's Web server, including AUX 3.1, BSDI 1.1 and 2.0, FreeBSD 2.1, HPUX 9.07, IRIX 5.3, Linux, NETBSD 1.1, SOLARIS 2.4, SunOS 4.1.3, UNIXWARE 1.1.2., and others.

Figure 2.1.
The Apache home page. Notice this site is mirrored around the world.

The Apache site provides links to various mirror sites from which you can download the software. Choose the one that is geographically closest to you from the various sites listed on the Apache home page.

To install Apache in its default location at /usr/local/etc/httpd, you may need to be the superuser. You'll need to know the root password of the machine in which you are installing Apache. If you don't know how to become root, please contact your local system administrator. Put the distribution archive in the /tmp directory. A sequence of commands to do the installation from /tmp might look like this:

```
mkdirs /usr/local/etc (your system may use 'mkdir -p /usr/local/etc' instead)
cd /usr/local/etc
mv /tmp/apache_1.1.1.tar.gz /usr/local/etc
gzcat apache_1.1.1.tar.gz ¦ tar -xf -
mv apache_1.1.1 httpd
```

If your system does not support gzcat, you may need to do a gunzip -c instead.

Note that depending on the version you are installing, you will be left with a directory called apache_x.x.x. Now you should have a tree under httpd that contains the complete distribution of Apache. This directory tree contains configuration templates and other resources that the server needs for its operation. Be sure not to move or rename any of the files and directories, unless you know what you are doing.

INSTALLING A PRECOMPILED SERVER

Apache has been compiled for many platforms, and chances are that a prebuilt copy of the server exists for your setup. If you are interested in compiling the source, you might want to skip to the section in this chapter titled "Installing from the Source," because it offers information on how to build the Apache HTTP server.

Installing a precompiled server is very similar to installing a source-only distribution. The only difference is that a compiled httpd binary already exists in the server's src directory. The compiled binary of the Apache server is called httpd. On binary distributions, the binary is usually labeled httpd-architecture, where architecture is the name of the OS you are installing. For Linux, the httpd binary is called httpd-linux.

Although it is perfectly fine to keep the binary in the src directory, I like to install the binary at the top of the distribution tree. In this example, that is /usr/local/etc/httpd/httpd. Sometimes, the binary distribution has not been stripped. Stripping removes extra symbol information that the linker left from the compilation linking process. Removing this extra information using strip usually makes the binary about 30 to 40 percent smaller. I also like to protect the executable from any user trying to alter it. An easy way to do this is by changing the owner and group of the executable to root and the group to wheel. Then remove all write privileges to the binary from everyone but the owner. To chown and chmod a file (*ch*ange *own*er and *ch*ange *mod*e) to root, you need to do this as the superuser. The following installation steps might look something like this:

1. cd /usr/local/etc/httpd
2. cp src/httpd-linux httpd
3. strip httpd
4. chown root.wheel httpd
5. chmod 755 httpd

If you are installing a precompiled server, you can skip to the section titled "Runtime Server Configuration Settings."

INSTALLING FROM THE SOURCE

Installing from the source is a little more time-consuming, but it will force you to get familiar with the source distribution of the Apache server. It will also give you the opportunity to customize the modules that are built into Apache. Many of these modules provide functionality that will make your server more powerful. All the files you will need to edit to build the binary are in the src directory. Building from the source is a three-step process:

1. Edit the one-time configuration file, src/Configuration.
2. Run the Configure script.
3. Run make.

EDITING THE CONFIGURATION FILE

Before you can compile the software, you need to edit the configuration file and set some compile-time options that address the peculiarities of your operating system (and, in some cases, the hardware on which you are going to be running the server). Apache supports the concept of modules that extend and enhance the functionality of the server. However, in order for some of these modules to work, they have to be enabled in the configuration file. The configuration file can be found in /usr/local/ etc/httpd/src. To make a copy of the configuration file, type in the following:

```
cd /usr/local/etc/httpd/src
cp Configuration.tmpl Configuration
```

Using your favorite editor, read and edit the configuration file you just created. A listing of the default configuration files is included at the end of this chapter for your reading enjoyment.

I kept all the default settings with the exception of changing the compiler and compilation options to match my hardware and operating system. This is executed by removing the comments (the # signs) from the AUX_CFLAGS and AUX_LIBS definitions found on the configuration file. Remember to comment out (put in a # in front of) other settings that may not apply to your system configuration.

RUNNING THE Configure SCRIPT

After you edit the configuration file, you need to run the Configure script. The Configure script is a Bourne shell script that uses the configuration file you edited (src/Configuration) to generate a new Makefile and modules.c to match the options you set in the compilation configuration file. To do this, type the following into your terminal program:

```
cd /usr/local/etc/httpd/src
./Configure
```

Tip

Configure allows you to specify a configuration file on the command line by using the -file flag:

```
Configure -file NEXTSTEP.configuration
Using alternate config file NEXTSTEP.configuration
```

This feature is useful if you need to maintain various different configurations for several different machines.

RUNNING make

If Configure proceeded normally, you should be able to build the server binary at this point. To build the binary, type this on your terminal:

```
make
```

After a few minutes, depending on the speed of your hardware, you will have a compiled version of the Web server. It is called httpd and is on the /usr/local/etc/apache/src directory. The current version of the Apache source code does not have an install target for make, so you'll have to copy and strip the executable by hand:

```
cp httpd ../httpd
cd
strip httpd
chown root.wheel httpd
chmod 755 httpd
```

RUNTIME SERVER CONFIGURATION SETTINGS

Apache reads its configuration settings from three files: access.conf, httpd.conf, and srm.conf. Primarily, this has been done to maintain backward compatibility with the NCSA server, but the reasoning behind this organization makes good sense. The configuration files reside in the conf subdirectory of the server distribution. Sample configuration files are included in the software distribution; they are named access.conf-dist, httpd.conf-dist, and srm.conf-dist, respectively. You will need to create copies of these files without the -dist portion:

```
cd /usr/local/etc/httpd/conf
cp httpd.conf-dist httpd.conf
cp access.conf-dist access.conf
cp srm.conf-dist srm.conf
```

After you've made your local copies, you are ready to configure a basic server.

Runtime configuration of your server is done by way of *configuration directives*. Directives are commands that set some option; use them to tell the server about various options that you want to enable, such as the location of files important to the server configuration and operation. Configuration directives follow this syntax:

```
Directive option option...
```

Directives are specified one per line. Some directives only set a value such as a filename; others let you specify various options. There are special directives, called *sections*, that look like HTML tags. Section directives are surrounded by angle brackets, such as `<directive>`. Sections usually enclose a group of directives that apply only to the directory specified in the section:

```
<Directory somedir/in/your/tree>
  Directive option option
  Directive option option
</Directive>
```

All sections are closed with a matching section tag that looks like `</directive>`. You will see some of these constructs in the `conf/access.conf` and in your `conf/httpd.conf` files. Note that section tags, like any other directive, are specified one per line.

EDITING `httpd.conf`

`httpd.conf` contains configuration directives that control how the server runs, where its logfiles are found, the User ID (UID) it runs under, the port that it listens to, and so on. You will need to edit some of the default configuration values to settings that make sense in your site. I kept most of the defaults found on my `httpd.conf`, with the exception of the following:

ServerAdmim
: The `ServerAdmin` directive should be set to the address of the webmaster managing the server. It should be a valid e-mail address or alias, such as `webmaster@your.domain`. Setting this to a valid address is important because this address will be returned to a visitor when there's a problem (see Figure 2.2).

User and Group
: The `User` and `Group` directives set the UID and Group ID (GID) that the server will use to process requests. I kept these to the defaults: `nobody` and `nogroup`. Please verify that the names `nobody` and `nogroup` exist in your `/etc/passwd` and `/etc/group` files, respectively. If you want to use a different UID or GID, go ahead; however, be aware that the server will run with the permissions you define here. The permissions for the specified UID and GID should be

very low because, in case of a security hole, whether on the server or (more likely) on your own CGI programs, those programs will run with the assigned UID. If the server runs as root or some other privileged user, someone may exploit the security holes and do nasty things to your site. Instead of specifying the User and Group directives using a name, you can specify them by using the UID and GID numbers. If you use numbers, be sure that the numbers you specify correspond to the user and group you want, and that they are preceded by the pound (#) symbol.

*Figure 2.2.
One of the error
messages the
server returns if
there's an error.
Note that the
ServerAdmin was
set to* alberto@
accesslink.com.

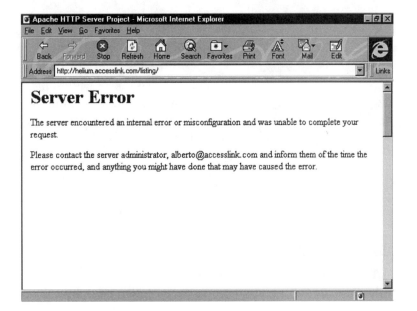

Here's how these directives would look if specified by name:

```
User nobody
Group nogroup
```

Here's the same specification, but by UID and GID:

```
User #-1
Group #-1
```

ServerName   The ServerName directive sets the hostname the server will return. Set it to a fully qualified domain name (fqdn). If not set, the server will try figure it out by itself and set to its canonical name. However, you may want the server to return a friendlier address such as *www.your.domain.*

Whatever you do, ServerName should be a real Domain Name System (DNS) name for your network. If you are administering your own DNS, remember to add a CNAME alias for your host. If someone else manages the DNS for you, ask her to do this for you. Your ServerName entry should look like this:

```
ServerName www.your.domain
```

Note

If you would like to install a Web server for test purposes on a standalone machine, you can do so by specifying a ServerName of localhost. You can then access the server as http://www.localhost from within the standalone machine. This may be a useful thing to do for trying out new configurations or Internet Web servers.

ServerRoot   This directive sets the absolute path to your server directory (where your httpd binary is located). This directive tells the server where to find all the resources and configuration files. Many of these resources are specified in the configuration files relative of the ServerRoot directory. If you installed your server using my examples, your ServerRoot directive will read:

```
ServerRoot /usr/local/etc/httpd
```

EDITING srm.conf

The srm.conf file is the resource configuration file. It controls settings related to the location of your Web document tree, the CGI program directories, and other resource configuration issues that affect your Web site. I kept most of the defaults found on my srm.conf. The most important directive on this configuration file is

DocumentRoot   Set this directive to the absolute path of your document tree. Your *document tree* is the top directory from which Apache will serve files. By default it is set to /usr/local/etc/ httpd/htdocs.

You may also want to set the UserDir directive to disabled. The UserDir directive defines the directory relative to a local user's home directory where they will put public HTML documents. It's relative because each user will have a public_html directory. Although this may give users at your site the freedom to create and maintain their own home pages, many users may not be aware of this fact, resulting in the possibility of their creating a public_html directory that contains private files.

Additionally, depending on the kind of users in your system and the server configuration, this may create potential security problems. It would make it possible for a user to publish your entire filesystem by creating a symbolic link to a directory outside of a Web document tree. By doing this, anyone would be able to read and navigate your filesystem freely.

Chapter 16, "Web Server Security Issues," discusses alternatives for providing this functionality that I feel are better from a security and maintenance standpoint.

A copy of the boilerplate `conf/srm.conf` file has been included at the end of this chapter.

EDITING `access.conf`

I kept all the defaults found in my `access.conf` file. `access.conf` is the global *access control file*; it configures the type of access users have to your site and the documents you make available, as well as security issues defining the extent to which users may alter the security settings you may have defined. The default configuration provides unrestricted access to documents in your `DocumentRoot`.

If you want to provide a more restrictive site, you may want to verify that all `<Directory path>` sections match the directories they list in your installation. The `Directory` sections specify a set of options, usually involving security issues, on a per-directory basis. In particular, you may want to remove the `Indexes` option that follows the `Options` directive on the section that looks like this:

```
<Directory /usr/local/etc/httpd/cgi-bin>
Options Indexes FollowSymLinks
</Directory>
```

The `Indexes` option allows for server-generated directory listings. You probably don't want anyone peeking at the contents of your `cgi-bin` directories.

Options that you implement on your global ACT can be overridden by the use of an `.htaccess` file. You can disable all `.htaccess` overrides by setting the directive `AllowOverride` to `None`, which is by default set to allow all overrides:

```
AllowOverride None
```

I discuss access control and security in Chapter 15, "Access Control and User Authentication."

CONFIGURING AN `inetd` SERVER

Normally, Apache runs in standalone mode or daemon mode. How it is run by the system depends on how it is configured by the `ServerType` directive in `conf/httpd.conf`.

A *standalone server* offers superior performance over inetd-run servers because usually there will be a server process ready to serve a request. When run under inetd (the Internet daemon), a new server is started every time a request is received on the HTTP port. There is a considerable amount of overhead in starting a new server process with each new request.

The default setting for ServerType is standalone; unless you have an extremely light traffic site, you should stick with this setting. inetd servers are good for information you want available, but to which you don't want to dedicate a computer.

Tip

> inetd servers are great for testing configuration settings because the server rereads all its settings every time there's a request. On standalone servers, you need to manually restart the server before it sees any changes you made to the configuration files.

To run a server from inetd, you'll need to modify conf/httpd.conf once more and change the ServerType directive from standalone to inetd:

```
ServerType inetd
```

The Port directive has no effect on an inetd server. A standalone server uses this configuration information to learn which port it should be listening to. Because inetd does the binding between the port and the software, this setting has no effect on an inetd configuration.

CONFIGURING inetd

inetd is the "Internet superserver." It gets started when the machines boots by /etc/rc. Once launched, inetd listens for connections on Internet socket ports. When it finds a connection, it starts up the program responsible for managing that port. When the request is served and the program exits, inetd continues to listen for additional requests on that port.

To make Apache work from inetd, you need to edit /etc/inetd.conf and /etc/services. Configuring an inetd server requires a bit more system configuration than a standalone server.

First, you need to edit your /etc/services file. The /etc/services database contains information about all known services available on the Internet. Each service is represented by a single line listing the following information:

Official service name
Port number
Protocol name
Aliases by which the service is known

Each entry is separated by a tab or spaces. An entry describing `httpd` will look like this:

```
http portnumber/tcp httpd httpd
```

UNIX

UNIX ports range from 0 to 65,535; however, the first 1,024 ports are reserved. A *reserved port* means that only processes owned by the superuser will be able to bind to them; if you want to run the server at port 80 (the default for `httpd`), `httpd` will need to be started by the superuser.

Set *portnumber* to the port number on which you want to run the server. Typically this will be port 80 for a standalone server. `inetd` servers run better at port 8080, so your entry will look like this:

```
http 8080/tcp httpd httpd
```

If you are running NetInfo, you can type this line into a temporary file, such as `/tmp/services`, and then run

```
niload services . < /tmp/services
```

Next, you need to edit `/etc/inetd.conf` to configure `inetd` to listen for `httpd` requests. Each line in `inetd.conf` contains the following information:

Service name
Socket type
Protocol
Wait/no wait
User the server program will run as
Server program
Server program arguments

My completed entry looks like this:

```
httpd  stream  tcp  nowait nobody  /usr/local/etc/httpd/httpd httpd -f /usr/
↪local/etc/httpd/conf/httpd.conf
```

Warning

The previous example will start the server as nobody. Typically, you will want a standalone server to be started by the root user so that the server is able to bind to port 80, the standard HTTP port, and be able to change the UID and GID of its children processes. When the standalone server starts up, it forks children processes. These children processes run with a UID of nobody and a GID of nogroup unless you specified a different setting with the User and Group directives. The children processes are the ones that handle HTTP requests. The main process, owned by root, has as its duty the creation and destruction of its children processes. This makes the standard, standalone server secure.

If you specify the root UID in this example with the intention of running the inetd server on port 80, the process handling the request is owned by root. This may create security problems; unlike a standalone server, the inetd server doesn't fork any children processes, so it handles requests with the UID and GID of the process owner.

After adding the httpd entry to /etc/inetd.conf, you'll need to restart inetd. You can easily do this by finding out the inetd process number with ps and sending it a HANGUP signal:

```
# kill -HUP InetdProcessID
```

Replace the InetdProcessID with the process number listed by the ps command. If the PID listed was 86, you would type kill -HUP 86.

inetd will restart, rereading its configuration file that will instruct it to listen for requests for port 8080.

RUNNING THE WEB SERVER FOR THE FIRST TIME

Before you can run the server for the first time, you need to create an HTML document. The standard Apache distribution includes such a file, but I have created another that is more useful and I am sure that you'll use time and again. Using your favorite text editor, create a file called index.html inside the htdocs directory with this content:

```
<HTML>
<HEAD>
<TITLE>Apache Server Survival Guide</TITLE>
</HEAD>
```

```
<BODY BGCOLOR="#ffffff" LINK="#000080" VLINK="#000080">
<H1><CENTER>Apache Server Survival Guide </CENTER></H1>
<H2><CENTER>Congratulations! Your Apache server was successfully
installed.</CENTER></H2>

<H3>Here are some interesting sites that host information about
the Apache server: </H3>

<UL>
<LI>The official homepage for the
<A HREF="http://www.apache.org">Apache Group</A>

<LI>The official homepage for
<A HREF="http://www.us.apache-ssl.com">Community Connexion</A>
developers of Stronghold: Apache-SSL-US (A Netscape compatible
SSL server based on Apache)

<LI>The official homepage for
<A HREF="http://www.algroup.co.uk/Apache-SSL">Apache-SSL</A>
(A Netscape compatible SSL server based on Apache - only available
to users outside of the United States).

<LI><A HREF="http://www.zyzzyva.com/server/module_registry/">
Apache Module Registry</A>, the place where you can find information
about 3<SUP>rd</SUP> party Apache modules and other development stuff.

<LI><A HREF="http://www.apacheweek.com">The Apache Week Home</A>,
here you will find an essential weekly guide dedicated to Apache server
➥information.

<LI><A HREF="http://www.ukweb.com">UK Web's Apache Support Center</A>

<LI><A HREF="http://www.fastcgi.com">The FastCGI Website</A>
</UL>

<P>
<STRONG>Deja News a very handy USENET news search engine:</STRONG>
<FORM ACTION="http://search.dejanews.com/dnquery.xp" METHOD=POST>

<P>
<CENTER>
<STRONG>Quick Search For:</STRONG> <INPUT NAME="query" VALUE="Apache" SIZE="37">
<INPUT TYPE="submit" VALUE="Search!"><INPUT NAME="defaultOp" VALUE="AND"
➥TYPE="hidden">
<INPUT NAME="svcclass" VALUE="dncurrent" TYPE="hidden">
<INPUT NAME="maxhits" VALUE="20" TYPE="hidden">
</CENTER>
</FORM>

</BODY>
</HTML>
```

Put this file in your `htdocs` directory. At this point you are ready to test the server.

The machine-readable text for the file you just created is included in `server/setup/index.html`, and it should be placed in *DocumentRoot*`/index.html`.

STARTING UP A STANDALONE SERVER

If you are running a standalone server, you'll need to start httpd manually. This is how you do it:

```
# /usr/local/etc/httpd/httpd -f /usr/local/etc/httpd/conf/httpd.conf
```

Please note that I started the standalone server from the root account, indicated by the pound sign (#) at the beginning of the line. Standalone servers need to be started by root so two important things happen:

◆ If your standalone server uses the default HTTP port (port 80), only the superuser can bind to Internet ports that are lower than 1025.

◆ Only processes owned by root can change their UID and GID as specified by the User and Group directives. If you start the server under another UID, it will run with the permissions of the user starting the process.

STARTING UP AN inetd SERVER

As you probably guessed, you don't need to start an inetd server. inetd will start httpd every time a request is received on the port assigned to the server. inetd servers make good development platforms because configuration settings are reread every time you send a request.

STARTING AND STOPPING THE SERVER

The Apache server, httpd, has a few command-line options you can use to set some defaults specifying where httpd will read its configuration directives. The Apache httpd executable understands the following options:

```
httpd [-d ServerRoot] [-f ConfigurationFile] [-x] [-v] [-?]
```

The -d option overrides the location of the ServerRoot directory. It sets the initial value of the ServerRoot variable (the directory where the Apache server is installed) to whatever path you specify. This default is usually read from the ServerRoot directive in httpd.conf:

The -f flag specifies the location of the main configuration file, conf/httpd.conf. It reads and executes the configuration commands found on ConfigurationFile on startup. If the ConfigurationFile is not an absolute path (doesn't begin with a /), its location is assumed to be relative of the path specified in the ServerRoot directive in httpd.conf. By default, this value is set to ServerRoot/conf/httpd.conf.

The -x option is used by the developers of Apache as a debugging aid and should not be used under normal server operation. It runs a single server process that does not create any children.

The -v option prints the development version of the Apache server and terminates the process.

The -? option prints the following usage information for the server:

```
Usage: httpd [-d directory] [-f file] [-v]
-d directory : specify an alternate initial ServerRoot
-f file : specify an alternate ServerConfigFile
```

THE start SCRIPT

I have developed a small start script that launches the server with all the command-line settings I use. This script saves me a little typing when I'm trying things that require me to start and stop the server.

You can create this script by just typing it into a file (one per script). When you are done entering it, to turn it into executable, type:

```
cd WhereEverYouEnterThem
chmod 755 start stop restart
```

You may want to store the script in a place where it is convenient, such as /usr/local/ bin. Here's the listing for the start script:

```
#!/bin/sh
/usr/local/etc/httpd/httpd -f /usr/local/etc/httpd/conf/httpd.conf
```

THE stop SCRIPT

The server is designed to stop gracefully when its sent a TERM (terminate) signal. Because when the server starts it spawns several children processes, it becomes a little more difficult to terminate. Apache automatically kills any children processes when the main process is killed. Luckily, the developers of Apache put the process ID of the main process in a file where you can easily obtain the ID of the process. My stop script makes use of the *PidFile* (/usr/local/etc/httpd/logs/PidFile) file.

This is the listing to the stop script:

```
#!/bin/sh
#Stop Apache Script
kill `cat /usr/local/etc/httpd/logs/httpd..pid`
```

THE restart SCRIPT

The server is designed to restart if it receives a -HUP (hangup) signal. On receiving this type of signal, the server stops and immediately restarts, rereading its configuration files.

Here's the listing for the restart script:

```
#!/bin/sh
#Restart Apache Script
kill -HUP `cat /usr/local/etc/httpd/logs/httpd.pid`
```

This is a very convenient script that automates the process. Any time you modify any of the configuration files, you need to restart the server to enable the changes. htrestart makes this easy to do.

AUTO-STARTING THE WEB SERVER AT BOOT TIME

You may be interested in automating the startup process of the server whenever you boot your machine. Doing so is very easy. On your /etc/rc.local file, add an entry like this:

```
#
# Run httpd server automatically
#
echo 'starting httpd server'
if [ -f /etc/rc.httpd ]; then
  sh /etc/rc.httpd
fi
```

Create a new file, /etc/rc.httpd, with the following contents:

```
#!/bin/sh -u
#
cd /usr/local/etc/httpd/
./httpd -d /usr/local/etc/httpd/ -f conf/httpd.conf
```

Although you can put the commands in /etc/rc.httpd in your /etc/rc.local, I find it convenient to be able to disable the server from loading by renaming the /etc/rc.httpd. When the computer boots, if /etc/rc finds a file named /etc/rc.httpd, it will execute the commands it finds there.

TESTING THE NEWLY INSTALLED SERVER

If your configuration files were edited properly, you should be able to point your Web browser to the machine running the server and see the page you created earlier, confirming that your server is running. Figure 2.3 shows what your screen should look like.

Tip

If you are running the server in a nonstandard port, such as 8080, you'll need to specify the port number as part of the URL:

```
httpd://yourhost.yourdomain.com:port
```

Figure 2.3.
The startup page
you created as
rendered by
Microsoft Internet
Explorer version
3.0.

If there was a problem with the server or a configuration, Apache is pretty good about giving you an indication about the problem. If Apache could not find some of the configuration files, it should give you a message like this:

```
httpd: could not open document config file /usr/local/etc/httpd/conf/httpd.conf
fopen: No such file or directory
```

Check for typos or incorrect path information on your command line or in the configuration files. Typically this problem appears if you have customized your installation to a different directory. Apache has compiled-in defaults that preset the location of ServerRoot. If you specify a relative path, the server prefixes the compiled-in ServerRoot instead.

Other problems may have dump values such as

```
httpd: could not bind to port
bind: Address already in use
```

If you get this message, more than likely there's another process using the port number you have defined. Other port binding problems can show up if you specify a reserved port number (one whose address is smaller than 1025). Only root processes can bind to reserved ports. The solution is to start the server as root so that the server can bind properly to the specified port (if you have followed my instructions, your server although started by root, runs as nobody).

If the server doesn't respond, check to see if it is running. Use the ps program to see what's going on:

ps -guax ¦ grep httpd (on BSD-type systems)

ps -ef ¦ grep httpd (on SVR4-type systems)

Don't get worried if you see several httpd processes running. Apache's server model runs several simultaneous processes coordinated by the parent process (the one owned by root).

Sometimes Apache returns enough information that will help you track a problem to a bad configuration setting. Other times, you'll have to hunt for the error. The first things to check are the logs/error_log and logs/access_log files for more information. While you're at it, you may want to check for any core files in the ServerRoot. If some problem is crashing Apache (I've never had one that dumped core), it's likely that it left a trace there.

CONFIGURATION FILE LISTINGS

For your convenience, here's a listing of the various configuration files I talked about in this chapter.

src/Configuration FILE

After you configure and build your server, you won't have to edit this file. At least not until you enable additional modules. You will then have to add them here, and repeat the configuration and binary building process again.

LISTING 2.1. THE Configuration.tmpl FILE.

```
# Config file for the Apache httpd.

# Configuration.tmpl is the template for Configuration. Configuration should
# be edited to select system type. Configuration.tmpl should only be changed
# when a new system or module is added, or an existing one modified.

# There are three types of lines here:

# '#' comments, distinguished by having a '#' as the first non-blank character
#
# Lines which set a Make option — these are simply copied into the Makefile
#
# Module selection lines, distinguished by having 'Module' at the front.
# These list the configured modules, in priority order (highest priority
# first).  They're down at the bottom.

# First, ordinary compile-time configuration.

# What to call the compiler:  For normal machines with ANSI compilers
# CC= cc
# For Suns or other non-ANSI platforms. Please make sure your gcc is
# 2.0 or later, as 1.40 seems to create bad code for the Sun 4.
CC= gcc
```

```
# CFLAGS, compile flags.

# -DMINIMAL_DNS is now obsolete. Use httpd.conf settings of
# HostnameLookups on
# or
# HostnameLookups off
#
# If you want to have more secure hostname resolution at the cost of some
# performance, use -DMAXIMUM_DNS.
# If you want setting the xbit of a file to cause it to be treated as
# server-included HTML (unless it is a CGI script), say -DXBITHACK.  Note
# that this is a run-time option, per-directory, either way (via the XBITHACK
# command); this option only sets the default.

# If you find that your OS can't cope with mmap (compiles OKAY but refuses
# to run and moans "httpd: Could not mmap memory" .. or similar) try
# disabling use of shared memory for process management (scoreboard with
# -DNO_MMAP

# Status Instrumentation
# In order for the status module to obtain full statistics Apache must
# be modified to keep track of various information.  This is not
# turned on by default. In order to enable full status details add -DSTATUS
# to the end of the CFLAGS line below.

# Using SOCKS
# Apache can be compiled to work over a SOCKS firewall by
# adding the following string to your CFLAGS define:
#
#   -Dconnect=Rconnect -Dselect=Rselect -Dgethostbyname=Rgethostbyname
#
# and by adding the following to the EXTRA_LIBS define:
#
#   -L/usr/local/lib -lsocks
#
# making sure that -L points to wherever you've put libsocks.a.

# [Some other former Apache compile-time options are now treated differently;
#  the virtual host code is always present; DBM auth is an optional module, and
#  may be configured out by changing the module config below, though it still
#  defaults in.  Note that this config file does not include DBM auth by
#  default --- configure it in below if you need it].

CFLAGS= -O2

# Place here any flags you may need upon linking, such as a flag to
# prevent dynamic linking (if desired)
LFLAGS=

# Place here any extra libraries you may need to link to.
# -lndbm is commonly required for DBM auth, if that is configured in.
EXTRA_LIBS=

# AUX_CFLAGS are system-specific control flags.
# NOTE: IF YOU DO NOT CHOOSE ONE OF THESE, EDIT httpd.h AND CHOOSE
# SETTINGS FOR THE SYSTEM FLAGS. IF YOU DON'T, BAD THINGS WILL HAPPEN.
```

continues

LISTING 2.1. CONTINUED

```
# For SunOS 4
#AUX_CFLAGS= -DSUNOS4
# For Solaris 2.
#AUX_CFLAGS= -DSOLARIS2
#AUX_LIBS= -lsocket -lnsl
# For SGI IRIX. Use the AUX_LIBS line if you're using NIS and want
# user-supported directories
#AUX_CFLAGS= -DIRIX
#AUX_LIBS= -lsun
# For HP-UX       n.b. if you use the paid-for HP CC compiler, use flag -Ae
#AUX_CFLAGS= -DHPUX
# For AIX
#AUX_CFLAGS= -DAIX -U__STR__
# For Ultrix
#AUX_CFLAGS= -DULTRIX
# For DEC OSF/1
#AUX_CFLAGS= -DOSF1
# For NeXT
#AUX_CFLAGS= -DNEXT
# For Sequent
#AUX_CFLAGS= -DSEQUENT
# For Linux -m486 ONLY IF YOU HAVE 486 BINARY SUPPORT IN KERNEL
#AUX_CFLAGS= -DLINUX
# For A/UX
#AUX_CFLAGS= -DAUX -D_POSIX_SOURCE
#AUX_LIBS= -lposix -lbsd -s
# For SCO ODT 3
# libcrypt_i available from sosco.sco.com, files /SLS/lng225b.Z and
# /SLS/lng225b.ltr.Z
# the -Oe option causes cc to die compiling mod_imap
➥(using 3.0.0a of the dev sys)
#CFLAGS= -Oacgiltz
#AUX_CFLAGS= -DSCO
#AUX_LIBS= -lPW -lsocket -lmalloc -lcrypt_i
# For SCO OpenServer Release 5
# -K noinline is needed to work around an optimiser bug which appears in
# http_bprintf.c
#AUX_CFLAGS= -DSCO5
#AUX_LIBS=-lsocket -lmalloc -lprot
#BROKEN_BPRINTF_FLAGS=-K noinline
# For SVR4
# Some SVR4 implementations will require SO_LINGER option to be set in order
# to guarantee buffer flushes. Dell, Esix, and UnixWare are a few of these.
# Use -DNEED_LINGER in addition to other AUX_CFLAGS for these.
#AUX_CFLAGS= -DSVR4
#AUX_LIBS= -lsocket -lnsl -lc
# For UnixWare 2.x, no longer just SVR4 (sigh) - use cc, not gcc
# AUX_LIBS= -lsocket -lnsl -lcrypt
# For Amdahl UTS 2.1
# -Xa enables ANSI mode, -eft is expanded types
#AUX_CFLAGS= -Xa -eft -DUTS21
#AUX_LIBS= -lsocket -lbsd -la
# For HP/Apollo Domain/OS
#AUX_CFLAGS= -DAPOLLO
# For NetBSD/FreeBSD/BSDI 2.x
# -m486 only if you are running on Intel 486/586
#AUX_CFLAGS= -m486
```

```
# BSDI doesn't need -lcrypt
#AUX_LIBS= -lcrypt
# For QNX
#AUX_CFLAGS= -DQNX
#AUX_LFLAGS= -N 0x20000
# For LynxOS
#AUX_CFLAGS= -DLYNXOS
#EXTRA_LIBS=-lbsd -ldes -lc_p
# For DG/UX 5.4
#AUX_CFLAGS= -DDGUX
#AUX_LIBS=

# For EMX OS/2 port
#AUX_CFLAGS= -Zbsd-signals -Zbin-files
#-DNO_KILLPG -DNEED_STRCASECMP -DNO_SETSID
#-g
#AUX_LIBS= -lsocket -llibufc -lgdbm -lbsd

################################################################
# Module configuration
#
# Modules are listed in reverse priority order — the ones that come
# later can override the behavior of those that come earlier.  This
# can have visible effects; for instance, if UserDir followed Alias,
# you couldn't alias out a particular user's home directory.

# The configuration below is what we consider a decent default
# configuration.  If you want the functionality provided by a particular
# module, remove the "#" sign at the beginning of the line. But remember,
# the more modules you compile into the server, the larger the executable
# is and the more memory it will take, so if you are unlikely to use the
# functionality of a particular module you might wish to leave it out.

## Basic modules (i.e., generally useful stuff that works everyplace):
## You should probably not comment out any of these unless you know what it
## does and you know you won't need it.

Module mime_module          mod_mime.o
Module access_module        mod_access.o
Module auth_module          mod_auth.o
Module negotiation_module   mod_negotiation.o
Module includes_module      mod_include.o
Module dir_module           mod_dir.o
Module cgi_module           mod_cgi.o
Module userdir_module       mod_userdir.o
Module alias_module         mod_alias.o
Module env_module           mod_env.o
Module common_log_module    mod_log_common.o

## The asis module implemented ".asis" file types, which allow the embedding
## of HTTP headers at the beginning of the document.  mod_imap handles internal
## imagemaps (no more cgi-bin/imagemap/!).  mod_actions is used to specify
## CGI scripts which act as "handlers" for particular files, for example to
## automatically convert every GIF to another file type.

Module asis_module          mod_asis.o
Module imap_module          mod_imap.o
Module action_module        mod_actions.o
```

continues

LISTING 2.1. CONTINUED

```
## Optional modules for NCSA user-agent/referer logging compatibility
## We recommend, however, that you migrate to the configurable logging
## module, below.

# Module agent_log_module    mod_log_agent.o
# Module referer_log_module  mod_log_referer.o

## This is a *replacement* for mod_log_common which supports a
## LogFormat directive which allows you to specify what goes into
## the TransferLog (if you want Referer, etc.)  source code for docs.
##
## If you play with this, remember to drop the standard
## mod_log_common — a server with both will work, but you'll get
## very confused trying to figure out what's going on...

# Module config_log_module    mod_log_config.o

## cern_meta mimicks the behavior of the CERN web server with regards to
## metainformation files.

# Module cern_meta_module    mod_cern_meta.o

## The status module allows the server to display current details about
## how well it is performing and what it is doing.  Consider also enabling
## -DSTATUS (see the CFLAGS section near the start of the file) to allow
## full status information.  Check conf/access.conf on how to enable this.

# Module status_module    mod_status.o

## The Info module displays configuration information for the server and
## all included modules. It's very useful for debugging.

# Module info_module    mod_info.o

## Optional authentication modules.
##
## The anon_auth module allows for anonymous-FTP-style username/
## password authentication.

# Module anon_auth_module    mod_auth_anon.o

## db_auth and dbm_auth work with Berkeley DB files - make sure there
## is support for DBM files on your system.  You may need to grab the GNU
## "gdbm" package if not.

# Module db_auth_module     mod_auth_db.o
# Module dbm_auth_module    mod_auth_dbm.o

## msql_auth checks against an MSQL database.  You must have MSQL installed
## and an "msql.h" available for this to even compile.  Additionally,
## you may need to add a couple entries to the CFLAGS line, like
##
##   -lmsql -L/usr/local/lib -L/usr/local/Minerva/lib
##
## This depends on your installation of MSQL.
```

```
# Module msql_auth_module     mod_auth_msql.o

## "digest" implements HTTP Digest Authentication rather than the less
## secure Basic Auth used by the other modules.

# Module digest_module  mod_digest.o

## Outright experiments — mod_dld defines commands which
## allows other modules to be loaded in at runtime, and mod_cookies
## uses Netscape cookies to automatically construct and log accurate
## click-trails from Netscape cookies, for Netscape-using clients who
## aren't coming in via proxy.

# Module dld_module  mod_dld.o
# Module cookies_module  mod_cookies.o

## Finally, the proxy module.  It's not as complete as it could
## be yet, so use at your own risk.

# Module proxy_module    mod_proxy.o
```

LISTING 2.2. THE SERVER CONFIGURATION FILE: conf/httpd.conf.

```
# This is the main server configuration file. See URL http://www.apache.org/
# for instructions.

# Do NOT simply read the instructions in here without understanding
# what they do, if you are unsure consult the online docs. You have been
# warned.

# Originally by Rob McCool

# ServerType is either inetd, or standalone.

ServerType standalone

# If you are running from inetd, go to "ServerAdmin".

# Port: The port the standalone listens to. For ports < 1023, you will
# need httpd to be run as root initially.

Port 80

# HostnameLookups: Log the names of clients or just their IP numbers
#    e.g.   www.apache.org (on) or 204.62.129.132 (off)
HostnameLookups on

# If you wish httpd to run as a different user or group, you must run
# httpd as root initially and it will switch.

# User/Group: The name (or #number) of the user/group to run httpd as.
#   On SCO (ODT 3) use User nouser and Group nogroup
User nobody
Group #-1
```

continues

Listing 2.2. continued

```
# ServerAdmin: Your address, where problems with the server should be
# e-mailed.

ServerAdmin you@your.address

# ServerRoot: The directory the server's config, error, and log files
# are kept in

ServerRoot /usr/local/etc/httpd

# BindAddress: You can support virtual hosts with this option. This option
# is used to tell the server which IP address to listen to. It can either
# contain "*", an IP address, or a fully qualified Internet domain name.
# See also the VirtualHost directive.

#BindAddress *

# ErrorLog: The location of the error log file. If this does not start
# with /, ServerRoot is prepended to it.

ErrorLog logs/error_log

# TransferLog: The location of the transfer log file. If this does not
# start with /, ServerRoot is prepended to it.

TransferLog logs/access_log

# PidFile: The file the server should log its pid to
PidFile logs/httpd.pid

# ScoreBoardFile: File used to store internal server process information
ScoreBoardFile logs/apache_status

# ServerName allows you to set a host name which is sent back to clients for
# your server if it's different than the one the program would get (i.e. use
# "www" instead of the host's real name).
#
# Note: You cannot just invent host names and hope they work. The name you
# define here must be a valid DNS name for your host. If you don't understand
# this, ask your network administrator.

#ServerName new.host.name

# CacheNegotiatedDocs: By default, Apache sends Pragma: no-cache with each
# document that was negotiated on the basis of content. This asks proxy
# servers not to cache the document. Uncommenting the following line disables
# this behavior, and proxies will be allowed to cache the documents.

#CacheNegotiatedDocs

# Timeout: The number of seconds before receives and sends time out
#   n.b. the compiled default is 1200 (20 minutes !)

Timeout 400

# KeepAlive: The number of Keep-Alive persistent requests to accept
# per connection. Set to 0 to deactivate Keep-Alive support
```

```
KeepAlive 5

# KeepAliveTimeout: Number of seconds to wait for the next request

KeepAliveTimeout 15

# Server-pool size regulation.  Rather than making you guess how many
# server processes you need, Apache dynamically adapts to the load it
# sees --- that is, it tries to maintain enough server processes to
# handle the current load, plus a few spare servers to handle transient
# load spikes (e.g., multiple simultaneous requests from a single
# Netscape browser).

# It does this by periodically checking how many servers are waiting
# for a request.  If there are fewer than MinSpareServers, it creates
# a new spare.  If there are more than MaxSpareServers, some of the
# spares die off.  These values are probably OK for most sites —

MinSpareServers 5
MaxSpareServers 10

# Number of servers to start --- should be a reasonable ballpark figure.

StartServers 5

# Limit on total number of servers running, i.e., limit on the number
# of clients who can simultaneously connect --- if this limit is ever
# reached, clients will be LOCKED OUT, so it should NOT BE SET TOO LOW.
# It is intended mainly as a brake to keep a runaway server from taking
# Unix with it as it spirals down...

MaxClients 150

# MaxRequestsPerChild: the number of requests each child process is
#  allowed to process before the child dies.
#  The child will exit so as to avoid problems after prolonged use when
#  Apache (and maybe the libraries it uses) leak.  On most systems, this
#  isn't really needed, but a few (such as Solaris) do have notable leaks
#  in the libraries.

MaxRequestsPerChild 30

# Proxy Server directives. Uncomment the following line to
# enable the proxy server:

#ProxyRequests On

# To enable the cache as well, edit and uncomment the following lines:

#CacheRoot /usr/local/etc/httpd/proxy
#CacheSize 5
#CacheGcInterval 4
#CacheMaxExpire 24
#CacheLastModifiedFactor 0.1
#CacheDefaultExpire 1
#NoCache adomain.com anotherdomain.edu joes.garage.com
```

continues

LISTING 2.2. CONTINUED

```
# Listen: Allows you to bind Apache to specific IP addresses and/or
# ports, in addition to the default. See also the VirtualHost command

#Listen 3000
#Listen 12.34.56.78:80

# VirtualHost: Allows the daemon to respond to requests for more than one
# server address, if your server machine is configured to accept IP packets
# for multiple addresses. This can be accomplished with the ifconfig
# alias flag, or through kernel patches like VIF.

# Any httpd.conf or srm.conf directive may go into a VirtualHost command.
# See alto the BindAddress entry.

#<VirtualHost host.foo.com>
#ServerAdmin webmaster@host.foo.com
#DocumentRoot /www/docs/host.foo.com
#ServerName host.foo.com
#ErrorLog logs/host.foo.com-error_log
#TransferLog logs/host.foo.com-access_log
#</VirtualHost>
```

LISTING 2.3. THE RESOURCE CONFIGURATION FILE: `conf/srm.conf`.

```
# With this document, you define the name space that users see of your http
# server.  This file also defines server settings which affect how requests are
# serviced, and how results should be formatted.

# See the tutorials at http://www.apache.org/ for
# more information.

# Originally by Rob McCool; Adapted for Apache


# DocumentRoot: The directory out of which you will serve your
# documents. By default, all requests are taken from this directory, but
# symbolic links and aliases may be used to point to other locations.

DocumentRoot /usr/local/etc/httpd/htdocs

# UserDir: The name of the directory which is appended onto a user's home
# directory if a ~user request is recieved.

UserDir public_html

# DirectoryIndex: Name of the file or files to use as a pre-written HTML
# directory index.  Separate multiple entries with spaces.

DirectoryIndex index.html

# FancyIndexing is whether you want fancy directory indexing or standard

FancyIndexing on

# AddIcon tells the server which icon to show for different files or filename
# extensions
```

```
AddIconByEncoding (CMP,/icons/compressed.gif) x-compress x-gzip

AddIconByType (TXT,/icons/text.gif) text/*
AddIconByType (IMG,/icons/image2.gif) image/*
AddIconByType (SND,/icons/sound2.gif) audio/*
AddIconByType (VID,/icons/movie.gif) video/*


AddIcon /icons/binary.gif .bin .exe
AddIcon /icons/binhex.gif .hqx
AddIcon /icons/tar.gif .tar
AddIcon /icons/world2.gif .wrl .wrl.gz .vrml .vrm .iv
AddIcon /icons/compressed.gif .Z .z .tgz .gz .zip
AddIcon /icons/a.gif .ps .ai .eps
AddIcon /icons/layout.gif .html .shtml .htm .pdf
AddIcon /icons/text.gif .txt
AddIcon /icons/c.gif .c
AddIcon /icons/p.gif .pl .py
AddIcon /icons/f.gif .for
AddIcon /icons/dvi.gif .dvi
AddIcon /icons/uuencoded.gif .uu
AddIcon /icons/script.gif .conf .sh .shar .csh .ksh .tcl
AddIcon /icons/tex.gif .tex
AddIcon /icons/bomb.gif core

AddIcon /icons/back.gif ..
AddIcon /icons/hand.right.gif README
AddIcon /icons/folder.gif ^^DIRECTORY^^
AddIcon /icons/blank.gif ^^BLANKICON^^

# DefaultIcon is which icon to show for files which do not have an icon
# explicitly set.

DefaultIcon /icons/unknown.gif

# AddDescription allows you to place a short description after a file in
# server-generated indexes.
# Format: AddDescription "description" filename

# ReadmeName is the name of the README file the server will look for by
# default. Format: ReadmeName name
#
# The server will first look for name.html, include it if found, and it will
# then look for name and include it as plaintext if found.
#
# HeaderName is the name of a file which should be prepended to
# directory indexes.

ReadmeName README
HeaderName HEADER

# IndexIgnore is a set of filenames which directory indexing should ignore
# Format: IndexIgnore name1 name2...

IndexIgnore */.??* *~ *# */HEADER* */README* */RCS
```

continues

LISTING 2.3. CONTINUED

```
# AccessFileName: The name of the file to look for in each directory
# for access control information.

AccessFileName .htaccess

# DefaultType is the default MIME type for documents which the server
# cannot find the type of from filename extensions.

DefaultType text/plain

# AddEncoding allows you to have certain browsers (Mosaic/X 2.1+) uncompress
# information on the fly. Note: Not all browsers support this.

AddEncoding x-compress Z
AddEncoding x-gzip gz

# AddLanguage allows you to specify the language of a document. You can
# then use content negotiation to give a browser a file in a language
# it can understand.  Note that the suffix does not have to be the same
# as the language keyword — those with documents in Polish (whose
# net-standard language code is pl) may wish to use "AddLanguage pl .po"
# to avoid the ambiguity with the common suffix for perl scripts.

AddLanguage en .en
AddLanguage fr .fr
AddLanguage de .de
AddLanguage da .da
AddLanguage el .el
AddLanguage it .it

# LanguagePriority allows you to give precedence to some languages
# in case of a tie during content negotiation.
# Just list the languages in decreasing order of preference.

LanguagePriority en fr de

# Redirect allows you to tell clients about documents which used to exist in
# your server's namespace, but do not anymore. This allows you to tell the
# clients where to look for the relocated document.
# Format: Redirect fakename url


# Aliases: Add here as many aliases as you need (with no limit). The format is
# Alias fakename realname

#Alias /icons/ /usr/local/etc/httpd/icons/

# ScriptAlias: This controls which directories contain server scripts.
# Format: ScriptAlias fakename realname

#ScriptAlias /cgi-bin/ /usr/local/etc/httpd/cgi-bin/

# If you want to use server side includes, or CGI outside
# ScriptAliased directories, uncomment the following lines.
```

```
# AddType allows you to tweak mime.types without actually editing it, or to
# make certain files to be certain types.
# Format: AddType type/subtype ext1

# AddHandler allows you to map certain file extensions to "handlers",
# actions unrelated to filetype. These can be either built into the server
# or added with the Action command (see below)
# Format: AddHandler action-name ext1

# To use CGI scripts:
#AddHandler cgi-script .cgi

# To use server-parsed HTML files
#AddType text/html .shtml
#AddHandler server-parsed .shtml

# Uncomment the following line to enable Apache's send-asis HTTP file
# feature
#AddHandler send-as-is asis

# If you wish to use server-parsed imagemap files, use
#AddHandler imap-file map

# To enable type maps, you might want to use
#AddHandler type-map var

# Action lets you define media types that will execute a script whenever
# a matching file is called. This eliminates the need for repeated URL
# pathnames for oft-used CGI file processors.
# Format: Action media/type /cgi-script/location
# Format: Action handler-name /cgi-script/location

# For example to add a footer (footer.html in your document root) to
# files with extension .foot (e.g. foo.html.foot), you could use:
#AddHandler foot-action foot
#Action foot-action /cgi-bin/footer

# Or to do this for all HTML files, for example, use:
#Action text/html /cgi-bin/footer

# MetaDir: specifies the name of the directory in which Apache can find
# meta information files. These files contain additional HTTP headers
# to include when sending the document

#MetaDir .web

# MetaSuffix: specifies the file name suffix for the file containing the
# meta information.

#MetaSuffix .meta

# Customizable error response (Apache style)
#   these come in three flavors
#
#     1) plain text
```

continues

LISTING 2.3. CONTINUED

```
#ErrorDocument 500 "The server made a boo boo.
#  n.b.  the (") marks it as text, it does not get output
#
#    2) local redirects
#ErrorDocument 404 /missing.html
#  to redirect to local url /missing.html
#ErrorDocument 404 /cgi-bin/missing_handler.pl
#  n.b. can redirect to a script or a document using server-side-includes.
#
#    3) external redirects
#ErrorDocument 402 http://other.server.com/subscription_info.html
#
```

LISTING 2.4. THE GLOBAL ACCESS CONFIGURATION FILE:
conf/access.conf.

```
# access.conf: Global access configuration
# Online docs at http://www.apache.org/

# This file defines server settings which affect which types of services
# are allowed, and in what circumstances.

# Each directory to which Apache has access, can be configured with respect
# to which services and features are allowed and/or disabled in that
# directory (and its subdirectories).

# Originally by Rob McCool

# This should be changed to whatever you set DocumentRoot to.

<Directory /usr/local/etc/httpd/htdocs>

# This may also be "None", "All", or any combination of "Indexes",
# "Includes", "FollowSymLinks", "ExecCGI", or "MultiViews".

# Note that "MultiViews" must be named *explicitly* — "Options All"
# doesn't give it to you (or at least, not yet).

Options Indexes FollowSymLinks

# This controls which options the .htaccess files in directories can
# override. Can also be "All", or any combination of "Options", "FileInfo",
# "AuthConfig", and "Limit"

AllowOverride None

# Controls who can get stuff from this server.

order allow,deny
allow from all

</Directory>
```

```
# /usr/local/etc/httpd/cgi-bin should be changed to whatever your ScriptAliased
# CGI directory exists, if you have that configured.

<Directory /usr/local/etc/httpd/cgi-bin>
AllowOverride None
Options None
</Directory>

# Allow server status reports, with the URL of http://servername/status
# Change the ".nowhere.com" to match your domain to enable.

#<Location /status>
#SetHandler server-status

#order deny,allow
#deny from all
#allow from .nowhere.com
#</Location>

# You may place any other directories or locations you wish to have
# access information for after this one.
```

SUMMARY

Congratulations! If you have reached this point, you should have a properly configured Apache server running. You can now continue to Chapter 3, "Organizing Your Web Site," where you will learn the tricks for putting together an effective site.

Apache server is easy to build and configure. Although there are no GUI-based tools available for the configuration (not yet anyway), configuration is not particularly difficult. A nice editor is all that is needed. Netscape servers, once they have a basic configuration, prompt the administrator to finish configuration details with a browser. See Chapter 8, "Apache Configuration Overview," for additional information on basic configuration.

CHAPTER 3

Organizing Your Web Site

Before you build your Web site, you may want to consider its organization. While more than likely you have thought of many ways of organizing your Web site's structure, you have probably thought about it from a navigational perspective. In addition to thinking about it from that angle, I would suggest that you also think about your Web site's structure from a maintenance point of view. What can you do to make your Web site easier to maintain? What conventions will simplify the structure of your pages?

The result of this early structuring process will help you set a standard to guide your efforts. Now that you have your server up and running, it would be a good opportunity to consider a few of the issues involved. By no means is this the only approach that you can use. Any thought-out logical system should serve you equally well. Many of the ideas presented here are used at accessLINK, inc., a small Web presence provider where I spend many hours of my day. AccessLINK develops several small- to medium-sized Web sites per week and maintains a few more on a daily basis. This chapter presents some of the ideas that I use for organizing our work. I will also address some other services, such as automatic support for personal Web pages, that your users will want you to implement.

Organizing your Web site is not about structuring a Web site so that visitors can find their way around. It's something you do for yourself; it's your filing mechanism. If you follow a few basic guidelines, the maintenance of your Web site will be much easier. Upgrading to new versions of the software will be a snap, and other administrative chores such as backups will require less time and effort.

AccessLINK's servers are closely guarded because they all have close control of what goes into the servers. We don't have end users setting up their own sites or writing their own programs. Because of this, accessLINK's needs are bound to be a little different from yours, but many of their structuring methodologies will help you build a better site. They are a Web presence provider. Simply put, they'll put your company on the Web. Their services range from designing and building a site to hosting your site on one of their servers, all while maintaining the same look and feel you would have if you had a Web server running in your own network. They handle all the issues a company faces when it first gets on the Net.

When you are building a site in-house, the responsibility for building and maintaining it will fall in the hands of the system administrator. System administrators are usually overworked, and to add to their responsibilities, the managing of a Web site of any size may be beyond some organization's means or policy. When possible, it is fair to say, the better prepared you are to maintain the site, the less bumpy the entire process will be. You should take it as a rule that unless you have a static Web site—one that won't change very often—development accounts for less than a third of the effort. Maintenance and future modifications comprise the real bulk of time.

SECURITY CONCERNS

Addressing security concerns is a very time-consuming task (not to mention costly). I find that many customers just want to get online and have someone else deal with the associated security problems. Security is the number one concern, and it should be because there's a lot to worry about. Setting up a Web site is like opening a window into your network. Many people will be very happy to windowshop. Others will try to snoop to see what they can find, and still others will try to force the window open. Scary.

Security concerns for a small to medium organization are not addressable in hours, and the costs associated are not small. Privacy of information and peace of mind are important. Just think about all the information that is stored on your systems. What sort of problems would you have if these records ended up in the wrong hands? What would happen if a vandal destroyed or corrupted your data?

To think about the security implications, without combining them with the pressure to be published on the Internet, is a good thing. Most organizations should not even consider going on the Internet unless they have implemented some sort of network security, such as a firewall. If you have pressure, go find a Web server provider to host your site while you resolve the security issues. An Internet Service Provider (ISP) is already set up to address these problems. Once you have figured out the implications and you are ready, they will be happy to help you migrate your Web site in-house.

STRUCTURING YOUR WEB SITE

I believe that organization starts in UNIX. If your system is not well organized or you have not followed a consistent method, you may want to consider why this is a good idea. Many new administrators take simple organizational methodologies, such as the location of added software, for granted. A few months later the result is that changes, such as upgrades, require additional time to install and troubleshoot. In the end, you may save a considerable amount of time by doing three very simple things:

- Put your local software in the `/usr/local` tree.
- Pick up a scheme for naming and storing your Web documents and programs.
- And most importantly, stick to your organizational scheme.

These won't make any sense unless you commit to them for the long haul. Spending a lot of time setting up an organizational scheme won't work unless you're able to do it. If you find that you cannot organize when you have a deadline, simplify what you pick and make it a part of our life.

LOCAL SOFTWARE

What is local software? Local software is *local*. It's not part of your original system distribution; it's the software that you've added. This is software that will need to survive future upgrades. Installation of your Web server software is a good example. You should store it in a way that makes it easy for you to upgrade both your operating system software and the software you have added.

Many software upgrades will replace, without impunity, programs that they find in the standard UNIX directories, such as `bin`, `etc`, and `usr`. If your modifications are to survive operating system upgrades, you'll need to find a place where these programs can happily coexist.

A good place is in the `/usr/local` tree. This directory can be the entry point for programs that you add. A good model to follow is to mirror your UNIX software like this:

```
bin
etc
lib
man
named
ftp
etc
Minerva
```

Put all binaries that you add in `/usr/local/bin`. This makes it easy for users to find and easy for you to maintain. If you upgrade a program to a new version, which is also included in your operating system release, keep the original in its place. Set `/usr/local/bin` in your path, ahead of the other system directories. You can do this by adding an entry to your PATH environment variable. Where this is done depends on the shell you are using. Typically, this will be in the `.profile` or `.cshrc` files in your home directory. Note that these files start with a period, so they normally will be hidden from view.

In the `.profile` file, the new path addition will look like this:

```
PATH=/usr/local/bin:/usr/ucb:/bin/...
```

Note that the paths to the directories that search for executables are separated by colons. Directories listed first are searched first.

If you are using the `csh` (c shell), you will want to put an entry into your `.cshrc` file. This is the same as your `.profile` entry, but the `csh` syntax for defining the environment variables is a little different:

```
set PATH=(/usr/local/bin /usr/ucb /bin ...)
```

Under the csh, multiple paths are separated by spaces and grouped together with parentheses.

Other directories, such as /usr/local/etc, contain the Web server tree. Storing it in its default place removes one source of potential problems. By keeping the default installation location, future upgrades will find the files in their standard locations. Moving default installation locations without having a really good reason for the change is asking for trouble. Future upgrades won't work properly because they will not be able to find supporting files, and you will be required to spend time hunting for the problem.

Having a written organizational policy will help cast in stone the structure of your site. If everyone decides on his own where to place files, you'll end up with a mess. Software will be installed and configured wherever someone felt that the files should go. Perhaps, they were installed on top of your system's distribution—a practice that often spells disaster if later you find out there's a bug, and the version that came with your operating system worked better!

An organizational scheme permits you to easily back up software you have added. If you need to install an additional machine and want to upgrade some of your customizations, the process is simplified and becomes really easy. All you need to do is copy the /usr/local tree, and everything is there. From that point, you can either opt to remove software you won't need or just keep it. The UNIX rdist command can be very helpful in maintaining multiple identically configured systems in sync.

Should you ever need a backup, a quick tar -cf /tmp/usrlocal.tar /usr/local will take care of the problem. You don't need to differentiate or select from various places that may contain files you added. It's all kept together.

FILE PACKAGES: ORGANIZING HTML AND RESOURCES

The concept of *page wrapper* was developed at accessLINK. A page wrapper is no more than a directory that keeps all relevant resources (images or additional HTML files) grouped together in a bundle. The concept is hierarchical, so ideally you would group a section of multiple page wrappers together into a section.

Grouping HTML files into a *page*.htmld directory is a good way of keeping tabs on files (accessLINK groups root trees in a *sitename*.ws wrapper; ws stands for Web site).

My experience has been that if I create a directory that contains all the necessary resources for an HTML document and group it all in a wrapper, it becomes easy for me to maintain that page. The system also enhances the recycling of disk space. If you are working on an HTML file and you remove a reference to an image that is stored in a different directory, it's likely to remain there. If it is near your HTML file, more than likely the file will be discarded, freeing disk space for other things.

This organizational scheme works best when several people are responsible for keeping a site running. When a document needs to be updated, the location of all the related resources are stored together and nicely packaged. The alternative is chaos. In a normal scenario where 40 HTML files are stored at the same directory level along with associated resources (such as images or videos), it becomes impossible to determine what needs to be done. To figure out referenced images in a file, you have to look at the HTML code and search for the tags for the image filename. With the wrapper, much of the chaos is removed and the structure is simplified. By simple inspection of the directory's contents, you can find what you are looking for.

It's no miracle that this basic structure also happens to follow the physical structure of the site. The directory structure mirrors the navigational structure, providing another level of reinforcing the way the site is organized for people who update and manage this site (see Figure 3.1). Just by navigating it, you have an understanding of the physical layout of a site.

Figure 3.1. The Web site directory hierarchy. All references are localized. Global items are placed at the top. Local items only used on a particular page remain close to their resources. The window capture shows the directory tree from htdocs *downward and describes the file organization scheme.*

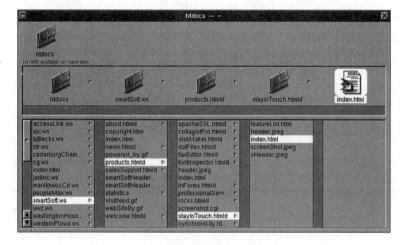

Figure 3.1 is a visual representation of the system. The htdocs tree contains a series of wrappers with a ws extension, which stands for Web site. Each of the sites listed lives in one of accessLINK's servers. One of them is for SmartSoft, Inc., a software development company. All files related to the SmartSoft site are stored inside the

smartSoft.ws wrapper. Each page is represented by an htmld wrapper. Wrappers nest according to the logical navigational structure of the site. On the end node you can appreciate the contents of a simple page. The stayInTouch.htmld wrapper holds a main HTML file (index.html) and a sibling file for feature information (featureList.html). Images and other supporting resources are found next to the files that reference them.

ADDITIONAL BENEFITS OF THE WRAPPER APPROACH

This approach works in several levels. It allows you to name graphics and resources generically, such as header.jpeg. However, the generic name works fine because more than likely there is only one header file, not a hundred. If you were using one general graphics directory, each graphic would need a unique name or some other cryptic-naming scheme. By localizing resources near their point of use, each name is descriptive, clear, and readable. This also removes a lot of the creativity involved in inventing filenames. The context of the file provides information about what it is, so you don't need to peek into the file to figure out what it contains.

This approach also allows you to create HTML template files. If you were going to add a product, it becomes a matter of duplicating one of the existing wrappers, updating new header.jpeg graphics and the new text. The rest remains the same. This makes you more efficient when you have to add or build a Web site because you can always leverage on previously done work.

From a maintenance point of view, the htmld approach helps to keep directories smaller and clutter-free. From a security standpoint, it also lets you clearly see suspicious files that you didn't put there. If you know where and what your files are, you'll have a better chance of noticing if you've had a break-in or if someone put something in the wrong spot. If you just throw it all in together and have 30 or 40 files per directory, it becomes difficult to figure out what is going on, and it takes more careful reading. Later the site will have many stale HTML files or graphics that are no being longer used. Cleaning up at this point is time-consuming because you have to think about what each of the files contain. If you remove any haphazardly, more than likely you'll break something.

FILENAMING SUGGESTIONS

When you are creative with your filenames, it becomes more difficult to know what a file contains. What is header2.gif? I don't know because there's no context, and I doubt that the person who created such a file could remember either. If it's all packaged, then you know who's the client of that resource, and you can create a visual and organizational association; you know what things are.

I title everything *firstSecondThird.type*. The first word is in lowercase letters. Any word after has its first letter in uppercase. I don't use spaces, dashes, or any other character that is not a letter or a number. Periods are used to separate file extensions. This makes it easy for me to read and type filenames, and it removes the possibility of any nonalphanumeric characters from becoming part of a filename.

WEB SITE DOCUMENTATION

While you are building your site, you may want to document clearly the standards used for creating a site. For example, it is useful to document colors used on an image. Better yet, create template files that can be used for creating new graphics. In Adobe Photoshop, this is really easy. Add a layer and enter the size of the text and font face that you used for a graphic title. This will allow future titles to be consistent and will save you a lot of time in generating artwork. Pass this information to those that create artwork for your site. You'll be glad if you do.

PERSONAL HTML DIRECTORIES

Many of your users will be interested in creating their own personal home pages. Apache provides support for this feature with its UserDir module. If you performed the installation instructions in Chapter 2, "Installing and Configuring the Apache Server," you'll recall that you disabled the UserDir functionality from your server. Requests for your users' home pages take the form of: http://host/~user, where *user* is the login name of the user.

On receiving a request for a user's home page, the default server configuration looks for the public_html directory inside of the user's home directory. I don't like this feature for security and convenience reasons.

If a user protects his directory, making it unreadable by the User ID (UID) of the server, then he doesn't have an opportunity to publish a home page. Other security implications are also possible, depending on the permissiveness of your configuration files and features such as automatic indexes. You can create a situation where a user could provide Web access to not only his files but to other directories in your system. This is something you really don't want to do!

Apache versions under 1.1 don't provide any configuration alternative, except for installing a third-party module that implements different functionality. If you are using version 1.1 or higher, you'll be glad to know that the version of the module allows you to specify a directory that contains all user's public HTML directories. Users are able to create and maintain their own Web pages while administrators are happy that their HTML directories are not located along with other potentially sensitive files.

An additional benefit of the improved module is that it allows you to create home page directories that don't necessarily match your internal usernames. Because this mechanism doesn't rely on a user account, it allows you to provide home pages even on a host that doesn't hold any user accounts, such as a *bastion host* for a site that has a firewall. Bastion hosts are machines that provide Internet services to the Internet.

You will need to provide some sort of mechanism to help users upload their information and publish it to the Web. In terms of security issues, you'll still have to deal with what they publish, but I'll leave that to your internal Web police. Let's assume that your organization doesn't have any disgruntled employees that would publish your most private secrets right off your Web site.

CGI LOCATION

CGIs are programs that interact with your server via the Common Gateway Interface—a convention used for exchanging data between the server and a program. CGIs are necessary on your Web if you want to implement things such as forms or any type of advanced functionality. On the default configuration you installed in Chapter 2, CGIs were disabled.

The problem with CGIs and other executable processes is that they are programs. Security problems are usually introduced by bugs in programs. While your Web server is fairly secure, programs that you implement may not take into account some of the treachery that some people will go through to break into your site. With that said, realize that someone may be able to exploit a weakness on a CGI program you create. (For detailed information on this subject, see Chapter 16, "Web Server Security Issues.")

My first suggestion is that until you understand the ramifications of permitting public CGIs, you should restrain from offering this capability to your users. There are a few questions that you'll need to address before you can really provide an evaluation:

- What does the CGI do?
- How does CGI do it?
- Could CGI present a security risk if it was terminated abruptly?
- What if the CGI receives unexpected input or more input than it can handle?
- Do you allow nonalphanumeric characters in your input?

Once you understand what you are installing and what you are protecting against, it becomes easier to define a policy regarding the use and location of CGI programs on your site. The easiest approach is to read the source code of each CGI before you install it. However, this obviously doesn't scale well on large installations, especially where a lot of users may be creating programs. It becomes unfeasible to look in close detail at what each CGI does and the security implications of the program.

To enable CGI, you will need to uncomment the ScriptAlias directive in your conf/ srm.conf file and restart the server. The ScriptAlias directive specifies a directory where the server can execute programs. By default, this is set to /usr/local/etc/ httpd/cgi-bin/. This provides a restrictive setup because the server will only execute programs that are found in this directory.

Because the server restricts the execution of CGI to designated directories, the organizational structure previously presented would require that all CGIs live in a central location. While this may be fine for a small site, you may have to consider other alternatives and their security implications:

◆ House your CGIs in the cgi-bin directory.

◆ House CGIs in a special cgi directory in the main tree for each site you host (inside your ws wrapper).

◆ Allow CGIs to live wherever they are needed.

These options are progressively lax on their security. I feel that the second option is a good compromise for the following reasons: It allows enough freedom for the site designer while at the same time keeps things orderly.

This mechanism fits into my belief system that a site should be portable—the .htmld approach. If the entire site tree moves, all the resources are properly referenced locally within the tree itself.

The first option I find too restrictive for any site that supports virtual hosts (multiple domains) such as accessLINK.

The third option is actually the one that I implement at accessLINK. I choose it because we have a tight control on our CGIs and what they do. If we had users on our system, this laissez-faire approach would not even be considered.

To enable CGI in predetermined directories, all you need to do is set an option that enables the execution of CGIs on a properly named directory. Use local-cgi for the name of local CGI directories. You can accomplish this with a <Directory> section in your global access control file, conf/access.conf, like in following example:

```
<Directory *.ws/local-cgi>
AllowOverride None
Options ExecCGI
</Directory>
```

This configuration will allow execution of CGIs only if they are stored in a subdirectory of a Web site wrapper called local-cgi.

USER CGI DIRECTORIES

If your users have more than a little technical inclination, it won't be long until you receive requests for setting up user-controlled CGI directories. This is often a source of headaches for you from a standpoint of establishing a security policy. Freedom equals problems. So the question is what do you do? If you give many people access and control over the CGIs they run, you've opened Pandora's box. My personal view is that as long as you are giving freedom, might as well give total freedom. Just make sure that freedom doesn't cause you other problems.

Another way of dealing with the problem may be to provide several CGIs that can be accessed publicly within your organization. CGIs provide functionality such as e-mail, generic form support, page counters, search tools, and so on. This way you'll eliminate a great portion of the need for public CGIs.

If a user needs to implement a form, have her use your generic form wrapper. This CGI should e-mail the form information. The user could then write a program that will process the e-mail information into something useful to her.

Another alternative is to place a machine outside of your firewall that doesn't have anything but user home pages. Then you could set restrictions like the following in your global access configuration file (conf/access.conf):

```
<Directory /usr/local/etc/httpd/public/*/user-cgi>
AllowOverride None
Options ExecCGI
</Directory>
```

Assuming that /public is your UserPath directory (using the UserPath module), users will be able to do what they want in their CGI directories. You can network mount the public directory so that it is easy for users to update and change what they want. However, in terms of access from the outside, no sensitive information would be available.

SUMMARY

Organizing your site will help you become more efficient at managing your Web site(s). As things get handed down from one person to another, a strong and workable framework will help maintain some sort of order, which will allow for efficient maintenance and growth.

As the number of users increases, you'll face security issues that are tough to predict in terms of the potential problems they may create. The purpose of the Internet is to disseminate information. Having either an overly restrictive or a loose policy creates problems. A happy medium is perhaps found on an isolated machine that has been sanitized for the function. Users can then create and maintain their own pages without much concern for security implications that may affect sensitive areas of your network.

- Virtual Hosts

- CGI (Common
  Gateway Interface)
  Programming

- Server Side
  Includes (SSI)

- Third-Party Modules

PART II

Beyond the Basics:
Advanced HTTP Server
Functionality

CHAPTER 4

Virtual Hosts

This chapter covers a powerful feature of the Apache server: virtual hosts. Virtual hosting allows a single instance of the Apache Web server to run several Web sites, each accessible by its own domain name. Apache was one of the first HTTP servers to provide support for building virtual sites. While servers from NCSA and others also provide virtual-site support, Apache provides better performance and has more features than the others.

At first glance, the main advantage of a virtual site seems mostly cosmetic: It allows many Web sites to be addressed by their own domain name on a single shared machine. However, this cosmetic advantage has several positive effects on the administration of your site and how others use it. Virtual hosts are frequently created with the intent to do the following:

◆ Make it easier for customers to access Web sites on leased servers. Because the lessee can use his own domain name, addresses tend to be shorter. This helps to project a professional identity to the world. Users are more likely to remember the shorter address since the domain name (hopefully) has some relevance to the corporate name.

◆ Reduce and maximize the computer and networking hardware. Several low-traffic sites can be housed in a single machine, thus reducing the costs of hosting the site.

◆ Reduce the human costs associated with system administration. Instead of managing and configuring a dedicated server for each domain, the webmaster only needs to maintain a few configuration files and a minimal number of boxes. This translates into a reduced number of systems that need to be upgraded or maintained, thus simplifying network maintenance.

Because most Web sites don't generate enough traffic to exhaust the resources of a single machine, it is desirable from an administrative point of view to allow a single server to masquerade and behave as several different machines. Instead of dedicating hardware and monetary resources to each site hosted, a few server configuration commands produce the same result: a virtual site. Because the expense required to set up a Web server can be shared between several sites, the time required to configure and manage Web sites is reduced dramatically.

Virtual hosts have the positive side effect of making Web pages portable. When a site is virtual, it's easy to move it to a different Web server in the same network or somewhere else. It becomes a matter of transferring the site's HTML pages to a new machine and modifying the site's Domain Name System (DNS) information to point to the new server. To accommodate DNS update lapses, simply create a redirection on the old server. This allows traffic to continue flowing without a lapse, which is an important issue with sites that thrive on traffic as a way of generating business.

Historically, when you wanted a site hosted using your domain, your only viable option was to purchase (or lease) a computer and have it configured as a Web server.

Incurred with these costs was the expense of managing the server. These costs, easily thousands of dollars, motivated Internet Service Providers (ISPs) to consider additional ways of supporting multiple Web sites in one host, which resulted in a few early solutions, such as the "home page" approach.

The home page approach was one early way to support multiple sites on a single Web server. This approach differentiates each site by adding extra address information, such as a user's home page.

The home page approach creates addresses that look like this:

```
http://www.isp.dom/~name
```

or, worse yet, uniform resource locators (URLs) that list some path to a directory on the server tree:

```
http://www.isp.dom/name
```

The home page approach is an appropriate way to serve local users' pages. But when it comes to serving corporate information that is going to be accessed more frequently and by a large number of viewers, this solution creates ugly addresses that are hard to remember, long to type, prone to user error, and not very professional looking.

Building a Virtual Site

The terms *virtual host*, *virtual site*, and *multihomed server* are generally used interchangeably to describe a server that supports multiple domain names. To make matters easier to understand, I find it best to limit the scope of these terms to their appropriate meanings: To create a virtual site, you need to configure a virtual host; for the virtual host to work, you may have to create a multihomed server; and obviously, there's a difference in tone. How you build a multihomed server depends on which version of Apache you are using and some other technical issues. "So what's the difference?" you ask. Semantics; but clarity here will help in describing the process.

A multihomed computer is one that can answer to multiple IP addresses. A computer that is accessible by multiple names (such as mailhost.foo.com and www.foo.com) that resolve to the same IP address is not a multihomed computer.

Aliasing a capability provided by DNS in a CNAME (canonical name) resource record, or by listing multiple machine names on the /etc/hosts file after an IP address, is just a convenience for people accessing a networked resource. In general, people have a hard time remembering names, and some names such as www or ftp are typically standardized for machines that host services with the same name. Users only need to remember the domain name when those resources use traditional names, such as www.apple.com, mailhost.apple.com, or ftp.apple.com. A multihomed computer needs more than that. It must answer to two or more different IP addresses such as 1.2.3.4. IP addresses are assigned by your Internet network provider when you sign up with them.

A *virtual site* is a Web site that resides on a server with other Web sites. Each Web site is accessible by its own name and shares all the hardware resources with other virtual sites. Although all requests are answered by the same HTTP server process, different home pages are returned for each site depending on the name or IP address used to access the information.

Another networking issue that you will have to address before you can multihome is the DNS; DNS provides the machine name to the IP translation service. While computers like to address each other using numbers, people prefer using names. DNS translates names into numbers and numbers into names. Chances are that if you have a connection to the Internet, you are running a name server. If you are not, someone else is running it for you. If you are not running your own DNS, you'll need to coordinate with your network administrator to implement any addition or change to the DNS. I have included a comprehensive DNS tutorial in Appendix E, "DNS and BIND Primer."

CONFIGURING A VIRTUAL HOST

A virtual site is configured by the `<VirtualHost>` directive, which allows you to override several configuration directives based on the site's name or IP address. This allows you to specify a different `DocumentRoot` directory for each virtual site, so a single instance of the HTTP server can return different Web sites for each of the virtual sites it hosts.

Right from the beginning, the Apache server provided the necessary infrastructure to allow server-side support for virtual hosts. The only requirement was that the server needed to answer to different IP addresses. This technique, which still works reliably, requires the creation of a multihomed server. Multihomed servers have a few downsides, including a built-in limit: The number of virtual hosts that can be supported depends on how many IP addresses you have available. Each virtual host requires its own unique IP address. This requirement made it easy for an ISP to swallow up scarce IP addresses with only a few customers.

In the current incarnation of the server, the Apache group introduced a non–IP-intensive solution. Using a new extension to the HTTP protocol, which requires the browser to report the name of the server being accessed (the `http://www.apple.com` portion of the URL) along with the resource to retrieve, the Web server can determine who the request is for. Before, a URL such as `http://www.apple.com/index.html` would have the `www.apple.com` portion removed from the request, making it impossible for the server to determine the name of the host as known by the user.

This new mechanism effectively added the infrastructure from which Apache could provide virtual site support without the need to create a multihomed computer. Non–IP-intensive virtual hosts make it possible to host an almost infinite number of virtual hosts easily, without the need to create a multihomed server.

THE <VIRTUALHOST> DIRECTIVE SECTION

The `<VirtualHost>` and `</VirtualHost>` section tags are used to group server configuration directives that only apply to a particular virtual host. Any directive that is allowed in a virtual host context can be used. When the server receives a request directed toward a virtual host, the configuration directives enclosed between the `<VirtualHost>` and `</VirtualHost>` section tags override directives found elsewhere. `<VirtualHost>` sections are found in the `httpd.conf` file.

You specify the host to which a `<VirtualHost>` section applies by specifying the IP of the virtual host or a fully qualified domain name. A minimal virtual host only needs to override the `DocumentRoot` directive:

```
<VirtualHost www.company.com>
DocumentRoot /www/docs/company
</VirtualHost>
```

The `<VirtualHost>` declaration for non–IP-intensive virtual hosts, based on the HTTP/1.1 feature previously described, is almost identical to the original IP-intensive version, except that you only supply a machine name that resolves to the same IP address as the real host. The server decides what to serve based on the machine name used to access the resource.

Apache 1.1

This approach only works with browsers that comply to the HTTP/1.1 specification, which is still a draft. Hopefully this will become part of the specification and will be more widely implemented.

For IP-intensive virtual hosts, each host IP identified by the `<VirtualHost>` directive must be unique and, in order for it to work, the computer must be configured to accept multiple IP addresses. This configuration, unlike that of the new non-IP virtual hosts, works regardless of the browser.

The `<VirtualHost>` section allows configuration of a virtual host as if it were a simple single-homed server; it allows you to implement customized server configuration settings on a per-site basis. Each site can tailor the server to its own needs.

A minimal virtual host configuration only needs to make use of the `DocumentRoot` directive. You can further customize the virtual server with `ServerName` directives, which will set the name the server will use when responding to requests. You are able to include many of the directives that can be specified in the server configuration file (`httpd.conf`) or in the resource configuration file (`srm.conf`). This gives total control over the configuration and behavior of the virtual server. You can even enable logging of the transaction to different log files. The following configuration presents a more complete and typical example:

```
#### Virtual machine configuration
#Bind Address (Address identifying this virtual host
BindAddress *
<VirtualHost>
#
#Server name returned to users connected to this host
ServerName www.company.com
#
#
#WebMaster for this host
#IF YOU USE A VIRTUAL DOMAIN FOR MAIL, REMEMBER TO
#CONFIGURE SENDMAIL TO ACCEPT THIS DOMAIN IN YOUR SENDMAIL.CF!!!
#
ServerAdmin  webmaster@company.com
#
#The document root for this virtual host
DocumentRoot /usr/local/etc/htdocs/company.htmld
#
#The location of the error log for the virtual host
ErrorLog /usr/local/etc/apache/logs/company/error_log
#
#The location of the access log for the virtual host
TransferLog /usr/local/etc/apache/logs/company/access_log
...
</VirtualHost>
#### End Virtual Machine configuration
```

Configuration using the <VirtualHost> directive is, as you can see, pretty straightforward. However, there are some mechanics that must be resolved prior to getting a server to multihome (namely, how to configure the server so that it answers to different IP numbers).

BindAddress

The BindAddress directive allows you to further refine where the server will listen for connections. The default behavior for the server is to listen for requests on all the IP addresses supported on the machine (BindAddress *) at the port specified by the Port directive. However, this may not be what you want. You may want to limit which addresses the server will serve. The BindAddress directive allows you to specify this. BindAddress allows you to specify the addresses to listen for (either the IP address or fully qualified hostname). These are examples for the various possibilities:

BindAddress 1.2.3.4

Or this specifies the fully qualified name of the machine:

BindAddress www.foo.com

To have the server listen to all IP addresses accepted by the host, use BindAddress *.

BindAddress * is also the default value if BindAddress is not specified.

Note that the server will only bind to requests on the port specified by the `Port` directive, which defaults to 80—the standard TCP port for HTTP servers.

Listen

The `Listen` directive is new for Apache 1.1. It has similar functionality to the `BindAddress`. This directive allows you to specify additional ports that the server will listen in for requests. This feature is useful in implementing internal servers that contain information you don't want others to see by default when they connect to your address. For example, you may want to have special information about your network available through the Web. Instead of running a separate server process to serve this information, you can have Apache listen in on multiple ports, such as port 8080.

This feature is used in the upcoming version of Stronghold—a commercial secure version of Apache that implements both an SSL and a standard server using one process. Instead of running two server processes (one for the secure server and another for the nonsecure one), you can have one process respond appropriately depending on the port used for the connection.

Technical Note

BindAddress and `Listen` don't implement virtual hosts. They simply tell the server where to listen for requests. `BindAddress` and `Listen` are used to build a list of addresses and ports that the server will listen for. If Apache is not configured to listen for a particular request, your virtual host won't be accessible.

MULTIHOMING: IP-INTENSIVE VIRTUAL HOSTS

This section does not apply if you are using Apache 1.1 non–IP-intensive virtual hosts. If you are using Apache 1.1 or better, you may want to skip this section because Apache 1.1 has a much easier way of developing a virtual host that doesn't require multihoming. (See "Apache Non-IP Virtual Hosts" later in this chapter.)

For a multihomed Web server to work, the host computer needs to be able to respond to multiple names or IP addresses. Traditionally, multihomed hosts were the only computers on a network that did this. Because they bridged two separate networks, they had the need to answer to two different addresses. To do this, these computers were usually fitted with two networking cards that allowed the computer to have two different network addresses. Each network knew the multihomed host by a different name. On the Web, multihomed computers don't connect to two networks, but they do need to answer to multiple names.

Most modern unices (plural for UNIX) provide the software tools needed to allow you to specify multiple IP addresses to a single interface. If your system does not include a version of `ifconfig` that supports the `alias` option, don't despair. Table 4.1 lists the major systems and how you can achieve multiple IP support.

TABLE 4.1. OPERATING SYSTEMS AND MULTIHOMING.

Operating System	Multiple IP Support
AIX 4.1	Built-in: `ifconfig alias`
BSDI	Built-in: `ifconfig alias`
Digital OSF/1	Built-in: `ifconfig alias`
Digital UNIX	Built-in: `ifconfig alias`
FreeBSD	Built-in: `ifconfig alias`
HPUX 10.x	Needs `ifconfig alias` patch
HPUX 9.x	Needs virtual interface (VIF) patch
IRIX 5.3	Needs SGI's `ifconfig alias` patch
Linux	Needs `ifconfig alias` patch
NeXTSTEP 3.3	Use PPP Interfaces to provide virtual interfaces
Solaris 2.3 and better	Built-in: `ifconfig` logical units
SunOS 4.x	Needs VIF patch
SunOS 5.3 and better	Built-in: `ifconfig` logical units
Ultrix	Needs VIF patch

If your system is not listed in Table 4.1, you might want to try the PPP approach described later in this chapter. Alternatively, you can opt for Apache's 1.1 non–IP-intensive virtual hosts, which remove the need to create a multihomed server altogether.

You can specify multiple IP addresses to a single interface by using the following:

◆ The `ifconfig alias`
◆ The VIF patch
◆ PPP

ifconfig alias

The `alias` option of `ifconfig` is the easiest way to implement a virtual host. The `ifconfig` command is used to set or display configuration values of a network interface. Not all vendors support the `alias` option.

You can make your Ethernet interface answer to an additional IP by issuing the following command:

```
ifconfig interface IP alias
```

Depending on your operating system, `interface` can be `en0` or `le0`, so you'll need to check your man pages for `ifconfig` to determine the appropriate name for your Ethernet interface. Set the IP parameter to a valid DNS address that you assigned to the virtual host. That's it! The interface will now accept packets destined for the virtual site.

Some operating systems in the preceding list don't offer the `alias` option by default, but patches are available from the vendor or the Net. Each patch distribution includes information on how to apply it, as well as any other specifics on its use. I have included some of these patches on the CD-ROM, but you may want to check for updates on them at the following locations:

♦ The `ifconfig alias` patch for HPUX 10.X can be found at `http://www.limitless.co.uk/hp_ifalias.html`. This patch has been included on the CD-ROM with the kind permission of its author, Julian Perry (`jules@limitless.co.uk`).

♦ You can find the `ifconfig` patch for IRIX 5.3 at `http://www.sgi.com`.

♦ The Linux `ifconfig alias` patch can be found at `ftp://ftp.mindspring.com/users/rsanders/ipalias`.

SOLARIS VIRTUAL INTERFACES

Solaris supports virtual interfaces in the form of logical units. You can have up to 255 logical units per network interface. To add a new virtual host to the primary interface, just type the following:

```
ifconfig le0:logicalunit 204.95.222.200 up
```

Replace `logicalunit` with a number from 1 to 255. You can check currently used interfaces by issuing `netstat -ia`.

THE VIF PATCH

The VIF patch was one of the first solutions available on the Internet to enable a single interface to handle multiple IP addresses. The VIF patch was originally developed by John Ioannidis in 1991 as part of a project related to his Ph.D. thesis at Columbia University. The patch was pared down in 1994 to allow a single interface to handle multiple IP addresses under SunOS. The patch was further enhanced for SunOS 4.1.*x* by Chuck Smoko and Bob Baggerman. Two separate Ultrix 4.3a ports have been developed, one by John Hascall and the other by Phil Brandenberger.

The VIF patch creates a virtual interface that, to the networking software, looks like a hardware interface. The VIF interface allows you to assign an address as well as to configure network interface parameters with `ifconfig`.

After the virtual interface has been configured, you may have to add routing entries to the routing table using the `route` command. However, some implementations do the right thing without this step. For more information, refer to the instructions for your operating system. The VIF allows requests to any of the host's addresses, real or virtual, to be answered by the real interface. Packets leaving the host use the real or virtual IP assigned to match where they are coming from.

Detailed instructions on how to build the patch and incorporate it into the kernel, and how to use VIF for each specific architecture, are included in the source. You can obtain the latest version of the VIF patch from this repository:

◆ John Hascall's latest ULTRIX modifications can be found at
`ftp://ftp.iastate.edu/pub/unix/ultrix/vif/`.

PPP

If your UNIX vendor didn't provide you with the sources to the kernel, then PPP software (used for establishing dial-up networking connections) may be your only viable alternative to create a multihomed host. NeXTSTEP, the operating system I use at accessLINK, doesn't come with the source to its Mach kernel, so I developed this workaround. The result is almost an equivalent to the VIF patch, and its effects are easily removed from a system. This solution should be very portable across various UNIX boxes.

PPP provides networking interfaces, which you can configure much in the same way as VIF interfaces, with these advantages:

◆ PPP's effects can be easily removed and isolated. If things are not working properly, you don't have to worry about irreversible changes made to the kernel.

- Some vendors' systems already ship with PPP software preinstalled, making it easy to implement.
- PPP is portable.

Tip

> The PPP in your distribution may already have one or two PPP interfaces available named ppp0 or ppp1. You can check the number of interfaces your vendor provides by executing the following command:
>
> `% netstat - ia`
>
> PPP interfaces will be listed as ppp0 though pppX. If you only need one or two virtual machines, you may be able to use your preinstalled version of PPP.

If you need additional interfaces, you will have to obtain the source code to the basic PPP software plus the system-specific changes for your operating system. You will also have to edit one of the header files to add the additional interfaces.

You can find the latest release to the source code for the PPP software at ftp:// dcssoft.anu.edu.au/pub/ppp and ftp://ftp.merit.edu/pub/ppp.

After you configure the software for your particular machine, modify the number of interfaces to match your needs. In the pppd.h file, found on the pppd distribution, find the line that contains the following definition:

```
#define NUM_PPP 2
```

The number to the right of NUM_PPP (in this case, 2) defines how many PPP interfaces are to be compiled into the software. Change this number to the number of interfaces you think you'll be needing plus a few more. I changed mine to add 25 interfaces.

In the NeXTSTEP-specific distribution of the PPP software, which is based on PPP-2.2, the defined NUM_PPP may be found on additional files. Do a grep to find them and change all instances to match the number of interfaces you want.

You should be able to build a customized version of your kernel or a kernel loader that adds supports for PPP. Read the installation instructions for your particular system. Once this is installed, you are ready to configure the interfaces.

CONFIGURING THE PPP INTERFACES

By default, PPP interfaces are named ppp0, ppp1, ppp2, and so on. It is a good idea to set up the interfaces right after the machine boots. This way you can be confident that the Web server will be accepting requests for all sites at boot time.

4

I suggest putting your configuration entries into your rc.local or, if you have many entries, creating your own rc.ppp.

To assign an address to an interface, I use the following commands. Your version of UNIX may provide additional or different options to these commands. Check the main page of your system prior to issuing any of these commands:

```
ifconfig ppp0 204.95.222.200 up netmask 255.255.255.0
route add host 1.2.3.4 1.2.3.4 0
arp -s 1.2.3.4 00:00:00:00:00 pub
```

In the previous example, I added a virtual host at address 1.2.3.4. Simply replace 1.2.3.4 with the address of your machine. Replace 255.255.255.0 with the netmask used in your network. Replace 00:00:00:00:00 with the Ethernet address of your networking card.

Warning

Make sure you update your DNS to include the virtual machine. Otherwise, a client won't be able to find the new virtual address!

The previous commands do the following:

◆ The ifconfig command assigns the IP and netmask to the ppp0 interface.

◆ The route command adds a static routing entry to the destination and gateway IP. Refer to the virtual IP address you assigned to the PPP interface.

◆ The arp command modifies the Internet-to-Ethernet address translation tables. The -s option was given to create an arp entry for the hostname, here specified in IP notation. The pub option will "publish" the arp for the host, even though the address is not its own (it's virtual!).

You can verify that the interfaces provided by PPP were incorporated into the kernel by issuing this:

```
/usr/etc/netstat -ia
```

You should be able to see a number of pppn interface names listed and be able to test whether the interfaces and the DNS are working properly. You will need to test from a machine other than the Web server. A limitation of PPP virtual hosts is that a virtual host is unreachable from the server that hosts it. However, that is not really a problem because your server is dedicated, right? To test that the virtual host is running, simply ping the virtual host. You should get a response like the following:

```
hydrogen:4# /etc/ping 1.2.3.4
PING helium: 56 data bytes
64 bytes from 204.95.222.2: icmp_seq=0. time=4. ms
64 bytes from 204.95.222.2: icmp_seq=1. time=2. ms
```

```
64 bytes from 204.95.222.2: icmp_seq=2. time=2. ms
64 bytes from 204.95.222.2: icmp_seq=3. time=2. ms
64 bytes from 204.95.222.2: icmp_seq=4. time=2. ms
64 bytes from 204.95.222.2: icmp_seq=5. time=2. ms
```

Replace *1.2.3.4* with the virtual IP address that you assigned earlier.

APACHE NON-IP VIRTUAL HOSTS

Starting with version 1.1, Apache added support for virtual hosts without the need for additional IP addresses. This greatly simplifies the management process of the server because it removes the hardest configuration problem from the list: how to get a machine to answer to multiple IP addresses.

Apache's implementation of non-IP virtual hosts depends on the client browser to provide information about the server being accessed. At the time of this writing, many browsers, including Netscape 2.0 or better and Microsoft's Internet Explorer 2.0 and better, support this feature.

The great advantage to non–IP-intensive virtual hosts is that now there are no limits to the number of virtual sites you can host. Before, the number of virtual hosts you could support was dependent on how many IP addresses you had available for hosts. Now, a single IP address can support an unlimited number of sites without having to rely on software, such as PPP or kernel patches, to get the machine to multihome.

The new modifications to the <VirtualHost> section look almost identical to the old version:

```
<VirtualHost www.company.com>
  ServerName www.company.com
  ServerAlias company.com *.company.com
  DocumentRoot /usr/local/htdocs/company
</VirtualHost>
```

Just add as many <VirtualHost> sections (one per virtual site as you need) to your httpd.conf configuration file and restart the server.

Additional directives can still be placed in the section. All you need to do to get the virtual server to work is add a DNS entry for www.company.com that points to your server's real address. Unlike IP-intensive virtual hosts, the IP of the virtual sites is the same as the real host.

A new directive, ServerAlias, allows you to reference a virtual host section configuration by other names. You must, of course, have DNS entries for each alias that points to the same IP address for this feature to work.

A WORKAROUND FOR CLIENTS THAT DON'T SUPPORT NON-IP VIRTUAL HOSTS

Client browsers that do not support the non-IP virtual hosts will get the server's real main page. A fully qualified path link to your server will let the client access your materials. If your link points to the same URL, you'll create an endless loop. With careful use of the new ServerPath directive, you can redirect traffic to the right place.

The ServerPath directive should be placed in the VirtualHost section. The directive looks like this:

```
<VirtualHost www.company.com>
ServerName www.company.com
DocumentRoot /usr/local/htdocs/company
ServerPath /company
</VirtualHost>
```

The preceding ServerPath directive will redirect all requests beginning with the /company path to /usr/local/htdocs/company, the correct place. Your HTML documents should contain only relative links; this will make your files accessible from any browser.

SUMMARY

With the ability to control most aspects of the server behavior on a per-virtual-host basis, multihoming is very powerful indeed. The downside of multihoming is that the load processed by a single machine is increased. One machine is going to handle all the requests for all the sites you host in it. If these requests require several connections per second, performance may degrade below acceptable levels depending on the supporting network and computer hardware. However, there are ways of eliminating these bottlenecks and obtaining the administrative benefits of a multihomed Web server.

The advantages of multihoming greatly outweigh any downsides. If your traffic load is heavy, you're probably interested in distributing the load. An infrastructure of multihomed distributed servers may be your best plan. By making all your servers clones of each other, you have in fact created a fault-tolerant information service. Should one machine go down, access to the site is unaffected. Other servers will handle requests for the non-operational server. This is good because it may reduce the urgency of a disaster situation and because it will allow you to maintain a high-level performance site at a low cost.

Using a single server to host various Web sites reduces the cost of the hardware, maximizes the use of computer and network hardware, and at the same time reduces the number of administrative chores. All this occurs because there is only one machine to set up, one machine to troubleshoot, one machine to upgrade, one machine to monitor, and one machine to back up.

One is a good number. The most valuable resource of a Web site is the time of the webmaster, so reducing his workload is an excellent thing. If you are running more than one HTTP server hosting different content, you may want to evaluate whether this feature can make your life easier as well.

CHAPTER 5

CGI (Common Gateway Interface) Programming

Any Web site that does more than just display pages will use Common Gateway Interface (CGI) programs. CGI programs provide support to many useful functions. Even basic things such as Hypertext Markup Language (HTML) forms require a CGI program to process the information and do something useful with it. Many people refer to CGI programs as *scripts*. For me, this term somehow diminishes the complexity that some CGI programs have. I prefer to call them CGI programs. CGI programs can exist as interpreted scripts or compiled binaries—in either form, they are programs.

The most popular languages used for developing CGI programs are sh (Bourne shell), Perl (Practical Extraction Report Language), and C. You can use any language from which you can access environment variables. Most, if not all, UNIX programming or scripting languages can do this because this support is really inherited from the shells. This means that, depending on the task at hand, you are free to choose a CGI development tool that matches your needs and program complexity—a good thing.

WHAT IS A CGI PROGRAM?

A *CGI program* is a program that conforms to certain conventions. Many people think that CGI is a protocol or a language or a specification. CGI is none of the above; it is a standard. In simplest terms, CGI is just a set of commonly used variables with the conventions used to access them. The variables provided by the CGI convention are used to exchange information between the HTTP server and a client program. In addition, CGI provides a means to return output to the browser. All output sent to stdout (the standard output stream) by a CGI program shows up on the Web browser, provided the right MIME-type header is sent by the CGI program.

If you want to execute a CGI program, you need to run a Web server like Apache because CGI transactions cannot be simulated by the browser. CGI calls happen only on the server side. On execution, most CGI programs will

◆ Process data sent by a browser;

◆ Return some sort of data; or

◆ Redirect the client to another URL containing some information.

At its most basic level, a CGI program will usually collect information from an HTML form, process data in the form, and then perform some action such as e-mailing data to a person. In its most complex form, there are virtually no limits to what can be done with a CGI program. CGI programs can interact with databases by fetching and storing various pieces of information to produce some sort of result.

Because of the stateless nature of the World Wide Web, there is no way to track a user from page to page using just conventional document-serving techniques. CGI allows communication, through a standard set of environment variables, between the HTTP server and a program running on the server computer—in this case, a CGI program. All sorts of things are possible with CGI that were not feasible with just HTML.

This basic capability of sending some data to a program via an HTTP server is responsible for a whole new way of creating client/server–type applications: the intranet. CGI programs permit the content of Web pages to be dynamic and relevant to what the user wants to see. I believe that in the future, many custom applications developed for private use by an organization (mission-critical applications) will be deployed as intranets—as Web-based applications. It makes sense. Instead of developing various versions of a program to match the mixed environment of today's office—PC, Macintosh, UNIX—you can develop a single version of your application that resides on a Web server. As long as there's a browser available for the machine you are using, you can access the application. Obviously, there are limitations, and some things are better done on the client side anyway. Java and other client-side programming tools will allow for more complex user-interface portions of the software to reside on the client, while the data persistence and other functionality happens on the server side.

Some environments, such as WebObjects from NeXT Software, Inc., provide many of the tools needed to create complex, real-world, Web-based applications today.

What Programming Language Should You Use?

CGI programs can be written in any language that has access to environment variables. However, you will find that most CGI programs are written in Perl, C, sh, or Tcl. Perl is widely used because of its strengths in text processing; currently, most Web applications are heavily weighted toward searching for and retrieving textual data. However, the language you choose will depend on your programming abilities and the complexity of your CGI. This chapter is by no means intended to be a programming reference. If you don't know how to program, there are many books that will help you get started. This chapter, however, will cover the basics regarding what makes a CGI program different. I will discuss how to access data passed from a browser in languages such as Perl, C, and sh. Many of the examples will be in Perl because it offers many facilities that make some of the basic CGI development tasks easier.

Perl

Perl is an excellent choice for CGI programs. In its current version, 5.002 as of this writing, it provides object-oriented modular programming, an excellent regular expression engine, and the best free support of any language I've seen. Perl allows for very rapid development. It originally was developed as an improved sh-sed-awk hybrid, but it has evolved into a feature-rich, structured, object-oriented language suitable for many programming tasks. Perl is great for text processing, and it has the extremely useful associative array data type built right into the language. An associative array is basically a key/value pair relationship. Unlike a list array, the key or index portion of the array is a string—a feature that makes it quite easy to work with the CGI environment variables.

There aren't too many downsides to Perl. One, however, is that it generally runs slower than a compiled language such as C. Perl is an interpreted language rather than a compiled language. This means that the Perl interpreter must parse, assemble, and compile the code each time a Perl program is called. This adds overhead (albeit small) to running a Perl program. Another downside is that Perl can't (yet) generate a standalone executable file. There is an effort underway to create a Perl compiler, and an alpha version has actually been released, but it is not yet the "accepted" way to run Perl programs. Another downside of interpreted versus compiled programs is that anyone with enough cleverness can view your Perl source code within the Web tree.

Overall, though, Perl is an excellent language for CGI programming, and the one on which I will focus in this chapter.

C

C has long been the industry-standard workhorse language for both small and large projects. Development of CGI programs in C usually takes a little longer, due to compiling time and the nature of C itself, but the resulting program runs orders of magnitude faster than any interpreted code. There aren't as many shortcuts as there are in Perl, however. For example, memory for dynamic arrays isn't automatically allocated or deallocated; you need to do all your housekeeping yourself. In contrast, Perl will grow an array automatically, freeing your time to do other things. Overall, though, C is very robust and is well-suited to CGI programming; and if your CGI program needs critical performance, it is a good candidate for the task.

SHELL (sh)

Some CGI programs are written as shell scripts. Although this may be quick and easy in some cases, sh is generally not suited for complicated programming. Use sh for the simplest of activities. Its advantages are that your system probably has an sh, or any of its variants, in it and, because sh is the environment, accessing environment variables is trivial.

The main problem with sh CGI programs is that it requires a bit of effort to decode encoded information sent to the CGI program via the QUERY_STRING environment variable or through the stdin or POST queries. There are a few tools on the Net that alleviate either of these problems quite a bit. I will cover these later.

WHERE TO LEARN MORE

You will find tons of useful information about programming for the Web on the Internet. The following are a few of my favorite sites and resources.

PERL

If you are interested in learning Perl, these four great books will provide about all the reference you will ever need:

- *Learning Perl* by Randal L. Schwartz, published by O'Reilly & Associates, Inc., ISBN 1-56592-042-2, is a great introduction to Perl with numerous tutorials to get you going quickly.

- *Teach Yourself Perl 5 in 21 Days* by David Till, published by Sams Publishing, ISBN 0-672-30894-0, is an ideal book for users who are interested in getting a basic understanding of Perl 4 and 5 with tutorials.

- *Perl 5 Unleashed* by Kamran Husain, published by Sams Publishing, ISBN 0-672-30891-6, takes a comprehensive look at Perl.

- *Programming Perl* by Larry Wall and Randal L. Schwartz, published by O'Reilly & Associates, Inc., ISBN 0-937175-64-1, is the authoritative guide to the Perl language. By the time this book is published, the second edition of *Programming Perl*, which covers Perl 5, should be out. Perl 5 is a complete overhaul of Perl 4; it provides a zillion new features. If you are running Perl 4, download the new version. It's better.

On the Internet, Usenet carries many things. Some of the newsgroups to check are

```
news:comp.lang.perl.announce
news:comp.lang.perl.misc
news:comp.lang.perl.modules
```

A special note about the newsgroups for Perl: Do NOT post CGI-related issues to the comp.lang.perl.* hierarchy. Rather, divert any CGI-related questions to comp.infosystems.www.authoring.cgi. Only post to the Perl newsgroups as a last resort. There are many common questions already answered in this frequently asked questions (FAQ) document:

```
http://www.perl.com/perl/faq/perl-cgi-faq.html
```

In addition to answering many commonly asked questions about Perl, this FAQ contains pointers for everything else you could possibly imagine about Perl.

The latest version of the Perl software is available from any of the Comprehensive Perl Archive Network (CPAN) sites listed. Its aim is to be the only Perl archive you will ever need. The CPAN archive can be found at various locations. Table 5.1 gives a list of all known sites, at the time of this writing, grouped by continent.

Table 5.1. Comprehensive Perl archive network sites.

Africa	
South Africa	`ftp://ftp.is.co.za/programming/perl/CPAN/`
Asia	
Hong Kong	`ftp://ftp.hkstar.com/pub/CPAN/`
Japan	`ftp://ftp.lab.kdd.co.jp/lang/perl/CPAN/`
Taiwan	`ftp://dongpo.math.ncu.edu.tw/perl/CPAN/`
Pacific	
Australia	`ftp://dongpo.math.ncu.edu.tw/perl/CPAN/`
	`ftp://ftp.mame.mu.oz.au/pub/perl/CPAN/`
New Zealand	`ftp://ftp.tekotago.ac.nz/pub/perl/CPAN/`
Europe	
Austria	`ftp://ftp.tuwien.ac.at/pub/languages/perl/CPAN/`
Belgium	`ftp://ftp.kulnet.kuleuven.ac.be/pub/mirror/CPAN/`
Czech Republic	`ftp://sunsite.mff.cuni.cz/MIRRORS/ftp.funet.fi/pub/languages/perl/CPAN/`
Denmark	`ftp://sunsite.auc.dk/pub/languages/perl/CPAN/`
Finland	`ftp://ftp.funet.fi/pub/languages/perl/CPAN/`
France	`ftp://ftp.ibp.fr/pub/perl/CPAN/`
	`ftp://ftp.pasteur.fr/pub/computing/unix/perl/CPAN/`
Germany	`ftp://ftp.leo.org/pub/comp/programming/languages/perl/CPAN/`
	`ftp://ftp.rz.ruhr-uni-bochum.de/pub/CPAN/`
Greece	`ftp://ftp.ntua.gr/pub/lang/perl`
Hungary	`ftp://ftp.kfki.hu/pub/packages/perl/CPAN/`
Italy	`ftp://cis.utovrm.it/CPAN/`
The Netherlands	`ftp://ftp.cs.ruu.nl/pub/PERL/CPAN/`

EUROPE

Poland	ftp://ftp.pk.edu.pl/pub/lang/perl/CPAN/
	ftp://sunsite.icm.edu.pl/pub/CPAN/
Portugal	ftp://ftp.ci.uminho.pt/pub/lang/perl/
	ftp://ftp.telepac.pt/pub/perl/CPAN/
Russia	ftp://ftp.sai.msu.su/pub/lang/perl/CPAN/
Slovenia	ftp://ftp.arnes.si/software/perl/CPAN/
Spain	ftp://ftp.etse.urv.es/pub/mirror/perl/
	ftp://ftp.rediris.es/mirror/CPAN/
Sweden	ftp://ftp.sunet.se/pub/lang/perl/CPAN/
Switzerland	ftp://ftp.switch.ch/mirror/CPAN/
UK	ftp://ftp.demon.co.uk/pub/mirrors/perl/CPAN/
	ftp://sunsite.doc.ic.ac.uk/packages/CPAN/
	ftp://unix.hensa.ac.uk/mirrors/perl-CPAN/

NORTH AMERICA

Canada	ftp://enterprise.ic.gc.ca/pub/perl/CPAN/
California	ftp://ftp.digital.com/pub/plan/perl/CPAN/
	ftp://ftp.cdrom.com/pub/perl/CPAN/
Colorado	ftp://ftp.cs.colorado.edu/pub/perl/CPAN/
Florida	ftp://ftp.cis.ufl.edu/pub/perl/CPAN/
Illinois	ftp://uiarchive.cso.uiuc.edu/pub/lang/perl/CPAN/
Massachusetts	ftp://ftp.iguide.com/pub/mirrors/packages/perl/CPAN/
New York	ftp://ftp.rge.com/pub/languages/perl/CPAN/
Oklahoma	ftp://ftp.uoknor.edu/mirrors/CPAN/
Texas	ftp://ftp.sedl.org/pub/mirrors/CPAN/
	ftp://ftp.metronet.com/pub/perl/
	ftp://ftp.sterling.com/CPAN/

SOUTH AMERICA

Chile	ftp://sunsite.dcc.uchile.cl/pub/Lang/perl/CPAN/

CGI

For CGI topics, you may want to check out *The CGI Book* by William E. Weinman, published by New Riders. Another good book is *CGI Programming Unleashed* by Dan Berlin, published by Sams Publishing. *HTML and CGI Unleashed* by John December and Mark Ginsburg, published by Sams.net Publishing, is a complete guide for the development of your Web content. Another good book, although already showing some age, is *Build a Web Site* by Net.Genesis and Devra Hall, published by Prima Online Books.

On the Internet, the following addresses are good resources to check:

- `news:comp.infosystems.www.authoring.cgi`—This newsgroup contains a lot of information about authoring CGI.
- `http://www.ncsa.uiuc.edu/Indices/WebTech/Docs.html`—This site has a lot of interesting information about CGI and other Web technologies.

WORLD WIDE WEB

`http://www.boutell.com`

Maintained by Thomas Boutell, this site has a lot of interesting Web information. It is also home to `MapEdit`, a PC and X Window map-creation tool; `Wusage`, a Web server statistics package; and `cgic`, a library of routines for programming CGI in C.

C AND SHELL (`sh`)

If you want to learn how to program in C, there are a few million books out there that will serve you equally well. The authoritative one, *The C Programming Language* by Brian W. Kernighan and Dennis M. Ritchie, published by Prentice-Hall, Inc., is a must.

Books are also available for `sh` programming; however, your system's online documentation may have enough to get you started. For those interested in using the `csh` as their command processor, check out *The UNIX C Shell Field Guide* by Gail and Paul Anderson, published by Prentice-Hall, ISBN 0-13-937468-X. This book is an excellent reference on `csh` and various UNIX commands that you can use to create powerful scripts that get real work done. Another helpful book is *UNIX Unleashed*, published by Sams Publishing, ISBN 0-672-30402-3. It covers UNIX commands, features, and utilities in depth.

HELLO WORLD!

The very first program most anyone writes in a new language is called Hello World!. The intention of Hello World! is to print the words Hello World, be it on the terminal or on a Web browser. I will provide you with three examples that say hello in Perl, C, and sh. Although I am not teaching you how to program, go get one of the books I've listed; these examples will show you what makes a CGI program different from other programs you may have developed.

The programs in listings 5.1, 5.2, and 5.3 could have been written more compactly, but I have opted for multiple print calls and for placing of HTML tags one per line (unless the tag closes on the same line) for the sake of clarity. (If you are writing CGI, I assume that you are familiar with HTML tags; otherwise you may be well over your head, and you should perhaps take a look at Appendix D, "HTML Reference Guide.")

LISTING 5.1. HELLO WORLD! AS A sh CGI.

```
#!/bin/sh
# HelloInSh - A trivial example of a shell CGI
# This program returns html content. The very first line of this
# listing
# Comments lines used for providing more information to the programmer
# or documentation lines have the '#' character as the first character
# in the line. The first # symbol is special, it's not a comment.
# It informs the operating system to use the program /bin/sh
# as the command interpreter for the script that follows.
# The very first thing, we do on our CGI is tell the server
# what type of data we are returning, in this case it is html:
#
echo Content-type: text/html
#
# then we need to add a single line blank line, that separates the
# 'header' from the actual stuff in our output:
#
echo
#
# At this point we need to provide 'body' that includes all the usual
# tags and structure required by html.
# because some of the characters such as the angle brackets
# are interpreted by the sh as a redirection, we need to enclose them
# with a single quote:
#
echo '<HTML>'
echo '<HEAD>'
echo '<TITLE> Hello World!</TITLE>'
echo '</HEAD>'
echo '<BODY>'
echo '<H1>Hello World!</H1>'
echo '</BODY>'
echo '</HTML>'
```

LISTING 5.2. HELLO WORLD! AS A PERL CGI PROGRAM.

```perl
#!/usr/local/bin/perl
# HelloInPerl, a trivial example of a CGI in Perl
#
# Output appropriate header for server, we included two newlines, the '\n'.
#
print "Content-type: text/html\n\n";
#
# Use a 'here' document format for easy readability and avoid need for many
# many printf() statements. All the lines following the print line are 'printed'
# verbatim, until the 'STOP' tag is found.
#
print <<STOP;
<HTML>
<HEAD>
<TITLE> Hello World!</TITLE>
</HEAD>
<BODY>
<H1>Hello World!</H1>
</BODY>
</HTML>
STOP
#
# Now we tell the operating system that this run of the program proceeded without
# any errors by 'exiting' with a zero status.
#
exit(0);
```

LISTING 5.3. HELLO WORLD! AS A C CGI PROGRAM.

```c
/* HelloInC - A trivial example of a CGI in C. */


#include <stdio.h>
int main (void)
{
  printf ("Content-type: text/html\n\n");
/* As our Perl or sh examples, the first thing to output is the Content-type */
  printf("<HTML>");
  printf("<HEAD>");
  printf("<TITLE>Hello World!</TITLE>");
  printf("</HEAD>");
  printf("<BODY>");
  printf("<H1>Hello World!</H1>");
  printf("</BODY>");
  printf("</HTML>");
  return;
}
```

The C version of the program is the one that looks the oddest of the three examples. For one thing, C is more structured, and its syntax is more rigid. C is a *compiled* program, meaning that after you enter the code, you need to convert it into an executable program before you can run it. C offers low-level access to the OS, making it a very powerful programming language. Although CGIs in C are harder to implement than the equivalent Perl programs, C does have its own advantages. C programs run fast—very fast. If your CGI is one that does many things and your server is under a heavy load, you may have no choice but to create an efficient program that creates the least impact on your system. C is a great tool for this.

Perl and sh are interpreted languages. *Interpreted* programs are executed by an interpreter—such as the Perl, sh (Bourne shell), or another shell type program. Both languages allow you to do several things, with very few commands that would take many lines of code in C. Both of these languages were designed with rapid development in mind.

In terms of debugging problems with your program, C may provide you with better tools that you can use to track problems in your code. Both Perl and sh provide you with ways to catch syntax errors, but certain types of errors may be a little harder to track.

RUNNING A CGI PROGRAM

I have talked about what a CGI is, and you have seen what a simple CGI looks like. At this point, you might be asking yourself how to run a CGI. If you have read this book in sequence, you will probably recall that execution of programs from the HTTP server can be a source of potential security problems, so CGI execution is usually restricted. By default, CGI programs exist in the /usr/local/etc/httpd/cgi-bin directory, or whatever other directory is defined by your ScriptAlias directive in your srm.conf file. The ScriptAlias directive is commented out from the default configuration. If you have not done so, you may want to remove the comment and restart the server. This will enable CGI execution for CGIs located in the cgi-bin directory.

Warning

Never, ever put a command interpreter such as Perl or any shell in your cgi-bin directory. Why? Think about it! That would make the executable available to anyone who wants to send it data. Even though the browser encodes data that is sent to the CGI, perverse minds will think of exploiting this security problem in their favor. In short, this is a huge security risk that is best avoided. Put your shells and command interpreters in a directory where the httpd daemon has no execution permission; /usr/local/bin is a very good place.

To test these CGI programs, just put them in your cgi-bin directory. Make sure your scripts are executable by setting the file mode to 755. You can do this easily from a command line by typing:

```
chmod 755 myscript
```

Replace *myscript* with the name of the file you want to make executable.

Also remember that the C version needs to be compiled before it is executed. Here's an easy way to compile it:

```
cc sourcefile.c -o binary
```

Replace *sourcefile.c* with the name of your C source file and *binary* with the name of the finished program. After a few seconds you should be left with an executable that you can run. If your system returns cc: command not found, you may want to try changing the command from *cc* to *gcc*.

If you named your CGIs as I suggested in the program comments in the listings, just move them to your cgi-bin directory and test the following URLs on your favorite browser:

```
http://localhost/cgi-bin/HelloInSh
http://localhost/cgi-bin/HelloInPerl
http://localhost/cgi-bin/HelloInC
```

You should get a result similar to the screen shown in Figure 5.1.

Figure 5.1.
The output for
any of the Hello
World! programs.

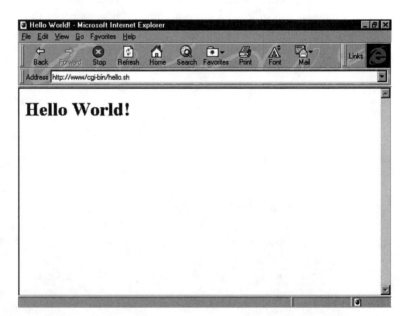

If you are having problems with the programs, see if you can get them to run on a terminal. If it will output the header and some HTML, and it doesn't give you an error, the problem may be with UNIX permissions. Recheck that your program is executable. If the problem is with a script, check that the location of the interpreter program is where I list it (the first line of the script). If it is not, change the first line to the absolute path of your command interpreter and try again. (If the program is found anywhere in any of the directories specified by your path, it will be listed by using the whereis command. For more information on how to use the whereis program, please refer to your UNIX documentation.) Note that ! and # are required symbols that tell the shell that the script should be run by the specified command processor.

STANDARD ENVIRONMENT VARIABLES

CGI programs run in an environment that is different from most programs. For one thing, most of the time they do not get input from stdin, the standard input stream. Because of this, input needs to be handled differently than in most programs. As I mentioned before, CGI passes values as *environment variables*. Environment variables are used extensively under UNIX as a way of communicating things like the location of your home directory and your mailbox, the capabilities of your terminal, and so on. When you execute a program, UNIX makes all of these settings available in case a program is interested in them.

In a similar manner to the UNIX shell, the HTTP server uses the environment mechanism to pass values to a CGI program. The HTTP server sets a number of environment variables prior to executing the CGI program. These variables provide information about the user, his software, and the server.

These environment variables can be accessed by name, and if your CGI calls other programs, these variables are inherited by the environment of the programs you call. The standard CGI 1.1 specification defines the variables discussed in the following sections.

AUTH_TYPE

The AUTH_TYPE variable is set to the type of authentication used to validate a request.

CONTENT_LENGTH

The CONTENT_LENGTH environment variable is set to the size of the data that was submitted with the request. The size of the data is specified in bytes. HTTP PUT and POST requests use this value to read that amount of bytes from stdin, the standard input stream. You shouldn't attempt to read any more data bytes than specified by this variable.

CONTENT_TYPE

The CONTENT_TYPE variable is set to the Multipurpose Internet Mail Extensions (MIME) type or format submitted with the request. The format is expressed with a *type/subtype* syntax. If the data was submitted using the HTTP POST method, the value of this variable is set to application/x-www-form-urlencoded. The amount of data submitted is specified by the CONTENT_LENGTH variable.

GATEWAY_INTERFACE

The GATEWAY_INTERFACE variable is set to the version of CGI that the server implements. The syntax of the version follows a pattern *CGI/version*: CGI/1.1. As new variables are added to the CGI standard, the version number is increased. Your program should be aware of this version number to ensure that the variables you use are available in the environment set up by the server you are using. This variable is set for all requests.

PATH_INFO

The PATH_INFO variable is set to the Uniform Resource Identifier (URI). For practical purposes, a URI is just a URL that follows the string identifying the CGI script, like the following example:

http://www.company.com/cgi-bin/mycgi/a/b/c will be set to /a/b/c.

Your program can use this information to do whatever it wants, perhaps to pass extra settings (switches) for the program to behave differently depending the situation, such as specifying extra arguments used for CGI configuration. It's up to your CGI program to use the values provided by this variable.

PATH_TRANSLATED

The PATH_TRANSLATED variable is set to the absolute path to the resource represented by the URL. In the case of http://www.company.com/index.html, PATH_TRANSLATED may hold a value such as /usr/local/etc/httpd/htdocs/index.html. This allows your CGI program to be able to read this file and do something with it if necessary.

QUERY_STRING

QUERY_STRING is one of the most important of all CGI environment variables. The QUERY_STRING variable is used for passing form information to a CGI. On CGIs that use the GET HTTP method, this variable will contain the query portion of the URL. Requests made to a CGI usually include a ? that is followed by the arguments to the query. In the URL http://www.company.com/cgi-bin/test?yes, the value of QUERY_STRING will be set to yes.

It is important to be aware that because QUERY_STRING is an environment variable, there are space limitations imposed by the operating system. Some systems limit the environment space anywhere from 250–8000 bytes. On my system, this limit is much larger—about 40,000 bytes. If your CGI handles a form that could potentially receive a large amount of data, you may want to consider using POST transactions to ensure portability and avoid overflows. POST transactions don't put values on QUERY_STRING; instead, the data comes into the CGI via the standard input stream.

Data in the QUERY_STRING is formatted as *key=value* pairs. *key* is the name assigned to the form widget using the NAME attribute in the HTML file. *value* is the value that the user assigned to the widget with a browser. Multiple *key=value* pairs are separated by ampersand (&) characters. In addition to this formatting, the browser will encode any nonalphanumeric character using a percent character plus the character's hexadecimal value. For example, %2C equals a comma (,) character. Spaces are encoded with a plus (+) character. The following QUERY_STRING is the result of two form fields, one called Name, the other called Address:

```
QUERY_STRING = Name=My+Name&Address=Some+Street+Rd.%0ACity%2C+State++12345&
↪name=Submit
```

The Name field contains the data

```
My+Name
```

The space between My and Name is encoded to a +.

The Address field contains

```
Some Street Rd.
City, State 12345
```

In the second field, spaces are also converted to + characters. In addition, the newline after Rd. is encoded to %0A. The %2C corresponds to a comma (,).

REMOTE_ADDR

The REMOTE_ADDR variable contains the IP address of the host making the request. IP addresses currently are written in dotted-decimal notation (four octets or 8-bit values represented in decimal, separated by dots). If you are concerned with security (and who isn't?), it is a good idea to log this variable in a logfile created specially for this form by your CGI program. You can also log REMOTE_HOST, REMOTE_IDENT, HTTP_USER_AGENT, and HTTP_REFERER. Although this takes up disk space, it also allows you to identify people (somewhat) who submit nasty, threatening, or malicious form data. For alternative logging suggestions, please see Chapter 13, "Web Accounting."

REMOTE_HOST

The REMOTE_HOST variable contains the hostname of the client making the request. It will be set only if reverse DNS lookups are enabled for your server. Reverse DNS lookups create an extra load on your server and should not be enabled on high-traffic servers. If your CGI needs to determine the hostname, you should be able to determine this information easily enough when you need it with a call to /usr/bin/host (part of the BIND release), with the IP address of the host in question from the REMOTE_ADDR variable.

REMOTE_IDENT

For clients running identd services, the REMOTE_IDENT variable will be set to the username of the user making the request. Many clients don't run this service and, as should be expected, you should never trust this information.

REMOTE_USER

Requests that require user authentication will set the REMOTE_USER variable to the name the user entered during the authentication session.

REQUEST_METHOD

The REQUEST_METHOD variable holds the name of the HTTP method used to make the request. Valid HTTP methods are GET, POST, HEAD, PUT, DELETE, LINK, and UNLINK. The Apache server implements only the first four methods, which specify where a CGI program will find its data. You can implement any of the other methods with CGI programs; however, be aware that those methods implement potential security holes. As their names suggest, PUT, DELETE, LINK, and UNLINK satisfy requests that put, delete, link, or unlink files. However, some of these methods may be very useful for implementing applications that allow a user to add information, such as adding a picture to a database.

SCRIPT_NAME

The SCRIPT_NAME variable contains the portion of the URI that identifies the CGI running. If your URL is http://www.company.com/cgi-bin/test, SCRIPT_NAME will be set to /cgi-bin/test.

SERVER_NAME

The SERVER_NAME variable holds the hostname, alias, or IP address of the server serving the request. You can use it to build self-referencing URLs. In cases where the server is configured to support virtual hosts, this variable will be set correctly to the name of the virtual host serving the request. This variable is set for all requests.

SERVER_PORT

The SERVER_PORT variable contains the TCP port where the server is running. You can use the SERVER_PORT value along with the SERVER_NAME to build self-referencing URLs if your server is using a nonstandard port. The default port for an HTTP server is 80.

SERVER_PROTOCOL

The SERVER_PROTOCOL variable contains the name and version of the HTTP protocol supported by the server. It has the format *HTTP/version*: HTTP/1.0. This value should be checked by your program to ensure that the server is compatible with your CGI program.

SERVER_SOFTWARE

The SERVER_SOFTWARE variable is the equivalent of your server's info box. This variable holds the name and version of the HTTP server software serving your request. The format is *name/version*: APACHE/1.1. This variable is set for all requests.

CLIENT HEADER LINES: HTTP_*

In addition to the standard variables, header lines received from a browser are put into the environment preceded by HTTP_. Any dash characters (-) are changed to underscores (_).

These headers may be excluded by the server if they are already processed or, if by including them, the system's environment limit would be exceeded. Some of the most popular ones are HTTP_ACCEPT, HTTP_USER_AGENT, and HTTP_REFERER.

HTTP_ACCEPT

The HTTP_ACCEPT variable is set to the MIME types that the client browser is able to accept. You can use this information to have your CGI return richer data, such as graphics, that is acceptable by the client.

HTTP_USER_AGENT

The HTTP_USER_AGENT variable is set to the name and version of the client browser in the format *name/version* library/version. This format string varies greatly from one browser to another. Because of the ranging capabilities of browsers, some sites provide various versions of the materials and return the one that it deems most appropriate based on information stored in this variable. This creates a situation in which some browsers do not get the "cool" version of a site. Some browser developers resolved this problem by making their wares impersonate other brands by supplying the HTTP_USER_AGENT string Mozilla (the Netscape Navigator user agent string).

Information regarding a proxy gateway is also contained here. A *proxy gateway* is a computer that sits between the client and the server. This proxy gateway is sometimes able to cache pages you request, reducing the amount of traffic generated from your site to that server.

HTTP_REFERER

The HTTP_REFERER variable holds the location the user visited that forwarded her to your site. Use of this variable may be useful to see which sites are linked to yours.

READING THE ENVIRONMENT

Reading environment variables in an sh is really easy—it's just like reading any other sh variable. The reason for this is that sh *is* the environment!

Environment variables are accessed by adding a $ before their name. To print the contents of the variable, use the echo command:

```
echo SERVER_SOFTWARE = $SERVER_SOFTWARE
```

The preceding line will print a line that looks like this:

```
SERVER_SOFTWARE = Apache/1.1.1
```

Listing 5.4 shows a simple sh CGI based on the test-cgi script included in Apache's cgi-bin directory that prints most of the environment variables.

LISTING 5.4. A SIMPLE sh CGI SCRIPT.

```
#!/bin/sh
echo Content-type: text/plain
echo
echo SERVER_SOFTWARE = $SERVER_SOFTWARE
echo SERVER_NAME = $SERVER_NAME
echo GATEWAY_INTERFACE = $GATEWAY_INTERFACE
echo SERVER_PROTOCOL = $SERVER_PROTOCOL
echo SERVER_PORT = $SERVER_PORT
echo REQUEST_METHOD = $REQUEST_METHOD
echo HTTP_ACCEPT = $HTTP_ACCEPT
echo PATH_INFO = $PATH_INFO
echo PATH_TRANSLATED = $PATH_TRANSLATED
echo SCRIPT_NAME = $SCRIPT_NAME
echo QUERY_STRING = $QUERY_STRING
echo REMOTE_HOST = $REMOTE_HOST
echo REMOTE_ADDR = $REMOTE_ADDR
echo REMOTE_USER = $REMOTE_USER
```

```
echo AUTH_TYPE = $AUTH_TYPE
echo CONTENT_TYPE = $CONTENT_TYPE
echo CONTENT_LENGTH = $CONTENT_LENGTH
```

The same CGI can be written in Perl, as shown in Listing 5.5.

LISTING 5.5. THE SIMPLE CGI SCRIPT IN PERL.

```perl
#!/usr/local/bin/perl

print "Content-type: text/plain\n\n";

print <<STOP;

SERVER_SOFTWARE = $ENV{SERVER_SOFTWARE}
SERVER_NAME = $ENV{SERVER_NAME}
GATEWAY_INTERFACE = $ENV{GATEWAY_INTERFACE}
SERVER_PROTOCOL = $ENV{SERVER_PROTOCOL}
SERVER_PORT = $ENV{SERVER_PORT}
REQUEST_METHOD = $ENV{REQUEST_METHOD}
HTTP_ACCEPT = $ENV{HTTP_ACCEPT}
PATH_INFO = $ENV{PATH_INFO}
PATH_TRANSLATED = $ENV{PATH_TRANSLATED}
SCRIPT_NAME = $ENV{SCRIPT_NAME}
QUERY_STRING = $ENV{QUERY_STRING}
REMOTE_HOST = $ENV{REMOTE_HOST}
REMOTE_ADDR = $ENV{REMOTE_ADDR}
REMOTE_USER = $ENV{REMOTE_USER}
AUTH_TYPE = $ENV{AUTH_TYPE}
CONTENT_TYPE = $ENV{CONTENT_TYPE}
STOP
```

The Perl program is similar to the C program, shown in Listing 5.6. The only notable difference is that the $ENV{variable_name} syntax is used to inform Perl that I am referring to an environment variable.

LISTING 5.6. THE SIMPLE CGI SCRIPT IN C.

```c
#include <stdio.h>
#include <stdlib.h>

main (int argc, char *argv[])
{
  char *p;

  // Keep the server happy. Put in a Content-type header:

  printf("Content-type: text/plain\n\n");

  /* Most versions of printf will handle a NULL pointer as "(Null
  // Pointer)" otherwise printf may crash. The solution is a macro that
  // always returns something valid. The macro below tests to see if
```

continues

LISTING 5.6. CONTINUED

```
// getenv returned something. If it returns NULL, it returns a
// "VARIABLE NOT SET" message, that should make old versions of printf
/* happy.

#define sgetenv(x) ((p = getenv(x)) ? p : "VARIABLE NOT SET")

printf("SERVER_SOFTWARE = %s\n", sgetenv("SERVER_SOFTWARE"));
printf("SERVER_NAME = %s\n", sgetenv("SERVER_NAME"));
printf("GATEWAY_INTERFACE = %s\n", sgetenv("GATEWAY_INTERFACE"));
printf("SERVER_PROTOCOL = %s\n", sgetenv("SERVER_PROTOCOL"));
printf("SERVER_PORT = %s\n", sgetenv("SERVER_PORT"));
printf("REQUEST_METHOD = %s\n", sgetenv("REQUEST_METHOD"));
printf("HTTP_ACCEPT = %s\n", sgetenv("HTTP_ACCEPT"));
printf("PATH_INFO = %s\n", sgetenv("PATH_INFO"));
printf("PATH_TRANSLATED = %s\n", sgetenv("PATH_TRANSLATED"));
printf("SCRIPT_NAME = %s\n", sgetenv("SCRIPT_NAME"));
printf("QUERY_STRING = %s\n", sgetenv("QUERY_STRING"));
printf("REMOTE_HOST = %s\n", sgetenv("REMOTE_HOST"));
printf("REMOTE_ADDR = %s\n", sgetenv("REMOTE_ADDR"));
printf("REMOTE_USER = %s\n", sgetenv("REMOTE_USER"));
printf("AUTH_TYPE = %s\n", sgetenv("AUTH_TYPE"));
printf("CONTENT_TYPE = %s\n", sgetenv("CONTENT_TYPE"));
printf("CONTENT_LENGTH = %s\n", sgetenv("CONTENT_LENGTH"));

exit(0);
}
```

The one notable thing occurring in this program is the use of the getenv(*variable_name*) function. This function returns the string stored in the environment variable matching the name of the argument provided. The following is an example:

```
string_pointer = getenv("HOME");
```

This call would return a pointer to a string describing the location of the home directory of the user running the program. If you look closely, you'll notice that I created a macro for the getenv function called sgetenv. This macro is a safeguard for users of older versions of the printf() function. If getenv returns a NULL pointer, ancient versions of printf may crash the program. My program safeguards against this condition by always returning a printable string. In this case, a NULL value will return the string VARIABLE NOT SET.

If you want to write CGI programs in C, probably the best way to write them would be to use Thomas Boutell's cgic library. This library is available from http://www.boutell.com. I have included a copy of the library on the CD-ROM for your convenience. I have written a similar Hello World! application using cgic, shown in Listing 5.7.

LISTING 5.7. HELLO WORLD! IN cgic.

```
/**********************************************************************
 *
 * HelloWorld.cgi
 *
 * This program prints out all the environment variables using Thomas
 * Boutell's cgic library.  Make sure cgic.h is in your current dir-
 * ectory, and that libcgic.a is installed in the usual place (most of
 * the time /usr/local/lib. Please follow the cgic installation
 * instructions.
 *
 **********************************************************************/

#include <stdio.h>
#include "cgic.h"

#define FIELD_SIZE 51
#define DEBUG 0

int cgiMain() {

#if DEBUG
/* Load a saved CGI scenario if we're debugging */
cgiReadEnvironment("/tmp/capcgi.dat");
#endif

cgiHeaderContentType("text/html");
fprintf(cgiOut, "<HTML><HEAD>\n");
fprintf(cgiOut, "<TITLE>Hello World!</TITLE></HEAD>\n");
fprintf(cgiOut, "<BODY><H1>Hello World!</H1>\n");
fprintf(cgiOut, "cgiServerSoftware=%s<BR>\n", cgiServerSoftware);
fprintf(cgiOut, "cgiServerName=%s<BR>\n", cgiServerName);
fprintf(cgiOut, "cgiGatewayInterface=%s<BR>\n", cgiGatewayInterface);
fprintf(cgiOut, "cgiServerProtocol=%s<BR>\n", cgiServerProtocol);
fprintf(cgiOut, "cgiServerPort=%s<BR>\n", cgiServerPort);
fprintf(cgiOut, "cgiRequestMethod=%s<BR>\n", cgiRequestMethod);
fprintf(cgiOut, "cgiPathInfo=%s<BR>\n", cgiPathInfo);
fprintf(cgiOut, "cgiPathTranslated=%s<BR>\n", cgiPathTranslated);
fprintf(cgiOut, "cgiScriptName=%s<BR>\n", cgiScriptName);
fprintf(cgiOut, "cgiQueryString=%s<BR>\n", cgiQueryString);
fprintf(cgiOut, "cgiRemoteHost=%s<BR>\n", cgiRemoteHost);
fprintf(cgiOut, "cgiRemoteAddr=%s<BR>\n", cgiRemoteAddr);
fprintf(cgiOut, "cgiAuthType=%s<BR>\n", cgiAuthType);
fprintf(cgiOut, "cgiRemoteUser=%s<BR>\n", cgiRemoteUser);
fprintf(cgiOut, "cgiRemoteIdent=%s<BR>\n", cgiRemoteIdent);
fprintf(cgiOut, "cgiContentType=%s<BR>\n", cgiContentType);
fprintf(cgiOut, "cgiAccept=%s<BR>\n", cgiAccept);
fprintf(cgiOut, "cgiUserAgent=%s<BR>\n", cgiUserAgent);

fprintf(cgiOut, "</BODY></HTML>\n");
return 0;
}
```

This program does not show off the true power of cgic, but you can see what's going on that's interesting.

First of all, notice that there is no main() function. Instead, cgic applications all have a cgiMain() function. Another difference is that instead of writing to stdout when you want some text to go to the browser, you write to a special file descriptor called cgiOut, defined in the cgic.h file. Where does cgiOut point? In almost every case it points to stdout. So why use cgiOut? It is mainly used to be compatible with future versions of cgic where stdout may not be where you want output to go.

You will also notice some debugging code in the program. This is a really nice feature of cgic that allows a developer to easily preserve an environment and run the CGI program with that environment from the command line or a debugger. It saves you the hassle of manually simulating the environment yourself. To use this feature you need to have the program capture compiled and located in your cgi-bin directory. Then, whenever you want to debug a cranky CGI program, just point the FORM ACTION tag to /cgi-bin/capture (make sure that capture is compiled with the default capture file set to something you want—/tmp/capcgi.dat would be good). This captures the environment and stores it in a file that can be read by using cgiReadEnvironment(). This is very useful and easier than manually running through and setting all the environment variables.

Finally, you'll notice that there are special variable names that refer to the environment variables. This is so that cgic's debugging feature will correctly write the environment to the capture file, as specified in the capture.c source code.

But cgic is much more than what you have seen. It includes functions for grabbing GET or POST form data of all types. In fact, if you're grabbing a numerical input from a form, cgic includes parameters for bounds checking. Included in the cgic documentation is an excellent HTML document that shows you exactly how to use the cgic functions.

Passing Data to a CGI Using the HTTP POST Method

The POST method, originally named and designated to refer to posting a message to a Usenet-like resource, is a better way to submit data from a form than GET. Unlike GET, the POST method has no restrictions on how much data can be submitted. The data from a POST submission is encoded in exactly the same way as GET; the main difference is that the string is not placed in QUERY_STRING. Instead, the string is read from stdin. How do you know when you reach the end of the string? The length is placed in the CONTENT_LENGTH environment variable. Other than these two differences, POST functions in exactly the same way as GET.

So why should you even bother with GET when POST is so much better? Well, you will use GET in the following situation: Say you want to have a text hyperlink within your HTML document to a CGI program, and you also need to pass some URL-encoded parameters to this program, such as color=red and size=large. The HTML code would be as follows:

```
<A HREF="/cgi-bin/somecgi.cgi?color=red&size=large">Run this</A>
```

The string after the ? is the URL-encoded string that is placed in QUERY_STRING as per the GET method. (You can also do a link this way with POST, but as far as I know, there is no way to make a Submit button a text link. You can make it an image by using the image tag, but for text, I don't know of a way to do it!)

Another instance where you might want to use GET over POST is when you are debugging a CGI program. You have probably faced many 500 Server Error messages when writing CGI programs. The reason for this uninformative message is security; however, that doesn't help your development efforts. The server swallows sterr and doesn't redirect it to anywhere useful. If you run the CGI program from the prompt, you will see the error messages and explanations generated by the CGI program that make debugging easier. (Thomas Boutell's cgic library provides a much nicer way of debugging CGI programs. Read on to find out more!)

CGI is nothing more than a set of environment variables. You can manually simulate a GET request in the following way:

```
% setenv 'REQUEST_METHOD' 'GET'
% setenv 'QUERY_STRING' 'color=red&size=large'
% somecgi.cgi
[results]
```

These commands assume that you are using csh, of course. If you are using the Bourne shell (sh), declare environment variables as follows:

```
% REQUEST_METHOD=GET
% QUERY_STRING="color=red&size=large"
% export REQUEST_METHOD
% export QUERY_STRING
% somecgi.cgi
[results]
```

Just set the environment variables yourself and run the CGI program from the prompt. Can you do the same thing with POST? After all, POST is done virtually the same way except for stdin. Well, this is what you'd have to do:

```
% setenv 'REQUEST_METHOD' 'POST'
% setenv 'CONTENT_LENGTH' '20'
% somecgi.cgi
(waiting for input)
color=red&size=large
% [results]
```

Aha! There's the gotcha! CONTENT_LENGTH needs to be set to the number of characters to read from stdin. Can you imagine what a pain it would be to have to count the number of characters each time you have a different form string? GET is much easier for debugging purposes. Use it until you are sure everything works; then make your form submit data via POST. (Or, if you are using C, use Boutell's cgic library debugging functions.)

As I've mentioned, most of the time CGI programs don't receive their information from the stdin stream. The POST method should be used for anything that has more than a few small input fields to avoid any problems with running out of space on the environment space.

However, requests of the type POST (or PUT) do put information after the header. Under these requests, some data will be sent to your program through stdin, which you need to read. However, unlike traditional UNIX programs, the HTTP server is not obligated to send an EOF (end of file) following CONTENT_LENGTH bytes of data. This means that you need to determine the amount of data that you are able to read beforehand. Luckily, the server will set the CONTENT_LENGTH variable to the amount of data you can safely read from stdin.

Data sent through stdin is encoded in the same way as values passed through QUERY_STRING.

Returning Data from a CGI Program

Output from your CGI program usually goes to stdout. This information can be raw HTML or some other MIME type that your program creates, or instructions to the client to retrieve the output (a redirection). The previous sample programs have been returning either text/plain or text/html MIME formats. When returning text/html, you need to make sure that the HTML you return is the correct HTML.

In addition, any content you return must be preceded by one of the following headers and two new lines.

Content-type

If you are returning content generated from within your CGI, you'll need to set the Content-type header to the MIME type of the data you are returning; typically this will be HTML or plain text. For example, CGIs that return text should set the content header like this:

```
Content-type: text\plain
```

CGIs that return HTML-formatted text should return a content header like the following:

```
Content-type: text\html
```

Location

Instead of returning data, you can use this header to specify that you are returning a reference or redirection instead of the actual document. When this header is set to a URL, the client will issue the redirect; the client (browser) is then responsible to fetch the document. If set to a virtual path, the server will intercept it and return the document listed:

```
Location: http://www.somewhere.com
```

When the server receives this header from a CGI, it will try to point the client browser to the http://www.somewhere.com URL.

Status

This is the result code returned to the client. It is composed of a three-digit code and a string describing the error or condition.

FORMS

The most basic thing you will ever do is collect data from an user and then process that data in some way. This will involve the use of HTML forms. *Forms* are a series of user-interface items that allow the user to set values: text fields, text boxes, radio buttons, check boxes, pop-up menus, and so on. Your HTML code is responsible for drawing these items and assigning them a name. A sample form looks like this in code:

```
<HTML>
<HEAD>
<TITLE>WhoAreYou</TITLE>
</HEAD>
<BODY BGCOLOR="#ffffff">
<FORM ACTION="/cgi-bin/printenv" ENCTYPE="x-www-form-encoded" METHOD="GET">
<HR>
<IMG SRC="1.gif" WIDTH="57" HEIGHT="77" ALIGN="MIDDLE">
<STRONG>Your name: </STRONG>
<INPUT NAME="Name" TYPE="text" SIZE="53"><BR>
<IMG SRC="2.gif" WIDTH="57" HEIGHT="77" ALIGN="MIDDLE">
<STRONG>Your Address: </STRONG>
<TEXTAREA NAME="Address" ROWS="6" COLS="50"></TEXTAREA>
<BR>
<HR>
<P><CENTER><INPUT NAME="name" TYPE="submit" VALUE="Submit"></CENTER>
</FORM>
</BODY>
</HTML>
```

This code produces a form that looks like Figure 5.2, when viewed under Microsoft's Internet Explorer version 3.

Figure 5.2.
A simple form
viewed with
Microsoft's
Internet Explorer
version 3.

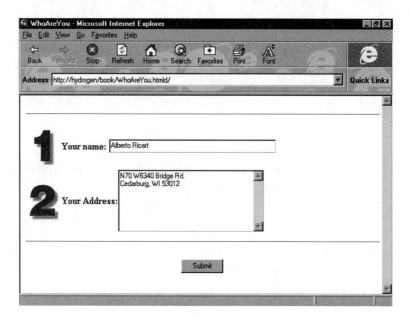

You can create forms by just typing the specifications, but sometimes it's a lot easier to use a graphical tool. Graphical tools allow you to lay out the form in an attractive and useful way. I like creating the basic form template in a program called Adobe PageMill. PageMill is an easy-to-use program for the Macintosh that generates HTML pages.

When you submit this form, your browser will return something similar to the following:

```
SERVER_SOFTWARE = Apache/1.1.1
GATEWAY_INTERFACE = CGI/1.1
DOCUMENT_ROOT = /NextLibrary/WebServer/htdocs
REMOTE_ADDR = 204.95.222.3
SERVER_PROTOCOL = HTTP/1.0
REQUEST_METHOD = GET
REMOTE_HOST = lithium
HTTP_REFERER = http://hydrogen/book/WhoAreYou.htmld/
QUERY_STRING = Name=Alberto+Ricart&Address=N70+W6340+Bridge+Rd.
➥%0D%0ACedarburg%2C+WI++53012&name=Submit
HTTP_USER_AGENT = Mozilla/2.0 (compatible; MSIE 3.0B; Windows 95;640,480
HTTP_ACCEPT = */*
HTTP_ACCEPT_LANGUAGE = en
SCRIPT_NAME = /cgi-bin/printenv
SCRIPT_FILENAME = /NextLibrary/WebServer/apache/cgi-bin/printenv
HTTP_PRAGMA = no-cache
SERVER_NAME = localhost
SERVER_PORT = 80
HTTP_HOST = hydrogen
SERVER_ADMIN = webmaster@ACCESSLINK.COM
```

Decoding `QUERY_STRING`

As you can imagine, before you can do anything useful with the QUERY_STRING you'll need to decode it. After you have decoded all encoded characters, you'll need to split them into key and value pairs.

The effort required to do this will depend on what you are using to develop a CGI. If you are using sh, you will run into some difficulties. You'll probably have to use an awk and sed script to preprocess your data; too much work! However, don't despair. Just because it's hard doesn't mean that someone didn't already go through these pains.

Steven Grimm has developed a package called Un-CGI that takes the hard work of decoding your program input. Un-CGI decodes the form input and places the decoded information in the environment as environment variables, which are very easy to access from a shell. I have reprinted Grimm's Un-CGI documentation in Appendix A, "Un-CGI Version 1.7 Documentation." Un-CGI makes it possible to easily write CGI using the sh or csh.

C will present you with similar challenges. You'll have to write a few decoding routines as well as a routine to split the data into simple key/value pairs that you can access, or you'll have to use Thomas Boutell's uncgic library.

Perl, by far, provides the easiest way of dealing with the decoding and conversion of the data into variables that you can access easily.

A Generic Form Wrapper for E-mail

Perhaps the most frequently asked question on all of the HTML and CGI newsgroups is, "How do I e-mail the contents of a form to myself?" The answer is contained in the following program listings. The first listing is a group of useful functions I wrote for developing CGI programs. It is a Perl package and must be imported into a program via the following statement:

```
require CGILIB;
```

Then, whenever you want to use a function in the library, first of all, make sure that CGILIB.pm is in the same directory or that it is in your @INC path. One function in CGILIB.pm is responsible for decoding the input string. This is the function parse_form(). It returns an associative array with all of the form keys and values. When you have this array, you can do anything with it that you want. In this case, you simply want to mail the contents of the array back to yourself.

The second listing is the actual Perl mailing program. It takes the user input values from an HTML form and mails the results to the address specified in the recipient field of the HTML form. It extracts some other various useful information for the e-mail response as well, such as client browser information, the date submitted, and information about the location from which the sender is submitting. This is all very relevant material, especially for simple security precautions.

To use this humble program, just install the programs in listings 5.8 and 5.9 in your cgi-bin directory and create a form whose ACTION target is cgi-bin/mail.cgi. Listing 5.10 is a sample form so you can see how it is done.

LISTING 5.8. CGILIB.pm.

```perl
package CGILIB;

################################################################
# Print the content-type header.
#
# &print_header;
sub print_header
{
 print "Content-type: text/html\n\n";
}

################################################################
# Print a canned header with title as argument.
#
#
sub canned_header
{
 my( $title ) = @_;

 print "<HTML>\n";
 print "<HEAD>\n";
 print "<TITLE>$title</TITLE>\n";
 print "</HEAD>\n";
}
################################################################
# Print the closing lines for an HTML document.
#
# &print_closing;
sub print_closing
{
 print "</BODY></HTML>\n";
}

################################################################
# Parse the HTML header and form
# information
#
# %ASSOC_ARRAY = &parse_form;
sub parse_form
{
 my ($buffer,$name,$value,%FORM);
 my ($content_length,$query_string,$request_method);

 $content_length = $ENV{'CONTENT_LENGTH'};
 $query_string = $ENV{'QUERY_STRING'};
 $request_method = $ENV{'REQUEST_METHOD'};
```

```perl
# If the REQUEST_METHOD was POST, read from stdin, else the string is in
➥QUERY_STRING
 if ($request_method eq 'POST') {
    read(STDIN, $buffer, $content_length);
 }
 else {
  $buffer = $query_string;
 }

   # Split the name-value pairs
   @pairs = split(/&/, $buffer);

   foreach $pair (@pairs)
   {
    ($name, $value) = split(/=/, $pair);

    # Un-Webify plus signs and %-encoding
  $name =~ tr/+/ /;
    $value =~ tr/+/ /;
    $value =~ s/%([a-fA-F0-9][a-fA-F0-9])/pack("C", hex($1))/eg;
  $name =~ s/%([a-fA-F0-9][a-fA-F0-9])/pack("C", hex($1))/eg;

    # Stop people from using subshells to execute commands
    # Not a big deal when using sendmail, but very important
      # when using UCB mail (aka mailx).
    $value =~ s/~!/ ~!/g;

     # Uncomment for debugging purposes
     # print "Setting $name to $value<P>\n";
    $FORM{$name} = $value;
    }

 %FORM;  # Returns %FORM to caller source...
} #End Sub form_mail


#############################################################################
#
# sub dump_env_vars
#
# Dumps the contents of %ENV in HTML
#
# INPUTS:  \%ENV
#
#############################################################################
sub dump_env_vars
{
 my ($ENV) = @_;

 foreach (keys %$ENV)
 {
  print "$_=$$ENV{$_}<BR>";
 }
}

# For require files
1;
```

LISTING 5.9. mail.cgi.

```perl
#!/usr/local/bin/perl -w
#
# mail.cgi: This is an CGI program that sends the results of the fill-out
# form to the recipient indicated in the form.
#
# Note: This CGI program relies on hidden variables in the form associated
# with this listing.

require CGILIB; #Use the lib included in book
use strict;    #Make sure we declare all our variables
$¦ = 1;        #Flush STDOUT

my( %FORM );   #Declare all the variables
my( $recipient, $sender, $thank_you );
my( $mailprog );

%FORM = CGILIB::parse_form();

$mailprog = '/usr/lib/sendmail';

# Location of thank_you page to be displayed after submitting form
$thank_you = $FORM{thank_you_location};

$recipient = $FORM{recipient};
$sender = $FORM{email};

#Grab some environment info
$FORM{Date} = 'date';
$FORM{ServerProtocol} = $ENV{'SERVER_PROTOCOL'};
$FORM{RemoteHost} = $ENV{'REMOTE_HOST'};
$FORM{RemoteAddress} = $ENV{'REMOTE_ADDR'};
$FORM{HTTPUserAgent} = $ENV{'HTTP_USER_AGENT'};

email_recipient();
say_thank_you();

exit(0);

######################################################################
#
# email_recipient() : calls the mail program and sends a message.
#
sub email_recipient
{
 my( $key );
 open (MAIL, "¦$mailprog $recipient") ¦¦ die "Cant open mail program: $!";

 print MAIL "To: $recipient\n";
 print MAIL "From: $sender ($FORM{name})\n";
 print MAIL "Reply-To: $sender ($FORM{name})\n";
 print MAIL "Subject: Email from Web Form :) \n\n"; #Need two \n's for

 foreach ( keys %FORM )
 {
  print MAIL "$_  : $FORM{$_}\n";
```

```
      }

      print MAIL "\n\n End of email message.\n";

      close( MAIL );
    }

    #########################################################################
    #
    # say_thank_you() : redirects user to the thank-you page.
    #
    sub say_thank_you
    {
      print "location: $thank_you\n\n";
    }
```

LISTING 5.10. form.html.

```
    <HTML>
    <HEAD>
    <TITLE>My Cool Email Form</TITLE>
    </HEAD>

    <BODY>
    <FORM METHOD="GET" ACTION="mail.cgi">
    <INPUT NAME="recipient" TYPE="hidden" VALUE="youremail@yourdomain.com">
    <INPUT NAME="thank_you_location" TYPE="hidden" VALUE="http://www.yourdomain.com/
    ➥thank_you.html">

    <P>
    <STRONG>Name:</STRONG><BR>
    <INPUT NAME="name" TYPE="text" SIZE=40>
    </P>

    <P>
    <STRONG>Email:</STRONG><BR>
    <INPUT NAME="email" TYPE="text" SIZE=40>
    </P>

    <P>
    <STRONG>Comments:</STRONG></BR>
    <TEXTAREA NAME="comments" COLS=40 ROWS=10></TEXTAREA>
    </P>

    <INPUT TYPE="submit">

    </FORM>
    </BODY>
    </HTML>
```

As you can see, I have included an example form. You may be wondering about the *thank_you.html* URL in the variable thank_you_location. Well, you have to create it. It is what your page visitors will see after they submit their form to the mail.cgi program. The process used is called *redirection*. A location header followed by two newline characters is sent, which redirects the user to the desired page.

The next program listing e-mails form results like the others, but uses Thomas Boutell's cgic library. Also, the form (shown in Listing 5.11) used is slightly different.

Listing 5.11. The form in cgic.

```c
/*************************************************************************
 *
 * email.cgi:
 *
 * This program reads the fields of the given form and emails
 * the contents to the destination, kept in the hidden field from within
 * the form. The program uses Thomas Boutell cgic library.
 *
 *************************************************************************/

#include <stdio.h>
#include <stdlib.h>
#include <unistd.h>
#include "cgic.h"

#define FIELD_SIZE 51
#define ADDRESS_SIZE 500
#define DEBUG1 0
#define TO "webmaster@foo.bar.com"   /* Substitute your address */
#define FROM "Web Fill-Out Form"

void printEnvironmentVariables();

int cgiMain()
{
 char name[FIELD_SIZE];
 char address[ADDRESS_SIZE];
 FILE* mailer;

#if DEBUG1
/* Load a saved CGI scenario if we're debugging */
cgiReadEnvironment("/tmp/capcgi.dat");
#endif

 cgiFormStringNoNewlines( "Name", name, FIELD_SIZE);
 cgiFormString( "Address", address, ADDRESS_SIZE);

 /* Open a pipe to sendmail */
 mailer = popen( "/usr/lib/sendmail -t", "w" );
 if (mailer <= 0)
  {
   perror( "Unable to open pipe to sendmail\n" );
   exit( 1 );
  }

#if DEBUG
printf( "popen: Done\n" );
#endif
```

```
  /* Now fill in the sendmail headers */
  fprintf( mailer, "To: " TO "\n" );
  fprintf( mailer, "From: " FROM "\n" );
#if DEBUG
printf( "From: Done\n" );
#endif
  fprintf( mailer, "Subject: Results of fill-out form for %s\n\n", name );

  /* Now give the results of the form */
  fprintf( mailer, "Name: %s\n", name );
  fprintf( mailer, "Address: \n%s\n", address );

  fprintf( mailer, "\nEnd of form submission.\n" );

  pclose( mailer );

  cgiHeaderContentType("text/html");
  fprintf(cgiOut, "<HTML><HEAD>\n");
  fprintf(cgiOut, "<TITLE>Form Mailed!</TITLE></HEAD>\n");
  fprintf(cgiOut, "<BODY><H1>Form Mailed!</H1>\n");
  fprintf(cgiOut, "Thank you, %s. Your email will be read ASAP!<BR>\n",
   name );

  printEnvironmentVariables();

  fprintf(cgiOut, "</BODY></HTML>\n" );

  return 0;
}

void printEnvironmentVariables()
{
  fprintf(cgiOut, "cgiServerSoftware=%s<BR>\n", cgiServerSoftware);
  fprintf(cgiOut, "cgiServerName=%s<BR>\n", cgiServerName);
  fprintf(cgiOut, "cgiGatewayInterface=%s<BR>\n", cgiGatewayInterface);
  fprintf(cgiOut, "cgiServerProtocol=%s<BR>\n", cgiServerProtocol);
  fprintf(cgiOut, "cgiServerPort=%s<BR>\n", cgiServerPort);
  fprintf(cgiOut, "cgiRequestMethod=%s<BR>\n", cgiRequestMethod);
  fprintf(cgiOut, "cgiPathInfo=%s<BR>\n", cgiPathInfo);
  fprintf(cgiOut, "cgiPathTranslated=%s<BR>\n", cgiPathTranslated);
  fprintf(cgiOut, "cgiScriptName=%s<BR>\n", cgiScriptName);
  fprintf(cgiOut, "cgiQueryString=%s<BR>\n", cgiQueryString);
  fprintf(cgiOut, "cgiRemoteHost=%s<BR>\n", cgiRemoteHost);
  fprintf(cgiOut, "cgiRemoteAddr=%s<BR>\n", cgiRemoteAddr);
  fprintf(cgiOut, "cgiAuthType=%s<BR>\n", cgiAuthType);
  fprintf(cgiOut, "cgiRemoteUser=%s<BR>\n", cgiRemoteUser);
  fprintf(cgiOut, "cgiRemoteIdent=%s<BR>\n", cgiRemoteIdent);
  fprintf(cgiOut, "cgiContentType=%s<BR>\n", cgiContentType);
  fprintf(cgiOut, "cgiAccept=%s<BR>\n", cgiAccept);
  fprintf(cgiOut, "cgiUserAgent=%s<BR>\n", cgiUserAgent);
}
```

The associated HTML code for the form is shown in Listing 5.12.

LISTING 5.12. THE NEW HTML CODE.

```
<HTML>
<HEAD>
<TITLE>WhoAreYou</TITLE>
</HEAD>

<BODY BGCOLOR="#ffffff">
<FORM ACTION="/cgi-bin/email.cgi" ENCTYPE="x-www-form-encoded" METHOD="GET">

<HR>
<IMG SRC="1.gif" WIDTH="57" HEIGHT="77" ALIGN="MIDDLE" SIZE=50>
<STRONG>Your name:</STRONG>
<INPUT NAME="Name" TYPE="text" SIZE="53"><BR>
<IMG SRC="2.gif" WIDTH="57" HEIGHT="77" ALIGN="MIDDLE">
<STRONG>Your Address:</STRONG>
<TEXTAREA NAME="Address" ROWS="6" COLS="50"></TEXTAREA><BR>
<HR>
<BR>

<P ALIGN=CENTER>
<INPUT NAME="name" TYPE="submit" VALUE="Submit">
</P>

</FORM>
</BODY>
</HTML>
```

As you can see from the C code, the only thing really different about calling sendmail using C is that you use the popen() system call within the unistd.h header file. This system call is actually also what Perl uses internally when you do an open() to a pipe.

RANDOM DATA

They say variety is the spice of life. Well, if that's true, then it is the lifeblood of any good Web site. People will be certainly more inclined to come back to your Web site if the information and look of your site changes over time. The problem with keeping your site fresh and different is that it requires a lot of maintenance if you code it statically—that is, you have to manually enter changes into one or more HTML files for display.

Randomizer programs can add a little variety to your Web site without a lot of tedious work. The two I discuss here are an image randomizer and a URL randomizer.

AN IMAGE RANDOMIZER

One good way to do this is through the use of an image randomizer program. Wouldn't it be nice if every time a user loaded one of your pages, he or she would see a different image depending on the context of the page?

Or perhaps you're the enterprising type and you want to get into the advertising business. You could statically display banners on each page, but that wouldn't be very flexible. You'd have to charge more for the most frequently hit pages, less for the lesser-hit pages, and most importantly, you'd have to manually rotate the image tags if you wanted a rotating display schedule! Well, what if you could guarantee an advertiser exposure on every page—say 1 in every 10 hits? Much more attractive to the advertiser and easier on your time.

I have created such a beast for inclusion with this book, shown in Listing 5.13. The image randomizer displays a random image from a configuration file with each hit on the page. Varying the frequency of each individual banner URL in the config file increases the chances of seeing that particular banner, thus allowing for rate schedules for advertisers wanting more exposure. The beauty of this scheme is that you can mix it with a static banner display scheme. Say, for example, one company wants to pay you a ton of money for placing its banner on your front page *all the time*. Well, that's fine; just statically code the URL. Done! The randomizer runs only when you tell it to. It doesn't have to be used on each page.

This program is written in Perl and must be run on a server with Server Side Includes enabled (see Chapter 6, "ServerSide Includes (SSI)"). Also, you need to specify a configuration file, which is a file consisting one or more lines of the following format:

```
"Link-URL","Image-URL","IMAGE_OPTIONS"
```

Briefly, "Link-URL" specifies a fully qualified URL for the destination the user is taken to upon clicking the banner, "Image-URL" is a fully qualified URL for the banner itself, and "IMAGE_OPTIONS" is a tag added to the <IMAGE> tag of the banner graphic. Any string of valid tags and values is acceptable here, the most important, perhaps, being the "BORDER=" tag, which is a Netscape extension to HTML specifying the size and presence of a hyperlink color border around an image.

So a sample graphics.conf would look something like this:

```
"http://www.foobar.com","http://www.yoursite.com/banners/foobar.gif","BORDER=0"
"http://www.anothersite.com","http://www.yoursite.com/banners/anothersite.gif",
➥"BORDER=0"
"http://www.foobar.com","http://www.yoursite.com/banners/foobar.gif","BORDER=0"
"http://www.foobar.com","http://www.yoursite.com/banners/foobar.gif","BORDER=0"
```

In this configuration file, there are only two advertisers who have banners. However, foobar.gif will be seen 75 percent of the time (3 out of 4), while anothersite.gif will be seen 25 percent of the time (1 out of 4). This allows for a schedule of rates, as I mentioned.

Listing 5.13. The Perl randomizer.

```perl
#!/usr/local/bin/perl -w
#
# random.cgi - prints a graphic at random from a configuration file
#
# $conf_file: the absolute path to your configuration file (your listing of
# URL's to the graphics.
#
# $ad_tag: the string outputted to the web page SSI location
#
# Call this script from a server-parsed html document (.shtml for example) and make
# sure that server-side includes are enabled.
#
# Use the following example code:
#
# <!--#exec cmd="/yourpath/random.cgi"-->
#
# Of course, substitute your actual path to the random.cgi for /
#yourpath.  Again,
# this won't work unless Server-Side Includes are activated for Apache...

use strict;     # Declare all our variables before using them
$| = 1;  # Flush the output buffer

#Variables
my( $conf_file, $URL, $graphic, $ad_tag, $border  );
my( @Graphics );
my( $num_graphics, $rand_graphic );

$conf_file = "/path-to-config-file/graphics.conf";

srand;

open( IN, $conf_file ) || die "Cannot open $conf_file: $!";
@Graphics = <IN>;
close( IN );

$num_graphics = @Graphics;  #Get length of @Graphics array
$rand_graphic = int( rand( $num_graphics - 1 ) );
($URL,$graphic,$border) = split( /,/, $Graphics[$rand_graphic] );

$URL =~ s/\"//g;
$graphic =~ s/\"//g;
$border =~ s/\"//g;

$ad_tag = "<A HREF=\"$URL\"><IMG SRC=\"$graphic\" $border></A>";

print $ad_tag;

exit( 0 );
```

A URL Randomizer

You can very easily adapt the image randomizer to act as a URL randomizer. What good is a URL randomizer? Well, it adds that ever-so-important quality of variety to your site, and it allows you to direct people to random, but related sites of interest.

Say you were writing a page about turtles—their habitats, behavior, variations, basically the whole "turtle thing." Being the thorough person you are, you decide to include hyperlinks to those resources in your page. Naturally, there are a lot of resources on turtles on the Internet. Yahoo! lists 31 entries on the query `turtle`—too many to include on a main page. So you decide to include the hyperlinks on a separate page called "Turtle Links." But this is away from the main page; you need something more eye-catching to draw people to other resources. Aha! Perhaps a "Link of the Day" at the top of your main page would look cool.

How could you use the image randomizer to do this? Well, the easiest way to do it is to simply create one image for "Random Turtle Link of the Day" and make it the default a clickable image for each hyperlink in the `graphics.conf` file. No modifications are necessary.

A Bulletin Board

Another useful application is a *bulletin board*, or message board. This provides a way for a user of your Web site to not only give feedback on various topics, but to see other people's opinions and ideas.

The program I have provided to illustrate this concept is very simple. (See Listing 5.14.) It provides a framework to which you can add the features you need. In its current working form, a user can add a message, clear the board of messages, or update the board to see new messages. Obviously, you don't want to give the user the capability to clear the board, and maybe you don't want her to be able to modify the message board file directly by posting the message to the message board without your review. You can make modifications to avoid this—for example, have all messages mailed to your address for review and censorship. Then, if a message is appropriate, you could post it to the board. This would solve all sorts of problems, such as people not conforming to the general theme of the board.

Another use of the board is as a chat vehicle. Two or more people could be given the address of the board, and then through the use of the Add and Update buttons, a "conversation" could be held. This is very useful if you want to have a conference call of more than two people, because IRC and `talk` are not options for everyone.

The program is written in Perl, as you can see from the source code, and it requires the `CGILIB.pm` library listed in Listing 5.8.

LISTING 5.14. THE PERL BULLETIN BOARD.

```perl
#!/usr/local/bin/perl -w
#
# board.cgi
#
# This program writes messages to a message board.
#
unshift (@INC,"/NextLibrary/WebServer/htdocs/perl/lib");
use strict;
require CGILIB;

# Parse the form data
my(%FORM) = CGILIB::parse_form();

# The location of the messageboard file. This should be something
# other than /tmp if you want the messages to hang around in case
# your system goes down.  However, /tmp is fine if all you want is
# a chat session.
my($board_file) = "/tmp/messageboard";

# Add a message
if ( $FORM{action} =~ /add/ )
{
 # Add message only if message body isn't empty
 if ( $FORM{message} ne "" )
 {
  add_message();
 }
}

# Clear the board of messages.
elsif ( $FORM{action} =~ /clear/ )
{
 system( "rm $board_file" );
}

# Default actions
display_form();
display_board();

exit(0);

####################################################################
#
# sub display_form()
#
# Prints out the header and the HTML for the form part of the page.
#
sub display_form
{
 CGILIB::print_header();

 print <<STOP;
<HTML>
<HEAD>
<TITLE>Message Board</TITLE>
</HEAD>
<BODY>
```

```
<H1>Message Board</H1>
<FORM METHOD="GET" ACTION="board.cgi">
<TEXTAREA NAME="message" ROWS=10 COLS=40 WRAP=VIRTUAL></TEXTAREA>
<BR>
<INPUT NAME="action" TYPE="submit" VALUE="add">
<INPUT NAME="action" TYPE="submit" VALUE="clear">
<INPUT NAME="action" TYPE="submit" VALUE="update">
</FORM>
<HR>
STOP
}

###################################################################
#
# sub display_board()
#
# Displays each message, in the order of most recent to least recent.
#
sub display_board
{
 my( @board );
 my( $count ) = 0;
 my( $message );

 # Check to see if messageboard file exists.
 if (-e $board_file)
 {
  # Load message file and slurp all the messages into an array.
  # One message per line.  Newline is the delineator.
  open( BOARD, $board_file ) || die "Cannot read $board_file: $_";
  @board = <BOARD>;
  close( BOARD );

  # Since messages are appended to the end of the file, simply
  # reversing the array will order them in most-recent-first.
  @board = reverse( @board );

  # Now traverse the array, printing each message
  foreach $message (@board)
  {
   $count++;
   print "<STRONG>Message $count:</STRONG>\n";
   print "<BLOCKQUOTE>$message\n";
   print "</BLOCKQUOTE><BR>\n";
  }
 }
 # Else message board is empty
 else
 {
  print "<EM>Message Board empty</EM>\n";
 }
 print "</BODY></HTML>\n";
}

###################################################################
#
# sub add_message()
```

continues

LISTING 5.14. CONTINUED

```
#
# Appends a message to the end of the messageboard file. Converts
# all newlines to <BR> tags for convenient processing.
#
sub add_message
{
 my( $message );

 # Open messageboard file for appending.
 open( BOARD, ">>$board_file" ) ¦¦ die "Cannot write $board_file: $_";

 $message = $FORM{message};

 # Convert newlines (\n) to <BR>
 $message =~ s/\n/<BR>/g;
 print BOARD "$message\n";

 close( BOARD );
}
```

SUMMARY

CGI is a very complex topic and one that is important for most Web applications. Instead of reinventing the wheel (that is, unless you think you can do it better), there are tons of tools out on the Net, such as cgic and Un-CGI, that can make your life much easier. Instead of reinventing, search. More than likely someone has already done what you are looking for.

While this chapter has discussed the generalities of how to write a CGI program, it didn't cover any of the issues you need to address when writing a *secure* CGI program. Before you write your first CGI program intended for public consumption, you may want to read Chapter 16, "Web Server Security Issues." The information there may be very enlightening.

If your site is CGI intensive (you run many CGI programs), you may benefit from learning about FastCGI. FastCGI is a replacement for the CGI mechanism that offers incredible performance gains with very little modification to what you have learned in this chapter. Information about FastCGI is covered in great detail in Appendix C, "FastCGI."

- Server Parsed HTML

- Extended Server Side
  Includes (XSSI)

CHAPTER 6

Server Side Includes (SSI)

SERVER PARSED HTML

Server Side Includes (SSI), also known as Server Parsed HTML (SPML), provides a convenient way of performing server-side processing on an HTML file before it is sent to the client. SSI provides a set of dynamic features, such as including the current time or the last modification date of the HTML file without developing a CGI program that performs this function. SSI can be considered as a server-side scripting language.

Server parsed HTML documents are parsed and processed by the server before they are sent to the client. Only documents with a MIME type of `text/x-server-parsed-html` or `text/x-server-parsed-html3` are parsed and processed. The resulting HTML is given a MIME type of `text/html` and is returned to the client.

You can include information such as the current time, execute a program and include its output, or include a document just by adding some simple SPML commands to your HTML page. When the HTML page is properly identified to the server as containing SPML tokens, the server parses the file and sends the result to the client requesting it.

Technical Note

Enabling Apache to Run Server Side Includes

By default, SSIs are not enabled on a standard Apache configuration. Before you can incorporate SSI commands into your HTML documents, you will have to add a few directives to your configuration files.

The first step is to uncomment (remove the # character at the beginning of a line) the two lines in your `srm.conf` file that enable the following directives:

```
AddType text/html .shtml

AddHandler server-parsed .shtml
```

If these directives are missing, simply add them to the configuration file. The `AddType` directive maps the extension `.shtml` to the MIME type `text/html`. The `AddHandler` directive maps the `.shtml` extension to a *handler*. Handlers allow the server to perform some action based on a file type. They *handle* the processing of the file before it is returned to the client. The `server-parsed` handler referenced in the `AddHandler` directive is predefined in the base Apache distribution.

The `AddType` and `AddHandler` directives enable the server to recognize and process files that contain SPML tokens. However, that alone is not enough to enable their use in Apache. Because SSI can execute programs and include other documents in your filesystem, processing of the SPML tokens is not allowed by default. To enable the processing

6

of SPML commands, you'll need to override the default set of options. The Options directive allows you to control which features are available in which server directory. This allows you to provide different security settings to different areas of your server document tree. If the server attempts to execute an SSI document in a directory that doesn't enable this functionality, the request fails.

By default the htdocs document tree allows only Indexes and FollowSymLinks, which enable the server to generate automatic directory listings and to follow symbolic links, respectively. Apache provides two different options that enable SSI execution:

♦ Includes

♦ IncludesNOEXEC

Includes activates all commands available to Server Side Includes (SSI). IncludesNOEXEC is a more restrictive option; it disables the exec and include commands. As their names suggest, the exec command executes programs and the include command inserts other documents into the requested HTML file.

Because of the obvious security implications associated with executing programs and including other documents, you should not enable SSI execution system wide, unless you are able to control what those SSI do.

The Options directive can be found inside a <Directory> section inside the global access configuration file, access.conf or in a per-directory access control file (.htaccess) files. For more information, see Chapter 9, "Apache Server Core Directives," which explains in great detail the <Directory> and Options directives.

An SPML document is parsed as an HTML document, with SPML commands embedded as Standard Generalized Markup Language (SGML) comments. The commands follow this syntax:

```
<!--#command option=value option=value ...-->
```

Each command has a different set of options that you can specify. Usually options have a value portion (a parameter). Currently the available commands include facilities to do the following:

♦ Execute programs

♦ Obtain file size and modification information

♦ Include text from other documents or from a program

♦ Configure the format used to display results from the various commands

SPML COMMANDS

The available SPML commands are

- ◆ config
- ◆ echo
- ◆ exec
- ◆ cmd
- ◆ fsize
- ◆ flastmod
- ◆ include

config

The config command controls various aspects of the parsing and establishes various formatting options for displaying errors, date-time strings, and file sizes. The valid options you can use are (note that quotes surround values)

errmsg="*message*"	*message* is the message returned to the client if an error occurs during the parsing of the document.
sizefmt=["bytes"] ¦ ["abbrev"]	These options set the format used to display a file size. Valid values are
	bytes for a size returned in bytes.
	abbrev for a size returned in KB or MB as appropriate.
timefmt="*format*"	*format* is a format string that specifies the format used to print the date. It is compatible with the strftime library available under most UNIX environments. The various strftime format options are
	%% identical to %; use it if you need a percent sign in the output.
	%a abbreviated weekday name
	%A full weekday name
	%b abbreviated month name
	%B full month name
	%c time and date using the time and date representation for the locale (the same as using the %X %x options together)

%d	day of the month as a decimal number (01–31)
%H	hour based on a 24-hour clock as a decimal number (00–23)
%I	hour based on a 12-hour clock as a decimal number (01–12)
%j	day of the year as a decimal number (001–366)
%m	month as a decimal number (01–12)
%M	minute as a decimal number (00–59)
%p	AM/PM designation associated with a 12-hour clock
%S	second as a decimal number (00–61)
%w	weekday as a decimal number (0–6), where Sunday is 0
%x	date using the date representation for the locale
%X	time using the time representation for the locale
%y	year without century (00–99)
%Y	year with century (for example, 1990)
%Z	time zone name or abbreviation, or no characters if no time zone is determinable.

echo

The echo command prints any of the include environment variables. If the specified variable doesn't have a value, it prints as (none). Printing of dates is subject to the currently configuration of timefmt. Valid options include the following:

var="*variable*"	*variable* is the name of the variable to print.

Beginning with Apache 1.1, the SSIs and CGIs you call from your SSI also have access to the CGI environment variables. For a complete listing, refer to Chapter 5, "CGI (Common Gateway Interface) Programming."

Apache 1.1

Beginning with Apache 1.2, Apache adopted the use of the XSSI module as their standard SSI processor. XSSI is discussed in detail in a section of this chapter titled, "Extended Server Side Includes (XSSI)."

Apache 1.2

exec

The exec command executes the specified shell command or CGI program. This option can be disabled by the IncludesNOEXEC option. The valid options are

cgi="*path*"
> *path* specifies the program to be run. If *path* is not an absolute path (one that begins with a /), then *path* is taken to be relative to the current document.
>
> The directory containing the program must be a CGI directory approved by either a ScriptAlias or by setting the ExecCGI option in the global access configuration file or on a per-directory access file.
>
> The program's environment includes the PATH_INFO and QUERY_STRING variables set to the values sent in the original request. The include variables are available to the script in addition to the standard CGI environment.
>
> Programs that return a Location: header have their output translated into an HTML anchor.
>
> Use of the include virtual element is preferred to exec cgi.

cmd="*string*"
> The server will execute *string* using /bin/sh. The environment includes the include variables and, beginning with Apache 1.1, the complete set of CGI environment variables.

fsize

This command inserts the size of the specified file, subject to the sizefmt format specification. The options to this command are

file="*path*"
> The value is a path relative to the directory containing the current document being parsed.

virtual="*path*"
> If *path* is not an absolute path (one that begins with a (/), *path* is taken to be relative to the current document.

flastmod

This command inserts the last modification date of the specified file, subject to the timefmt format specification. The options for this command are

file="*path*"
> The value is a path relative to the directory containing the current document being parsed.

virtual="*path*"
> If *path* is not an absolute path (one that begins with a /), it is taken to be relative to the current document.

include

This command inserts another document into the parsed file. Included files are subject to any access-control settings governing their access, including any restrictions to CGI program execution. If there is a permissions restriction, the file or program output won't be included.

An option specifies the document's location; an inclusion is done for each option given to the `include` command. Valid options are as follows:

`file="filename"`   *filename* is a filename relative to the directory containing the current document being parsed. It cannot contain `../`, nor can it be an absolute path. The `virtual` option should always be used in preference to this one.

`virtual="urlpath"`   *urlpath* is a path relative to the current document being parsed. The URL cannot contain a scheme or hostname, only a path and an optional query string. If *urlpath* is not an absolute path (one that begins with a `/`), *path* is taken to be relative to the current document.

A URL is constructed from the option, and the output the server would return if the URL were accessed by the client is included in the parsed output; included files can be nested.

INCLUDE VARIABLES

These variables are provided for includes and to any program invoked by the document:

`DATE_GMT`   The current date in Greenwich Mean Time (GMT).

`DATE_LOCAL`   The current date in the local time zone.

`DOCUMENT_NAME`   The filename of the document requested by the user. `DOCUMENT_NAME` does not include any path information.

`DOCUMENT_URI`   The path of the document requested by the user.

`LAST_MODIFIED`   The document's last modification date.

In Apache 1.1, you can access the CGI environment variables (for a complete list, refer to Chapter 5) in addition to the include variables. The standard CGI 1.1 specification defines the several variables. Some are filled for all requests (`SERVER_SOFTWARE`, `SERVER_NAME`, and `GATEWAY_INTERFACE`). Others are request specific and may not be defined. A third category is added by the client program. These variables start with `HTTP`.

With this information you can create some pretty useful SPML pages that start to act more like a CGI program than a SPML. Two omissions from the Apache SSI module are conditional execution and user-defined variables. Howard Fear has developed a full replacement for the Apache SSI module, adding this missing functionality. This module is called XSSI. It is available from the CD-ROM included with this book, and is part of the standard Apache distribution for 1.2, which at the time this book was written, is yet unavailable.

SSI EXAMPLE

Here's an example, shown in Listing 6.1 and then in Figure 6.1, that puts it all together. You may want to implement something like this on your own site. The page returned is generated at random, based on a small database of quotes (in my programs the database is referred to as `quotes.conf`). Each entry in the database is a single line of text. Each record in the quote database is separated by a newline.

LISTING 6.1. `quote.shtml`.

```
<HTML>
<HEAD>
<TITLE> Random Quote </TITLE>
</HEAD>
<BODY>
<P ALIGN=CENTER>
<FONT SIZE=7><EM>Random Quote</EM></FONT>
</P>
<HR>
<BLOCKQUOTE>
<FONT SIZE=5><EM>
<!--#exec cmd="cgi/quoteoftheday.cgi"-->
</EM>
</FONT>
</BLOCKQUOTE>
<HR>
<!--#exec cmd="cgi/envvar.cgi"-->
<P>
<!--#config timefmt="%A, %B %d %Y"-->
<!--#echo var="DATE_LOCAL"-->
</BODY>
</HTML>
```

The `quoteoftheday.cgi` program returns a random line from the quote database (see Listing 6.2). The quote database is just a simple text file with one quote per line. The CGI returns one line, which the server inserts into the HTML stream returned to the client.

Figure 6.1.
Quote of the day.

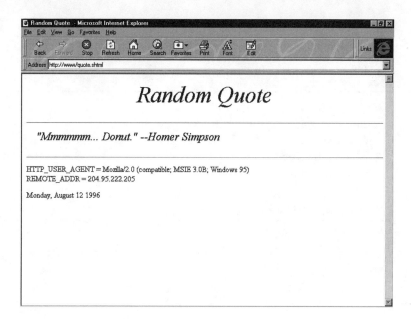

LISTING 6.2. quoteoftheday.cgi.

```perl
#!/usr/local/bin/perl -w
#
# quote.cgi - prints a quote at random
# $conf_file: the absolute path to your configuration file
# $ad_tag: the string outputted to the web page SSI location
# Call this script from a server-parsed html document (.shtml for example)
➥ and make
# sure that server-side includes are enabled.
#
# Use the following example code:
# <!--#exec cmd="/yourpath/random.cgi"-->
#
# Of course, substitute your actual path to the random.cgi for /
➥yourpath.   Again,
# this won't work unless Server-Side Includes are activated for Apache...
use strict;    # Declare all our variables before using them
$| = 1;  # Flush the output buffer

#Variables
my( $conf_file, $quote );
my( @Quotes );
my( $num_quotes, $rand_quote );
$conf_file = "/NextLibrary/WebServer/htdocs/AccessLink.htmld/cgi/quotes.conf";
srand;

open( IN, $conf_file ) || die "Cannot open $conf_file: $!";
@Quotes = <IN>;
close( IN );
$num_quotes = @Quotes;   #How many quotes are there?
```

continues

LISTING 6.2. CONTINUED

```
$rand_quote = int( rand( $num_quotes - 1 ) );
$quote = $Quotes[$rand_quote];
print $quote;
exit( 0 );
```

Finally, `envvar.cgi` is a trivial Perl program that prints out two of my CGI environment variables. (See Listing 6.3.) If you are using Apache 1.1.1's SSI module or XSSI, CGI variables are available as any of the standard SSI variables, so there's no need for this program.

LISTING 6.3. `envvar.cgi`.

```
#!/usr/local/bin/perl -w
#
use strict;     # Declare all our variables before using them
$¦ = 1;  # Flush the output buffer

print "HTTP_USER_AGENT = $ENV{HTTP_USER_AGENT}<BR>\n";
print "REMOTE_ADDR = $ENV{REMOTE_ADDR}<BR>\n";
```

EXTENDED SERVER SIDE INCLUDES (XSSI)

To circumvent some of the limitations of the standard SSI Apache module, Fear developed an extended SSI module that provides additional functionality and directives.

XSSI is a plug-in replacement module for the built-in `mod_include` module. Extended Server Side Includes (XSSI) enhances the Server Side Includes syntax and provides serveral additional features, including

◆ Conditional inclusion with `if-then-else` constructs

◆ User-defined variables

◆ Additional output directives

◆ Regular expression support

The SSI module is available on the CD-ROM included with this book. The latest version can be found at `http://pageplus.com/~hsf/xssi`.

VARIABLES

XSSI supports the notion of user-defined variables that you can use on all value tags, with the exception of `var=`, which you can use on all directives.

To define a variable, you use the `set` directive:

```
<!--#set var="variableName" value="variable_value"-->
```

For example, to define a variable *program* that holds the value `"/cgi-bin/printenv"`, you would set the following:

```
<!--#set var="program" value="/cgi-bin/printenv" -->
```

You can then use this variable on any value tag, except on the `var=` tags:

```
<!--#exec cgi="$program" -->
```

Alternatively, you can specify additional arguments by enclosing the variable in braces like the following:

```
<!--#exec cgi="${program} additional_text"-->
```

In addition to the variables defined for SSI, you can use any of the CGI environment variables (for a complete listing of these variables, please refer to the Chapter 5), which help create very simple, yet powerful, SSI programs without the need to write a CGI program.

It's worth noting that the `$` syntax to denote variable names may cause problems in `exec cmd` constructs where the `$` may be used by another program to denote an argument. For example:

```
<!--#exec cmd="/usr/local/etc/httpd/cgi-bin/finger @${HOST_NAME} ¦/bin/
➥awk '{print $1}'" -->
```

This SSI won't work as expected. The `$1` is set to a null value, which causes `awk` to print the complete line instead of the first word as intended. The solution to this minor inconveniece is to have an `sh` script handle all the output properly and return the data to you.

OUTPUT COMMANDS

In addition to the `echo`, `fsize`, and `flastmod` commands, which work as I've described, XSSI provides `printenv`, which prints all variables currently set (this includes CGI environment variables):

```
<!--#printenv -->
```

FLOW CONTROL

XSSI provides you with basic flow control with the following directives:

```
<!--#if expr="condition" -->
<!--#elif expr="condition" -->
```

```
<!--#else -->
<!--#endif -->
```

The `if` constructs work as they do in any programming language. If `condition` evaluates to `true`, all text specified until the next `elif`, `else`, or `endif` is included in the output. If `condition` evaluates to `false`, text specified after the `else` statement is included in the output.

The `elif` `condition` is evaluated if the preceding `if` statement evaluated to `false`. Statements specified after an `elif` statement are included in the output if the `elif` expression evaluates to `true`.

All conditional constructs must be terminated by an `endif` construct.

Any token that is not recognized as a variable or an operator is treated as a string. Strings can be quoted; variable substitution is done within quoted strings (if you need a $ within a string, you can escape it by preceding it with a backslash character). Unquoted strings cannot contain whitespace because spaces are used to separate other tokens. `condition` can be any of the following:

`string`	Evaluates to `true` if the string or variable is not empty
`stringA = stringB`	Evaluates to `true` if `stringA` is equal to `stringB`
`stringA != stringB`	Evaluates to `true` if `stringA` is not equal to `stringB`
`(condition)`	True if the condition evaluates to `true`
`!condition`	True if the condition is `false`
`conditionA && conditionB`	True if both conditions are `true`
`conditionA || conditionB`	True if either `conditionA` or `conditionB` is true

More interesting than a straight comparison is that XSSI enables you to test using regular expressions that follow the UNIX `egrep` syntax. In Table 6.1, `character` excludes newline.

TABLE 6.1. egrep SYNTAX.

Syntax	Effect
`\character`	Matches that character.
`^`	Matches the beginning of a line.
`$`	Matches the end of a line.
`.`	Matches any character.
`[string]`	Matches any single character in the string. You can abbreviate ranges of ASCII character codes as `a-z0-9`. A `]` may occur only as the first character of the string. A literal (a character) must be placed where it can't be mistaken as a range indicator.

Syntax	Effect
character	Matches that character, as long as that character doesn't have another meaning on a regular expression.
expresion*	Matches a sequence of 0 or more matches of the regular expression.
expresion+	Matches a sequence of 1 or more matches of the regular expression.
expresion?	Matches a sequence of 0 or 1 matches of the regular expression.
expression expression	Two regular expressions concatenated match a match of the first followed by a match of the second.
expression¦expression	Two regular expressions separated by ¦ or a newline can match either the first or the second.
(expression)	A regular expression enclosed in parentheses matches the regular expression definition.
	The order of precedence of operators at the same parenthesis level is [], then *+?, then concatenation, and then ¦ and newline.

The following example shows you how to output HTML based on the browser detected:

```
<!--#if expr="${HTTP_USER_AGENT} = /Mozilla/" -->
Output NETSCAPE specific HTML
<!--#else --> Output HTML 2.0 compliant formatting
<!--#endif -->
```

SUMMARY

The benefits of Server Parsed HTML don't come gratis. The parsing process is costly in terms of server performance and also adds some security issues. If you are concerned about security, you may want to disable the IncludeNoExecs option, which allows SPML but disables the #exec and #include commands from SSI. Obviously, this severely hampers the usefulness of SSI severely. For more information on the security issues involved, take a look at Chapter 16, "Web Server Security Issues."

In terms of programming, SPML gives you the capability to embed some "programming" into your pages. However, there are many features that have to be lacking for it to become a serious option to CGI programs.

If you are interested in pursuing HTML scripting type languages, of which SSI is a member, you may want to explore PHP/FI, which is another HTML-embedded scripting language. For more information on PHP/FI, check its home page at http://www.vex.net/php.

- mod_auth_cookies_file

- mod_auth_cookies_msql

- mod_userpath

- mod_cgi_sugid

- mod_auth_sys

- mod_perl and
  mod_perl_fast

- mod_auth_external

- mod_auth_kerb

- mod_auth_dbi

- mod_rewrite

- mod_neoinclude

- mod_xinclude (XSSI)

- mod_php

CHAPTER 7

Third-Party Modules

There is a wide range of modules developed by third parties for Apache that extend the functionality of the server in some useful way. Following the belief that it is better to reuse and enhance than to re-create, this chapter covers some of the third-party modules registered with the Apache Module Registry. The registry can be found at `http://www.zyzzzyva.com/server/module_registry` (see Figure 7.1).

Figure 7.1.
The home page of the Apache Module Registry.

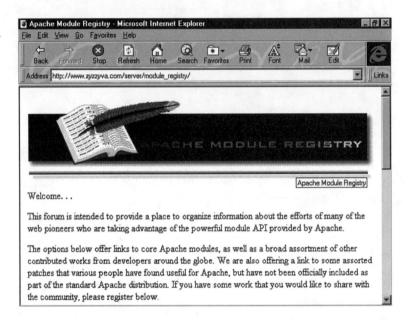

mod_auth_cookies_file

Source: `mod_auth_cookie_file.c`
Author: Dirk-Willem van Gulik
Type: User authentication/Access control
Home: `http://med.jrc.it//~dirkx/mod_auth_cookie_file.c`

This module is designed to allow transparent authentication to users who have previously registered with your site. Suppose that you want to have visitors register with you before they access your software download area. By collecting information from them and then issuing a persistent cookie, the next time they visit your download area they can forgo the authentication procedure.

Technical Note

Cookies are a Netscape extension. The official reference for Netscape cookies can be found at `http://home.netscape.com/newsref/std/cookie_spec.html`.

A cookie enables the browser to identify itself every time it makes a request. A cookie is no more than a ticket. When you go to your dry cleaner and give them clothes for cleaning, they give you a ticket. That ticket identifies you as having brought clothes in for cleaning; it associates you with your clothes. You can think of the dry cleaner's ticket as a cookie.

There are two types of cookies: persistent and temporary. Persistent cookies get recorded in the visitor's computer for use later. When the browser makes subsequent requests to the same URL, it first checks to see if it has a cookie for it. If it does, the browser includes this information in the HTTP request header where a program in the server (a CGI or a module) can use this information for any purpose it wants. Temporary cookies are only used during the duration of the visit, after which they are discarded.

A Netscape persistent cookie is set with an HTTP header like the following:

```
Set-Cookie: Name=value; [Expires=date;] [Path=path;] [Domain=domainname;]
[Secure]
```

The `Set-Cookie` header can be embedded in an HTML document in a `META` tag, like the following, or from a CGI:

```
<META HTTP-EQUIV="Set-Cookie" CONTENT="Customer=John Doe";
➥Path=/; Domain=www.domain.com">
```

When sent from a CGI, this information must be sent as part of the HTTP header. For more information on how to form a header, please refer to Chapter 5, "CGI (Common Gateway Interface) Programming."

`Name` specifies the name identifier for the cookie.

`value` can be any information you want to keep track of.

The `Expires` option sets a date that will be used for expiring the cookie. If not specified, the cookie will expire at the end of the current session, making it a temporary cookie. The format is `Wdy, DD-Mon-YY HH:MM:SS GMT`. `Wdy` is the day of the week; possible values for `Wdy` are `Mon`, `Tue`, `Wed`, `Thu`, `Fri`, `Sat`, or `Sun`. `DD` is the day of the month; possible values are `01`–`31`. `Mon` is the month; possible values for it are `Jan`, `Feb`, `Mar`, `Apr`, `May`, `Jun`, `Jul`, `Aug`, `Sep`, `Oct`, `Nov`, or `Dec`. `YY` is the last two digits of the year, without the century (1996=96). `HH` specifies the hour in a 24-hour format. `MM` specifies the minutes, and `SS` specifies the seconds. The date should be specified in the Greenwich Mean Time (GMT) time zone. Previously issued cookies can be expired by sending a new cookie with the same name using an expiration date that has already past. Expiration depends on the visitor's clock time, which may be far off from the real time.

The Path option specifies the document hierarchy where the cookie is valid. This is typically set to / so that it is valid for all documents in the document hierarchy. The browser uses this information to determine if there are any cookies already stored in the visitor's computer that are associated with *path*. If there are, the browser returns a Cookie: header along with the cookie *Name* and *value* along with the request. Multiple cookies matching the path will be sent with semicolons separating them.

Domain specifies the Internet domain where the cookie is valid. You can specify a fully qualified domain name such as *host.domain.com*.

When Secure is specified, the cookie will only be sent if the connection is secure by using a Secure Socket Layer (SSL) server, such as Stronghold.

The mod_auth_cookies_file module requests a named cookie from the client that contains the authentication information, which gets verified against an htpasswd like database.

DIRECTIVES

mod_auth_cookie_file provides five directives:

◆ Cookie_Access

◆ Cookie_AuthFile

◆ Cookie_Authorative

◆ Cookie_MustGive

◆ Cookie_EncryptedCookies

Cookie_Access

Syntax: Cookie_Access [on]|[off]
Default: Cookie_Access off

This directive sets cookie access authentication.

Cookie_AuthFile

Syntax: `Cookie_AuthFile authFile`
Default: `Cookie_AuthFile NULL` (no file specified)

The format of the authentication file (`authFile`) is a list of colon (`:`)-separated values following this format:

`userId:name:value`

where `userID` is the user's name, `name` is the cookie name, and `value` is the cookie value.

Cookie_Authorative

Syntax: `Cookie_Authorative [on]|[off]`
Default: `Cookie_Authorative off`

If the cookie fails, no authorization is given (authorization is final.) The user will have to re-register with the site before she is able to log in.

Cookie_MustGive

Syntax: `Cookie_MustGive [on]|[off]`
Default: `Cookie_MustGive off`

When set to `on`, the client must present a cookie prior to authenticating.

Cookie_EncryptedCookies

Syntax: `Cookie_EncryptedCookies [on]|[off]`
Default: `Cookie_EncryptedCookies on`

This module specifies if the cookie value is encrypted using `crypt`—the program used by UNIX to encrypt passwords.

mod_auth_cookies_msql

Source: `mod_auth_cookie_msql.c`
Author: Dirk-Willem van Gulik
Type: User authentication/Access control
Home: `http://med.jrc.it//~dirkx/mod_auth_cookie_msql.c`

This module is similar to `mod_auth_cookie_file`, but uses mini-SQL (mSQL) to store its authentication data. It is designed to allow transparent authentication to users who have previously registered with your site. Suppose that you want to have visitors register with you before they access your software download area. By collecting information from them and then issuing a persistent cookie, the next time they visit your download area they can forgo the authentication procedure.

This module will request a named cookie from the client that contains the authentication information, which gets verified against tables in a mSQL database.

Directives

Mod_auth_cookie_msql provides 10 directives:

◆ Cookie_Access

◆ Cookie_Authorative

◆ Cookie_EncryptedCookies

◆ Cookie_MSQL_table

◆ Cookie_MSQLcookie_namefield

◆ Cookie_MSQLcookie_valuefield

◆ Cookie_MSQLdatabase

◆ Cookie_MSQLhost

◆ Cookie_MSQLuid_field

◆ Cookie_MustGive

Cookie_Access

Syntax:　Cookie_Access [on]|[off]

Default:　Cookie_Access off

This directive sets cookie access authentication.

Cookie_Authorative

Syntax:　Cookie_Authorative [on]|[off]

Default:　Cookie_Authorative off

If the cookie fails, no authorization is given (authorization is final). The user will need to re-register with the site.

Cookie_MustGive

Syntax:　Cookie_MustGive [on]|[off]

Default:　Cookie_MustGive off

When set to on, the client must present a cookie prior to authenticating.

Cookie_MSQL_table

Syntax:　Cookie_MSQL_table *tableName*

`Cookie_MSQL_table` sets the name of the mSQL table that contains the username and cookie fields used for authentication.

Cookie_MSQLcookie_namefield

Syntax: `Cookie_MSQLcookie_namefield cookieFName`

`Cookie_MSQLcookie_namefield` sets the name of the field from which the module will fetch the name of the cookie.

Cookie_MSQLcookie_valuefield

Syntax: `Cookie_MSQLcookie_valuefield valueFName`

`Cookie_MSQLcookie_valuefield` sets the name of the field from which the module will fetch the value of the cookie.

Cookie_MSQLdatabase

Syntax: `Cookie_MSQLdatabase database`

`Cookie_MSQLdatabase` sets the name of the mSQL database that contains the `Cookie_MSQL_table` where the authentication information is stored.

Cookie_MSQLhost

Syntax: `Cookie_MSQLhost [FQHN] | [IPAddress] | [localhost]`

This directive sets the name of the host machine running the mSQL server. The name of the host can be specified using its fully qualified domain name, its IP address, or `localhost` to specify that the server running the database is the same as the Web server.

Cookie_MSQLuid_field

Syntax: `Cookie_MSQLuid_field uidFName`

`Cookie_MSQLuid_field` sets the name of the field from which the module will fetch the `username` or the `uid`.

Cookie_EncryptedCookies

Syntax: `Cookie_EncryptedCookies [on]|[off]`
Default: `Cookie_EncryptedCookies on`

This directive specifies if the cookie value is encrypted using `crypt`—the program used by UNIX to encrypt passwords.

mod_userpath

Source: mod_userpath.c
Author: Simon Wilkinson
Type: Resource location/Uniform Resource Identifier (URI) rewriting
Home: http://www.tardis.ed.ac.uk/~sxw/apache/mod_userpath.c

Apache 1.1

This module is a replacement for the mod_userdir module distributed with versions of Apache earlier than 1.1. The version of mod_userdir distributed with Apache 1.1.1 provides this functionality and more.

mod_userpath rewrites the URI of requests following the pattern:

http://machine/~username

This module enables you to specify a directory where the server will look for a user's home page. This module has the added benefit of allowing you to create home page directories that don't necessarily match your internal usernames. Because this mechanism doesn't rely on user accounts, it allows you to provide home pages on machines that don't contain any user information.

If you incorporate this module into Apache, you should remove mod_userdir because both of these modules will attempt to rewrite the URI, and which one will win is anyone's guess.

DIRECTIVE

mod_userpath adds one directive:

◆ UserPath

UserPath

Syntax: UserPath *pathToUserPages*
Default: UserPath /usr/local/etc/httpd/htdocs/

Requests ending in a username will have UserPath prepended before they are processed by the server. For example:

http://machine/~username

will be translated into

http://machine/usr/local/etc/httpd/htdocs/~username

mod_cgi_sugid

Source: mod_cgi_sugid.c
Author: Philippe Vanhaesendonck
Type: CGI UID/GID execution options
Home: http://linux3.cc.kuleuven.ac.be/~seklos/mod_cgi_sugid.c

This module is a replacement for the standard Apache CGI module, mod_cgi. It provides the capability to run CGI under the User ID (UID) and Group ID (GID) of a different user. UID and GID can be specified inside the <Limit> sections. <Limit> sections are specified under <Location> or <Directory> sections in the global access configuration file. By default, this module does not allow the use of its directives from within per-directory access control files (.htaccess). Also, if the module fails to change the UID/GID of a CGI, the script is aborted. As you should expect, this module won't run CGI with a root UID.

DIRECTIVES

mod_cgi_sugid adds two directives:

◆ UserId

◆ GroupId

UserID

Syntax: UserID [*user*]

The UserID directive sets the UID used to run a CGI. This directive rejects requests to run a CGI with the root UID.

GroupID

Syntax: GroupID [*group*]

The GroupID directive sets the GID used to run a CGI.

mod_auth_sys

Source: mod_auth_sys.c
Author: Franz Vinzenz
Type: Authentication

mod_auth_sys allows you to authenticate a user using the UNIX calls getpwnam_r and getgrnam_r to retrieve password and group information for that user. This allows you to use your existing UNIX authentication scheme, such as /etc/passwd files, Network

Information Service (NIS), NIS++, and so on. This module does not provide any directives.

To call the module, just put an entry like the following in your global access configuration file or in a per-directory access file (omit the `<Directory>` section on per-directory access files):

```
<Directory somedir>
AuthType Basic
<Limit GET POST>
  require valid-user
</Limit>
</Directory>
```

The only concern with this module is the transmission of login and password information across the Internet because basic authentication does not encrypt the login transaction in any way. If anyone obtained this information en route, he would have full access to that user's account.

mod_perl AND mod_perl_fast

Authors:	Doug MacEachern
Type:	Embedded interpreter
Home:	`http://www.osf.org/~dougm/apache`

`mod_perl` and `mod_perl_fast` provide an alternative method for executing Perl programs. `mod_perl` and `mod_perl fast` are not CGI, so the way you program them is a little different.

At the time of this writing, programs that you write to take advantage of these modules don't run from the command line without the aid of the `CGI::Switch` Perl module. `CGI::Switch` is available from your nearest CPAN archive at `modules/by-module/Apache/CGI-XA-0_22305-alpha_tar.gz`.

These modules embed a Perl interpreter in the Web server. Because the Perl interpreter is embedded, the server can run Perl scripts by itself, and your Perl programs will run much faster. The embedded interpreter eliminates much of the expense associated with running CGI on your Web server. Also, scripts that run under these modules have full access to the Application Programming Interface (API) of the server, giving you the option of writing modules using Perl.

These modules differ in the way they function. `mod_perl` allocates and constructs a Perl interpreter for each request. This interpreter parses and executes the script. On completion, the Perl interpreter is destroyed, freeing the resources that it consumed.

`mod_perl_fast` allocates and constructs one Perl interpreter when the server starts. It also loads and parses a Perl script that is persistent.

mod_auth_external

Source: mod_auth_external.c
Author: Nathan Neulinger
Type: Authentication
Home: http://www.umr.edu/~nneul/

mod_auth_external allows you to specify an external program that will handle user and group authentication. The specified program will receive authentication information the visitor entered in the authentication panel via the USER and PASS environment variables. In addition, when doing group authentication, the group name is passed in the environment variable GROUP. The external authentication program is expected to return 0 to indicate successful authentication, or a nonzero result as an indication of a failed authentication session or an error in the authentication program.

This is a simple way of interfacing Apache to any authentication system.

DIRECTIVES

mod_auth_external adds four directives:

- ◆ AddExternalAuth
- ◆ AuthExternal
- ◆ AddExternalGroup
- ◆ GroupExternal

AddExternalAuth

Syntax: AddExternalAuth *token userAuthenticator*

Adding the AddExternalAuth directive to your httpd.conf file will register *userAuthenticator* under *token*. You can have multiple AddExternalAuth directives.

AuthExternal

Syntax: AuthExternal *token*

This directive is used inside a <Limit> section to specify the authenticator to use in this context. *token* gets matched to the AddExternalAuth directive, and the appropriate authenticator is launched:

```
<Directory somedir>
AuthName authentication realm description
AuthType Basic
AuthExternal token
<Limit GET POST>
```

```
    require valid-user
</Limit>
</Directory>
```

AddExternalGroup

Syntax: AddExternalGroup *token groupAuthenticator*

Adding the `AddExternalAuth` directive to your `httpd.conf` file will register *groupAuthenticator* under *token*. You can have multiple `AddExternalGroup` directives.

ExternalGroup

Syntax: ExternalGroup *token*

This directive is used inside a `<Limit>` section to specify the authenticator to use in this context. *token* gets matched to the `AddExternalGroup` directive, and the appropriate authenticator is launched:

```
<Directory somedir>
AuthName authentication realm description
AuthType Basic
ExternalGroup token
<Limit GET POST>
  require group groupA
</Limit>
</Directory>
```

mod_auth_kerb

Source: mod_auth_kerb.c
Author: James E. Robinson, III
Type: Authentication
Home: http://www2.ncsu.edu/ncsu/cc/rddc/projects/mod_auth_kerb/
           mod_auth_kerb.c

`mod_auth_kerb` provides kerberos authentication to Apache. *Kerberos* is a network security system designed at MIT that guarantees that users and services are who they claim to be without the need to ask a user for his password whenever he requests access to additional services. If the user's browser does not support kerberos directly, `mod_auth_kerb` will authenticate the user based on the User ID and password supplied to the browser.

DIRECTIVES

`mod_auth_kerb` provides the following directives:

   ◆ AuthType

◆ KrbAuthRealm

◆ RedirectHttps

AuthType

Syntax: AuthType [KerberosV4] | [KerberosV5]

This directive tells Apache and the browser which kerberos protocol to use when validating the user. This is the only directive necessary for the module to be functional.

KrbAuthRealm

Syntax: KrbAuthRealm *realm*

The KbrAuthRealm directive takes one argument: a string specifying the kerberos *realm* name that the server should use for authentication. For example, KrbAuthRealm MIT.EDU sets the authentication realm to MIT.EDU.

RedirectHttps

Syntax: RedirectHttps [On] | [Off]

This directive tells Apache to redirect the user's request to an SSL Web server running on the same host, if the original request was not under SSL. This allows for increased security on browsers that do not support kerberos directly by preventing clear text passwords from being sent over the network.

mod_fontxlate

Source: mod_fontxlate.c and Apache server patches
Author: Warwick Heath
Type: Eastern European font conversion
Home: http://www.rcc-irc.si/eng/fontxlate

mod_fontxlate is a configurable font-conversion module that determines if a request needs to be converted. Eastern European countries such as Slovenia use a variety of characters to represent local non-ASCII characters. Proper functioning of this module requires that Apache be patched. The advantage of this module is that it does its conversion very quickly.

For additional information, please refer to the documentation included in the module's source.

mod_cntr

Source:	`mod_cntr.c`
Author:	Brian Kolaci
Type:	Page counter
Home:	`ftp://ftp.galaxy.net/pub/bk/webcounter.tar.gz`

This module and ancillary CGI provide a transparent way of implementing Web counters. The module will keep track of the page access count on ASCII or DBM databases. Because the Web server keeps count of page access, there's no possible spoofing of the pages. To be counted, a page needs to be delivered. This module comes with several different number styles.

When the page counter databases have been set with the provided utilities, displaying the counter is very easy. On the Web page, you put an entry such as

```
<img src="/cgi-bin/count?type=subdirectory length=numDigits">
```

where `type` specifies the subdirectory for the number type used and `length` is the number of digits to put in the output, including any padding.

mod_sucgi

Source:	`mod_sucgi.c`
Author:	Jason A. Dour
Type:	CGI under different UID
Home:	`http://www.louisville.edu/~jadour01/mothersoft`

This module is a drop-in replacement for the `mod_cgi` provided in the Apache release. It allows you to transparently change the UID of CGI scripts to match that of a user.

To enable the functionality, just add the following to your global access configuration file (`access.conf`):

```
<Directory userdir/*/cgi-bin>
Options ExecCGI
</Directory>
```

When the server receives a CGI request, it checks it see if it came from a `UserDir`. If it did, it will pass the request to a supporting CGI program, `suCGI`, which will check the request and run it with the UID of the appropriate user.

mod_auth_dbi

Source:	`mod_auth_dbi.c`
Author:	Doug MacEachern
Type:	Authentication
Home:	`http://www.osf.org/~dougm/apache`

This module provides Perl DBI authentication. Database interface (DBI) provides a set of functions, variables, and conventions that you can use to access a database. This programming interface is independent of the database in use. For additional information on DBI, check `http://www.hermetica.com/technologia/DBI`.

DIRECTIVES

Mod_auth_dbi adds the following directives:

- ◆ AuthDBIAuth
- ◆ AuthDBIDB
- ◆ AuthDBIDriver
- ◆ AuthDBINameField
- ◆ AuthDBIPasswordField
- ◆ AuthDBIUser
- ◆ AuthDBIUserTable

AuthDBIAuth

Syntax: AuthDBIAuth *password*

This directive sets the DBI password. It is optional, depending on the driver used.

AuthDBIDB

Syntax: AuthDBIDB *databaseName*

This directive sets the name of the database to use.

AuthDBIDriver

Syntax: AuthDBIDriver *nameOfDBIDriver*

AuthDBIDriver sets the name of the DBI driver (for example, Oracle).

AuthDBINameField

Syntax: AuthDBINameField *fieldName*

This directive sets the fieldname within the AuthDBIUserTable in the AuthDBIDB database where the username can be found.

AuthDBIPasswordField

Syntax: AuthDBIPasswordFiled *fieldName*

This directive sets the fieldname within the `AuthDBIUserTable` in the `AuthDBIDB` database where the user's password can be found.

AuthDBIUser

Syntax: AuthDBIUser *userName*

This directive sets the user's DBI username. It is optional depending on the driver used.

AuthDBIUserTable

Syntax: AuthDBIUserTable *tableName*

This directive sets the tablename within the `AuthDBIDB` database where the user and password fields can be found.

mod_rewrite

Source: mod_rewrite.c
Author: Ralf S. Engelschall
Type: URI rewriting
Home: http://www.engelschall.com/sw/mod_rewrite

This is a killer module that even has its own Web site (see Figure 7.2). It uses a regular expression parser to rewrite requested URLs and can use external databases in both ASCII or DBM format for mapping support. This module has been incorporated into the Apache 1.2 release (not yet made public at the time of this writing). Apache 1.2 incorporates a built-in regular expression library. The latest version of mod_rewrite uses this library, which further reduces its impact on Apache.

mod_rewrite can replace several modules, including some of the default Apache modules (when properly configured). This is great because it can provide more comprehensive functionality while reducing the number of modules needed and the size of the Apache executable.

This module can easily replace mod_alias, mod_userdir (both Apache core modules), mod_userdir_virtual (not covered in this book), mod_userpath, and mod_uri_remap.

If you don't have use for a fully configurable URI rewrite module, there's an additional module that will replace the mod_alias and mod_userdir. This module, mod_rewrite_compat, uses mod_rewrite to provide a plug-and-play replacement to those other two modules.

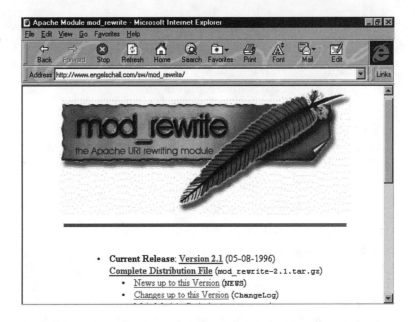

*Figure 7.2.
This module also
has a nice home
page.*

Oh, yes—and this is not a minor detail—mod_rewrite, together with the FastCGI module documentation, is by far the best-documented piece of software available for Apache. This one edges out the FastCGI docs a bit and is easier to use, so it takes first place on my list. Documentation for both these modules is commercial grade, matching documentation produced by Apple Computer or NeXT Software, Inc. (the best documentation I have ever used). Most other modules feature rather thin information that requires users and authors alike to spend a lot of time experimenting with software before they can get it to work. This usually means diving into the source code to determine what really is going on. I didn't have to do that with this one.

For information on mod_rewrite, see Chapter 10, "Apache Modules."

mod_neoinclude

Authors: Karl Lehenbauer, George Porter, Randy Kunkee, and
          Horace Vallas
Type: Tcl-based, secure server-side scripting language
Home: http://www.neosoft.com/neoscript

The neoinclude module processes NeoWebScript—a server-side scripting language based on Tcl. NeoWebScript programs can perform sophisticated data processing and dynamic HTML generation safely, without compromising the system. For comprehensive information on this module, please visit http://www.neosoft.com/neoscript.

mod_xinclude (XSSI)

Source: `mod_xinclude.c`
Author: Howard Fear
Type: SSI module replacement
Home: `ftp://pageplus.com/pub/hsf/xssi`

This module implements and extends SSI functionality. In Apache 1.2, it replaces the standard SSI module (`mod_include`). This module provides additional functionality and directives over the Apache SSI module, including the following:

- ◆ User-defined variables
- ◆ An additional output directive, `printenv`
- ◆ Flow-control directives

XSSI (Extended SSI) supports the notion of user-defined variables, which you can use on all value tags with the exception of `var=` constructs. In addition to the `echo`, `fsize`, and `flastmod` commands, XSSI provides `printenv`, which prints all variables currently set (this includes CGI environment variables). XSSI also provides basic flow control. For more information on this module, refer to Chapter 6, "Server Side Includes (SSI)."

mod_php

Author: Rasmus Lerdorf
Type: Server-parsed scripting language with RDBMS support
Home: `http://www.vex.net/php`

This is a powerful SSI-type scripting language that provides a C-like syntax. Its main features include the following:

- ◆ Is supported via standard CGI, FastCGI, and Apache modules
- ◆ Access logging capabilities
- ◆ Built-in GUI-based configuration
- ◆ mSQL, Postgres95, and DBM support
- ◆ Supports a wide range of variables, arrays, and Perl-like associative arrays that can be passed from page to page
- ◆ Supports conditionals and `while` loops
- ◆ Supports regular expressions
- ◆ Provides raw HTTP header control for doing things like redirections
- ◆ Has on-the-fly GIF image support, with Thomas Boutell's GD library

For more information, please visit the PHP/FI home page listed at the top of this section.

SUMMARY

While modules are great, remember that they get incorporated into the server binary. The more modules you add, the bigger the binary will get, which will increase the resources needed by your system to run the server efficiently. Remember that the server runs multiple copies of the Web server. So increasing the footprint by 100KB may translate into several megabytes depending on the number of server processes you have running. Your production server should only include the default Apache modules and any additional modules you absolutely need.

- Apache Configuration Overview

- Apache Server Core Directives

- Apache Modules

P A R T III

Complete Reference: Apache Configuration in Detail

CHAPTER 8

Apache Configuration Overview

The Apache server loads most of its configuration settings from a series of files at runtime when the server starts up. These files specify directives that control the behavior of the server. As you explore and exploit additional functionality of your server, you will be referring to the main configuration files for your changes.

Understanding the structure of the configuration files may help you find what you need more effectively. Although you could create a giant master configuration file, this usually doesn't work from a practical point of view because you'll spend a lot of time searching through a single, large file for what you need. Some of the configuration files are already several pages in length. If you were to combine them, it would only make searching a more complicated task.

APACHE CONFIGURATION FILES

Apache reads its configuration from several files located in the `conf` directory of your server root:

◆ `httpd.conf`

◆ `srm.conf`

◆ `access.conf`

◆ `mime.types`

httpd.conf

`httpd.conf` contains the main server configuration information. The basic behavior of the server is contained in this file, such as how it runs, User IDs (UIDs) it runs under, what port it listens to, performance issues, and information on how to find other configuration files.

srm.conf

`srm.conf` is the server's resource configuration file. The directives in this configuration file define the namespace that users can access on your server and the settings that affect how requests are serviced and formatted. The directives in this file control the location of the various resources that the server will access to retrieve information, such as `DocumentRoot`, the path to user's home pages, the location of the `cgi-bin` directory, the file the server looks for when the URL ends in a directory, the icons and format the server uses for displaying automatic directory listings, and so on. Directives in this file also map other areas of your UNIX file system into the server's document tree. This allows you to store resources, such as your `cgi-bin` directory, and make them available as if they were located within the directory specified by `DocumentRoot`.

access.conf

`access.conf` is the server's global access-configuration file. This file defines the types of services that are allowed and under what circumstances. Careful configuration of this file is important because many security issues can be avoided if you do your configuration correctly. `access.conf` defines whether the server will handle Server Side Includes, execute CGI programs, follow symbolic links, or generate automatic indexes of directories when an `index.html` file is not found. Many aspects can be overridden by allowing use of per-directory access files (`.htaccess` files); however, this has a very adverse consequence on the performance of the server. If you can manage it, it is much better to handle all access-configuration issues in the global access-configuration file.

mime.types

The `mime.types` file more than likely won't ever need configuration from you. This file maps MIME formats to file types that the server uses to know which files comply with which MIME standard. Remember that your browser always sends a header like

```
HTTP_ACCEPT = image/gif, image/x-xbitmap, image/jpeg, image/pjpeg, */*
```

that informs the server of the various types it is able to handle. This file provides the crucial mapping that allows your server to understand the content of a file from its extension.

ORGANIZATION OF THE CONFIGURATION DIRECTIVES

It's hard to group directives into descriptive categories. The Apache approach has been to classify directives based on whether their functionality is part of the server core or added by optional modules.

Core directives are directives that are always available; the code and modules that incorporate core functionality are built in. This functionality is central to the operation of the Apache Web server.

Other directives is a broad category that includes everything else that is not part of the core. These directives enhance the server. Many of them are actually included in the default server configuration (also called the base) because they are incredibly useful. Directives that are part of the base build are available for use without the need to recompile the server.

In addition to core and other directives, there are many other directives provided by optional modules. I call these *specialized directives* because they add specialized functionality that not all servers will need.

I find this broad classification not clear in terms of providing a good description of what is available right out of the box. I have further classified directives into subgroups (see Tables 8.1 and 8.2). I hope this will help portray the overall set of directives more clearly. Some directives may fit into one or more categories, but for clarity, I included them in only one category each.

TABLE 8.1. APACHE CORE AND BASE DIRECTIVES.

Directive	*Type*	*Implemented In*	*Base*
ErrorLog	Accounting	Core	
HostNameLookups	Accounting	Core	
PidFile	Accounting	Core	
TransferLog (mod_log_common)	Accounting	mod_log_common	Yes
ResourceConfig	Additional configuration files	Core	
AccessConfig	Additional configuration files	Core	
AccessFileName	Additional configuration files	Core	
TypesConfig	Additional configuration files	mod_mime	Yes
AddDescription	Automatic indexing	mod_dir	Yes
AddIcon	Automatic indexing	mod_dir	Yes
AddIconByEncoding	Automatic indexing	mod_dir	Yes
AddIconByType	Automatic indexing	mod_dir	Yes
DefaultIcon	Automatic indexing	mod_dir	Yes
FancyIndexing	Automatic indexing	mod_dir	Yes
HeaderName	Automatic indexing	mod_dir	Yes
IndexIgnore	Automatic indexing	mod_dir	Yes
IndexOptions	Automatic indexing	mod_dir	Yes
ReadmeName	Automatic indexing	mod_dir	Yes
DirectoryIndex	Automatic indexing	mod_dir	Yes
PassEnv	CGI	mod_env	Yes

Directive	Type	Implemented In	Base
SetEnv	CGI	mod_env	Yes
ErrorDocument	Error handling	Core	
ServerAdmin	Error handling	Core	
Action	MIME, language, or handler management	mod_actions	Yes
Script	MIME, language, or handler management	mod_actions	Yes
AddHandler	MIME, language, or handler management	mod_mime	Yes
SetHandler	MIME, language, or handler management	mod_mime	Yes
DefaultType	MIME, language, or handler management	Core	
AddEncoding	MIME, language, or handler management	mod_mime	Yes
AddLanguage	MIME, language, or handler management	mod_mime	Yes
AddType	MIME, language, or handler management	mod_mime	Yes
ForceType	MIME, language, or handler management	mod_mime	Yes
LanguagePriority	MIME, language, or handler management	mod_negotiation	Yes
XBitHack	MIME, language, or handler management	mod_include	Yes
CacheNegotiatedDocs	Proxy server/Cache management	mod_negotiation	Yes
ScriptAlias	Resource location	mod_alias	Yes
Alias	Resource location	mod_alias	Yes
Redirect	Resource location	mod_alias	Yes
UserDir	Resource location	mod_userdir	Yes
KeepAlive	Resource management	Core	
KeepAliveTimeout	Resource management	Core	
MaxClients	Resource management	Core	
MaxRequestsPerChild	Resource management	Core	

continues

TABLE 8.1. CONTINUED

Directive	Type	Implemented In	Base
MaxSpareServers	Resource management	Core	
MinSpareServers	Resource management	Core	
StartServers	Resource management	Core	
TimeOut	Resource management	Core	
<Directory>	Security/Access control	Core	
<Limit>	Security/Access control	Core	
<Location>	Security/Access control	Core	
AllowOverride	Security/Access control	Core	
AuthName	Security/Access control	Core	
AuthType	Security/Access control	Core	
Options	Security/Access control	Core	
require	Security/Access control	Core	
IdentityCheck	Security/Access control	Core	
Group	Security/Access control	Core	
User	Security/Access control	Core	
allow	Security/Access control	mod_access	Yes
deny	Security/Access control	mod_access	Yes
order	Security/Access control	mod_access	Yes
AuthGroupFile	Security/Access control	mod_auth	Yes
AuthUserFile	Security/Access control	mod_auth	Yes
ImapBase	Server-side image map	mod_imap	Yes
ImapDefault	Server-side image map	mod_imap	Yes
ImapMenu	Server-side image map	mod_imap	Yes
BindAddress	Server I/O configuration	Core	
Listen	Server I/O configuration	Core	
Port	Server I/O configuration	Core	
<VirtualHost>	Server I/O configuration	Core	
ServerAlias	Server I/O configuration	Core	
ServerName	Server I/O configuration	Core	
ServerType	Server I/O configuration	Core	
ServerPath	Server I/O configuration	Core	

TABLE 8.2. APACHE SPECIALIZED DIRECTIVES.

Directive	Type	Implemented In
CookieLog	Accounting	mod_cookies
AgentLog	Accounting	mod_log_agent
LogFormat	Accounting	mod_log_config
TransferLog	Accounting	mod_log_config
RefererIgnore	Accounting	mod_log_referer
RefererLog	Accounting	mod_log_referer
LoadFile	External module loading	mod_dld
LoadModule	External module loading	mod_dld
MetaDir	Meta header	mod_cern_meta
MetaSuffix	Meta header	mod_cern_meta
CacheDefaultExpire	Proxy server/Cache management	mod_proxy
CacheGcInterval	Proxy server/Cache management	mod_proxy
CacheLastModified	Proxy server/Cache management	mod_proxy
CacheMaxExpire	Proxy server/Cache management	mod_proxy
CacheRoot	Proxy server/Cache management	mod_proxy
CacheSize	Proxy server/Cache management	mod_proxy
NoCache	Proxy server/Cache management	mod_proxy
ProxyPass	Proxy server/Cache management	mod_proxy
ProxyRemote	Proxy server/Cache management	mod_proxy
ProxyRequests	Proxy server/Cache management	mod_proxy
Anonymous	Security/Access control	mod_auth_anon
Anonymous Authoritative	Security/Access control	mod_auth_anon
Anonymous LogEmail	Security/Access control	mod_auth_anon

continues

TABLE 8.2. CONTINUED

Directive	Type	Implemented In
Anonymous VerifyEmail	Security/Access control	mod_auth_anon
AuthDBGroupFile	Security/Access control	mod_auth_db
AuthDBUserFile	Security/Access control	mod_auth_db
AuthDBMGroupFile	Security/Access control	mod_auth_dbm
AuthDBMUserFile	Security/Access control	mod_auth_dbm
Auth_MSQL_Authorative	Security/Access control	mod_auth_msql
Auth_MSQL_EncryptedPasswords	Security/Access control	mod_auth_msql
Auth_MSQLdatabase	Security/Access control	mod_auth_msql
Auth_MSQLgrp_field	Security/Access control	mod_auth_msql
Auth_MSQLgrp_table	Security/Access control	mod_auth_msql
Auth_MSQLhost	Security/Access control	mod_auth_msql
Auth_MSQLnopasswd	Security/Access control	mod_auth_msql
Auth_MSQLpwd_field	Security/Access control	mod_auth_msql
Auth_MSQLpwd_table	Security/Access control	mod_auth_msql
Auth_MSQLuid_field	Security/Access control	mod_auth_msql
AuthDigestFile	Security/Access control	mod_digest

As you can see, Apache is well equipped right from a basic configuration, and the specialized directives add a myriad of features. These additional modules enhance existing functionality by providing additional ways to perform a function, such as user authentication, or add completely new server features. Some modules such as mod_proxy implement a totally different kind of server, a proxy server.

Directives can be subclassified as

- ◆ Accounting directives
- ◆ Additional configuration file directives
- ◆ Automatic indexing directives
- ◆ Error-handling directives
- ◆ MIME type, language, and handler directives
- ◆ Resource-location directives
- ◆ Resource-management directives
- ◆ Security and access-control directives

- ◆ Server I/O configuration directives
- ◆ Server-side image map directives
- ◆ Proxy server and cache-management directives

ACCOUNTING DIRECTIVES

These directives set the location of log files where Apache will record data about the server operation, such as server access information.

ADDITIONAL CONFIGURATION FILE DIRECTIVES

The server will look for additional configuration information in the files specified by these directives. The server has compiled in defaults settings for these directives so if a directive is not overridden, the server will attempt to read additional configuration information from the compiled-in defaults.

AUTOMATIC INDEXING DIRECTIVES

These directives control what gets returned when a request is for a directory: `http://localhost/directory/`. First, the server will try to return a user-generated index file in `directory` that matches the `DirectoryIndex` file specification. If a user-generated index is not found, the server will automatically create an index file. Typical automatic indexes look like directory listings, but they can be quite fancy and graphical. Listings can associate an icon and description based on the file type or name and incorporate headers and readme information.

ERROR-HANDLING DIRECTIVES

Apache can be configured to provide informational error messages. It provides a directive that lets you customize what gets returned when an error is generated from a request.

MIME, LANGUAGE-MANAGEMENT, OR HANDLER-MANAGEMENT DIRECTIVES

These directives allow you to map a file extension into a MIME type. Some of the MIME types are processed by a program prior to returning data to the server. Programs that perform this processing are called *handlers*. For example, CGI programs that live in a `cgi-bin` directory or have a `.cgi` extension are processed by the `mod_cgi` module. The server passes execution to a handler program that knows how to deal with the special file type or condition.

RESOURCE LOCATION DIRECTIVES

These directives help the server find files. They define places where you can put CGI programs, or where documents you publish on the Web live.

RESOURCE-MANAGEMENT DIRECTIVES

Resource-management directives control issues that affect the performance of the server. Default settings for many of these directives should not be changed unless there's a good reason for it, and you understand what you are doing. Apache manages many of its resources dynamically. Arbitrarily modifying these default settings can adversely affect the performance of the server.

SECURITY AND ACCESS-CONTROL DIRECTIVES

Directives of this kind affect the security of your site in one way or another. They set the UID and GUI the server runs as, control who has access to what resources, and implement access control and user-validation measures. The `<Directory>`, `<Limit>`, and `<Location>` sections allow you to group a series of settings on a directory or URL basis.

SERVER I/O CONFIGURATION DIRECTIVES

These directives control the IP and the port the server listens to for requests, as well as some other basic (and not-so-basic) things regarding the normal operation of the server.

SERVER-SIDE IMAGE MAP DIRECTIVES

Apache has a built-in module to handle server-side image maps. Traditionally, image maps have been implemented with CGI programs. Incorporating image map handling into the server core provides a significant enhancement in performance. This functionality is really a subcategory of the MIME, language management, or handler management directives, but its functionality is distinct enough to merit its own category.

PROXY SERVER AND CACHE-MANAGEMENT DIRECTIVES

Starting with Apache 1.1, Apache is able to function as a caching proxy server. This allows the server to make transactions on behalf of a browser and store the results in a cache. Future requests to the same URL by a different user in the network are satisfied from the cache, reducing the load of the network. These directives control the cache management: how long files will be cached, and how big the cache can grow.

SUMMARY

The next two chapters will explain with great detail all the directives available in Apache. When searching for a directive, you may want to reference the tables in this chapter because the next two chapters organize directives alphabetically and by module for ease of reference.

CHAPTER 9

Apache Server Core Directives

The main server module is called the *core*. It implements what the Apache online server documentation describes as a "barely functional HTTP server." The core implements the basic support for the HTTP protocol as well as the foundation framework that allows for Apache's modular design.

AccessConfig

Syntax: `AccessConfig` *filename*
Default: `AccessConfig conf/access.conf`
Extent: server configuration, virtual host
Status: core

The `AccessConfig` directive defines the location of the global access control file. A filename can be specified relative to the `ServerRoot` pathname or as a full pathname. Traditionally, this file contained `<Directory>` sections and other directives that affected access control and user authentication; today, however, you can put any server-configuration directives allowed in the server configuration context.

If not defined, the default is

```
AccessConfig conf/access.conf
```

The `AccessConfig` directive can also be specified inside a `<VirtualHost>` section. Only one `AccessConfig` directive is allowed in the `http.conf` file unless the additional directives are part of a `<VirtualHost>` section, and then only a single `AccessConfig` directive is allowed per `<VirtualHost>` section.

To disable reading configuration settings from `conf/access.conf`, set `/dev/null` as the filename parameter. The file specified by `AccessConfig` is read after the file specified by `ResourceConfig`.

AccessFileName

Syntax: `AccessFileName` *filename*
Default: `AccessFileName .htaccess`
Extent: server configuration, virtual host
Status: core

The `AccessFileName` directive allows you to change the default name Apache uses for per-directory access control files.

If not defined, the default is

```
AccessFileName .htaccess
```

Before returning a document to the client, Apache looks for additional per-directory access control files (ACF) in all directories in the path of the request.

The effects of any access control directive specified by an ACF can be disabled with an `AllowOverride None` directive specified in a `<Directory>` section on the global ACF (`conf/access.conf`).

AllowOverride

Syntax: `AllowOverride [All] | [None] | [AuthConfig] [FileInfo] [Indexes] [Limit]`
            `[Options]`
Default: `AllowOverride All`
Context: directory
Status: core

The `AllowOverride` directive specifies the extent to which a per-directory access control file can override defaults set in the global ACF `conf/access.conf`. If security is a concern, you will probably want to specify a setting of `None`.

This directive is specified inside a `<Directory>` section in the global ACF. The various options are as follows:

`All`	Allows all overrides
`AuthConfig`	Allows use of the directives used to control user authentication and access control: `AuthName`, `AuthType`, `AuthGroupFile`, `AuthUserFile`, `AuthDBMGroupFile`, `AuthDBMUserFile`, and `require`
	Apache 1.1 adds several additional AuthConfig directives: `AuthDBGroupFile`, `AuthDBUserFile`, `Auth_MSQL.pwd_table`, `Auth_MSQL_Authorative`, `Auth_MSQL_EncryptedPasswords`, `Auth_MSQL_nopasswd`, `Auth_MSQLdatabase`, `Auth_MSQLgrp_field`, `Auth_MSQLgrp_table`, `Auth_MSQLhost`, `Auth_MSQLpwd_field`, and `Auth_MSQLuid_field`
`FileInfo`	Allows you to use the directives that control document types: `AddEncoding`, `AddLanguage`, `AddType`, `DefaultType`, and `LanguagePriority`
`Indexes`	Allows you to use the directives that control directory indexing: `AddDescription`, `AddIcon`, `AddIconByEncoding`, `AddIconByType`, `DefaultIcon`, `DirectoryIndex`, `FancyIndexing`, `HeaderName`, `IndexIgnore`, `IndexOptions`, and `ReadmeName`
`Limit`	Allows you to use the directives that control host access: `allow`, `deny`, and `order`
`None`	Disables all override directives for the directory
`Options`	Allows you to use the directives that control specific directory features: `Options` and `XBitHack`

Apache 1.1

AuthName

Syntax: AuthName *label*
Default: none
Context: directory, .htaccess
Status: core

The AuthName directive allows you to label an access-controlled resource. *label* is displayed in the user authentication panel (login) that is displayed to the user when he is trying to access a controlled resource. If *label* is omitted, there is no default.

label can contain spaces:

AuthName This is a secured resource, please login first.

This directive requires the use of the AuthType and require directives, and requires that directives such as AuthUserFile and AuthGroupFile or any of their derivatives work properly.

AuthType

Syntax: AuthType [Basic] | [Digest]
Context: directory, .htaccess
Status: core

The AuthType directive controls the type of authentication used. Basic authentication provides no encryption to the authentication session. Password information is transmitted in code form but not encrypted, making it quite simple to decode.

Digest authentication uses RSA MD5 encryption, which makes the authentication process more secure because the authentication session is encrypted. The login and password entered by the user are also encoded so that they are only good for retrieving the requested URL. On requesting a different URL within the authentication realm, the browser will encode a new key (password) to retrieve those materials.

These directives require the use of the AuthName and require directives. In addition, if you are using Basic authentication, you need to use directives such as AuthUserFile and AuthGroupFile or any of their derivatives. When using Digest authentication, you'll need to use AuthDigestFile.

BindAddress

Syntax: BindAddress [*] | [*IP*] | [*fully qualified domain name*]
Default: BindAddress *

Context: server configuration
Status: core

The `httpd` server can listen for connections to the host's IP address or to multiple IP addresses if the server is multihomed. If given a `BindAddress`, the `httpd` server will listen only for connections to the IP address specified by this directive. `BindAddress` can be specified by IP, such as

```
BindAddress 204.12.123.123
```

or by the fully qualified name of the machine, such as

```
BindAddress www.foo.com
```

To have the server listen to all IP addresses accepted by the host, use

```
BindAddress *
```

This is also the default value if not specified.

DefaultType

Syntax: DefaultType `mime-type`
Default: DefaultType `text/html`
Context: server configuration, virtual host, directory, `.htaccess`
Override: `FileInfo`
Status: core

When a client requests a document, the server is responsible for setting the document type of the requested document in the HTTP header. If a client asks for a document type that the server does not recognize (either because the extension of the document is missing or because the extension is not registered as a valid MIME type), the server returns the `mime-type` defined by `DefaultType`.

If you have a directory that contains many Graphical Interchange Format (GIF) files that are not properly named with a `.gif` extension, an entry in an `.htaccess` such as

```
DefaultType image/gif
```

would ensure that the client browser would handle unknown files as GIFs. Some browsers are fairly smart and actually identify a type based on the encoding and format of the file.

DocumentRoot

Syntax: DocumentRoot `path`
Default: DocumentRoot `/usr/local/etc/httpd/htdocs`

Context: server configuration, virtual host
Status: core

The `DocumentRoot` directive specifies the server's document root. The server will append *path* to all requests prior to executing them, unless the paths are matched by an `Alias` directive. Do not terminate the path with a trailing slash (`/`):

```
DocumentRoot /usr/local/etc/httpd/htdocs
```

A request for `http://www.foo.com/index.html` will translate into `/usr/local/etc/htdocs/index.html`.

ErrorDocument

Syntax: `ErrorDocument error-code [pathname] | [URL] | [message string]`
Default: none
Context: server configuration, virtual host
Status: core

This is one of the great features of Apache. Instead of returning the standard error responses, Apache can be configured to return customized error messages or to redirect the request to a local or external URL that can handle the request.

You can specify that a file be retrieved by putting in the complete pathname to the file:

```
# Error code 404 - file not found
ErrorDocument 404 /error/filenotfound.html
```

Or you can specify a message on-the-fly:

```
ErrorDocument 404 "This file is not on this server. Go away.
ErrorDocument 500 "Your request failed, because: %s. Oh well...
```

If you provide the characters `%s` in *message string*, Apache inserts further information about the error if available.

You can also force the client to redirect to an external site by specifying a complete URL:

```
ErrorDocument 404 http://www.server.com/filex.html
```

Tip

Redirecting is especially useful for debugging CGI. If you code your CGI so that debugging and error output are stored in one file, you can have the server return the error file whenever your program fails. This saves you the step of manually testing for error responses.

With Apache 1.1, you can place `ErrorDocument` directives in per-directory access control files (`.htaccess`). This setting is toggled with the `FileInfo` option in `AllowOverrides`.

ErrorLog

Syntax:	`ErrorLog filename`
Default:	`ErrorLog logs/error_log`
Context:	server configuration, virtual host
Status:	core

This directive specifies the location of the error-log file. The *error log* is, not surprisingly, the file where the `httpd` server logs errors. An error can be any request that timed out, or any request that the server could not fulfill because of an access- or resource-availability error. As system administrator, you should check error logs often, especially after upgrading or adding a new CGI program. Many problems of which you may be unaware get logged here, and checking the error log may be the only way to see if someone is trying to attack your server.

If the filename specified in this directive is not an absolute path (a path starting with a /), the `filename` location is assumed to be relative to the path indicated by `ServerRoot`.

To turn off error logging, execute

```
ErrorLog /dev/null
```

Group

Syntax:	`Group GID`
Default:	`Group #-1`
Context:	server configuration
Status:	core

The `Group` directive sets the Group ID (GID) that the server will use to answer any requests. In order to use this directive, the standalone server needs to be started as root because only the superuser is able to change the real and effective GID of a process.

When started by root, the parent `httpd` process will have root GID (usually wheel). However, `httpd` requests are served by child processes that use the GID assigned by the `Group` directive. If started by a user other than root, the GID is inherited from the user that started the `httpd` process.

Warning

> If root doesn't start the httpd daemon, the Group directive will fail to change the GID of the child processes, leaving you with a potential security problem.
>
> The GID under which you run the server is a very important security-configuration setting. The server should execute under a GID that has very low UNIX privileges. Also, to avoid potential security problems, the server should not be able to execute any programs not intended for use over the Web.

You can supply the GID in number format by preceding it with a #, like this:

Group #-1

You can also specify a valid group name as an argument:

Group nogroup

On my system, nogroup has a GID of -2. On many systems, however, nogroup has a GID of -1, which is the default setting for Apache.

Tip

> When assigning a GID by number, you should examine the /etc/group file for the proper GID of the group under which you want the httpd daemon to run. On most systems, the GID you want is listed in the third field. The field delimiter for the group file is a colon (:).

Warning

> If the server is started by root, you should make sure that neither the User directive nor the Group directive is set to root. Otherwise, you'll be seriously compromising security.

IdentityCheck

Syntax: IdentityCheck [on] | [off]
Default: IdentityCheck off
Context: server configuration virtual host, directory, .htaccess
Status: core

The IdentityCheck directive determines whether the username of the remote user is logged to the transferlog. For this feature to work, the remote machine must be running an RFC931-compliant identity daemon. It should be obvious that this information should not be trusted outside of your network. The transferlog file is defined by the TransferLog directive.

This directive creates an additional server load because the server tries to determine the identity of each user making a request.

Only one IdentityCheck directive is allowed in your server-configuration file. If omitted, the default is

```
IdentityCheck off
```

Apache 1.1 enhances the IdentityCheck directive. It can now be used on a per-directory basis. The new version of IdentityCheck is RFC1413-compliant.

KeepAlive

> Syntax: KeepAlive *numrequests*
> Default: KeepAlive 5
> Context: server configuration
> Status: core

The KeepAlive directive enables multiple transactions to be sent by the server over a single TCP connection, otherwise known as a *persistent connection*. Persistent connections greatly enhance the performance of the transaction because the overhead of establishing a new connection for each request is reduced or eliminated. The *numrequests* limit is imposed to prevent a client from grabbing all the server resources.

The following criteria must be met in order for this feature to work:

◆ The client must support this feature. All leading browsers, including Netscape Navigator and Microsoft Internet Explorer, support this feature.

◆ The length of the resources being transmitted must be known beforehand. That means that most CGI scripts, Server Side Includes files, and directory listings won't be able to take advantage of this protocol.

KeepAliveTimeout

> Syntax: KeepAliveTimeout *seconds*
> Default: KeepAliveTimeout 15
> Context: server configuration
> Status: core

This directive sets the maximum amount of time, in seconds, that the server will wait for subsequent requests before closing the connection. The time-out period starts the moment a request is received by the server. (*See* KeepAlive.)

Listen

Syntax: Listen *IP_address*[:*port*]
Context: server configuration
Status: core

This directive is similar to the BindAddress directive. The Listen directive instructs Apache to listen to more than one IP address or port; by default it listens in for requests on all interfaces, but only on the port given by the Port directive (Port is by default set to 80, the standard HTTP port). New versions of Stronghold (see Chapter 14, "Secure Web Servers") will use this feature to implement both SSL and standard servers in a single process. (Currently, you need two servers running: one for standard requests and another for SSL requests.)

MaxClients

Syntax: MaxClients *number*
Default: MaxClients 150
Context: server configuration
Status: core

This directive specifies the maximum number of connections that the httpd server will handle. Connections beyond *number* get put on a wait state until the server is freed. *number* should be changed with care, because setting it too low will place new connections on a wait state, and setting it too high will rapidly exhaust server resources. The default setting is probably fine for the typical server. High-performance servers may benefit from setting *number* higher, as long as the hardware resources are able to cope with the additional load.

MaxRequestPerChild

Syntax: MaxRequestsPerChild number
Default: MaxRequestsPerChild 30
Context: server configuration
Status: core

This directive specifies how many requests an individual child httpd process will handle before getting terminated. MaxRequestPerChild was initially developed to autokill processes that had aged longer than a certain number of requests with the intention of limiting the number of memory leaks that the process could consume. This option is still valuable on many systems such as Solaris, where memory leaks in the libraries still exist.

MaxSpareServers

Syntax: `MaxSpareServers number`
Default: `MaxSpareServers 10`
Context: server configuration
Status: core

The `MaxSpareServers` directive sets the maximum number of idle child processes. *Idle processes* are `httpd` server processes not currently fulfilling HTTP requests.

Should the number of idle processes increase above what is specified by `number`, the parent process will terminate the excess processes.

Extremely busy sites can benefit from increasing the default setting of `10`, in case there's a drop in usage for a few seconds. If usage drops, idle processes will go up, which the server will then kill. When usage resumes, the system will be scrambling to find resources to fulfill the requests. Unless you have a very good reason for altering it, don't change the default setting.

(*See* `MinSpareServers` and `StartServers`.)

MinSpareServers

Syntax: `MinSpareServers number`
Default: `MinSpareServers 5`
Context: server configuration
Status: core

The `MinSpareServers` directive controls the minimum number of idle child server processes that are available at any one time. Idle processes are server processes not currently handling HTTP requests. If the idle-process count should decrease below the amount designated by `MinSpareServers`, the parent process will create new child processes. New processes are created at one-second intervals.

This setting should not be changed from the default value unless you have a very good reason for the change.

(*See* `MaxSpareServers` and `StartServers`.)

Options

Syntax:	Options [All] | [None] | [ExecCGI] [FollowSymLinks] [Includes] [IncludesNOEXEC] [Indexes] [MultiViews] [SymLinksIfOwnerMatch]
Context:	server configuration, virtual host, directory, .htaccess
Override:	Options
Status:	core

The Options directive controls which server options are available in a particular directory:

All	Enables all options except MultiViews.
ExecCGI	Execution of CGI programs is allowed.
FollowSymLinks	Following of symbolic links is allowed.
Includes	Use of Server Side Includes (SSI) is allowed.
IncludesNOEXEC	SSI is allowed with the following restrictions: the #exec and #include commands are disabled.
Indexes	Enables the return of directory listings in cases where a client requests a directory for which there is no DirectoryIndex file (index.html).
MultiViews	Enables content negotiation based on document language. (*See* LanguagePriority.)
SymLinksIfOwnerMatch	Following of symbolic links is allowed if the target file or directory is owned by the same user as the link. This setting offers better security than the FollowSymLinks option.

When multiple <Directory> sections that contain Options directives match a request, the Options in the best match are applied. As the following script shows, Option settings are not cumulative:

```
<Directory /usr/local/etc/htdocs/miscfiles>
Options Indexes
</Directory>

<Directory /usr/local/etc/htdocs>
Options MultiViews
</Directory>
```

For requests in the /usr/local/etc/htdocs/miscfiles tree, the only option enforced is MultiViews.

PidFile

Syntax: PidFile *filename*
Default: PidFile logs/httpd.pid
Context: server configuration
Status: core

This directive specifies the location of a file that contains the process ID of the main httpd process on a standalone configuration. The contents of this file are very useful if you need to stop or start the server. A convenient way to restart the server is to run the following:

```
# kill -HUP 'cat pathToPidFile'
```

If you are running your server using inetd instead of standalone, the contents of this file are bogus.

A *filename* is set to be relative to ServerRoot if it's not an absolute path specification (begins with a slash).

Port

Syntax: Port *number*
Default: Port 80
Context: server configuration
Status: core

The Port directive sets the port where a standalone server listens for requests. The standard port for the HTTP protocol is 80.

The *number* is a TCP port, and as such it has certain restrictions. Ports numbered below 1024 are reserved for the system. Nonroot users cannot bind to reserved ports. If you want to use the default HTTP port (80), httpd must be started by root.

require

Syntax: require *option name name*...
Context: directory, .htaccess
Override: AuthConfig
Status: core

This directive sets the selection criteria used to determine which authenticated users may access a restricted resource.

require also selects which authenticated users can access a directory. The allowed options are as follows:

user	Only users named in the list can access the resource:
	`require user1 user2 ...`
group	Only users that are members of the groups specified in the list can access the resource:
	`require group1 group2 ...`
valid-user	Any valid user can access the resource:
	`require valid-user`

If the `require` directive appears inside a `<Limit>` section, it restricts access to the named HTTP methods; otherwise, access is restricted for all methods:

```
AuthType Basic
AuthName somedomain
AuthUserFile /web/users
AuthGroupFile /web/groups
Limit <GET POST>
require group admin
</Limit>
```

To work properly, this directive requires the use of the `AuthName` and `AuthType` directives, and directives such as `AuthUserFile` and `AuthGroupFile` or any of their derivatives.

ResourceConfig

Syntax: `ResourceConfig filename`
Default: `ResourceConfig conf/srm.conf`
Context: server configuration, virtual host
Status: core

The `ResourceConfig` directive defines the location of a secondary configuration file. `filename` can be specified relative to the `ServerRoot` or as a full pathname. Traditionally, this file contained most configuration directives with the exception of the server configuration and `<Directory>` sections. This file can contain any directive with a context of server configuration.

If not defined, the default is

`ResourceConfig conf/srm.conf`

The `ResourceConfig` directive can also be specified inside a `<VirtualHost>` section. Only one `ResourceConfig` directive is allowed in the server configuration file unless the additional directives are part of a `<VirtualHost>` section, and then only a single `ResourceConfig` directive is allowed per `<VirtualHost>` section.

To ignore the default setting for the `ResourceConfig`, define `/dev/null` as the `filename` parameter. The file specified by `ResourceConfig` is read after the server configuration file.

ServerAdmin

Syntax: ServerAdmin *emailaddress*
Default: none
Context: server configuration, virtual host
Status: core

The ServerAdmin directive sets the e-mail address of the webmaster that will be returned to a client in case of an error.

If you are hosting virtual domains, this directive gives you an opportunity to effectively add information; in some cases, it may be valuable to set up more elaborate aliases (such as ServerAdmin webmaster-smartsoft@accesslink.com) so that you know which server caused the problem. When you receive e-mail addressed to webmaster-smartsoft@accesslink.com, you know immediately that the sender was at SmartSoft's Web site.

For a more sophisticated method of handling e-mail aliases, please see Appendix B, "Managing Virtual Domains with sendmail V8."

ServerAlias

Syntax: ServerAlias *host1 host2...*
Context: server configuration, virtual host
Status: core

The ServerAlias directive sets additional names the server will respond to for requests. This directive is intended for use with non-IP intensive virtual hosts. For more information, please refer to Chapter 4, "Virtual Hosts," for the section titled, "Non-IP Virtual Hosts."

ServerName

Syntax: ServerName *hostname*
Default: ServerName (Deduced from IP; may not be what you want)
Context: server configuration, virtual host
Status: core

This directive sets the name returned by your server. *hostname* should be a fully qualified domain name; it should be a valid DNS name.

ServerPath

Syntax: `ServerPath path`
Context: server configuration, virtual host
Status: core

The `ServerPath` directive is used as a workaround for browsers that don't support non-IP virtual hosts. Non-IP virtual hosts are supported by a browser by including an extra HTTP header, `HTTP_HOST`, that contains the name of the server requested. Because older browsers don't include this information, requests for a non-IP virtual host will end up in your real server's home page, where the virtual host shares its IP address.

`ServerPath` provides you with a mechanism to redirect requests to the proper place by using additional path information. Please refer to Chapter 4 for additional information on how to use and implement non-IP intensive virtual hosts.

ServerRoot

Syntax: `ServerRoot path`
Default: `ServerRoot /usr/local/etc/httpd`
Context: server configuration
Status: core

The `ServerRoot` directive specifies where the server directory tree lives. `path` is appended to all relative path definitions. Many of the server resources are expected to be found in this tree.

The location of this tree can also be specified by using the `-d` option to the `httpd` executable.

ServerType

Syntax: `ServerType [standalone] | [inetd]`
Default: `ServerType standalone`
Context: server configuration
Status: core

The `ServerType` directive sets how the HTTP server is run by UNIX. The server can be run from `inetd` (which listens for socket connections to the Internet ports and then passes the request to the appropriate software) or in standalone mode (where the server itself listens and handles requests to its port).

`inetd` runs a new copy of the server per request. After the request is processed, the server exits. Standalone servers fork several server processes that handle several connections before being disposed of by the main server process. This reuse of existing processes provides for increased efficiency.

inetd-run servers are considered by many administrators to be more secure and less prone to attack than standalone servers.

To have inetd start the Web server, you need to edit /etc/inetd.conf and /etc/services. For more information, please refer to Chapter 2, "Installing and Configuring the Apache Server."

StartServers

Syntax: StartServers *number*
Default: StartServers 5
Context: server configuration
Status: core

The StartServers directive specifies the number of child server processes that are forked at server startup. The actual number of server processes at any one time is dynamically controlled by the server load and the MaxSpareServers, MinSpareServers, and MaxClients directives.

There's no need to change this parameter from its default setting.

TimeOut

Syntax: TimeOut *seconds*
Default: TimeOut 1200
Context: server configuration
Status: core

This directive sets the maximum amount of time, in seconds, that the server will wait for a request to be completed. If it is set too low, the server will terminate the connection before a large transfer is completed. Note that unless you are downloading huge pages, the default is set to 20 minutes. If you notice problems with many stuck-open connections, reducing this number will increase performance of your site.

User

Syntax: User *uid*
Default: User #-1
Context: server configuration
Status: core

The User directive sets the User ID (UID) the server will use to answer requests. In order for the server to change UIDs, the server needs to be started as root because only the superuser is able to change the real and effective UID of a process.

When started as root, the owner of the parent server will remain as root. However, requests are handled by child processes that will run under the UID assigned by this directive.

Warning

If root doesn't start the server, the User directive will have no effect, leaving the server running under the UID of the user that started the server process.

To set the UID of httpd to nobody, use

```
User nobody
```

or

```
User #-1
```

where # is followed by the UID. You may find nobody to have a UID of -1 on many systems. The default for the User directive is -1. On my system, nobody has an UID of -2.

When specifying UIDs by number, verify the /etc/passwd file for the proper UID of the user under which you want the httpd daemon run. On most systems, the format of the passwd file is

```
login:encryptedPassword:UID:GID:realname and other info:home directory:shell
➥program
```

As seen in the preceding /etc/passwd sample entry, UID is the third field. All fields on the passwd file are separated by colons (:).

Warning

If the server is started by root, ensure that the UID is not set to root.

<Directory>

Syntax: <Directory dir>...</Directory>
Context: server configuration, virtual host
Status: core

A <Directory> section is a group of control directives enclosed by a <Directory *dir*> and </Directory> tag pair. Control directives inside a <Directory> section apply only to the document tree specified by *dir*. The effects of a <Directory> section apply to any subdirectories in the tree.

You can use any directive in a <Directory> section that is allowed in a directory context. *dir* is specified either as a full path or as a wildcard string. Wildcard strings can use ? and * characters, with results similar to a shell; ? matches any single character, whereas * matches any sequence of characters.

Because a directory may match various <Directory> sections, the directives are applied in the order of the shortest match first:

```
<Directory /usr/local/etc/htdocs>
AllowOverride None
</Directory>

<Directory /usr/local/etc/htdocs/public/*>
AllowOverride AuthConfig Limit
</Directory>
```

For a request to /usr/local/etc/htdocs/public/project/foo.html, the preceding directives get applied in the following order:

- ◆ Apply AllowOverride None, which disables per-directory access control files.
- ◆ Apply AllowOverride and AuthConfig Limit directives to /usr/local/etc/htdocs/public/project, which enables the use of the user authentication and host access control directives.
- ◆ Apply any AuthConfig and Limit directives found on the /usr/local/etc/htdocs/public/project/.htaccess file.

<Directory> sections are usually found in the global ACF conf/access.conf, or inside a <VirtualHost> section. However, you can put them in any configuration file, with the exception of per-directory ACFs (.htaccess). <Directory> sections cannot nest or appear inside a <Limit> section.

You can specify *dir*, using a regular expression. For information on creating regular expressions, please see Table 6.1.

Apache 1.2

<File>

Apache 1.2

Syntax: <File *filepath*>...</File>
Context: server configuration, virtual host
Status: core

The <File> section provides for access control on a per-file basis. It functions exactly like the <Directory> section; however, instead of using a directory specification, it specifies a file in a directory.

You can specify *filepath*, using a regular expression. For information on creating regular expressions, please see Table 6.1.

<Limit>

Syntax: `<Limit method method...>...</Limit>`
Context: any
Status: core

A `<Limit>` section is a group of access control directives, enclosed by a `<Limit>` and `</Limit>` tag pair, which applies only to listed HTTP access methods such as GET, POST, HEAD, and so on.

Typically, you use a `require` directive nested by limit tags to specify authentication requirements before the request is served:

```
...
  <Limit Get>
    require valid-user
    order deny,allow
    deny from all
    allow from domain
  </Limit>
...
```

Any HTTP request that uses the GET or POST method will be processed by the server only if the user authenticates (other authentication directives are not shown) and is a member of the group *groupname*.

<Location>

Apache
1.1

Syntax: `<Location URI>...</Location>`
Context: server configuration, virtual host
Status: core

The `<Location>` section provides for access control on a per-file or per-URL basis. It functions exactly like the `<Directory>` section, but instead of using a filepath specification, it uses a URI for its target.

URI is a URL without the `http://servername` portion. *URI* is specified either as a full path or a wildcard string. Wildcard strings can use ? and * characters, with results similar to a shell. ? matches any single character; * matches any sequence of characters.

<Location> sections are evaluated in the order listed after <Directory> sections and .htaccess files have been evaluated.

You can specify *URI*, using a regular expression. For information on creating regular expressions, please see Table 6.1.

(*See* <Directory>.)

<VirtualHost>

Syntax:	<VirtualHost *host*[:*port*]>...</VirtualHost>
Context:	server configuration, virtual host
Status:	core

The <VirtualHost> and </VirtualHost> section tags are used to group directives that apply only to a particular *host*. Any directive that is allowed in a virtual host context can be used. The server receives a request directed toward a virtual host; the configuration directives enclosed in the <VirtualHost> and </VirtualHost> section tags override directives found elsewhere.

You can specify the host to which the section applies by specifying the IP address of the virtual host, or by specifying a fully qualified domain name (fqdn). In addition, you can specify the TCP port for the configuration. This way virtual hosts can return different content solely on the basis of the port used to access it.

```
<VirtualHost www.company.com>
ServerAdmin webmaster@company.com
DocumentRoot /www/docs/company
ServerName www.company.com
ErrorLog logs/company.error_log
TransferLog logs/company.transfer_log
</VirtualHost>
```

New in Apache 1.1 is support for non-IP intensive virtual hosts. The declaration of the directive is identical to the original IP-intensive version. The difference in implementation is that the IP of the virtual host must be the same as that of the main host. This new functionality works in conjunction with an HTTP/1.1 protocol, which requires the browser to send the name used for addressing the server.

For IP-intensive virtual hosts, each host IP identified by the VirtualHost directive must be unique; in order for the host to work, the computer must be configured to accept multiple IP addresses. This configuration, unlike the new non-IP virtual hosts, works regardless of the browser.

For more information on how to build virtual hosts, refer to Chapter 4.

CHAPTER 10

Apache Modules

Apache's modular structure has simplified the way that functionality is added to the server. Its generalized Application Programmer's Interface (API) greatly simplifies the process of adding new or enhancing existing functionality. Modules are usually developed in a single source code file named after the module. Many of these modules are so useful that they are included on a default server configuration. Modules that are included in this fashion are part of the *Base* release. Other modules are not included in the Base release either because they are in the initial stages of development or have not received a methodical testing to ensure that they are of production quality. The lack of inclusion should not be a deterrent to their use, however. The DBM Authentication module is not part of the Base release, yet it is heavily used in many sites.

The following sections describe all the modules shipped with Apache and the directives they provide. For a list of modules provided by third parties, take a look at Chapter 7, "Third-Party Modules."

THE mod_access MODULE

Source: mod_access.c
Base: Yes
Type: Security/Access Control

The mod_access module is built into Apache by default. It provides host-based (or domain-level) access control security options.

Host-based access control grants or denies access on the basis of the Internet Protocol (IP) address of the machine generating a request. Machines matching an allow or deny description are allowed or denied access as appropriate. Flexible descriptions can be formed by the combination of both lists and the use of the order directive.

mod_access DIRECTIVES

The mod_access module provides three directives for building the allow and deny criteria:

◆ allow from

◆ deny from

◆ order

These directives are typically specified in the <Directory>, <Limit>, or <Location> sections or inside an .htaccess file. <Location> sections are available only in Apache 1.1 or better.

allow from

Syntax:	allow from *host host*...
Override:	AllowOverride Limit
Context:	directory, .htaccess

`allow from` specifies hosts that are allowed to access the protected resource. You can specify more than one host or network by separating the additional host specifications with a space. *host* can be specified in any of the following formats:

all	This option allows all hosts to access the resource.
FQDN	You can specify a host using its fully qualified domain name. A fully qualified domain name must include a hostname, subnets (if any), and a domain name, such as www.xyc.com.
PDN	You can specify a group of hosts by using a partial domain name, which allows you to group several hosts in a particular domain. An entry such as xyc.com would match any host in the xyc.com domain.
	A more selective grouping could be specified by using a network subnet. If available, group.xyc.com would match any host in the *group* subnet in the xyc.com domain.
IP	You can also specify machines by their IP address. This option may provide tighter security than name-based specifications; however, names are easier for humans to maintain.
PIP	You can also specify partial IP patterns, 1–3 bytes of the IP address, to define groups of hosts. Hosts matching the IP description are included in the group. If 204.95.160.0 is a class C address, specifying 204.95.160 as the *PIP* would match any host from that network. If the network is subdivided into subnets, you can specify the subnet number to create a more restrictive grouping within a network.

Here's an example of the `allow from` directive:

```
allow from .cs.uwm.edu bar.com 204
```

All hosts from the specified domain are allowed access. Note that the comparison is based on the entire name. The entry for bar.com would not match foobar.com.

deny from

Syntax:	deny from *host host*...
Override:	AllowOverride Limit
Context:	directory, .htaccess

deny from specifies hosts that are to be denied access to the resource. You can specify more than one host or network by separating additional host specifications with a space. *host* can be specified in any of the following formats:

all   This option allows all hosts to access the resource.

FQDN   You can specify a host using its fully qualified domain name. A fully qualified domain name must include a hostname, subnets if any, and a domain name, such as www.xyc.com.

PDN   You can specify a group of hosts by using a partial domain name. This allows you to group several hosts in a particular domain. An entry like xyc.com would match any host in the xyc.com domain.

     A more selective grouping could be specified by using a network subnet, if available. group.xyc.com would match any host in the group subnet in the xyc.com domain.

IP   You can also specify machines by their IP address. This option may provide tighter security than name-based specifications; however, names are easier for people to maintain.

PIP   You can also specify partial IP patterns, 1–3 bytes of the IP address, to define groups of hosts. Hosts matching the IP description are included in the group. If 204.95.160.0 is a class C address, specifying 204.95.160 as the *PIP* would match any host from that network. If the network is subdivided into subnets, you can specify the subnet number to create a more restrictive grouping within a network.

Here's an example of the deny directive:

```
deny from .cs.uwm.edu bar.com 204
```

All hosts from the specified domain are denied access. Note that comparison is based on the entire name. The entry for bar.com would not match foobar.com.

order

Syntax: order [deny,allow] | [allow,deny] | [mutual-failure]
Default: order deny,allow
Override: AllowOverride Limit
Context: directory, .htaccess

The order directive specifies the order in which the allow from and deny from directives are evaluated within a <Limit>, <Location>, or <Directory> section. Possible options are

deny,allow   Evaluates the deny from directive first and then grants exceptions based on the allow from directive.

allow,deny	Evaluates the `allow from` directive first and then grants exceptions based on the `deny from` directive.
mutual-failure	Evaluates so that only hosts that appear in the `allow from` directive and do not appear on the `deny from` directive are granted access.

Here's an example of the `order` directive:

```
order deny,allow deny from all allow from aol.com
```

In this example, requests from America Online users would be allowed. All other hosts are denied access.

THE mod_actions MODULE

Source:	mod_actions.c
Base:	Yes
Type:	Handler management

The `mod_actions` module is compiled into Apache by default. It adds the functionality of setting user-defined handlers that execute CGI programs based on the MIME type of a request or the HTTP access method used for the request.

mod_actions DIRECTIVES

`mod_actions` adds two directives:

◆ Action

◆ Script

Action

Syntax:	Action *mime-type cgi*
Context:	Server configuration, virtual host, directory, .htaccess
Override:	AllowOverride FileInfo

The `Action` directive adds a handler that runs *cgi* when *mime-type* is requested. The `Action` directive sets the URL and filepath of the request using the standard CGI environment variables PATH_INFO and PATH_TRANSLATED, respectively. The CGI program can then perform whatever action it needs to handle the request.

Script

Syntax:	Script *http-method cgi*
Context:	Server configuration, virtual host, directory, .htaccess
Override:	AllowOverride FileInfo

The Script directive adds a handler that runs *cgi* when a file is requested using the *http-method*. Supported HTTP methods are GET, POST, PUT, or DELETE. The Action directive sets the URL and filepath of the request using the standard CGI environment variables PATH_INFO and PATH_TRANSLATED, respectively. The CGI program can then perform whatever action it needs to handle the request.

Script handlers only define default actions. If some resource is capable of handling the request internally, that resource will be called. GET requests are passed to a handler only when they have query arguments—that is, the query string contains a question mark (?). This directive provides you with a way of implementing the PUT or DELETE methods in Apache.

THE mod_alias MODULE

Source:	mod_alias.c
Base:	Yes
Type:	Resource location

This module is compiled into Apache by default. It provides directives that allow you to map document and CGI program directories that are in the local filesystem, but outside of DocumentRoot, into the server's document tree. This allows clients to reference these resources as if they were inside your DocumentRoot. The alias module also provides facilities for *uniform resource locator* (URL) redirection, which allows you to redirect the request to a different URL, perhaps in a different network.

mod_alias DIRECTIVES

The directives provided are

- ◆ Alias
- ◆ Redirect
- ◆ ScriptAlias

Typically, these directives are specified in the conf/srm.conf configuration file.

Alias

Syntax:	Alias *url-path directory-filename*
Context:	Server configuration, virtual host

The Alias directive allows you to reference directories in your local filesystem that are outside of your DocumentRoot as if they were located inside it. The Alias directive maps the request to *url-path* into the directory tree specified by *directory-filename*:

```
Alias /icons/ /usr/local/etc/httpd/icons/
```

A request for `http://www.mydomain.com/icons/text.gif` will be mapped by the server to the file `/usr/local/etc/httpd/icons/text.gif`.

Redirect

Syntax: `Redirect url differenturl`
Context: Server configuration, virtual host, and `.htaccess` (in Apache 1.1 or better)

The `Redirect` directive allows you to map one URL into another. It can redirect a local request to a different Web server or an external URL. When the server receives a request for `url`, it returns `differenturl` to the client along with a `redirect` HTTP response code. Better clients automatically re-request the materials from the new URL:

```
Redirect /projectA http://www.domain.dom/projectA
```

> ## Tip
>
> Use `Redirect` if you change the name of an often-accessed file. That way the error logs won't fill up with requests for the file from users who have bookmarked the URL, and visitors will have less trouble finding the new location.

Apache 1.1 enables you to use the `Redirect` directive from an `.htaccess` file if the `FileInfo` option is enabled by the `AllowOverride` directive.

> ## Tip
>
> `Redirect` directives take precedence over `Alias` and `ScriptAlias` directives.

ScriptAlias

Syntax: `ScriptAlias path URL`
Context: Server configuration, virtual host

The `ScriptAlias` directive is similar to the `Alias` directive. The `ScriptAlias` directive enables you to reference a CGI directory that is stored outside of your `DocumentRoot`, but in your local filesystem, as if it were inside your `DocumentRoot`. The difference is that the server marks the directory as containing CGI programs and permits their execution:

```
ScriptAlias /cgi-bin/ /usr/local/etc/httpd/cgi-bin/
```

In this example, a request for `http://www.mydomain.com/cgi-bin/foo.cgi` will make the server run the program `/usr/local/etc/httpd/cgi-bin/foo.cgi`.

THE `mod_asis` MODULE

Source: `mod_asis.c`
Base: Yes
Type: Handler management
Context: Server configuration

The `mod_asis` module is built into Apache by default. This module enables you to specify *type* as a filetype that is to be sent without HTTP headers except for date and server headers. This module is internally used to send server redirects and other responses without the need for a CGI or a no parse header (nph) program.

Because the server does not return headers, you'll need to add them yourself. You'll need to return a status header (a three-digit HTTP response code) followed by a message. Apache can return any of the following HTTP response codes:

`200`: OK
`302`: Found
`304`: Not Modified
`400`: Bad Request
`401`: Unauthorized
`403`: Forbidden
`404`: Not Found
`500`: Server Error
`503`: Out Of Resources (Service Unavailable)
`501`: Not Implemented
`502`: Bad Gateway

Here's an example of how to enable `mod_asis`:

Syntax: `AddType httpd/send-as-is type`

The following example defines the filetype `.asis` as a send-as-is filetype:

```
AddType httpd/send-as-is asis
```

Here's an example that implements redirection using the send-as-is feature. A *redirection* makes the client look for the requested resource in a different location:

```
Status: 302 Site closed, go to a different server.
Location: http://www.mirror.com/index.html
Content-type: text/html

<HTML>
<HEAD>
<TITLE>This portion of our site is currently under remodeling,
```

```
➥please visit a mirror site.</TITLE>
</HEAD>
<BODY>
<H1>This portion of our site is currently under remodeling,
you can find a mirror of this site
<A HREF="http://www.mirror.com/index.html">here</A></H1>
</BODY>
</HTML>
```

THE mod_auth MODULE

Source:	mod_auth.c
Base:	Yes
Type:	Security/Access Control

The mod_auth module is built into Apache by default. This module provides user authentication by using text files.

User authentication allows you to control access to a document tree on an individual user basis, using user and password lists to provide the necessary authentication verification. When a user requests a restricted resource, the server requires him to log in by specifying a username and a password. If the user supplies the proper information, access is granted to roam across the site without additional login requests. Also, you should be aware that this process is repeated for every document you request (your password and User ID (UID) are sent with every page request, thus your password is sent not once, but many times).

mod_auth DIRECTIVES

mod_auth provides you with the following directives:

◆ AuthGroupFile

◆ AuthUserFile

These directives enable you to specify the location of your password and group files. Password files that are usable by this module are maintained with the htpasswd program included in the server's support directory. For more information on how to use the htpasswd program, see Chapter 15, "Access Control and User Authentication."

AuthGroupFile

Syntax:	AuthGroupFile *filename*
Context:	Directory, location, .htaccess

The AuthGroup directive allows you to specify the location of the group file. *filename* should be specified with an *absolute path*—a path beginning with a slash (/)—that is outside of your Web server's DocumentRoot. For security reasons, it is important that `filename` resides outside of the directory it is trying to protect:

```
AuthGroupFile /usr/local/etc/httpd/passwords/mygroupfile
```

The group file is an ASCII file with the following format:

```
groupname: username1 username2 username3...
groupname2: username1, username3
...
```

groupname is the name of your group followed by a colon (:) and then followed by a list of valid usernames that appear in the user file. Use your favorite editor to maintain this file.

Tip

Use `AuthGroupFile` to authenticate a large group of users, such as a workgroup. This way, you can easily manage multiple levels of access with just one directive.

AuthUserFile

Syntax: `AuthUserFile filename`
Context: directory, location, .htaccess

The `AuthUserFile` directive enables you to specify the location of the user/password file. `filename` should be an absolute path outside of `DocumentRoot`. For security reasons, it is important that `filename` is outside of the directory it is trying to protect:

```
AuthUserFile /usr/local/etc/httpd/passwords/.htpasswd
```

The password file is maintained with the `htpasswd` program. The file format of the password file is similar to the `/etc/passwd` file: it contains a username followed by a colon (:) and a `crypt()`-encrypted password. For information on how to maintain password files, please see Chapter 15.

Tip

Use the DBM authentication module when the number of users is greater than 100. It will speed up things greatly.

The mod_auth_anon Module

Source: mod_auth_anon.c
Base: No
Type: Security/Access Control

The mod_auth_anon module enables you to have an FTP-style *anonymous* login. This will allow visitors that are not registered with your site to gain access if they provide the appropriate information, typically their e-mail addresses.

mod_auth_anon Directives

◆ Anonymous

◆ Anonymous_LogEmail

◆ Anonymous_VerifyEmail

◆ Anonymous_NoUserID

◆ Anonymous_Authorative

Anonymous

Syntax: Anonymous *login login2...*

This directive allows you to specify various acceptable anonymous names. Typical logins include: Anonymous, guest, or visitor. These logins are not case sensitive. Because there's no default, be sure to include Anonymous.

Anonymous_MustGiveEmail

Syntax: Anonymous_MustGiveEmail [on] | [off]
Default: Anonymous_MustGiveEmail off

The Anonymous_MustGiveEmail directive specifies that the password field must not be left empty. Typically users will be required to enter their e-mail address.

Anonymous_LogEmail

Syntax: Anonymous_LogEmail [on] | [off]
Default: Anonymous_LogEmail on

The Anonymous_LogEmail directive specifies that the password field should be logged in the server's access log.

Anonymous_VerifyEmail

Syntax: Anonymous_VerifyEmail [on] | [off]

Default: Anonymous_VerifyEmail off

The Anonymous_VerifyEmail directive specifies that the password field must contain a valid e-mail address. That is, it will be checked syntactically for resemblance to an e-mail address. It must contain at least one @ and a period (.).

Anonymous_NoUserID

Syntax: Anonymous_NoUserID [on] | [off]

Default: Anonymous_NoUserID off

The Anonymous_NoUserID directive permits anonymous logins without entering any values in the user or password fields.

Anonymous_Authorative

Syntax: Anonymous_Authorative [on] | [off]

Default: Anonymous_Authorative off

The Anonymous_Authorative directive returns a denies access message if the UID entered doesn't match one of the anonymous logins specified by Anonymous. The ultimate order of the modules, by which login information is processed, depends on the linking order of the various authentication modules. Modules that appear later in the src/Configuration file can override those that come earlier in the file.

mod_auth_anon CONFIGURATION EXAMPLE

This excerpt, from an access.conf, permits anonymous logins so long as a proper e-mail address is entered in the password field.

```
Anonymous anonymous guest
Anonymous_MustGiveEmail on
Anonymous_VerifyEmail on
Anonymous_NoUserId off
AuthName This resource contains restricted materials.For guest entry use
➥'anonymous' in the login prompt, and enter you email address as the password.
AuthType basic
<Limit get,post>
order deny,allow
allow from all
require valid-user
</Limit>
```

The mod_auth_db Module

Source:	mod_auth_db.c
Base:	No
Type:	Security/Access Control

The mod_auth_dbm module is not built into Apache by default. In order to use any of its directives, you need to reconfigure Apache to include this module and recompile the server. This module provides user authentication using Berkeley DB (BSD) files. It is very similar to mod_auth_dbm and should be used as an alternative to mod_auth_dbm on those systems that support DB and not DBM.

mod_auth_db Directives

mod_auth_db provides you with the AuthDBGroupFile and AuthDBUserFile directives that you can use to specify the location of your password and group files. Password and group files are maintained with the dbmmanage program included in your server's support directory. For more information on how to use the dbmmanage program, see Chapter 15.

AuthDBGroupFile

Syntax:	AuthDBroupFile *dbfilename*
Context:	Directory, location, .htaccess
Override:	AllowOverride AuthConfig

The AuthDBGroupFile directive enables you to specify the location of the user/password/group file. *dbfilename* should be an absolute path outside of DocumentRoot. For security reasons, it is important that *filename* is outside of the directory it is trying to protect:

```
AuthDBGroupFile /usr/local/etc/httpd/passwords/passworddb
```

DB password files store username, password, and group information. Typically you'll reference *dbfilename* on both the AuthDBGroupFile and AuthDBUserFile directives. User information in the group file is maintained using the dbmmanage program included in the server's support directory. You'll need a copy of Perl to run dbmmanage. For information on how to use the dbmmanage program, see Chapter 15.

AuthDBUserFile

Syntax:	AuthDBUserFile *dbfilename*
Context:	Directory, location, .htaccess
Override:	AllowOverride AuthConfig

10

APACHE MODULES

The AuthDBUserFile directive enables you to specify the location of the user/password/ group file. *dbfilename* should be an absolute path outside of DocumentRoot. For security reasons, it is important that *filename* is outside of the directory it is trying to protect:

```
AuthDBUserFile /usr/local/etc/httpd/passwords/passworddb
```

DBM password files store username, password, and group information. Typically you'll reference *dbfilename* on both AuthDBGroupFile and AuthDBUserFile directives. User information in the group file is maintained using the dbmmanage program included in the server's support directory. You'll need a copy of Perl to run dbmmanage. For information on how to use the dbmmanage program, see Chapter 15.

THE mod_auth_dbm MODULE

Source:	mod_auth_dbm.c
Base:	No
Type:	Security/Access Control

The mod_auth_dbm module is not built into Apache by default. In order to use any of its directives, you need to reconfigure Apache to include this module and recompile the server.

This module provides user authentication using DBM files. *User authentication* enables you to control access to a document tree on an individual user basis, using user and password lists to provide the necessary authentication verification. When a user requests a restricted resource, the server requires him to log in by specifying a username and a password. If the user supplies the proper information, access is granted to roam across the site without additional login requests.

DBM files provide a significant performance improvement over the authentication routines provided by mod_auth. If your password file has more than 100 entries, you should use the mod_auth_dbm module and its directives instead.

mod_auth_dbm DIRECTIVES

mod_auth_dbm provides you with the AuthDBMGroupFile and AuthDBMUserFile directives that you can use to specify the location of your password and group files. Password and group files are maintained with the dbmmanage program included in your server's support directory. For more information on how to use the dbmmanage program, see Chapter 15.

AuthDBMGroupFile

Syntax:	AuthDBMGroupFile *dbmfilename*
Context:	Directory, location, .htaccess
Override:	AllowOverride AuthConfig

The AuthDBMGroupFile directive allows you to specify the location of the user/password/ group file. *dbmfilename* should be an absolute path outside of DocumentRoot. For security reasons, it is important that *filename* is outside of the directory it is trying to protect:

```
AuthDBMGroupFile /usr/local/etc/httpd/passwords/passworddbm
```

DBM password files store username, password, and group information. Typically you'll reference *dbmfilename* on both the AuthDBMGroupFile and AuthDBMUserFile directives. User information in the group file is maintained using the dbmmanage program included in the server's support directory. You'll need a copy of Perl to run dbmmanage. For information on how to use the dbmmanage program, see Chapter 15.

AuthDBMUserFile

Syntax: AuthDBMUserFile *dbmfilename*
Context: Directory, location, .htaccess
Override: AllowOverride AuthConfig

The AuthDBMUserFile directive enables you to specify the location of the user/password/ group file. *dbmfilename* should be an absolute path outside of DocumentRoot. For security reasons, it is important that *filename* is outside of the directory it is trying to protect:

```
AuthDBMUserFile /usr/local/etc/httpd/passwords/passworddbm
```

DBM password files store username, password, and group information. Typically you'll reference *dbmfilename* on both AuthDBMGroupFile and AuthDBMUserFile directives. User information in the group file is maintained using the dbmmanage program included in the server's support directory. You'll need a copy of Perl to run dbmmanage. For information on how to use the dbmmanage program, please see Chapter 15.

THE mod_auth_msql MODULE

Source: mod_auth_msql.c
Base: No
Type: Security/Access Control

The mod_auth_msql module is not built into Apache by default. In order to use any of its directives, you need to reconfigure Apache to include this module and recompile the server.

mod_auth_msql enables you to provide access control using the mini SQL (mSQL) relational database engine, which can be obtained from ftp://ftp.bond.edu.au/pub/ Minerva/msql. mSQL is not free for commercial or private use. Price for the engine is U.S. $170 for commercial organizations and $50 for private use. For more information, please visit the mSQL FTP site. Online documentation for the server can be found at http://Huges.com.au and http://cscsun1.larc.nasa.gov/~beowulf/msql/msql.html.

mod_auth_msql Directives

mod_auth_msql provides you with several directives that allow you to map the various authentication pieces of information to tables and fields within an mSQL database.

- ◆ Auth_MSQLhost
- ◆ Auth_MSQLdatabase
- ◆ Auth_MSQLpwd_table
- ◆ Auth_MSQLgrp_table
- ◆ Auth_MSQLuid_field
- ◆ Auth_MSQLpwd_field
- ◆ Auth_MSQLgrp_field
- ◆ Auth_MSQL_nopasswd
- ◆ Auth_MSQL_Authorative
- ◆ Auth_MSQL_EncryptedPasswords

Auth_MSQLhost

Syntax: Auth_MSQLhost [*FQDN*] | [*IPaddress*] | [localhost]

The Auth_MSQLhost directive sets the address of the host that is running the mSQL server. The host's address can be specified as the fully qualified domain name (*FQDN*), by IP address (*IPaddress*), or by specifying localhost, when the Web server host is also the database server. The localhost option forces the use of the faster interface /dev/msql instead of a slower socket connection.

Auth_MSQLdatabase

Syntax: Auth_MSQLdatabase *databasename*

The Auth_MSQLdatabase directive sets the name of the mSQL database that contains the various authentication tables.

Auth_MSQLpwd_table

Syntax: Auth_MSQLpwd_table *passwd-table*

The Auth_MSQLpwd_table directive sets the name of the table that contains the fields defined by Auth_MSQLuid_field and Auth_MSQLpwd_field.

Auth_MSQLgrp_table

Syntax: Auth_MSQLgrp_table *group-table*

The `Auth_MSQLgrp_table` directive sets the name of the table that contains the fields defined by `Auth_MSQLgrp_field` and `Auth_MSQLuid_field`.

Auth_MSQLuid_field

Syntax: `Auth_MSQLuid_field` *uid-name*

The `Auth_MSQLuid_field` directive sets the name of the field that holds the username in the `Auth_MSQLpwd_table` and `Auth_MSQLgrp_table`.

Auth_MSQLpwd_field

Syntax: `Auth_MSQLpwd_field` *pwd-name*

The `Auth_MSQLpwd_field` directive sets the name of the field that holds the password in the `Auth_MSQLpwd_table`.

Auth_MSQLgrp_field

Syntax: `Auth_MSQLgrp_field` *pwd-name*

The `Auth_MSQLgrp_field` directive sets the name of the field that holds the group membership in the `Auth_MSQLgrp_table`.

Auth_MSQL_nopasswd

Syntax: `Auth_MSQL_nopasswd [on] | [off]`
Default: `Auth_MSQL_nopasswd off`

The `Auth_MSQL_nopasswd` directive sets whether the password authentication is skipped when `Auth_MSQLpwd_field` is empty (NULL). The default is set to disable this feature.

Auth_MSQL_Authorative

Syntax: `Auth_MSQL_Authorative [on] | [off]`
Default: `Auth_MSQL_Authorative on`

The `Auth_MSQL_Authorative` directive, when set to `off`, makes it possible to fall through to other authentication modules. If authentication fails, the server will pass control to other authentication modules such as `mod_auth_anon`. If authentication fails when set to `on`, the user is denied access. The default is set to `on`.

Auth_MSQL_EncryptedPasswords

Syntax: `Auth_MSQL_EncryptedPasswords [on] | [off]`
Default: `Auth_MSQL_EncryptedPasswords on`

10

APACHE MODULES

When set to on, the password field is assumed to be encrypted with the crypt function. Incoming passwords are encrypted before they are compared. When set to off, the passwords are assumed to be in plain text format and are compared directly.

THE mSQL PASSWORD DATABASE

Please refer to your mSQL database manual for information on how to install and run the database server. This information assumes that you have some understanding of mSQL and SQL syntax. You can create the mSQL password database by typing the following commands:

```
msqladmin create passwords
msql passwords
-> create table user (
-> uid char(32) primary key,
-> pwd char(32) not null,
-> grp char(32) null
-> ) \g
```

To enter records on the password database, type the following:

```
-> insert into user
-> values ('User Name', 'asdflkjwer2223', 'registered')
-> \g
```

Note that for this example the password field is not encrypted.

To reference the previous table for authentication, enter the following on your conf/access.conf in a <Directory> section or in a per-directory (.htaccess) file:

```
Auth_MSQLhost localhost
Auth_MSQLdatabase passwords
Auth_MSQLpwd_table user
Auth_MSQLuid_field uid
Auth_MSQLpwd_field pwd
Auth_MSQLgrp_field grp
Auth_MSQL_Authorative on
Auth_MSQL_EncryptedPassords off
Auth_Name secured area
Auth_Type basic
<Limit GET POST>
  order deny,allow
  allow for all
  require valid-user
</Limit>
```

For more information, please see Chapter 15.

THE mod_cern_meta MODULE

Apache 1.1

Source:	mod_auth_msql.c
Base:	No
Type:	Meta header

The `mod_cern_meta` module is not built into Apache by default. In order to use any of its directives, you need to reconfigure Apache to include this module and recompile the server.

`mod_cern_meta` provides you with the ability to include additional HTTP headers into the requested document. This module was originally developed to provide additional compatibility to users of the CERN Web server who were migrating to Apache.

`mod_cern_meta` DIRECTIVES

`mod_cern_meta` provides two additional directives:

◆ MetaDir

◆ MetaSuffix

MetaDir

Syntax:	MetaDir *directoryName*
Default:	MetaDir .web
Context:	Server configuration

The `MetaDir` directive will set the name of the directory the server will search for additional Meta information files. To have the server search the same directory as the request, set *directoryName* to a period (.).

MetaSuffix

Syntax:	MetaSuffix *fileExtension*
Default:	MetaSuffix .meta
Context:	Server configuration

The `MetaSuffix` directive will set the file extension of the file containing the additional header information.

MetaSuffix EXAMPLE

This is a sample configuration:

```
MetaDir .
MetaSuffix .meta
```

For a request like `http://somehost/index.html`, the server will look for a file called `index.html.meta` in the same directory as the request. The contents of `index.html.meta` will be included as additional MIME-header information.

THE mod_cgi MODULE

Source:	mod_cgi.c
Base:	Yes
Type:	Handler management

The mod_cgi module is built into Apache by default.

This module enables the execution of CGI programs. Files ending in .cgi or inside a directory defined by ScriptAlias will be processed as a CGI program and run by the server. Output of CGI programs is returned to the client.

When a CGI program is run by the server, the server will add the following variables to the environment:

DOCUMENT_ROOT	This variable will be set to the value of DocumentRoot.
REMOTE_HOST	This variable is added only if the server was not compiled with MINIMAIL_DNS or if the new HostnameLookups runtime directive was enabled in Apache 1.1.
REMOTE_IDENT	This is set to the name of the user if IdentityCheck is enabled and the user is running an RFC931- or RFC1413-compliant identity daemon.
REMOTE_USER	This variable is set to the name of the user if the CGI program is subject to user authentication.

The mod_env module adds additional environment variables. For more information, see the mod_env module later in this chapter.

THE mod_cookies MODULE

Source:	mod_cookies.c
Base:	No
Type:	Administration

The mod_cookies module is not built into Apache by default. In order to use any of its directives, you need to reconfigure Apache to include this module and recompile the server.

Cookies help a Web server to maintain persistent state by handing the browser a unique identifier. Maintaining state has been one of the tedious programming issues for anyone developing a Web site. The Web is, by design, stateless: The server receives a request, answers the request, and disconnects. It doesn't care what you were doing. It doesn't know where you've been or where you are going.

Initial efforts at maintaining state were put on the server side. Although that works great, it adds to the load and to the complexity of programming Web-based applications. Netscape developed an extension to the HTTP protocol that implements cookies, which off-load the persistence issue off to the client—a better thing to do. Although cookies are great, they are not part of the HTTP specification; however, browsers from Netscape, Microsoft, and others support them. For a better description of Netscape cookies, please refer to Chapter 7.

The mod_cookies module handles the process of generating and handing out cookies. When a request is received, the server looks for a Cookie: header. If one isn't found, the server assumes that the user has not visited the site in the current session, so it sends a Set_Cookie: header out with the request. Additional requests from the client will maintain the Cookie header sent by the server. Apache generates cookies with every request, no matter which browser was used to make the request. Unique cookie tags are generated by making a new tag by using the process ID of the server, the time, and the host IP of the client.

Although cookies are generated automatically by the server, it is up to your software to do something useful with them. You can use cookies to implement shopping carts or create meaningful logs that track users. The possibilities are almost endless.

THE mod_cookies DIRECTIVE

The mod_cookies module provides a directive you can use to log cookies: CookieLog.

Versions of Apache prior to 1.1 support only hands-out cookies to Netscape browsers. Apache 1.1 generates cookies for every request no matter what the browser.

THE CookieLog DIRECTIVE

> Syntax: CookieLog *filename*
> Context: Server configuration, virtual host

The CookieLog directive sets the *filename* where the server will log cookies and the request that accompanied them. *filename* is relative of the path specified by the ServerRoot directive.

Tip

This directive does not log the initial request—the request that generated the cookie.

THE mod_digest MODULE

Source: mod_digest.c
Base: No
Type: Security/Access Control

The mod_digest module is not built into Apache by default. This module adds a new form of authentication called *Digest* authentication, which uses RSA MD5 encryption technology. Digest authentication encrypts and encodes the password the visitor provided so that it is useful only for retrieving the requested URL. The browser generates encodes a new password for each request. This ensures that if the password sent was compromised, it would only be useful for retrieving one URL only. Use of Digest authentication requires the use of a supporting Web browser. Be aware that unless you are using a secure server to access your documents, the information that you transmit is still sent in world-readable form.

Digest authentication requires a compatible browser to operate the work.

THE mod_digest DIRECTIVE

The mod_digest module adds one directive:

◆ AuthDigestFile

AuthDigestFile

Syntax: AuthDigestFile *filepath*
Context: Directory, .htaccess

The AuthDigestFile directive specifies the file that contains the user and password information. This file is created with the htdigest utility found in the support subdirectory of the Apache server distribution. htdigest is similar in functionality to the htpassword utility.

htdigest

Usage: htdigest [-c] *filepath realm username*

The -c flag creates a new password file in *filepath*.

realm is the server realm being protected (set with the AuthName directive).

username is the name of the user to add an entry.

The htdigest program will prompt you for the password to add.

CONFIGURING THE SERVER TO USE DIGEST AUTHENTICATION

Using Digest authentication is very simple. Set authentication the way you normally would (see Chapter 15). Use `AuthType Digest` and `AuthDigestFile` instead of `AuthType Basic` and `AuthUserFile`. All else should remain the same.

THE `mod_dir` MODULE

Source:	`mod_dir.c`
Base:	Yes
Type:	Automatic indexing

The `mod_dir` module is built into Apache by default. This module provides directives that control the handling of requests ending in a directory name.

The `mod_dir` module controls the resource and formatting returned by the server when the request is for a directory. Directory indexes can be generated by a file written by a user, typically called `index.html`, or on-the-fly by the server (an automatic directory listing).

The `DirectoryIndex` directive sets the default name for the user-generated index file. The server looks for this file on any request for a directory.

The additional directives control the formatting of server-generated indexes, such as the embellishment of a listing by adding icons and descriptions to filenames. The filename-mapping conventions are very flexible. You can use wildcard expressions to make any file matching a pattern or content type display a particular description and icon next to its name.

`mod_dir` DIRECTIVES

`mod_dir` provides a number of directives that help you associate icons, descriptions, header and footer files, and the selective inclusion of files and other information on a listing, as well as the name of user-generated index files:

- `AddDescription`
- `AddIcon`
- `AddIconByEncoding`
- `AddIconByType`
- `DefaultIcon`
- `DirectoryIndex`
- `FancyIndexing`

10

APACHE MODULES

- ◆ HeaderName
- ◆ IndexIgnore
- ◆ IndexOptions
- ◆ HeaderName
- ◆ ReadmeName

AddDescription

Syntax: AddDescription *description file [file]...*
Context: Server configuration, virtual host, directory, .htaccess
Override: AllowOverrides Indexes

AddDescription maps a description to a filename or a filetype. *description* is displayed next to the filename on server-generated indexes when the FancyIndexing directive is set to on. *description* is a text string enclosed by double quotes ("). *file* can be described by a

file extension:	.gif—This would match files with a .gif extension.
partial filename:	Readme—This would match any file called Readme anywhere in the server.
full filename:	/usr/local/etc/httpd/htdocs/myfile.doc
wildcard expression:	ASG??MAR.doc—The ? character matches a single character. The * character matches any sequence of characters. This would provide a match for ASG01MAR.doc, ASG02MAR.doc, and so on.

Here's an example of the AddDescription directive:

```
AddDescription "This is a Graphics Interchage Format" *.gif
AddDescription "Read This file before you do anything else" readnow
AddDescription "This is a picture of my boat" boat.gif
```

AddIcon

Syntax: AddIcon [*iconfile*] | [(*description,iconfile*)] *file file* ...
Context: Server configuration, virtual host, directory, .htaccess
Override: AllowOverrides Indexes

This directive sets the icon displayed next to a file listing on server-generated indexes when the FancyIndexing directive is set to on. *iconfile* can be a relative URL to the icon file or can follow the format (*description,iconfile*) where *description* is the text provided to nongraphical browsers.

The *description* string is enclosed by double quotes ("). *file* can be specified by a

file extension:	`.gif`—This would match files with a `.gif` extension.
partial filename:	`Readme`—This would match any file called `Readme` anywhere in the server.
full filename:	`/usr/local/etc/httpd/htdocs/myfile.doc`
wildcard expression:	`ASG??MAR.doc`—The `?` character matches a single character. The `*` character matches any sequence of characters. This would provide a match for `ASG01MAR.doc`, `ASG02MAR.doc`, and so on.

file can be either

◆ `^^DIRECTORY^^` for directories

◆ `^^BLANKICON^^` for blank lines (to format the list correctly)

◆ A file extension, wildcard expression, partial filename, or complete filename

Here's an example of the `AddIcon` directive:

```
AddIcon(image,/icons/image.gif) .gif .jpg .xbm
AddIcon /icons/dir.gif ^^DIRECTORY^^
AddIcon /icons/text.gif *.txt
```

Use of the `AddIconByType` directive is preferred over `AddIcon`.

AddIconByEncoding

Syntax:	`AddIconByEncoding` [*iconfile*] | [(*description,iconfile*)] *mime-encoding mime-encoding ...*
Context:	Server configuration, virtual host, directory, `.htaccess`
Override:	Indexes

When the `FancyIndexing` directive is set to on, `AddIconByEncoding` sets the icon displayed next to the file with *mime-encoding* on a server-generated index. *iconfile* can be a relative URL to the file containing the icon or of the format (*description,iconfile*) where *description* is the text provided to nongraphical browsers.

mime-encoding is a wildcard expression matching the content encoding of the file. An example includes the following:

```
AddIconByEncoding (CMP,/icons/compressed.gif) x-compress x-gzip
```

AddIconByType

Syntax:	`AddIconByType` [*iconfile*] | [(*description, iconfile*)] *mime-type mime-type ...*
Context:	Server configuration, virtual host, directory, `.htaccess`
Override:	Indexes

This directive sets the icon displayed next to a file of type *mime-type* on server-generated indexes when the `FancyIndexing` directive is set to `on`. *iconfile* can be a relative URL to the file containing the icon or of the format (*description,iconfile*) where *description* is the text provided to nongraphical browsers.

mime-type is a wildcard expression matching the required MIME types. The following is an example of this:

```
AddIconByType (IMG,/icons/image.gif) image/*
```

DefaultIcon

    Syntax: `DefaultIcon iconfile`
    Context: Server configuration, virtual host, directory, `.htaccess`
    Override: Indexes

When the `FancyIndexing` directive is set to `on`, this directive sets the icon displayed next to a file that has not been given an icon with any of the other directives on server-generated indexes. *iconfile* can be a relative URL to the file containing the icon or of the format (*description,iconfile*) where *description* is the text provided to nongraphical browsers.

Here's an example of the `DefaultIcon` directive:

```
DefaultIcon /icon/unknown.gif
```

DirectoryIndex

    Syntax: `DirectoryIndex url url ...`
    Default: `DirectoryIndex index.html`
    Context: Server configuration, virtual host, directory, `.htaccess`
    Override: Indexes

The `DirectoryIndex` directive identifies which resources to look for when a request ends in a directory name. `DirectoryIndex` provides a list of files to return if such a request is made.

Here's an example of the `DirectoryIndex` directive:

```
DirectoryIndex index.html readme.txt
```

If a request is made to a directory, the server would first try to return `index.html`. If that file does not exist, it tries to return a file called `readme.txt`. If that file doesn't exist, it returns a server-generated index.

URLs don't need to be relative to the directory. In the following example, the output from a program that tells you your fortune would be returned if the first two files didn't exist:

```
DirectoryIndex index.html readme.txt /cgi-bin/fortune.cgi
```

FancyIndexing

> Syntax: `FancyIndexing [on] | [off]`
> Context: Server configuration, virtual host, directory, `.htaccess`
> Override: `AllowOverrides Indexes`

The `FancyIndexing` directive sets the `FancyIndexing` option for a directory. It can be set to `on` to enable the display of icons and other adornments or to `off` to provide more generic listings.

The `IndexOptions` directive described in the following section should be used instead of `FancyIndexing`, because it gives better control over the format of server-generated indexes. This directive is provided for National Center for Supercomputing Applications (NCSA) `httpd` server compatibility.

HeaderName

> Syntax: `HeaderName` *filename*
> Context: Server configuration, virtual host, directory, `.htaccess`
> Override: `AllowOverrides Indexes`

The `HeaderName` directive specifies the name of the file to include at the top of a server-generated listing. *filename* is the name of the file to include, and it is taken to be relative to the directory being indexed. The server first tries to include *filename*`.html` as an HTML document. Otherwise, it includes *filename* as an ASCII document:

```
HeaderName README
```

When generating a server index for `/usr/local/htdocs`, the server will include the file `/usr/local/htdocs/README.html` if such a file is found. Otherwise, it will try to include `/usr/local/htdocs/README` if it exists.

This is a great way of posting information about a series of documents. (*See also* `ReadmeName`.)

IndexIgnore

> Syntax: `IndexIgnore` *file file* ...
> Context: Server configuration, virtual host, directory, `.htaccess`
> Override: Indexes

The `IndexIgnore` directive specifies the files to omit on server-generated indexes.

file can be specified by a

file extension:	.gif—This would match files with a .gif extension.
partial filename:	Readme—This would match any file called Readme anywhere in the server.
full filename:	/usr/local/etc/httpd/htdocs/myfile.doc
wildcard expression:	ASG??MAR.doc—The ? character matches a single character. The * character matches any sequence of characters. This expression would provide a match for ASG01MAR.doc, ASG02MAR.doc, and so on.

Here's an example of the IndexIgnore directive:

```
IndexIgnore README core *~
```

By default, IndexIgnore ignores *dotfiles*—files that are normally hidden from directory listings. Dotfiles start with a period (.), such as .cshrc, .mailrc, and so on.

IndexOptions

Syntax: IndexOptions *option option* ...
Default: No options enabled
Context: Server configuration, virtual host, directory, .htaccess
Override: Indexes

The IndexOptions directive controls the features available on server-generated indexes. *option* can be

FancyIndexing	This enables fancy indexing of directories.
IconsAreLinks	This makes the icons part of the anchor for the filename. For fancy indexing, clicking on the icon would have the same effect as clicking on the filename (it would retrieve the file).
ScanHTMLTitles	This enables reading the title from HTML documents for fancy indexing. If the file does not have a description associated with an AddDescription directive, the server will scan the document for the value of the <TITLE> tag. Needless to say, this is CPU and disk intensive.
SuppressLastModified	This will suppress display of the last modification date in fancy indexing listings.
SuppressSize	This will suppress the file size in fancy indexing listings.

SuppressDescription	This will suppress the file description in fancy indexing listings.

The default doesn't enable any options. When multiple `IndexOptions` apply to a directory, only the most specific one is used; the options are not cumulative.

Here's an example of the `IndexOptions` directive:

```
<Directory /usr/local/etc/httpd/htdocs/
IndexOptions FancyIndexing
</Directory>
<Directory /usr/local/etc/httpd/htdocs/projectA>
IndexOptions ScanHTMLTitles
</Directory>
```

In this example, `ScanHTMLTitles` is the only option used in requests for `/usr/local/etc/httpd/htdocs/projectA`.

ReadmeName

Syntax:	ReadmeName *filename*
Context:	Server configuration, virtual host, directory, `.htaccess`
Override:	AllowOverrides Indexes

The `ReadmeName` directive specifies the name of the file to include at the bottom of a server-generated listing. *filename* is the name of the file to include, and it is taken to be relative to the directory being indexed. The server first tries to include *filename*`.html` as an HTML document. Otherwise, it includes *filename* as an ASCII document, as in this example:

```
ReadmeName README
```

When generating an index for `/usr/local/htdocs`, the server will include the file `/usr/local/htdocs/README.html` if such a file is found. Otherwise, the server will try to include `/usr/local/htdocs/README` if it exists.

This is a great way to post information about a series of documents. (See also `HeaderName`.)

THE mod_env MODULE

Source:	mod_env.c
Base:	Yes
Type:	CGI

This module extends the environment variables passed to CGI and SSI scripts. It permits CGI and SSI scripts to inherit all environment variables from the shell that invoked the `httpd` process. It was originally developed to provide additional compatibility to users migrating from the CERN Web server.

mod_env DIRECTIVES

mod_env provides two additional directives:

- ◆ PassEnv
- ◆ SetEnv

PassEnv

Syntax: PassEnv *environmentVariable*
Context: Server configuration, virtual host

The PassEnv directive enables you to define an environment variable, from the server's own environment, that will be passed to CGI and SSI scripts. For example:

PassEnv PATH

SetEnv

Syntax: SetEnv *environmentVariable value*
Context: Server configuration, virtual host

The SetEnv directive enables you define an environment variable that will be passed to CGI and SSI scripts. For example:

SetEnv SERVER_TOOL_PATH /usr/lib/tools

THE mod_dld MODULE

Source: mod_dld.c
Base: No
Type: External Module Loading

The mod_dld module is not built into Apache by default. In order to use any of its directives, you need to reconfigure Apache to include this module and recompile the server.

mod_dld is a proof of concept module—that is, it is experimental code. It allows for the loading of modules at server-configuration time instead of statically linking them in at compile time. This option may be useful to someone developing modules to reduce the compile and linking process. Its use requires GNU's dynamic linking library, DLD. As with any other dynamic linking, the httpd binary and the modules you are dynamically loading should not have their symbols stripped (see strip in your UNIX manual).

mod_dld Directives

The mod_dld module provides two directives:

◆ LoadFile

◆ LoadModule

LoadFile is for loading support libraries. LoadModule loads modules and properly inserts the module in the server's module list.

LoadFile

> Syntax: LoadFile *filename filename ...*
> Context: Server configuration

The LoadFile directive links at runtime the named object code files or libraries listed in *filename* at server configuration. The LoadFile directive is used to link additional code that may be required by a module. *filename* is relative to ServerRoot. Here's an example of the LoadFile directive:

```
LoadFile /lib/libc.a
```

LoadModule

> Syntax: LoadModule *module filename*
> Context: Server configuration

The LoadModule directive links in the object file or library filename and adds the module structure named *module* to the list of active modules. *module* is the name of the external variable of type module in the file. The following is an example of this:

```
LoadModule cookies_module modules/mod_cookies.o
```

The mod_imap Module

> Source: mod_imap.c
> Base: Yes
> Type: Server-side image map

The mod_imap module is built into Apache by default. It replaces the image map CGI program for server-side processing of image map (.map) files.

mod_imap Directives

New with Apache 1.1 is an enhanced image map module. The new enhanced dmodule provides three directives:

◆ ImapMenu

◆ ImapDefault

◆ ImapBase

ImapMenu

Syntax: ImapMenu [none] | [formatted] | [semiformatted] | [unformatted]
Context: Server configuration, virtual host, directory, .htaccess
Override: Indexes

The ImapMenu directive controls the behavior taken when an image map is called without valid coordinates, such as when a nongraphical browser accesses it. Here are the valid options:

none   If set to none, no menu is generated and the default action is performed. The default action can be set by the ImapDefault directive or by a default entry in the image map itself.

formatted   Generates the simplest menu: A header, a rule (HR), and the link are printed (one per line).

semiformatted   This menu also includes any comments in the image map file. Comments are lines that begin with a pound character (#). They can include HTML tags. Blank lines in the map are turned into HTML BR tags. This menu does not print a header or a rule like the formatted menu.

unformatted   This is the most flexible menu format. Comments are lines that begin with a pound character (#). They can include HTML tags. Blank lines are ignored. All content sent to the client must be specifically included in the image map file. Headers and breaks should be included as comments in the image map file.

ImapDefault

Syntax: ImapDefault [error] | [nocontent] | [map] | [referer] | [url]
Default: ImapDefault nocontent
Context: Server configuration, virtual host, directory, .htaccess
Override: Indexes

The ImapDefault directive sets the default for image map files. This default can be overridden by a default directive inside the image map file.

error	Returns a 500 Server Error.
nocontent	This option returns a 204 No Content HTTP status code, which keeps the client focused on the original page.
map	Sets the default action to the URL of the image map itself. This option will generate a menu, unless ImapMenu is set to none.
referer	Sets the default action to the URL of the referring document. If no referer header is available, the default URL is set to the server's DocumentRoot.
url	A URL.

ImapBase

Syntax: ImapBase [map] | [referer] | [URL]
Default: ImapDefault DocumentRoot-URL
Context: Server configuration, virtual host, directory, .htaccess
Override: Indexes

The ImapBase directive sets the base URL used in the image map files. This directive will be overridden by the value of the base directive in the image map file. If omitted, the default is set to the server's DocumentRoot.

USING SERVER-SIDE IMAGE MAPS

Map files define regions within a graphic that behave as a link when clicked on by the user. Regions are defined as simple shapes: circles, rectangles, or polygons.

Documents tagged as being MIME-type application/x-httpd-imap are processed by this module, which offers better performance and more flexibility than the original CGI program used for this purpose. This functionality is compiled into the server, so no external CGI server transaction is generated. To get this module to process .map files, you'll need to associate a MIME-type format to a file extension using the AddType directive in an entry such as

```
AddType application/x-httpd-imap map
```

An entry like this already exists in the Apache configuration templates provided, so you don't need to alter this unless you want to use a different filename.

The image map module adds some new features that were not possible with previously distributed image map programs:

◆ URL can reference documents relative to the Referer: information (relative of the current document).

◆ Default <BASE> assignment through a new map field base_uri, which appears in imagemap files.

◆ Eliminates the need for the `imagemap.conf` file, a configuration file that associates `.map` files to the images. You can now just reference the relevant map file in your HTML document.

◆ Supports point references.

`base_uri` options appear in an image map and include:

map	Provides the default and old behavior of map relative reference
Referer	Uses the `Referer:` header information to reference a URL relative to the current document
http://URL	Has the effect of setting `<BASE>` to that URL, which makes all references relative to that `<BASE>`

A MAP FILE EXAMPLE

Here's an example of an `imagemap` file:

```
default http://lincoln/
base_uri referer
rect .. 0,0 77,27
poly http://www.inetnebr.com/ 78,0 194,27
circle http://www.inetnebr.com/lincoln/feedback/ 195,0 305,27
rect search_index 306,0 419,27
point http://www.zyzzyva.com/ 420,0 549,27
```

REFERENCING THE MAP FILE

Map files are referenced right from the HTML page:

```
<A HREF="http:/maps/imagmap1.map">
<IMG ISMAP SRC="http:/images/imagemap1.gif">
</A>
```

THE `mod_include` MODULE

Source:	mod_include.c
Base:	Yes
Type:	Handler management

The `mod_include` module is built into Apache by default. It provides support for server-parsed HTML (SPML) documents.

SPML documents are processed by the server before they are sent to the client. Those with MIME-type `text/x-server-parsed-html` or `text/x-server-parsed-html3` are parsed. The resulting HTML document is sent to the client.

SPML COMMAND FORMAT

The document is parsed as an HTML document with commands embedded as Standard Generalized Markup Language (SGML) comments. The commands can

- ◆ Execute programs
- ◆ Obtain file size and modification information
- ◆ Include text from other documents or from a program
- ◆ Configure the format used to display results from the various commands

Commands follow this syntax:

```
<!--#command option=value option=value ....-->
```

SMPL COMMANDS

The available commands are

- ◆ config
- ◆ echo
- ◆ exec
- ◆ cmd
- ◆ fsize
- ◆ flastmod
- ◆ include

A plug-in replacement module called Extended Server Side Includes (XSSI) extends the server-side includes syntax (which adds conditional inclusion with if-then-else constructs), adds the capability to set and use variables, and provides regular expression support. This package is available at `http://pageplus.com/~hsf/xssi/`.

For complete documentation on how to use Server Side Includes and its commands, see Chapter 6.

THE mod_include DIRECTIVE

mod_include adds one directive:

- ◆ XBitHack

XBitHack

Syntax: XBitHack [off] | [on] | [full]
Default: XBitHack off

Context: Server configuration, virtual host, directory, .htaccess
Override: Options

The XBitHack directive controls processing of ordinary HTML documents. The following options are available:

off   No special treatment of HTML files marked as executable.

on   Any .html file that has the user-execute bit set will be parsed by the server.

full   The same as for on, but also test the group-execute bit. If it is set, then the server will set the last-modified date of the returned file to be the last-modified time of the file. If the group-execute bit is not set, no last-modified date is sent. Setting this bit allows clients and proxies to cache the result of the request because it is possible to determine the date of the document's last modification.

THE mod_info MODULE

Apache
1.1

Source: mod_info.c
Base: No
Type: Server information

The mod_info module is not built into Apache by default. In order to use its functionality, you need to reconfigure Apache to include it and then rebuild the server. mod_info displays all your server configuration settings. The report includes modules and all runtime configuration settings in a nicely formatted HTML file. It's way cool!

Once you rebuild your server, you'll need to add the following directives to your conf/access.conf configuration file:

```
<Location /configuration>
SetHandler server-info
</Location>
```

If you want to keep your server configuration private—an important thing because this report will list all your settings—add a Limit section specifying some access restrictions (see Chapter 15 for more information). Restart the server and point your Web browser to http://yourhost/configuration. The server will return its very detailed configuration report.

THE mod_log_agent MODULE

Source: mod_log_agent.c
Base: No
Type: Logging

The mod_log_agent module is not built into Apache by default. In order to use any of its directives, you need to reconfigure Apache to include this module and then recompile the server. This module is provided for compatibility with NCSA 1.4.

This module enables logging of the client user agents—the browsers used for accessing your site. This feature is not very reliable. Because many sites provide different pages to different browsers, there is a trend with some browsers to fake their identity to obtain the more elaborate versions of the site. The faked agent is usually Mozilla, the Netscape Navigator browser.

THE mod_log_agent DIRECTIVE

mod_log_agent adds one directive:

♦ AgentLog

AgentLog

> Syntax: AgentLog [*filename*] | [¦*program*]
> Default: AgentLog logs/agent_log
> Context: Server configuration, virtual host

The AgentLog directive specifies the file where the server logs the UserAgent header on incoming requests. The options are either *filename* or ¦*program*.

♦ *filename* is the name of a file relative of ServerRoot.

♦ ¦*program* is the pipe symbol (¦) followed by path to a program capable of receiving the log information on standard input (stdin).

As with any program started by the server, the program is run with the UID and GID of the user that started the httpd daemon. If the user starting the program is root, be sure that the user directive demotes the server privileges to those of an unprivileged user such as nobody. Also, make sure the program is secure.

THE mod_log_common MODULE

> Source: mod_log_common.c
> Base: Yes
> Type: Logging

The mod_cgi module is built into Apache by default.

This module logs requests made to the server using the Common Logfile Format. For more information, please see Chapter 13, "Web Accounting."

LOGFILE FORMAT DESCRIPTION

The Common Logfile Format logs each request in a separate line. A line is composed of several fields separated by spaces:

```
host ident authuser date request status bytes
```

Null fields (fields that have no values) contain a dash (-).

The following options are available:

host	The host field contains the fully qualified domain name or, if the name was not available, the IP of the machine that made the request.
Ident	If IdentityCheck is enabled and the client machine is running an identity daemon, this field contains the name of the user that made the request.
Authuser	If the request requires authentication, this field contains the login of the user who made the request.
date	This field contains the date and time of the request. The date format used is day/month/year:hour:minute:second timezone.
request	The request line from the client enclosed in double quotes (").
status	The three-digit HTTP status code returned to the client.
bytes	The size of the transfer in bytes returned to the client, not counting header information.

mod_log_common DIRECTIVES

The mod_log_common module provides the following directive to set the file where the log information is stored:

◆ TransferLog

TransferLog

Syntax: TransferLog [filename] | [¦program]
Default: TransferLog logs/transfer_log
Context: Server configuration, virtual host

The TransferLog directive specifies the file where the server logs request information on incoming requests. The options are filename or ¦program.

◆ filename is the name of a file relative of ServerRoot.

◆ ¦program is the pipe symbol (¦) followed by a path to a program capable of receiving the log information on standard input (stdin).

As with any program started by the server, the program is run with the UID and GID of the user that started the `httpd` daemon. If the user starting the program is `root`, be sure that the user directive demotes the server privileges to those of an unprivileged user such as `nobody`. Also, make sure the program is secure.

THE `mod_log_config` MODULE

Source: mod_log_config.c
Base: No
Type: Administration

The `mod_log_config` module is not built into Apache by default. In order to use any of its directives, you need to reconfigure Apache to include this module and recompile the server.

This module allows the logging of server requests using a user-specified format. This module is experimental in nature. It implements the `TransferLog` directive (same as the `mod_log_common`) and an additional directive, `LogFormat`.

The argument to the `LogFormat` directive is a string that can include literal characters copied into the log files as well as `%` directives:

`%h`	Remote host.
`%l`	Remote logname (from `identd`, if supplied).
`%u`	Remote user from `auth`; may be bogus if return status (`%s`) is 401.
`%t`	Time, in common log format time format.
`%r`	First line of request.
`%s`	Status. For requests that got internally redirected, this is the status of the original request.
`%>s`	Status. For requests that were internally redirected, this is the status of the last request.
`%b`	Bytes sent.
`%{Header}i`	Inserts the contents of the HTTP header *Header* that was received from the client.
`%{Header}o`	Inserts the contents of the HTTP header *Header* that was sent back to the client.

You can specify the conditions for inclusion of a particular field by specifying an HTTP status code between the `%` and the letter code for the field. You can specify more than one by separating them with a comma (,):

```
%400,500{User-agent}I
```

10

APACHE MODULES

This line of code logs User-Agent headers as only Bad Request or Not Implemented errors.

You also can specify that an item should be logged, if a certain HTTP code is not returned by adding an exclamation symbol (!) in front of the code you want to see:

```
%!200,304,302{Referer}i
```

This line of code logs Referer header information on all requests not returning a normal return code.

If any condition is not met, the field is null. As with the common log format, a null field is indicated by a dash (-) character.

Virtual hosts can have their own LogFormat and/or TransferLog. If no LogFormat is specified, it is inherited from the main server process. If the virtual host doesn't have its own TransferLog, entries are written to the main server's log.

To differentiate between virtual hosts that are writing to a common log file, you can prepend a label to the log format string like in this next example:

```
<VirtualHost xxx.com>
LogFormat "xxx formatstring"
...
</VirtualHost>
<VirtualHost yyy.com>
LogFormat "yyy formatstring"
...
</VirtualHost>
```

mod_log_config DIRECTIVES

mod_log_config provides two directives:

◆ LogFormat

◆ TransferLog

LogFormat

Syntax: LogFormat *string*
Default: LogFormat "%h %l %u %t \"%r\" %s %b"
Context: Server configuration, virtual host

This sets the format of the log file.

TransferLog

Syntax: TransferLog [*filename*] | [¦*program*]
Default: TransferLog logs/transfer_log
Context: Server configuration, virtual host

The `TransferLog` directive specifies the file where the server logs all request transactions. The options are *filename* or ¦*program*:

◆ *filename* is the name of a file relative of `ServerRoot`.

◆ ¦*program* is the pipe symbol (¦) followed by a path to a program capable of receiving the log information on `stdin` (standard input).

As with any program started by the server, the program is run with the UID and GID of the user that started the `httpd` daemon. If the user starting the program is `root`, be sure that the user directive demotes the server privileges to those of an unprivileged user such as `nobody`. Also, make sure the program is secure.

The `mod_log_referer` Module

Source:	`mod_log_refer.c`
Base:	No
Type:	Administration

The `mod_log_referer` module is not built into Apache by default. In order to use any of its directives, you need to reconfigure Apache to include this module and recompile the server.

This module provides logging of documents that reference documents on the server.

Logfile Format Description

The logfile contains a separate line for each reference. Each line has the format

uri -> document

where *uri* is the URI for the document that references the one requested by the client, and *document* is the local URL to the document being referenced.

`mod_log_referer` Directives

◆ `RefererIgnore`

◆ `RefererLog`

RefererIgnore

Syntax:	`RefererIgnore` *string string ...*
Context:	Server configuration, virtual host

The `RefererIgnore` directive adds to the list of strings to ignore in `Referer` headers. If any of the strings in the list are contained in the `Referer` header, no information will be logged for the request. An example of this is as follows:

```
RefererIgnore webcrawler.com
```

This avoids logging requests from `webcrawler.com`.

RefererLog

Syntax:	`RefererLog [filename]` | `[¦program]`
Default:	`RefererLog logs/referer_log`
Context:	Server configuration, virtual host

The `RefererLog` directive specifies the file where the server logs `referer` information. The options are `filename` or `¦program`:

◆ `filename` is the name of a file relative of `ServerRoot`.

◆ `¦program` is the pipe symbol (¦) followed by a path to a program capable of receiving the log information on `stdin`.

As with any program started by the server, the program is run with the UID and GID of the user that started the `httpd` daemon. If the user starting the program is `root`, be sure that the user directive demotes the server privileges to those of an unprivileged user such as `nobody`. Also, make sure the program is secure.

This directive is provided for compatibility with NCSA `httpd` 1.4.

The mod_mime Module

Source:	`mod_mime.c`
Base:	Yes
Type:	MIME

The `mod_mime` module is built into Apache by default.

This module maps MIME-encodings of documents based on their filenames. Filenames are composed of a basename followed by one or more extensions:

`base.type.language.encoding`

The `type` sets the document type; an HTML document has an `.html` type. The `language` extension describes the language in which the document is written. `encoding` specifies if the document has been processed by a program, such as a compression program.

This module is used to map the MIME types of documents based on their type, language, and encoding extensions. MIME types requiring some special processing by the server are handed down to the appropriate modules, such as the `mod_imap` module which processes `.map` files or the `mod_include` module, which processes SPML documents. Types not requiring any processing, such as `.gif` or `.html`, are returned to the client where the browser can process the document as needed.

mod_mime DIRECTIVES

mod_mime adds the following directives:

- ◆ AddEncoding
- ◆ AddLanguage
- ◆ AddType
- ◆ TypesConfig

The following directives are available only in Apache 1.1 or better:

- ◆ AddHandler
- ◆ ForceType
- ◆ SetHandler

AddEncoding

Syntax: AddEncoding *mime-enc extension extension...*
Context: Server configuration, virtual host, directory, .htaccess
Override: FileInfo

The AddEncoding directive maps file extension's *extension* to the encoding type *mime-enc*. The following is an example:

```
AddEncoding x-gzip gz
AddEncoding x-compress Z
```

The preceding example will mark files ending in .gz as encoded using the x-gzip encoding, and files ending in .z as encoded with x-compress encoding.

AddLanguage

Syntax: AddLanguage *mime-lang extension extension...*
Context: Server configuration, virtual host, directory, .htaccess
Override: FileInfo

The AddLanguage directive maps language extension's *extension* to the language type *mime-lang*. *mime-lang* is the MIME language of the files after any encoding formats have been removed. An example of this is as follows:

```
AddEncoding x-gzip gz
AddLanguage en .en
AddLanguage fr .fr
```

Then the document document.en.gz will be treated as being a gzipped-compressed English-language document. The AddLanguage directive is useful in content negotiation, where the server selects from several documents one that is appropriate for the client's language preference.

AddType

Syntax: AddType *mime-type extension extension...*
Context: Server configuration, virtual host, directory, .htaccess
Override: FileInfo

The AddType directive maps filename extension's *extension* to the content type *mime-type*. *mime-type* is the content encoding of the file, after any encoding formats and language extensions have been removed. The following is an example:

AddType image/gif GIF

You should add new MIME types using the AddType directive instead of modifying entries in the TypesConfig file (conf/mime.types).

> **COMPATIBILITY**
>
> Unlike the NCSA httpd, the AddType directive cannot be used to set the type of particular files.

TypesConfig

Syntax: TypesConfig *filename*
Default: TypesConfig conf/mime.types
Context: Server configuration

The TypesConfig directive specifies the location of the MIME-types configuration file. *filename* is a relative of ServerRoot. This file contains the default list of filename extension mappings to content types. Don't alter this file unless you know what you are doing. Use the AddType directive in conf/srm.conf instead.

The MIME-types configuration file contains lines in the format of the arguments to an AddType command:

mime-type extension extension...

Extensions are specified in lowercase. Blank lines and lines beginning with a pound sign (#) are ignored.

AddHandler

Syntax: AddHandler *handler-type file-type*
Context: Server configuration, virtual hosts, directory, .htaccess

The AddHandler directive specifies the handler that will process the filetype. *handler* is nothing more than a program that knows how to handle the specified filetype. For example, CGI programs are handled by the `cgi-script` handler. Server Side Includes are handled by the `server-parsed` handler.

In addition to `cgi-script` and `server-parsed` handlers, the following handlers are available:

`send-as-is`	Sends files with HTTP headers. *See* `mod_asis`.
`imap-file`	Processes image map files. *See* `mod_imap`.
`server-info`	Informs you of the server configuration. *See* `mod_info`.
`server-status`	Informs you of the server status. *See* `mod_status`.
`type-map`	Parses type maps for content negotiation information. *See* `mod_negotiation`.

To add a handler that will process CGI programs with a *.program* extension, you might specify in your `conf/srm.conf` or `httpd.conf`:

```
AddHandler cgi-script program
```

Once the server is restarted, any file with the program extension will be treated as a CGI.

ForceType

Syntax: `ForceType MIME-type`
Context: Directory, location, .htaccess

The `ForceType` directive specifies the MIME-type format that will be applied to files matching a `<Directory>` or `<Location>` section. This directive is useful to remap many files of a particular type that don't sport the appropriate extension. The following is an example:

```
<Location /images>
ForceType image/gif
</Location>
```

Any request in the `/images` directory will send any file, regardless of filetype extension, as a GIF.

SetHandler

Syntax: `SetHandler handler-type`
Context: Directory, location, .htaccess

The `SetHandler` directive specifies the handler that will process a particular request based on access to a directory or location. Requests matching the directory or location specification will be processed by the handler. This is how you enable the status module (`mod_status`):

```
<Location /status>
SetHandler server-status
</Location>
```

Requests for the /status URI will return a status report.

THE mod_negotiation MODULE

Source:	mod_negotiations.c
Base:	Yes
Type:	MIME

The mod_negotiation module is built into Apache by default.

This module provides for content negotiation. Any document with MIME type application/x-type-map will be processed by this module.

Content selection is the selection of the document that best matches the client's capabilities from several equivalent documents. There are two ways of providing this functionality.

One way is through a *type map* (a file with the MIME type application/x-type-map), which lists equivalent files.

The other way to provide this functionality is through a MultiViews search (enabled by the MultiViews option), which forces the server to perform a filename pattern match and choose from the resulting list.

TYPE MAPS

A *type map* uses the same format as RFC822 mail headers that contain document descriptions separated by blank lines. Lines beginning with a pound (#) are treated as comments.

The description consists of several of these headers. Records may be continued on additional lines if the additional lines start with spaces. The leading space will be deleted and the lines concatenated.

A *header record* consists of a keyword name, which always ends in a colon, followed by a value. Whitespace is allowed between the header and the value, and between the tokens of value. The headers allowed are

Content-Encoding	The encoding of the file. Currently only two encodings are recognized by HTTP; x-compress for compressed files and x-gzip for gzipped files.
Content-Language	The language of the variant as an Internet standard language code, such as en (English).

Content-Length	The length of the file in bytes. If this header is not present, the actual length of the file is used.
Content-Type	The MIME media *type* of the document with optional parameters. Parameters are separated from the media type and from each other by semicolons. Parameter syntax is *name=value*. Allowed parameters are

Level	The value is an integer that specifies the version of the media type. For text/HTML, this defaults to 2; otherwise, 0.
qs	The value is a floating-point number with a value between 0 and 1. It indicates the quality of this variant.
	Example: Content-type: image/jpeg; qs=0.8

URI	The path to the file containing this variant, relative to the map file.

MultiViews

A MultiViews search is enabled by the MultiViews option (Options MultiViews). When the server receives a request for a file and it does not exist, the server searches for a file using the name requested as a basename (without any extensions) and tries to match the name to a list of files that use basename as a name.

Here's a sample request:

.../path/file

The server searches for files matching the pattern

.../path/file.*

By using the filetype, language, and encoding-mapping information, the server effectively builds a type map from which to select the best match for the client's requirements, which it will then return to the client.

mod_negotiation DIRECTIVES

The mod_negotiation module adds the following directives:

- ◆ CacheNegotiatedDocs
- ◆ LanguagePriority

CacheNegotiatedDocs

> Syntax: `CacheNegotiatedDocsmime-lang...`
> Context: Server configuration

When set, content-negotiated requests are cachable by proxy servers.

LanguagePriority

> Syntax: `LanguagePriority mime-lang mime-lang...`
> Context: Server configuration, virtual host, directory, `.htaccess`
> Override: `FileInfo`

The `LanguagePriority` directive sets the precedence of language encodings in cases when the client does not express a preference. The list of *mime-lang* is in order of decreasing preference. The following is an example:

`LanguagePriority en fr de`

In a request for `index.html`, where the browser did not specify a language preference but only the French and German versions of the document were available, the server would return the French version.

THE mod_proxy MODULE

Apache 1.1

> Source: `mod_proxy.c`
> Base: Yes
> Type: Proxy server/cache management

A proxy server is a Web server that sits between a local client and an external Web server. It acts as an intermediary to the client and fetches information from other Web servers. Instead of having a client connect to a server on the Internet directly, it establishes a connection with a proxy server in the user's local network. The proxy server then retrieves the resources requested and serves them to the client as if the resources were its own.

Caching proxy servers can be a powerful tool in your arsenal to increase the performance of your internal Web traffic. While originally developed as a way of allowing access to the Web through a firewall, proxy servers have also been used to reduce the traffic your organization generates to popular Web sites.

For additional information on proxy servers, please see Chapter 12, "Web Server Performance Tuning."

mod_proxy DIRECTIVES

`mod_proxy` supplies a variety of directives to help you manage the behavior of the server and its cache:

- CacheegotiatedDocs
- CacheDefaultExpire
- CacheGcInterval
- CacheLastModified
- CacheMaxExpire
- CacheRoot
- CacheSize
- NoCache
- ProxyPass
- ProxyRemote
- ProxyRequests

ProxyRequests

Syntax: ProxyRequests [on] | [off]
Default: ProxyRequests off
Context: Server configuration

The ProxyRequests directive enables or disables the proxy functionality of the server. A proxy server is one that is able to act as an intermediary to fulfill requests from a browser to another Web server. It is frequently used as a way of providing access to the Web to clients behind a firewall without compromising the security requirements of the organization.

Tip

Disabling the ProxyRequest functionality does not disable the ever cool ProxyPass directive functionality provided with the module.

ProxyRemote

Syntax: ProxyRemote [pattern] [remote-server]
Context: Server configuration

The ProxyRemote directive enables you to specify remote proxies to this proxy server. Its configuration is based on a pattern specified as a partial URL that the remote server can understand. To indicate that a specified server should be contacted for all requests, specify a dollar sign ($) as the URL.

ProxyRemote http://www.company.com/ http://mirror.somewhere.com

10

You can specify a server that runs in a different port as:

```
ProxyRemote  http://www.company.com/  http://mirror.somewhere.com:8080
```

ProxyPass

Syntax: ProxyPass [*path*] [*URL*]
Context: Server configuration

This is a very cool directive. ProxyPass enables you to map a remote server into your local server's document tree, much as if you were mounting the remote document tree into your server's document tree. The local server appears as a mirror of the remote server. ProxyPass takes two arguments: *path* is the file path you want to use for inserting the remote server into your document tree; and *URL* is the address of the real server that the proxy request should be sent to:

```
ProxyPass /SmartSoft.htmld  http://www.smartsoft.com/
```

In this case, a request such as

```
http://proxy/SmartSoft.htmld/index.html
```

will get translated into a proxy request to

```
http://www.SmartSoft.com/index.html
```

You can specify as many ProxyPass directives as you like.

CacheRoot

Syntax: CacheRoot [*directory-path*]
Context: Server configuration

CacheRoot specifies the directory that the server should use to store cache information. The server must be able to write to the directory specified by *directory-path*. Because this means that user nobody must have write privileges to this directory, this typically translates into a directory that is world writable.

Tip

> If you are concerned about security, you may wish to have the server run under a special UID that has low permissions. This would allow you to create a directory that is writable by the server but not by the world.

CacheSize

Syntax:	CacheSize [*size*]
Default:	CacheSize 5
Context:	Server configuration

This directive specifies the maximum size of the cache in kilobytes (1024 byte units). While the cache *will* grow beyond the amount specified by *size*, at garbage collection intervals, the server will remove cached documents until the space consumed is at or below the amount specified by this directive. The garbage collection interval is specified by the CacheGcInterval directive.

CacheGcInterval

Syntax:	CacheGcInterval [*time*]
Context:	Server configuration

The garbage collection interval is specified by the CacheGcInterval directive. At this time the server will check the disk space consumed by the cache. It will then prune the cache until the disk space consumed is less or equal to the space specified by the CacheSize directive.

time is specified in hours.

CacheMaxExpire

Syntax:	CacheMaxExpire [*time*]
Default:	CacheMaxExpire 24
Context:	Server configuration

The CacheMaxExpire directive controls how long (in hours) cacheable documents will be kept in the cache without re-requesting documents from the original server.

In effect this setting controls the maximum amount of time that documents could potentially be served out of date because it is feasible that changes may be introduced into documents while they are in cache.

The CacheMaxExpire directive is enforced even when a document has an expiration date supplied in a meta tag within.

CacheLastModifiedFactor

Syntax:	CacheLastModifiedFactor [*factor*]
Default:	CacheLastModifiedFactor 0.1
Context:	Server configuration

10

APACHE MODULES

The `CacheLastModifiedFactor` directive supplies an expiration time for a document based on the formula:

`expiry = timeOfLastModification * factor`

If a document was modified in the last 24 hours and the factor is set to the default, the expiry period will be set to 2.4 hours (24 x 0.1 = 2.4 hours; 2 hours and 24 minutes).

If the expiration time specified by `CacheMaxExpire` arrives sooner, it takes precedence over the expiry time calculated by `CacheLastModifiedFactor`.

CacheDefaultExpire

Syntax: `CacheDefaultExpire [time]`
Default: `CacheDefaultExpire 1`
Context: Server configuration

If a protocol does not supply an expiration time, the value specified by `CacheDefaultExpire` is used. This expiration time is not overridden by `CacheMaxExpire`. Currently, the proxy module only provides proying capabilities for FTP and HTTP (both HTTP/0.9 and HTTP/1.0) protocols.

NoCache

Syntax: `NoCache [host] | [domain] ...`
Context: Server configuration

The `NoCache` directive provides you with a mechanism to specify a list of hosts or domains that you don't want cached by the proxy server. You can specify hosts and/ or domain names in a list form where each host or domain is separated by spaces:

`NoCache foo.xxxx.com bar.com`

This directive is particularly useful if you know a site is dynamic, and you don't want stale information ever to be served for it.

THE mod_status MODULE

Source: `mod_status.c`
Base: No
Type: Server status

The `mod_status` module is a great tool for informing the server administrator what the server is doing. It takes a snapshot of all the server processes and creates an HTML report that can be viewed with a browser. The report includes a wealth of information including the following:

- ◆ The number of children processes and their status
- ◆ Transfers performed by each child
- ◆ The average number of requests per second
- ◆ The average number of bytes served per second
- ◆ The amount of resources utilized by each child and by the entire group
- ◆ Current clients and the requests being served.

mod_status is not included by default; you'll need to reconfigure and rebuild the server. Once built, you'll need to add the following directives to your conf/access.conf configuration file:

```
<Location /status>
SetHandler server-status
</Location>
```

If you want to keep your server statistics private, add a Limit section specifying some access restrictions (see Chapter 15 for more information). Restart the server and point your Web browser to http://yourhost/status. The server will return its detailed status report.

THE mod_userdir MODULE

Source:	mod_userdir.c
Base:	Yes
Type:	Resource location

The mod_userdir module is built into Apache by default. It provides a mechanism through which users can publish their own home page information.

This module specifies the directory, relative of a local user's home directory, where public HTML documents and home pages can be found. Requests for user's home pages take the form of

```
http://www.somedomain.com/~user
```

mod_userdir DIRECTIVES

The only directive provided by this module is UserDir.

UserDir

Syntax:	UserDir [disabled] | *directoryname*
Default:	UserDir public_html
Context:	Server configuration, virtual host

The UserDir directive sets the directory name relative of a local user's home directory where public HTML documents may be found. This feature can be disabled by specifying the disabled option to the directive. If omitted, it defaults to

```
UserDir public_html
```

Although this may be a useful directive to allow users in a UNIX environment to specify their own home pages, some users may not be aware of this fact, resulting in the possibility of them creating a directory named public_html that contains private files. Additionally, depending on the kind of users in your system, this can create some security problems.

Apache 1.1 enhances this module to redirect home page requests to a different directory, removing the security concerns previously raised. By specifying an absolute path such as the following

```
UserDir /Users/homepages
```

the server will look for a directory matching the request in /Users/homepages. Requests for http://www.somedomain.com/~x will be retrieved from /Users/homepages/x.

Warning

If you have enabled Options FollowSymLinks or AllowOverrides Options for the directory containing your users' home directories, any users could attach, via a link, any portion of your filesystem to their public_html directory. This, in effect, would make private materials from your organization available to anyone outside of your organization. This might not be what you want, and might be a good reason to scan logs frequently.

Here's an example of the UserDir directive:

```
UserDir public_html
```

A request for http://www.somedomain.com/~user will return the file http://www.somedomain.com/~user/index.html.

SUMMARY

This chapter serves as a reference guide for Apache modules. In the next chapters, you will learn about system administration, including the basics, Web server performance tuning, and Web accounting.

- Basic System Administration

- Web Server Performance Tuning

- Web Accounting

P A R T IV

Keeping Up: Web Server System Administration

CHAPTER 11

Basic System Administration

HTTP servers provide information; however, if your servers are unreachable, no one can get at this information. Your job as a system administrator is to ensure that your computers and networks are running smoothly. You must be both proactive and reactive. A proactive system administrator monitors his system resources to prevent basic problems, such as running out of disk space or some other disaster. A reactive system administrator has a contingency plan ready to be implemented in case of a disaster.

Proactive system administration is better than reactive system administration. Proactive administration can help you avoid the unpleasant experience of responding to a barrage of users' complaints about services that are down. However, should such a situation arise, your efficiency in resolving the matter (reactive administration) will affect how those complaining users perceive you and your level of competence. Therefore, it is your responsibility to maintain a close watch on all that is under your control.

The system administrator's central task is to orchestrate and choreograph the installation, setup, and maintenance of all hardware and software. Ancillary obligations can include setting up additional systems that help users obtain more information regarding access patterns and logs (HTTP logs and other UNIX logs).

The key word here is *maintenance*. This word can mean several different things: backing up your computers, pruning logfiles, and ensuring that name servers and HTTP servers are running. The most important of these is backing up your computers. If your system catastrophically failed, how long would it take you to get it up and running again? If it took you weeks to set up and install everything the first time, doing it over is not acceptable and definitely not fun. Instead, do it once and back it up. In case of a failure, replace the hardware or software that caused the failure with your backups.

If your information system is critical to your organization, any downtime is unacceptable. This means that you must build redundant systems that guarantee the trouble-free, continuous operation of your site. How much you can do depends on your budget.

MAKING BACKUPS

Backing up is not hard to do, and if you want to keep your job as a system administrator, you should consider it an essential task. Although backing up is not difficult, it is tedious and time-consuming, especially when the disks you are backing up are large.

How can you back up a heavily used resource without taking it down and making it unavailable? How often should these backups occur? The answer to both of these questions is that *it depends*. A server that constantly has new information on it needs to be backed up more often than one that rarely changes. If your server is also a fileserver on which users or other programs store data, all bets are off. You don't have the luxury of determining what is a good interval; you will have to back it up daily.

Some technologies, such as Redundant Arrays of Inexpensive Disks (RAID), can provide automatic reliability, in case of media failure, and uninterrupted operation during hardware replacement. If a single drive on a RAID configuration fails, the data can be reconstructed from the information stored in the other drives and the redundant parity or Error Correcting Code (ECC) information. However, this feature will not help much if the root of the problem is a bad disk controller or some other problem that compromises the integrity of your data. RAID reliability is dependent on only a single drive going bad. RAID-6 arrays address this problem by allowing up to two disk failures without compromising the data. However, these multidimensional disk arrays have never been commercially implemented. Because of the auto-correcting nature of RAID, problems with the disk array are often found only when a second drive goes bad. By that time it's usually too late, and the likelihood of irreparable data loss is great. I suggest that you monitor your RAID array on a daily basis and back it up to ensure that you have a way to restore your files.

The good news is that Web servers don't change too often. If your machine is dedicated to just serving pages, your site will change when someone modifies it by adding, deleting, or updating information on the pages. The site also will change when you configure your server or install some new piece of software. How often you do backups depends on how much you are willing to lose. Keep in mind that your server logs may contain valuable information that takes time to accumulate, and unless you back them up, they will be lost. If your server also handles any sort of commercial transactions, you may want to make sure that the point-of-sale information is safely backed up.

How you handle your backup strategy is really a matter of personal preference. If you establish policies, such as describing what you back up, it becomes easier to do many system-administration tasks. Also, it is important to have the right hardware for making backups. By *right hardware* I mean that the disks you back up must fit into a convenient backup medium; otherwise, you'll have more tapes than you'll know what to do with. If you can afford it, buy a tape drive. This medium is inexpensive and can hold a lot of data. Other backup solutions may work on your network, depending on how much data you need to back up.

11

BASIC SYSTEM ADMINISTRATION

Backup Media

There is an incredible array of choices for backup media these days:

◆ Floppy disks

◆ Floptical disks

◆ Magneto-optical (MO) disks

◆ Quarter-inch Cartridge tapes (QIC)

◆ Travan tapes

◆ Write-once CD-ROMs

◆ Iomega Jaz and Zip drives

◆ Nine-track magnetic tapes

◆ 4mm Digital Audio Tapes (DAT)

◆ 8mm cartridge tapes

Floppy Disks

Floppy disks are the most convenient backup medium available because your system likely has a built-in floppy disk drive. The standard capacity is 1.44MB. Some 2.88MB drives made it into the market a few years back, but they never caught on. The drawback of floppy disks is that they are slow, fairly expensive (about 50¢ to 60¢ per disk), and not very useful for backing up anything that is larger than a couple disks.

Floptical Disks

These higher-capacity disks take advantage of optical tracking technology to improve head positioning, and therefore maximize the amount of data that can be packed onto the surface of a disk. Floptical drives can read standard 1.44MB and 720KB floppy disks. Density of information can be anywhere from a few megabytes to 200MB per disk.

Magneto-Optical Disks

Magneto-optical disks have a plastic or glass substrate coated with a compound that, when heated to its Curie point, allows a magnetic source to realign the polarity of the material. Once the material cools, its polarity is frozen. The material can be repolarized by a subsequent write operation.

Data is read by a lower-intensity beam, and the polarization pattern is interpreted as a byte stream. A wide variety of these devices are commercially available, ranging in format from 5 1/2 inches to 3 1/2 inches. These devices can store information ranging in size from 128MB to more than 2GB.

Read speed on these devices is as fast as that on a hard disk. Write operations usually take a little longer, but are still faster than write operations on a slow hard disk. Media reliability is very high.

QUARTER-INCH CARTRIDGE TAPES (QIC)

A QIC tape is a low-end, PC-market backup storage solution that uses .25-inch tape. Some vendors, including IBM, are pushing the format to store up to 1600MB by-using a .315-inch format; these tapes are commonly known as Travan tapes.

Standard QIC tapes can hold anywhere from 11MB to 150MB, and are usually designated as QIC-11, QIC-24, and QIC-150, depending on the amount of storage space they provide. Storage space in megabytes is indicated by the number following the QIC portion of the designation.

Sometimes tapes created on one vendor's drive are not readable by another vendor's drive. This is due to byte ordering and other special formatting issues. Within a vendor, tapes are usually backward compatible, meaning that you may be able to read lower-density tapes on a higher-density drive; however, you should verify this before you upgrade to a new drive in the same product line.

TRAVAN TAPES

Travan tapes are similar in size to QIC tapes, but store anywhere from 120MB to 1600MB per tape depending on the type of tape drive mechanism used. Travan tapes are compatible with the QIC tape formats, making them attractive if you have legacy QIC tapes.

WRITE-ONCE CD-ROMs

New technology and price drops have made the write-once CD-ROM a popular choice with multimedia enthusiasts. Write-once CD-ROMs use a technology similar to a CD burner. CDs created by write-once CD-ROMs are not as rugged as pressed CDs, but will last forever if you take care of the disk. These disks are compatible with any desktop system that has a CD-ROM, which has helped in making this a popular Write Once Read Many (WORM) format. Current capacity is about 600MB. Recording speed is slow. New formats for CD-ROMs that are currently in the works will yield 17GB storage, making it a very interesting solution to backup and archival tasks.

IOMEGA JAZ AND ZIP DRIVES

Zip is a popular removable disk drive. They are very inexpensive: around $200 for the drive and $10 to $15 per disk. Each disk holds about 100MB. They are available in SCSI and parallel flavors.

Jaz drives are a higher-performance, higher-capacity version of the Zip drives. Jaz drives are a bit more expensive, about $599, and require a SCSI interface. Disks cost more than $99 and pack 1GB of fast storage space. You can back up 1GB of information in about 5 minutes on PC platforms. This is a hot product.

NINE-TRACK MAGNETIC TAPES

This is an old format of tape written at 800, 1600, or 6250BPI (bits per inch) density. This format is not in great use today except by old mainframes.

4MM DATS

A DAT, which stores 1.3GB of information on a 60-meter tape, was originally designed for the audio market. Digital data storage (DDS), the computer version of DAT, provides the smallest storage solution of all. You can store about 2GB of data per cartridge. Drives with hardware compression can store up to 8GB. DDS is the preferred tape backup system for most UNIX users.

8MM CARTRIDGE TAPES

8mm cartridges (also known as "Exabytes" for the company that first produced them) are the same size as their video counterparts. Many administrators purchase high-quality "video grade" tapes instead of the premium data versions. Drives can store 2–5GB, and versions boasting hardware compression can pack up to 10GB into a single tape. Because fewer tapes are needed, this is a very convenient format. Next to the 4mm format, this is the best storage solution.

A BACKUP STRATEGY

Doing incremental backups under UNIX means using the `dump` utility. This utility is powerful, but somewhat dangerous. Using it incorrectly can cause serious problems. However, `dump` can handle backups that span multiple tapes. If you can fit your entire backup onto a single tape, you'll be able to automate backups. Just start up the backup, and let it run.

Web sites have a slightly different usage pattern from your typical server. Because Web sites don't have users creating files all the time, the filesystem doesn't change very often (unless your server provides some sort of intranet application that uses a database for persistence, or you want to back up your logfiles).

A *production server*, the server people connect to in order to obtain information, is very different from a *development server*. Development servers contain an individual's work. They should be backed up often! Incremental backups should be used to minimize the media and time required to perform them.

If you have been following my suggestions, you will probably agree that the server documents (`.html` files) should reside on a separate disk. If you cannot afford another disk, a separate partition may offer the same benefits. *Partition* is just a fancy word for a smaller logical unit (smaller disk) of a big disk. Partitioning a large disk can offer many advantages:

◆ Partitions are smaller in size, more likely to fit into a single tape, and much faster to back up because they contain less data.

◆ Partitions protect your system from a runaway program that fills up a disk.

On the negative side, if you fill up a partition, UNIX doesn't provide you with a way to enlarge or shrink it. What you choose is what you live with. Don't go partition-crazy either; if you have too many little partitions, you'll probably find that some of your partitions need more space. A two-partition scheme works well. It is a good idea to partition a disk so that the base operating system fits easily into one partition and allows 15 to 25 percent of the partition space for future growth. This is the *system* partition. The second partition is allocated to a single user area. Any customizations or added third-party software should go there. If you cannot afford a second disk for user-generated files, you can store them in the second partition as well.

Separate disks or partitions help the backup process because both can be dumped separately to tape. If you are unable to partition or have multiple filesystems, your backups will take a little longer.

If you follow this scheme, you'll need to back up only software and configuration files that you add or modify, instead of having to back up the whole system. Likewise, the user partition can be backed up separately.

My strategy is to back up production servers at well-defined times:

◆ Right after the system software is installed, but before anything is configured

◆ After the server software is installed and configured

◆ Any time additional software is installed and configured

If your operating-system software distribution comes on a CD-ROM or some other easily installed medium, the first backup you make after installing your system software doesn't need to go to tape. If you send it to `/dev/null`, you'll be able to create a backup set that doesn't include your system's software distribution. This will set the beginning of time for the `dump` utility to operate. The backup level for this dump should be at level 0; it must include everything in the newly installed system.

If the installation of basic software is problematic, you should probably direct the backup to a tape and save it for future disaster recovery. If you need to reinstall your distribution software, simply restore it to a clean disk instead of rebuilding a kernel or something else.

11

Basic System Administration

Subsequent backups should be performed at level 9; this will effectively back up everything that has been modified in the machine since the first backup was made.

To restore files stored in a tape created with the dump utility, use the restore program.

THE dump COMMAND

The dump command uses the following syntax:

```
/usr/etc/dump [options [argument ...] filesystem]
```

The dump command tracks the scope of a backup by assigning each backup a level. Levels range from 0 to 9. Level 0 copies the entire filesystem. Subsequent dump levels copy only files that have changed since the most recent dump with a lower-level number.

If you dump a disk at level 5, it includes all files that have changed since the date of the last dump with the next lowest level (in this case, last level 4 dump, or lower if no dump level 4 was performed). When executed with the u flag, dump tracks the backup level along with the date and time the backup was performed.

The typical strategy is to begin with a level 0 dump and then make incremental backups at regular intervals. Level 0 dumps should be performed with extreme care; they should be run with the machine in single-user mode, and fsck, the filesystem consistency checker, should run before the dump to verify that the filesystem is consistent. This is important because most of the files you restore will come from dump level 0 tapes!

One disadvantage worth noting is that dump is unable to back up single directories or files. It can only be used to back up an entire filesystem. To back up individual files or directories, use the programs tar or cpio. For information on how to use these programs, refer to your UNIX documentation.

Note that tapes created under one hardware/software configuration are not usually portable to other operating systems or drives. On some environments, even tapes created with older versions of the dump program are unreadable by newer versions of the restore program.

dump EXAMPLES

The following command will create a level 0 dump (specified by the 0) of the specified disk, /dev/rsd0a:

```
dump 0u /dev/rsd0a
```

Replace rsd0a with the appropriate name for your raw disk device. This dump will include all the files found on the device. If you specify the u option and the backup finishes successfully, dump will remember the date, time, and level of this backup. This effectively sets a reference point that can be used to evaluate which files need to be dumped next time.

To create a partial backup that includes only files modified since the last backup of a lower level, in this case 0, use a level 9 dump:

```
dump 9u /dev/rsd0a
```

By default, dump writes its output to the default tape unit, in this case /dev/rxt0. The /dev/rxt0 is a rewinding interface to the tape drive. When the backup is finished, the tape will be automatically rewound. To finish the backup and prevent the tape from rewinding, use the nonrewinding device. On my system, this is called /dev/nrxt0. For the name of this device, please check the dump UNIX manual page. To specify a different backup device or file, use the f option:

```
dump 9uf /tmp/backup /dev/rsd0a
```

The preceding command will create a file called backup in the /tmp directory. To redirect dump's output to stdout (standard output), specify a dash (-) instead of a filename:

```
dump 9uf - /dev/rsd0a | gzip > /tmp/backup.gz
```

In the preceding example, output from dump was sent to stdout and piped to the gzip program to be compressed. If your tape doesn't provide hardware compression, using the preceding command can be an effective way of increasing tape capacity.

For complete information on the myriad of options that dump provides, read your system's documentation.

restore

To extract files backed up with dump, use restore. restore copies files stored in a dump tape or file to the current directory. Note that using restore can and will clobber existing files with matching names. restore will also create any directories or directory trees that it needs before extracting a file. This feature is powerful if you know what you are doing. If in doubt, restore to an empty directory and move the files by hand. restore has the following syntax:

```
/usr/etc/restore [options [argument ...]]
```

By default, restore will use the tape drive at /dev/rxt0 (check your man page). If you want to override this device, use the f option.

restore has an easy-to-use interactive shell-like interface that allows you to navigate through the dump tape as if you were in a filesystem. The interactive session is started by using the i option.

`restore` EXAMPLES

To restore all files from a tape, use this:

```
restore r
```

To restore a particular file, use this:

```
restore x /Users/demo/file.rtf
```

The preceding command will extract (x) the file specified (`/Users/demo/file.rtf`) from the tape. If the directories don't exist, it will create them. It's a good idea to direct `restore` to put recovered files on an empty directory, and then move the files to their final destination.

To restore from a compressed `gzip` archive, use this:

```
gzcat /tmp/backup.gz ¦ restore f -
```

To create a catalog from files on a `dump` tape, use the `t` option. It is always a good idea to create a catalog from your tape. This will ensure that the backup tape you made contains the correct information and that the tape is readable.

Listing 11.1 is a script I use to automate backups. It is called from `cron` (see your UNIX documentation) with the level for the backup. Customizing it to fit your needs should not be very hard. Just read over all the options and make sure that the commands in your system are located in the same place. Also verify that the `/dev` files I reference match your configuration and change accordingly. This script automatically creates a catalog of the backups; it will also send a message notifying you if the backup was successful.

LISTING 11.1. AN AUTOMATED BACKUP SCRIPT.

```
#!/bin/csh -f
# Simple backup csh program. Takes one argument, the dump level.
# The goal of a backup is not only to save the data in case of disaster,
# but to minimize the time and grief required to get the system
# running again...
# ©Alberto Ricart, 7/1/1996
#
# This example backups 2 disks /dev/rsd1a and /dev/rsd0a, in order of preference.
# /dev/rsd1a contains a lot of user data, if the tape were to fill up in the
# middle of
# the second backup, we are assured that the important data copied OK.
# as a peace of mind, this script generates a listing of all the files. This is
# just
# a test to verify that the tape can be read. Also helpful for locating files.
# Please verify that these commands have the same significance as yours.
# Also, more than likely you'll have to change the /dev/rsd1a and /dev/rsd0a to
# point to
# your raw disk device, as well as your tape device /dev/nrxt0 on our case.

set LOGGER = '/usr/ucb/Mail '
set DUMP_LOG = '/usr/local/adm/dump.log'
```

```
set DUMP = '/usr/etc/dump'
set DUMP_ARGS = ''$1'ufs /dev/nrxt0 1200000'
set GZIP = '/usr/bin/gzip -9'
set RM = '/bin/rm'
set TAPE = '/bin/mt -f /dev/nrxt0'
set PRINTCAT = '/usr/etc/restore t'
set CATDIR = '/usr/local/amd/Tape_Catalogs'
set DATE = `/bin/date ¦ /bin/awk '{print $1":"$2":"$3":"$6 }'`
set OPERATOR = 'webmaster'


if ($#argv == 1) then

        $DUMP $DUMP_ARGS /dev/rsd1a ¦& $LOGGER $DUMP_LOG ¦¦ mail -s DISK1_
        ➥BACKUP_FAILED $OPERATOR
        $DUMP $DUMP_ARGS /dev/rsd0a ¦& $LOGGER $DUMP_LOG ¦¦ mail -s DISK0_
        ➥BACKUP_FAILED $OPERATOR
        $TAPE rewind
        $PRINTCAT > $CATDIR/$DATE.rsd1a.dump.$1
        $TAPE fsf 1
        $PRINTCAT > $CATDIR/$DATE.rsd0a.dump.$1
        $TAPE rewind
        mail -s BACKUP_OK $OPERATOR
        exit (0)
else
        echo "Backup script had no dump level, aborting" ¦ mail -s BACKUP_
        ➥ABORTED $OPERATOR
        exit (1)
endif
exit (1)
```

MONITORING DISK SPACE

UNIX provides tools for monitoring your disk space as well as for monitoring the load incurred by your disk: df and iostat, respectively.

df (disk free) displays various statistics regarding all currently mounted disks on your system. It reports on capacity, used amount, and free amount, in kilobytes and percentage formats:

```
% df
Filesytem     kbytes  used    avail   capacity  Mounted on
/dev/sd0a     1014845 397882  515478     44%    /
/dev/sd0b     1014845 329337  584023     36%    /usr/local
```

iostat displays information about disk performance, including the number of characters read and written to terminals for each disk, the number of transfers per second, and other information.

From this information you can glean the load affecting your disks:

```
% iostat
tty              sd0          cpu
tin tout bps tps msps us ni sy id
0      6  80  14  0.5  2  0  5 93
```

One of the main reasons to monitor disk space is because if the logs are not checked periodically, they will fill up your filesystem. You should monitor what's in logs as well as the size of the logs.

ROTATING THE LOGS

If there's one thing that logs do, it's grow. The bigger they are, the longer it takes to process them. Organizing and managing your logs is a good thing to do because it provides you with a systematic way of naming and storing the logs. Once the logs are properly named, you can dump them to tape and forget about them. Should you ever need them, you can quickly retrieve them.

Small sites may not need their logs rotated more often than once a month. Heavy-traffic systems should really consider not logging at all. However, if logging is absolutely necessary, resetting the logs on a daily basis can produce a more manageable logfile.

To give you an idea of how quickly logs grow, the typical access log entry contains 85 bytes per request. Not much. However, on a site that handles 5 million requests a day at 85 bytes per request, this translates into 405MB of log data per day! You should rotate logs at an interval that gives you a manageable file size.

RESETTING THE LOGS

Resetting logs is a bit tricky. Apache won't start logging on to a new file until it restarts. The easiest way to accomplish the rotation is through a script that renames the logfile and then sends the server a HUP (hangup) signal. However, the problem with this approach is that all the current connections to the server will be terminated.

A simple script is shown in Listing 11.2.

LISTING 11.2. RESETTING THE LOGFILE.

```
#  This script resets the log file, the log is renamed with todays date
# ©1996 Alberto Ricart
# This script assumes that the PID file exists in its default location
# Bugs: Should handle a list of filenames, instead of just one.
#
set OPERATOR = 'webmaster'
set DATE = `/bin/date ¦ /bin/awk '{print $1":"$2":"$3":"$6 }'`

if ($#argv == 1) then
  if (-e $1) then
    mv $1 $1$DATE.weblog
    kill -HUP `cat /usr/local/etc/httpd/logs/apache.pid`
    exit (0)
  else
    echo "Logfile $1 doesn't exist." ¦ mail -s LOG_ROTATION_ABORTED $OPERATOR
```

```
    exit 1
  endif
else
  echo "You didn't provide a path to a log file." ¦ mail -s LOG_ROTATION_
  ➥ABORTED $OPERATOR
  exit 1
endif
exit 0
```

Apache 1.1 ships with a utility program called `rotatelogs` that can be used to automatically reset the log without having to stop the server. As a side benefit, the program also names files incrementally.

Apache 1.1

To use `rotatelogs`, you'll need to compile it. You can do this easily by issuing the following commands:

```
cd /usr/local/etc/httpd/support
cc -o rotatelogs rotatelogs.c
strip rotatelogs
```

After a few moments, the program `rotatelogs` will be built. Next, you'll need to specify that output to the logfiles should be redirected to `rotatelogs`. The `rotatelogs` program uses the following syntax:

```
rotatelogs logfilename time
```

where `logfilename` is the path to a logfile. `logfilename` will be used as the base name for the log. It's followed by a number that represents the system time. A new logfile will be started at the end of `time`. `time` specifies the rotation time in seconds.

To rotate the access and error logs every 24 hours, you'll need to modify the `TransferLog` and `ErrorLog` directives in your `httpd.conf` file like this:

```
TransferLog "¦/usr/local/etc/httpd/support/rotatelogs
➥/usr/local/etc/httpd/logs/access_log 86400"
ErrorLog "¦/usr/local/etc/httpd/support/rotatelogs
➥/usr/local/etc/httpd/logs/error_log 86400"
```

UPGRADING THE SERVER

Upgrades are always a cause for concern in production environments. The overall strategy should be to install any new versions of the server in a test environment prior to putting the server into production. Always read the distribution documentation to see if some behavior has changed from previous versions.

KEEPING THE OLD SERVER AROUND

To be on the safe side, you should keep an old version of the server on hand just in case the new one causes some problems. An easy way to do this is to install the new

11

BASIC SYSTEM ADMINISTRATION

server after you rename the old one to `httpd.old`, and restart the server. If you discover any problems, you can quickly put the old server back online by renaming `httpd.old` to `httpd` and restarting the server again.

Making Sure It Is All Running

One of the biggest concerns you'll have is making sure that your machines are working correctly. Automated periodic testing of your site can help you ensure that it is accessible. A good setup has internal and external testing systems.

The best type of testing is actually the type that you don't have to do. For a small fee, some companies monitor your site every few minutes. If there's a problem, they call your beeper and inform you that something is afoot. They even go so far as making sure that your Web page is accessible. One such service can be found at `http://www.redalert.com`.

Having an external source test the accessibility of your Web site is a great idea because it confirms to your customers that users are able to access your site. You will know within a reasonable amount of time if your network becomes unreachable because of a problem with your provider.

Monitoring Your Hosts and Network Interfaces

The easiest way for you to test whether your server is reachable is to use the `ping` command. The `ping` command will send an ECHO_REQUEST datagram to a host or network interface. On reception, the packet is returned with an ECHO_RESPONSE datagram. While this test does not verify that your server is operating correctly, it does verify that the networking portion of it is reachable.

The format of the command is

`/etc/ping ipaddress packetsize pingcount`

Typically, you will want to use the `ping` command to send a datagram to the host to verify that your network interface is running. Once this is verified, you can start `test` from other hosts and gateways farther away.

Monitoring HTTP: `httpd_Monitor` and the STATUS_MODULE

When you monitor HTTP, you ensure that the server is running and you assess its current load. Apache has implemented a series of child processes that are semipersistent. Unlike some servers, which fork a new server process with each request and then kill off the new process as the request is satisfied, Apache implements a system that tracks all idle and busy server processes. If more server processes are needed, it creates more to handle the load (up to a limit). If the count of idle server processes exceeds a certain amount, the extra httpd processes are killed. This avoids a condition in which too many server processes compete for resources and effectively kill the machine. If the machine starts swapping, it becomes unusable and it is brought to its knees.

Apache's server implementation makes it harder to ascertain the current status of the server. To circumvent this problem, Apache has implemented a scoreboard status file. The scoreboard file enables all the various server processes to write status information on a designated portion of a file. A special program, httpd_monitor, located in the support subdirectory of the Apache distribution, is able to read the scoreboard file and display information regarding the server:

```
Usage: httpd_monitor [-d config-dir] [-s sleep-time]
Defaults: config-dir: /usr/local/etc/httpd/
          sleep-time: 2 seconds
```

Here's a sample run on a quiet server:

```
% httpd_monitor
sssss (0/5)
```

httpd_monitor displays the status of all child processes and whether they are sleeping (s), starting (t), active (R) or dead (_). In the preceding example, there are five processes, all of them sleeping.

If you are running version 1.1 or better, there's a easier way of obtaining server status information. The status_module shipped with Apache can display a nice HTML report that you can access with a browser.

To enable this module, just uncomment this line from your src/Configuration file:

```
Module status_module     mod_status.o
```

For more descriptive status reports, also add the -DSTATUS flag to the CFLAGS section near the start of the file. Build and install the new version of Apache by issuing the following commands:

```
cd /usr/local/etc/httpd/src
./Configure
make
strip httpd
mv httpd ../
```

In addition to building the new program, you'll have to edit your conf/access.conf file and add an entry like this one:

```
<Location /status>
SetHandler server-status
order deny,allow
```

```
deny from all
allow from yourdomain
</Location>
```

Change *yourdomain* to your Internet domain. As you should be able to tell from this configuration, the server will supply status information to requests that originate only within your domain name. Once the server is restarted, a request for the for /status on your server (http://www/status) will return a nicely formatted report that looks like Figure 11.1.

Figure 11.1.
A server status
report generated
by the
status_module.

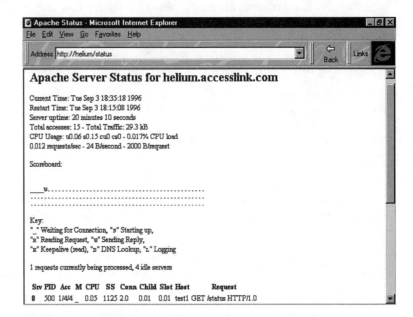

You can have the status information (produced by the status_module) updated every few seconds by typing

http://your.server.name/status/?refresh=*N*

Replace *N* with the number of seconds between updates.

In addition, you can access a machine-readable ASCII version of the report by requesting:

http://your.server.name/status/?auto

MONITORING YOUR NAME SERVER

The Berkeley Internet Name Domain (BIND) system includes a utility called name daemon control (ndc) interface, which allows you to easily send various signals to the name server. It also allows you to start, restart, or stop the name server. Even better, it allows you to display many status settings, as well as display cache and query log information. For extensive information on what a name server does, see Appendix E, "DNS and BIND Primer."

To check if your name server is running, just enter the following commands on a shell:

```
% ndc status
3170 ? SW 0:00 named
```

This displays a short line with process-status information.

From this line I know that my process is running, sleeping, and swapped out of memory. For more information on what this output means, check out the man page for ps.

If your server was not running, it would display a line such as this:

```
named (no pid file) not running
```

or this:

```
named (pid 3262?) not running
```

A better way to monitor the name server is to look at the logfiles. named uses the syslog facility to log problems. To see where syslog logs named messages, run this command:

```
grep daemon /etc/syslog.conf
```

Check the lines that contain named. An easy way to do this is to do a grep on named. It should be obvious when the problem is due to an incorrectly defined dbfile because named should echo a descriptive message to this effect. It is important to look for these errors because some of them may lead to your server stopping. An unreachable message can result in a secondary name server declaring that the data is stale and refusing to serve it. malformed type errors usually mean that some server provided a malformed response.

DEALING WITH DNS OUTAGES

The worst thing that could happen (besides your processor catching fire) is that your domain name server stops running. If the DNS goes, your network grinds to a halt. External users will be unable to reach it, and internal users will be unable to contact external resources.

There are several solutions to this problem:

◆ Make sure that you have at least two DNS servers running. If your pre-ferred DNS machine fails, each new request to your site will time-out for 4

11

BASIC SYSTEM ADMINISTRATION

seconds. After 4 seconds, DNS servers that you listed as alternatives for your site will be queried for the information. However, this will work for a certain amount of time only. After a while, if the only server running is not a primary server, the information will be declared stale, and the secondary server will refuse to serve it.

◆ One way to ensure that your DNS is always running is to have several servers. Some of the servers should be in your local network; others should be in a completely different network.

◆ DNS servers should also be located in stable and protected environments; do not trust prerelease software unless you know it is stable for both named and your operating system. Protect your server against power outages and other similar problems.

SUMMARY

This chapter covers some basic system administration points as they relate to the management of your Web site. Preventive action in terms of backups and the monitoring of processes and resources signal issues before they become a problem. The tools covered in this chapter are universally available to most unices. Commercial products are also available that address network monitoring. However, these tools are costly; some of the most popular tools cost thousands of dollars.

An inexpensive, efficient way to automate the generation of the server and network status information is by having a Web page that summarizes the information from the commands described in this chapter. When used under cron, you can ensure systematic testing of the various systems.

CHAPTER 12

Web Server
Performance Tuning

If there's one thing there is never enough of, it's speed. Speedy delivery of your content is one way to enhance your site's appeal. Slow sites usually get clicked away because computers are good at eliminating patience from their users. A computer will never be fast enough. As a webmaster, it is your responsibility to maintain and tune your system to meet the performance needs of your users. Many of the things you can do will depend on the size of your budget. Dream systems and high-speed networks are available, but at a premium.

Performance tuning is an art. Where you spend money in terms of hardware can make a big difference in the cost and performance of your site. Performance enhancements also raise the initial cost of hardware, which gets cheaper and more powerful everyday. Some performance tuning issues don't cost anything; they relate more to the design of your site and how users navigate it. Other issues involve tuning your software so that your system can run optimally. Another option involves the organization of your systems; arranging your network in a certain way can provide certain benefits that enhance the overall performance of your site.

Here are the four performance issues you'll explore in this chapter:

◆ Hardware tuning

◆ Software tuning

◆ Network-topology tuning

◆ Content tuning

If you are willing to spend the time, fine-tuning your kernel can make all the difference in the world in terms of performance. However, you should be very careful to have a bootable kernel available in case you manage to kill the system. The best advice regarding kernel configuration is *don't do it* unless you know exactly what you're doing.

Other than tuning your kernel and server software, there's only so much you can do to enhance the performance of your server. Performance is really an input/output issue, and it affects all aspects of your system and network. Think of your system as plumbing: The bigger the pipes, the faster the drain. No matter how much water you have, it can only drain so quickly. To make matters worse, ultimate transfer rates are determined by the smallest segment of the pipe, no matter how fast your server is.

All performance issues are interrelated. When some subsystems get maxed out before others, a cascading effect usually occurs; a system with insufficient memory will swap, slowing the processing speed and the network I/O. A server with really fast networking hardware but slow disk access won't be able to match its networking subsystem, so the networking hardware's potential is never realized.

HARDWARE TUNING

Your Web server's performance depends on the following hardware and associated software subsystems:

- CPU
- Disk
- Memory
- Network

CPU SUBSYSTEM TUNING

Processing speed is how fast your computer can process a request in terms of CPU usage. The Web doesn't create a very strenuous demand on most capable systems unless they are subjected to a very intense load. A Pentium box running Linux can swamp a DS-1 (T-1) line way before the hardware even feels it. Chances are that the networking bottlenecks are going to be noticed. Assuming that traffic increases proportionally to the size of your wide area network (WAN) interface, bigger WAN interfaces require more processing to handle requests.

DISTRIBUTED SERVERS

Distributed Web servers are a way of increasing the performance of your Web site when the bottleneck causes an intense load on your Web server. Assuming that your gateway bandwidth is greater than the performance of your computer, you may be able to obtain better performance by evenly distributing the load over several servers.

Instead of having all traffic directed to one system, the load is distributed as evenly as possible across an array of servers (mirrors). This allows heavy traffic sites to maximize the performance of their servers and at the same time reduce the delays associated with slow server response due to an overloaded host.

The technique I will describe is a Domain Name System (DNS) technique that provides a different server for each new connection. When a client contacts DNS to find the IP address of the server, it will answer with a rotating list of IPs so each request will be replied with a different machine in a round-robin fashion. This allows for a more equal load distribution across the number of hosts you provide because each connection will be served by a different host.

For moderate traffic sites, a two-server machine will offer better performance at peak times. Some busy sites, such as www.yahoo.com, have more than nine Web servers serving requests for their main entry point, http://www.yahoo.com.

As far as users are concerned, there's only one machine, www.yahoo.com. However, the distribution helps tremendously because sites such as www.yahoo.com have very intense computational CGI loads. This positively affects responsiveness of the site.

The technique for distribution is almost trivial to implement. And while it is not guaranteed to be supported in the future because, according to the DNS Request For Comment (RFC) papers, this round-robin behavior is not defined, this solution works, and it works well. I believe many sites use this feature, and eventually the Berkeley Internet Name Domain (BIND) system release and associated RFCs will address it in a more formal way. For now, let's hope that the developers of BIND don't fix what isn't broken.

Here's a snippet of a simple db.file that implements distribution of its Web server over three different hosts (for information about setting up DNS, see Appendix E, "DNS and BIND Primer"):

```
www  IN CNAME www1.domain.COM.
     IN CNAME www2.domain.COM.
     IN CNAME www3.domain.COM.
www1 IN A    4.3.2.1
www2 IN A    4.3.2.2
www3 IN A    4.3.2.3
```

This simple setup would rotate the three addresses. However, if you observed closely and are aware of DNS caching, you'll know that this would only work for new DNS requests. Remember that DNS requests are cached for the duration of the Time To Live (TTL) delay. This delay is usually set to 24 hours (86,400 seconds). In order to avoid this caching, you'll most certainly want to set the TTL anywhere between 180–600 seconds (3–10 minutes). This will force some clients to re-request the IP of your server when the TTL has expired, forcing requests to be more evenly balanced across machines. On the downside, this setting creates a bigger DNS load. But any DNS load is minor in contrast to the volume of data that your server will move around.

It is worth mentioning that many Web browsers (Netscape included) cache DNS address/name mappings internally and disregard TTL altogether. This means that one client, once he begins accessing a given server, will stick with that particular address until the next time it is restarted. However, the distribution effect is still achieved over many different clients, and that is what is important.

For busier sites, you could implement multilevel rotations by specifying a setting such as the following:

```
www  IN CNAME www1.AccessLink.COM.
     IN CNAME www2.AccessLink.COM.
     IN CNAME www3.AccessLink.COM.
www1 IN A    4.3.2.1
     IN A    4.3.2.11
     IN A    4.3.2.21
www2 IN A    4.3.2.2
```

```
        IN A    4.3.2.12
        IN A    4.3.2.22
www3 IN A    4.3.2.3
        IN A    4.3.2.13
        IN A    4.3.2.23
```

This setup would require nine separate servers and would implement a two-level rotation. The first rotation occurs at the CNAME level and the second at each A (Alias) level.

While any server rotation technique may only be useful on heavily loaded sites, it is very useful when combined with multihomed Web servers. By making distributed servers multihomed, you have the ability to build a more reliable Web service. Not only would the load be distributed between machines, but in case of a failure, one of the mirror servers could take over transparently. Even if the system administrator didn't become aware of the problem immediately, the virtual (or real) sites would continue to operate by providing uninterrupted service. Naturally, this robustness is equally valuable for distributed single-homed sites. But because the likelihood of a server failure is greater on a multihomed host (Murphy's Law), preparing for such a disaster and implementing a fault-tolerant service may be the best tool to use to avoid a server outage.

RAM

Because Web servers are RAM hogs, RAM is the one hardware addition that will pay off big. RAM helps every part of your system. The more RAM you have, the better your system works.

How much RAM is enough? There isn't a single administrator who wouldn't love to have 256MB of RAM on his server. So it depends. If you have a RISC machine, you'll probably need double the memory of an equivalent CISC box. Some smaller sites with limited traffic can do very well with less than 16MB of RAM. A good starting point probably is 32MB. You can then start monitoring your server for bottlenecks and add RAM as needed.

One easy way to test for memory bottlenecks is to use the vmstat (or vm_stat) command, which will display virtual memory statistics for your system. You want to watch the number of pageins and pageouts, which tell you how much swapping your system is doing. If it gets so bad that you can hear the machine constantly swapping (the disk is making constant accesses), you are in trouble. Go buy some RAM.

One way to reduce the amount of RAM your system consumes is to limit the number of services that are running on the server. If your Web server is a busy one, and you are also running a myriad of other services such as DNS, NFS, NNTP, SMTP, shell accounts, and FTP, your system will have to divide its resources between those tasks. Running only the necessary services on your server box will allow you to maximize your resources. If the machine is not a mail server, you can probably have `sendmail`, the mail daemon, run under `inetd`. Do the same for any other services that you may want available but are nonessential. You may want to consider using separate boxes to provide all the other services, thus freeing resources for the Web server to do its thing.

If you have a Web server that makes heavy use of CGI, the performance of your server will decrease. One way to alleviate this problem is to recode the CGI program to a compiled language instead of an interpreted script. Both programs do the same thing, but the speed and efficiency of a compiled binary can be several orders of magnitude greater. The section in this chapter titled, "CGI Program Tuning," discusses the CGI impact in more detail.

DISK TUNING

Disk speed is probably one of the first bottlenecks you'll run into. The speed of a modern hard disk does not even begin to match the capacity of some of the most common processors. Disks are the turtles of the system, and Web servers demand a lot from them. After all, all requests end up generating a disk access of some sort. The faster your processor is able to read the disk and process it, the faster it can go handle another request.

Although purchasing a faster disk can help a lot, adding a dedicated disk subsystem to handle swapping (your server should not really swap anyway), log files, and data files will help even more. For real performance, a RAID solution may be the only way to go for data storage in a heavily loaded server.

RAID

The concept of RAID was developed at the University of California at Berkeley in 1987 by Patterson, Gibson, and Katz in a paper titled, "A Case for Redundant Arrays of Inexpensive Disks (RAID)."

The idea behind RAID is to combine several small, inexpensive disks into a battery of disk drives, yielding performance exceeding that of a Single Large Expensive Drive (SLED). All disks in the array appear as a single logical storage unit, or a single disk, to the computer. Because the disk controller(s) and the host processor are able to request or initiate read or write operations more quickly than any disk can satisfy them, having multiple disks allows some degree of parallelism and concurrency between transactions. Another important consideration is that by spreading a single data file on various disks (striping), all disks can work concurrently. This provides better load balancing than would be otherwise possible. Without this improved load balancing, some disks would end up doing most of the work. By distributing the load, requests can be fulfilled more quickly because each disk has less to do. This allows each drive to work on a different read/write operation and maximizes the number of simultaneous I/Os that the array can perform, thus increasing the transfer rate.

Although RAID offers a big enhancement in performance, your mileage may vary depending on the RAID configuration implemented. Also, it is important to note that using more hardware increases the likelihood of a failure; given that data is spread across multiple disks, a drive failure could be catastrophic. RAID can achieve increased reliability by mirroring data on duplicate drives or by using error-recovery technology that allows on-the-fly data reconstruction. However, this redundancy comes with a performance trade-off.

RAID systems usually allow for the hot-swapping of drive components without having to halt the system. On replacement, most RAID implementations reconstruct data that was stored on the failed drive, allowing the array to continue operation at optimal speeds. On the current commercial RAID offerings, an array will tolerate the loss of a single drive, but multiple drive failures in the array will destroy data. Most catastrophic array failures are due to the system administrator's lack of awareness of a drive going bad; failure of a second drive is what causes the devastating consequences.

STRIPING

The basis for RAID is *striping*, which is a method of integrating several disk drives into a single logical storage unit that offers parallelism in the I/O (see Figure 12.1).

Figure 12.1.
Striping disk
drives. Data
stripes from disks
A, B, and C are
interleaved to
create a single
logical storage
unit.

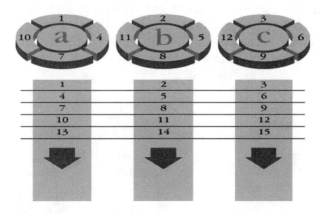

The same way normal (non-stripe) storage space is organized into sectors on a single disk, the RAID system is able to partition drives into stripes. These stripes start on one disk and continue to the next. Unlike adjacent disk sectors, adjacent stripe sectors are located on different disks. This allows the individual drives to fetch portions of the data at the same time.

Stripes can be as small as one sector (512 bytes) or as large as several megabytes; the size of the stripe determines how responsive the array is. Large stripes allow for concurrent access to different files because the data is not necessarily spread across all disks. Small stripes provide quick data transfers without the concurrency because the data has to be retrieved from all drives. The stripes are interleaved in a round-robin fashion so that the storage space is composed of stripes in each drive. For each read or write transaction, each drive reads or writes its own stripe. When the stripes are combined, you have the complete data.

Unlike storage that is on separate disks, which is never balanced (data stored in one disk may be used more frequently than data on another disk), data striping divides work evenly among all drives. Balancing the disk I/O across all the drives greatly reduces the time required to access files.

Single-user systems benefit from small stripes (512 bytes) because they help ensure that most of the data spans across all drives in the array. Small stripes also help to access large files because most of the operations can occur concurrently. The negative effect of a small-stripe partition is that if the drives are not synchronized, performance worsens relative to the number of drives in the array. This is because the I/O operation is not completed until the last disk drive has finished its read or write operation.

There are several different RAID topologies, labeled RAID 0 through 7.

RAID 0: NON-REDUNDANT STRIPED ARRAY

RAID 0 is a non-redundant group of striped disk drives. That means that if one drive fails, the entire array fails. Failure is an important concern of any RAID strategy. Under a RAID setup, the Mean Time Between Failures (MTBF) rating listed by a drive should be divided by the number of drives in the setup. A diagram of RAID 0 can be found in Figure 12.2.

Figure 12.2. Non-redundant striped array. Data stripes from disks A, B, and C are interleaved to create a single logical storage unit. Reads and writes can occur concurrently on all drives.

The best performance in any RAID configuration is on a RAID 0 configuration. This is because no data-integrity processing is done on read or write operations, and because disks can perform concurrently. The array can have two or more disks.

RAID 0 supports multiple concurrent read and write transactions on short requests. Longer read and write transactions can be split and handled concurrently.

RAID 1: MIRRORED ARRAYS

RAID 1 provides disk mirroring—information is duplicated to both disks. Each adapter manages two drives. There is no striping between the two disks; information is duplicated to both disks. However, you can stripe several RAID 1 arrays together. A diagram of RAID 1 can be found in Figure 12.3.

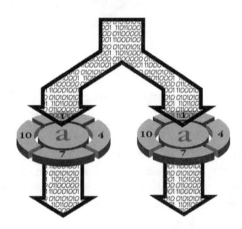

Figure 12.3. A mirrored array. Data is written in duplicate to drives A and B. Different read transactions can occur concurrently on either drive.

To maintain the mirroring, both disks write the same data. Therefore, RAID 1 offers no performance gains on write accesses. However, different read transactions can occur simultaneously, with a performance increase of 100 percent. RAID 1 delivers the best performance of any RAID in a multi-user environment. It provides faster short- and long-read transactions because the operations can resolve to either of the disks.

Write transactions are slower because both disks must write the same amount of data. Implementing RAID 1 can be quite expensive because it requires double the number of disks and double the storage capacity.

RAID 2: PARALLEL ARRAY WITH ERROR-CORRECTING CODE (ECC) DATA PROTECTION DISK

RAID 2 uses a sector-stripe array. Data is written to a group of drives with some drives storing the ECC. Because most modern drives store ECC information at the end of a sector, this configuration offers no particular advantage over a RAID 3 configuration. A diagram of RAID 1 can be found in Figure 12.4.

Figure 12.4. Parallel array with ECC. Multiple drives are striped for data storage. ECC is stored on one or more drives. Read and write transactions span all drives.

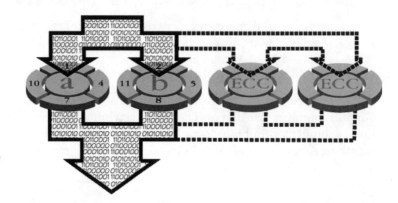

The ECC is calculated from the multiple-disks stripe and stored in a separate drive. Reads happen at normal speed. Writes are slower than normal because of the ECC that needs to be calculated and stored.

RAID 3: PARALLEL ARRAY WITH PARITY

RAID 3, like RAID 2, sectors data into stripes across a group of drives. Error detection is dependent on the ECC stored in each sector on each drive. If a failure is detected, data consistency is assured by mathematically calculating the correct data from information stored on the remaining drives. Files usually span all drives in the array, making disk transfer rates optimal. However, I/O cannot overlap because each transaction affects all drives in the array. This configuration provides the best performance for a single-user workstation. To avoid performance degradation on short-file accesses, synchronized drives, or *spindles*, are required. A diagram of RAID 3 can be found in Figure 12.5.

RAID 4: STRIPED ARRAY WITH PARITY

The configuration of RAID 4 is the same as that of RAID 3, but the size of the stripes is larger, which allows read operations to be overlapped. Write operations have to update the parity drive and cannot be overlapped. This configuration offers no significant advantage over a RAID 5 configuration. RAID 4 disk arrays can have three or five disks. A diagram for RAID 4 can be found in Figure 12.6.

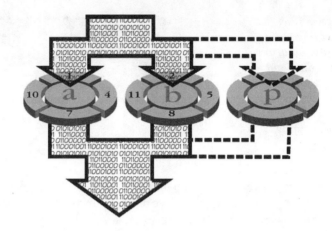

Figure 12.5.
Parallel array
with parity.
Multiple drives
are striped for
data storage.
Parity is stored
on one drive.
Read and write
transactions span
all drives. In the
event of a
hardware failure,
the data from the
failed drive can
be reconstructed
on-the-fly from
the data stored on
the other drives.

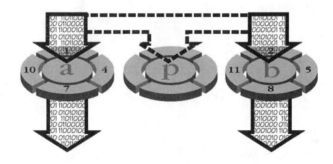

Figure 12.6.
Striped array
with parity.
Stripes in this
configuration are
larger, so read
and write
transactions can
occur concur-
rently. Because
there is only a
single-parity
drive, all write
transactions need
to update the
parity drive.

RAID 5: ROTATING PARITY ARRAY

RAID 5 implements a rotating parity array that eliminates the bottleneck of the single-parity drive configuration used in RAID 4. RAID 5 uses large stripes to enable the overlap of multiple I/O transactions. Each drive takes a turn storing parity for a stripe. Most write operations access only a single data drive and the current parity drive. Write operations can overlap. A diagram for RAID 5 can be found in Figure 12.7.

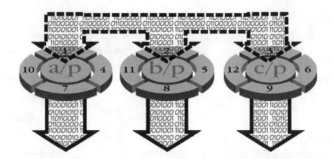

Figure 12.7. Rotating parity array. All drives store data and parity information. Reads and writes can occur concurrently.

This is the best configuration for a fault-tolerant setup in a multi-user environment that is not performance sensitive or that performs few write operations. Disk arrays can have between three and seven disks. RAID 5 is efficient because it uses parity information instead of duplicating data. However, because parity information must be calculated for all drives with each write operation, write operations are not as efficient. This setup is not recommended for applications that write data. Read operations, such as those sustained by a Web server, are better with RAID 5 than with the RAID 1 counterpart. For a Web server application, RAID 5 provides the best performance and reliability.

RAID 6

RAID 6 describes a scheme involving a two-dimensional disk array that promises to tolerate any two-drive failure; however, no commercial implementation of RAID 6 exists as of this writing.

RAID 7

RAID 7 is a marketing term created by Storage Computer, Inc. Information on the Internet about RAID 7 indicates that while some of RAID 7's performance claims may be worthwhile, RAID 7 is controversial because of its use of a cache. A few major vendors have started to introduce RAID 7 products. RAID 7 is basically just RAID with caching.

SOFTWARE STRIPING

Some operating systems include software striping options, which allow your system to effectively implement RAID. However, there is a trade-off in performance, as well as additional CPU overhead, when these options are used. Some of the vendors and operating systems that offer software striping options include Silicon Graphics, Linux, Hewlett-Packard, and Sun. For more information, check your UNIX documentation.

NETWORK TUNING

For a busy site, network tuning will be the second major performance issue you'll face. Even if your disk subsystem is tuned for optimal performance, its impact will be limited unless you are able to push data through the wire quickly enough. Here are a few issues to consider:

◆ The size of your connection to the Internet backbone and the speed of your WAN interface. Increasing these is the most costly enhancement, but any serious Web service requires ISDN or better. An ISDN service may be more than adequate for personal Web servers, but typically, network bandwidth of less than a DS-1 (T-1) won't be able to handle any sort of intense traffic. Large providers will need DS-3 connections.

◆ The speed of your local Ethernet network, 10Mbps (Megabits per second) Ethernet or 100Mbps Ethernet. This factor dictates how long network transactions will take and is affected by local traffic on your local area network (LAN). If you have a large number of systems on your network, chances are your network is not performing well. Add traffic from the outside, and it's no wonder the network seems slow! There are hardware and organizational solutions to this problem; the organizational solutions are described in the "Network Topology Tuning" section later in this chapter.

These issues can be addressed by limiting traffic to well-defined sections of your network or by adjusting the size of your network plumbing to match your needs. The bigger the pipes and the pumps, the better the performance.

NETWORK SERVICES (WAN)

How much bandwidth you have depends on the type of service to which you subscribe. For Internet information providers, this is generally some sort of leased line. The faster the line, the more expensive it is. Top-of-the-line DS-3 services cost tens of thousands of dollars per month. This figure doesn't even include the initial cost of the networking hardware, which can easily be over $80,000, plus any other setup fees and the rental of the line! New technologies are going to increase bandwidth for consumers, and if the pricing is attractive, many providers may begin looking at them as possible additions to or replacements for their current leased lines. (See Table 12.1.)

Telephone companies, with their huge infrastructure, are in a position to bring the price of this technology down, making it affordable to almost anyone. Network plumbing varies greatly in price and performance. For a graphical comparison of the various options, see Figures 12.8 and 12.9. The shaded areas are proportional to the amount of data they can carry. Table 12.1 presents the various services available for a WAN interface and the monthly costs associated with them.

Figure 12.8. Relative size comparison of 100Mbps Ethernet, DS-3, and 10Mbps Ethernet.

Figure 12.9. Relative size comparison of 10Mbps Ethernet, DS-1, ISDN, DS-0, and 28.8 modems.

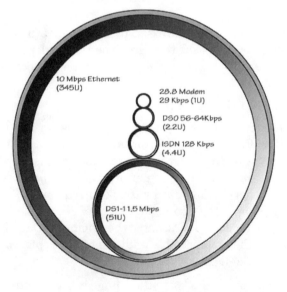

TABLE 12.1. SERVICE AND PRICE COMPARISON FOR DEDICATED SERVICES.

Service Type	Bandwidth	Price/Month
DS-3/ATM	45,000Kbps	>$25,000
ADSL/DMT Modems* (downloading)	1,500-8,000Kbps	Unknown
T-1 or DS-1 (Digital Service 1)	1,500Kbps	$770–$950
ISDN	128Kbps	$325–$450
ADSL/DMT Modems* (uploading)	64-768Kbps	Unknown
DS-0 (Digital Service 0)	56-64Kbps	$180–$225
28.8 Modem	29Kbps	$95–$150

The Price/Month column doesn't include costs related to leasing the line that connects you to the Internet Service Provider (ISP). Typically, you could approximate costs by figuring that a single voice line is $30/month. 28.8 modems, DS-0, and ADSL/DMT lines* take a single line. Any other service requires multiple lines. An ISDN line requires two lines ($60/month); a DS-1 line requires 24 lines ($720/month); a full DS-3 needs around 672 lines ($20,160/month).

Dedicated network connections vary in price depending on your geographic location, your distance from the provider, the length of your contract, and other factors. The following sections describe the most common services.

DS-0 (DIGITAL SERVICE 0)

DS-0 service is used to enhance two- or four-wire voice or analog data, providing a single transmission channel between the end user and the provider. It can also be used as a dedicated link between two remote office locations.

DS-1 (DIGITAL SERVICE 1)

A DS-1 service has a capacity of 1.544Mbps and can carry up to 24 64Kbps voice-grade signals. This service is also known as a T-1, referring to the "T Carrier" digital communication system.

DS-3 (DIGITAL SERVICE 3)

A DS-3 circuit has the capacity of 44.736Mbps. It is the equivalent of 28 DS-1 circuits, having a capacity of 672 voice-grade signals. This service is also known as a T-3. This is a very high-capacity service.

---

* ADSL/DMT modems are not available at the moment, but they promise to provide incredible performance using a single telephone line.

DISCRETE MULTITONE ASYMMETRICAL DIGITAL SUBSCRIBER LINE (ADSL)

New technology, such as Discrete Multitone ADSL, promises to deliver incredible performance inexpensively. The technology, intended for consumer Internet access, has varying rates of bandwidth depending on the direction of the transfer. Downloads that operate from DS-1 to almost Ethernet speeds are sure to be hot with consumers. Uploads range from 64Kbps to half of a DS-1 line—respectable performance, considering that it operates over existing copper lines.

INTEGRATED SERVICES DIGITAL NETWORK (ISDN)

ISDN is a service that allows the combination of voice and data connections over a single high-speed connection. The quality of the voice line is better than the standard voice line because the service is digital. This service works over existing copper wires and requires a modem-like device. The typical consumer ISDN modem costs around $300.

LOCAL NETWORKS: ETHERNET LANs

The type of LAN you implement on your network will greatly affect the performance and reliability of your server.

An Ethernet network is a well-behaved, polite group of computers. If one talks, the others listen. However, that means that the more systems there are on the wire, the more time computers are going to spend waiting to talk. If two talk at the same time, a packet collision occurs. On detecting a collision, all computers will randomly reset their talk interval to avoid a *deadlock*, which is a condition where the collision continues to occur due to a predetermined silence period.

One way to improve performance is to have a faster Ethernet. The faster the network, the quicker the packets travel and the more opportunity each system has to talk and deliver its message. Ethernet LANs come in two flavors: 10Mbps and 100Mbps.

In contrast to most WAN interfaces, Ethernet networks are very fast. However, Ethernet network capacity is only 60 to 80 percent of the rated bandwidth. On a 10Mbps Ethernet network, a server responding to 100 requests per second (each request having an average size of 7KB) is using roughly 60 percent of the available bandwidth. A network experiencing this sort of activity should have a 100Mbps Ethernet backbone support.

SOFTWARE TUNING

Software tuning will allow your system to operate optimally when given a load. There are several configuration details that will make your system more efficient; they are discussed in the following sections.

HTTP SERVER

The HTTP server software is critical. The Apache server in its default configuration is already tuned very well. Apache provides you with configuration directives that allow you to address just about every issue that could affect the performance of your server. These directives cover issues relating to the life of the HTTP children processes, the maximum and minimum number of processes the server runs, whether to enable Server Side Includes (SSI) or per-directory access control files, and so on. Configurability is one of the big strengths of the Apache server. If the server does it, you can configure it.

You will achieve maximum performance for your HTTP server by following these tips:

◆ Run a standalone server. The overhead of starting a server under inetd just won't work for any sort of real traffic.

◆ Don't log anything unless you need to. Logging takes time and resources. If you need to log, you might want to consider some of the special logging options that Apache provides. Configurable logging is one way of building audit trails that are important.

◆ If you log, don't force the DNS lookups. Requesting reverse DNS lookups takes extra work from the server. Don't use them unless you really need them. Also, log into a different disk (not just a different partition). This will allow the server to access files and write the log files almost concurrently, almost always yielding a performance enhancement for servers that do some logging.

◆ Server Side Includes. In a word: *Don't*! SSI increases disk access. In order to return a requested page, the server has to parse the SSI page, perform some computations, and then return results to the client. How much this increased disk access matters depends on the type of SSI you have. Including big files won't affect your server much, but including many small files will result in several disk accesses. If your SSI includes a header and a footer, that alone accounts for three accesses. In that same amount of time, your server could have returned the same three documents to three separate clients. Consider instead having a script that adds header and footer information to a static HTML file. The script would run under cron every so often and produce a page that the server can return without preprocessing it. Needless to say, an SSI which also makes a CGI call is twice as expensive.

◆ Per-directory access control files generate a lot of server load because the server looks for an `.htaccess` file in every directory in the path of a request, which can be very painful for deeply nested requests. As an alternative, consider putting any access restrictions in the global-access control file, `conf/access.conf`.

◆ Don't let httpd processes expire too soon. Although it does provide some benefit in terms of memory use to expire the processes every so often (some unices, notably Solaris, leak memory in some of the libraries, making a more frequent process expiration a must), that benefit comes at a cost: a new process needs to be forked to replace the old one. Forking is expensive, especially when your server is under a heavy load.

◆ If you need user authentication, use any of the database-authentication modules that Apache provides. The `dbm` module provides incredible performance gains. If you have many users on your system (I would go to `dbm` for any number of users greater than 30, although you may not notice any improvements until you have 200+ users), using one of the database-authentication systems will provide a great speed enhancement over the inefficient flat-file version. A complete description of all user-authentication modules is given in Chapter 15, "Access Control and User Authentication." If you use one of these enhanced modules, the server will spend less time checking for permissions and serving pages. These savings can be considerable on very large `htpasswd` files.

◆ Server-generated indexes are expensive. If the server needs to find out what files are on a directory before returning a list, this adds to the load. Create an `index.html` file instead, listing the contents you want to make available. If you absolutely need automatic directory indexing, you may consider writing a small program that can create an index page every so many hours versus having the server generate them on-the-fly.

◆ Don't use CGI unless you have to. If you need something that is generated on-the-fly, think about how often the data changes. There may be another way of providing an up-to-date result without having to build the page from a CGI every time. If you have some data that changes every few hours, or even every few minutes, prebuild a page that contains the same data. Requests will be fulfilled much more quickly, and the server load created by the CGI will be eliminated.

◆ If you need to use CGI, determine how server intensive your CGI is. Not all CGI programs are equal. The load generated by a Perl CGI script is several times greater than that generated by a C program. To access the load your program creates, run it by hand and use the UNIX `time` command to compute the resources. For more information, consult the time command in the first section of the manual. If you are using a csh, the `time` command is built-in. However, its output is a little different. Check your UNIX manual for more information on csh.

◆ If you are using server-side image maps, don't forget that Apache has a built-in module to handle them. Performance of the built-in module versus the CGI version is much better, and it's provided on the default Apache configuration free of charge. Even better, consider a client-side image map. However, note that client-side image maps have a different syntax from regular maps. For more information, please refer to Appendix D, "HTML Reference Guide."

TCP/IP TUNING

Your operating system's TCP/IP implementation determines the number of connections, the connection rate, and the maximum throughput that your system will achieve. Some of the default settings for your kernel may not be adequate for a high-traffic Web server.

Before you attempt to fix anything, you should try to determine whether your system has a problem. The `netstat` program provides a wealth of information that you can use to determine what is going on.

The following sections explain the enhancements you'll need to do yourself, presented system by system.

LISTEN BACKLOG (SOMAXCONN)

A frequent source to TCP/IP performance problems is attributed to the system call `listen()`. The `listen()` call is responsible for enabling incoming connections for a socket. The source of the problem is that the call sets a `backlog` parameter that specifies the maximum size that the queue of pending connections may reach. If the number of waiting connections grows beyond the defined size, the client will receive an error message that will prompt the client to issue a new request. Typically, the `backlog` parameter is set to 5, which is hopelessly inadequate.

To determine whether your system is running into trouble because of the listen backlog, type the following command:

```
netstat -n ¦ grep SYN_RCVD
```

If you continually don't get any lines listed, the listen backlog issue is not causing you grief. However, if you regularly get six or seven lines, you may be running into trouble.

The only ways to fix this problem are to rebuild the kernel or to apply a runtime kernel patch that increases the value of the `backlog` variable. If your Web server is a busy one, you definitely want to address this problem. Please note that the valid ranges for each OS are different. A great majority of operating systems can only use 256 as the maximum value.

Warning

If you rebuild your kernel, make sure you have a backup of your old kernel plus any necessary files, such as `/vmunix`. That way, in case of trouble, you can boot your computer using the old kernel. For more information on rebuilding your kernel, look at your system documentation. If you make changes to your kernel and do not have the hardware resources to match your settings, it is very likely that your computer will boot to a kernel panic.

APPLE UNIX (A/UX)

A/UX has a hardwired SOMAXCONN. You will need the patch `BNET-somax.tar.gz`, available from `ftp://ftp1.jagunet.com/pub/aux/`.

This patch is just a simple `ksh` script that patches the runtime kernel using `adb`. The documentation included in the patch specifies how to install it at system startup time.

BSDI AND FreeBSD

Look for the SOMAXCONN definition:

```
#define SOMAXCONN 5
```

which is typically found in

```
/usr/include/sys/socket.h
/usr/src/sys/sys/socket.h
```

Change the value from 5 to 32. After you make your changes, you will have to rebuild your kernel and reboot your system.

DIGITAL UNIX

You need to patch the kernel's global variable `somaxconn` using `dbx -x`. The default value is set to 8, but you can bump it up all the way to 32767. Servers with high traffic shouldn't even consider values that are less than 2048. Digital's Alta Vista servers get 5 million hits per day, and they probably have set theirs to 32767.

Digital has also published some patches that address the listen backlog and other related performance issues regarding Web servers. The patch ID is 0SF350-146. This patch improves the performance of the network subsystem for machines used as Web servers.

LINUX

Modify the following lines in `/usr/src/linux/net/inet/af_inet.c`:

```
...
if ((unsigned) backlog > 5)
backlog = 5;
...
```

Replace both instances of 5 with the size of the listen queue you want. A valid number ranges from 0 to 255, but some experts suggest not exceeding 128. Then rebuild your kernel.

SUN

On Solaris 2.4 and 2.5, you can patch the running kernel using the `ndd` command. To patch SOMAXCONN, type

```
/usr/sbin/ndd -set /dev/tcp tcp_conn_req_max N
```

where N is a number. On Solaris 2.4, the maximum value of N is 32. Solaris 2.5 defaults to 32, and the limit is 1024. You will probably want to patch this value automatically at system startup time. Do so in `/etc/rc2.d/s69inet`, putting the preceding command at the end of the file. For more information on `ndd`, check the man page.

Under SunOS 4.1.3, things are not as easy. Unless you have licensed the kernel code, you will have to patch the object code file that defines those values. The object code file is

```
/sys/sun4m/OBJ/uipc_socket.o
```

Warning

Of course, you should make a backup of the `uipc_socket.o` file before you proceed.

These modifications involve changing a value stored at octal locations 0727, 0737, and 0753 in the preceding file. You can change these values using the following program:

```
/*This program was originally developed by Mark Morley (mark@islandnet.com),
➥and was copied with permission*/
#include <stdio.h>
```

```
main()
{
  FILE* fp;
  fp = open("/sys/sun4m/OBJ/uipc_socket.o", "r+");
  if (fp != NULL){
    fseek(fp, 0727, 0 );
    putc( 128, fp );
    fseek( fp, 0737, 0 );
    putc( 128, fp );
    fseek (fp, 0757, 0 );
    putc( 128, fp );
    fclose( fp )
  printf("/sys/sun4m/OBJ/uipc_socket.o was successfully patched.
➡You need to rebuild your kernel and restart\n");
    exit(0);
  }
  printf("Sorry /sys/sun4m/OBJ/uipc_socket.o could not be open\n");
  exit(-1);
}
```

FILE SYSTEM TUNING

Most HTTP requests will involve a disk access, so the performance of your file system will be tested. Some systems allow you to implement RAID in software at the cost of some additional processing overhead.

CGI PROGRAM TUNING

If a significant number of the requests processed by your server involve CGI execution, the performance of your Web server will be closely related to the performance of the CGI programs.

CGI is inherently inefficient; request requires the server to fork a process. The process then needs to initialize itself, execute, and exit. If the CGI is based on some interpreted programming language, such as Perl or Tcl, the process is even more demanding because an interpreter will have to be launched, the script compiled, and then finally executed.

Porting your CGI to a compiled language is one way of improving the performance of your programs. Another way of enhancing program performance is by using FastCGI or an embedded interpreter, or in some cases, by developing a server module that accomplishes what you need.

If you have a server that frequently incurs hits from CGI programs, you might want to consider one of these solutions:

◆ Compiled CGI
◆ FastCGI

- ◆ Embedded Interpreters
- ◆ Distributed CGI servers

COMPILED CGI

Porting the most-used CGI to C or some other compiled language will increase performance a lot. You may want to take a look at server-side compiled JavaScript or WebObjects as an environment to develop Web applications (intranets).

WebObjects offers some very interesting technology. WebObjects was developed by NeXT Software, Inc. (http://www.next.com), a leader in object-oriented software development technology. The WebObjects package currently runs under Windows NT, Sun Solaris, NeXTSTEP, and OPENSTEP for Mach. A version will be available for Hewlett-Packard's HPUX in the near future.

WebObjects is an environment for interfacing objects to the Internet via the Web. WebObjects' object technology is based on NeXT's OPENSTEP technology. It uses NeXT's *Enterprise Objects Framework* (EOF) for database access and *Portable Distributed Objects* (PDO) for object distribution. PDO provides automatic load balancing of CGI between various CGI servers. It all happens automatically, and is fully compatible with any HTTP server with a CGI, ISAPI, or NSAPI interface (including Apache). WebObjects allows you to publish dynamic content and materials obtained from a database or some other dynamic source through the Web.

WebObjects provides the scripting language WebScript. It will also provide full support for VBScript, Perl, and JavaScript in the very near future.

FASTCGI

Of the various options, FastCGI may be the one you'll want to explore first because it can potentially provide you with the greatest benefits while requiring the least efforts. For more information, check out Appendix C, "FastCGI."

FastCGI is a high-performance extension to the CGI standard that offers a significant improvement in performance over the existing CGI program interface. FastCGI is improved CGI; however, the programming methods are virtually the same. FastCGI accomplishes its performance enhancement by having the CGI be a long-lived process. The long-lived process remains ready to serve requests until it is destroyed by the system administrator or the server stops running.

This difference can have a dramatic effect on the performance of your programs and the servers that run them. The performance savings are really noticeable especially if your program needs to establish a connection with a database or some other process. A FastCGI application will maintain a connection to the database server, eliminating this time-consuming step. FastCGI requests are almost as fast as requesting a static document, and that is a tremendous improvement!

DISTRIBUTED CGI SERVERS

Another way of reducing the CGI load is to dedicate servers for CGI execution. Netscape runs CGI servers on their network.

FastCGI can be used for this purpose as well. It can connect to any process via a TCP/IP connection. This means that you have your Web server separate from your FastCGI servers.

Some CGI development systems offer automatic CGI load balancing. WebObjects allows you to use distributed objects that provide services to any processes on your network. The system is distributed by design. When a process looks for a service, it will bind to the first server process that answers the request. This has the effect of making the least utilized servers the ones more likely to answer first, hence the load distribution. Not only can one item be distributed, but different objects can seamlessly bind to other objects in the network, making the application truly distributed.

DATABASES

More and more applications of Web server technology involve intranet technology. An *intranet* is an internal application deployed over the Web. Web technology is proving to be a viable solution for implementing client-independent mission-critical applications. Any system capable of using a browser has access to the corporate information. This scales well when you consider that a typical network houses systems of various architectures and operating systems. Software development on the server side ensures a great reduction in software-development costs. Intranet applications ultimately depend on the performance of the database server and the CGI programs used to access the data.

KERNEL TUNING

Although there are a few well-known ways to increase your Web server's performance, such as the SOMAXCOMM kernel variable discussed in the preceding section, there are other software bottlenecks that are less known.

As operating-system vendors are learning about these bottlenecks, they are quickly fixing them. Some of these kernel enhancements offer Web server speed improvements of 33 percent or better over previous versions of the operating system. One of the best things you can do as a webmaster is keep informed of these updates and evaluate whether these changes will enhance your system.

A/UX

You might want to update the NMBUFS kernel variable if you are finding many connections with a TIME_WAIT status. You can easily determine how many connections have this status by running the netstat command. The value you need for NMBUFS should be a lot higher than you might think. Mid-transfer disconnections will make sockets unavailable for several minutes, impeding the formation of new good connections. A good value for NMBUFS is 4096.

BSDI AND FreeBSD

You may want to up the maxusers kernel variable. This variable controls several things, including

◆ The maximum number of system processes

◆ The maximum number of processes per user

◆ The maximum number of open files

◆ The maximum number of files that processes can have open

If your server is heavily loaded, you might want to consider upping maxusers to 256, but make sure that you have enough RAM resources for that. The maxusers variable will increase the value of several other kernel variables. For information on the values derived from the maxusers variable, see the file /usr/src/sys/conf/param.c.

If you find that there are many connections with a TIME_WAIT status when you run the netstat command, you may want to up the NMBCLUSTERS value. The value you need for this should be a lot higher than what you might think. Mid-transfer disconnections will make sockets unavailable for several minutes, impeding the formation of new good connections. A good value for NMBCLUSTERS is 4096.

Linux

In the file /usr/src/kernel/linux/include/fs.h changes NR_OPEN from 256 to 1024 and NR_FILE from 1024 to 2048.

Network Topology Tuning

The number of hosts that you have on your network will affect your network's overall performance. By rethinking and reorganizing the layout of your network, you might be able to reduce your network traffic, allowing the server to send and receive data.

12

NETWORK PLUMBING 99

Before discussing how the size of the pipe affects your data speed, it is useful to understand just what travels through your pipe. After all, you cannot be a plumber until you know about water. The water in your network is the data, and its motion through the wire on the Internet is controlled by a set of networking protocols known collectively as *TCP/IP*. TCP/IP is named after the two main protocols used: Transmission Control Protocol (RFC793) and Internet Protocol (RFC791).

The success of TCP/IP is attributed to its design. It was developed under an open standard, which means the protocol is independent of any particular operating system or hardware. Because of this independence, TCP/IP is able to run over a dial-up connection, Ethernet, X.25 Net, token rings, or virtually any other physical medium.

The TCP fits into a layered protocol architecture above the Internet Protocol. The Internet Protocol provides TCP with a mechanism to send and receive data packets of variable length that have been prepackaged in an Internet envelope, also called a *datagram*.

The datagram provides a way of addressing the sender and recipient TCP packets in different networks.

The layers used by the protocol are

- ◆ The Application Layer
- ◆ The TCP Layer
- ◆ The IP Layer
- ◆ The Network Layer

THE NETWORK OR COMMUNICATION LAYER

The *Network Layer* is responsible for handling the specifics of moving a piece of data through the underlying hardware. This layer also manages electrical voltages and interfaces (connectors), as well as packet sizes and structures required to transfer a packet from one point to another through a particular network. This portion of the protocol is not part of TCP; rather, it is merely used by the protocol. Hardware designers are responsible for implementing the details necessary for the TCPs to be able to use the underlying hardware.

THE INTERNET PROTOCOL LAYER

The *Internet Protocol Layer*, or *Routing Layer*, is the foundation of the Internet. It defines the transmission unit, the datagram, and the addressing scheme; connects the Network Layer to the TCP Layer, routes datagrams between hosts, and splits and reassembles datagrams into sizes appropriate for the underlying network hardware.

A datagram, as I mentioned, is the envelope used for delivering the data. It contains several pieces of information, including the source address that generated the datagram, the destination of the datagram, a serial number so that the data can be reassembled in the right order, and a check sum value that can be used to determine whether the datagram arrived intact.

When a datagram is sent between two hosts, if the recipient host is outside of the local Net, it gets forwarded to a gateway. This gateway is typically a router. It in turn forwards the datagram to other gateways until the datagram is delivered to a gateway that knows how to deliver it to its final destination—a host or another device local to that network.

A *router* is a specialized computer that forwards datagrams across networks. Although this might seem like a simple task, it is in fact quite involved. Packets not acknowledged within the given time period will get re-sent, requiring the router to figure out where to process and forward packets rapidly. Routers build dynamic tables to help forward datagrams to different networks. If a router has various ways of forwarding the datagram, it will forward (unless directed by a static route) the packet in the most efficient way possible.

In order for one device to communicate with another on an IP network (be it the Internet or your local TCP/IP network), each device must know three different pieces of information:

◆ An Internet Protocol (IP) address
◆ A network submask
◆ The broadcast address

IP ADDRESSES

An IP is an address format used on TCP networks and the Internet. It is composed of four or more 8-bit numbers represented as octets. A new standard allows addressing 2^{128} computers, roughly—my calculator doesn't go that far!—3.40282367^{38}, which is a huge number! It has been said that under this scheme there are enough addresses to put 10 computers per square meter all over the world. For simplicity's sake, I'll stick to the old 32-bit implementation for these examples. Each octet can represent values ranging from 0 to 255, allowing 256 unique values. Each octet is separated by a period. Here's a sample IP address: `1.2.3.4`

The maximum number of hosts that you can address on an IP network is set by the *class* of the address. There are currently three address classes: A, B, and C. (See Table 12.2.)

TABLE 12.2. IP NETWORK CLASSES.

Address Class	Network Portion	Hosts Allowed Per Network
A	`1.-127.`	More than 16 million
B	`128.0-191.255.`	65,536
C	`192.0.0-223.255.255`	255

RESERVED ADDRESSES

In order for a device to work on a network, it needs to know three addresses:

◆ The IP address

◆ A network mask

◆ A broadcast address

The *IP address* is the address of the device. Outside networks don't know anything about your subnet mask, which is just an internal organization tool for you. Instead, outside networks reference the device by its IP address. The *network mask* tells your router how to interpret the IP address, specifying which portion of the address corresponds to the network address and which portion corresponds to the host portion of the address.

The *broadcast address* is a special address to which all devices on the network listen. Routing information is propagated this way, as are messages you send using the UNIX `wall` (write-all) program. Typically, address 0, or the first address in the subnet range, belongs to the address of the network or subnet. Address 255, or the last address available to the subnet range, is used as the broadcast address. (See Table 12.3.) What this means to you is that when you add a subnet, you give away two IPs per subnet for overhead in exchange for the organizational and performance benefits of subnetting.

TABLE 12.3. MASKS AND THEIR EFFECT ON A C-CLASS ADDRESS.

Address Class	Default Mask
255.255.255.0	The C-class address mask. Hosts' numbers range from 1–254. 0 and 255 are reserved for the network and broadcast addresses, respectively.
255.255.255.128	2 subnets with hosts numbered: 1-126, 129-254 0 & 127 are reserved for the network address; 127 and 255 are reserved for broadcast address.

Address Class	Default Mask
255.255.255.192	4 subnets: 1-62, 65-126, 129-190, 193-254.
255.255.255.224	8 subnets, each with 30 possible hosts.
255.255.255.240	16 subnets, each with 14 possible hosts.
255.255.255.248	32 subnets, each with 6 possible hosts.

The number of hosts available listed in Table 12.3 takes into account the requirement for network and broadcast addresses.

Typically, unless you are a large organization, your IP address will be a C-class address. Even if your gateway to the Internet is through a DS-1 line, having a 100Mbps Ethernet network may improve the performance and responsiveness of your servers, as well as help you maximize the potential of your DS-1 line.

SUBNETTING

Another way to improve performance is to reduce the amount of traffic that gets into your network in the first place. If you have a busy Web server, network traffic to and from the server will slow your local network activity. By segmenting your network into various smaller networks, you allow each of the segments to operate at peak performance. If you have high traffic, you might want to consider putting your Web server on its own subnet.

Subnetworks require the installation of additional hardware, namely bridges or routers. Routers don't grab packets that are not destined for their LAN. By subnetting, you are basically reducing the number of hosts you can have on each subnet, thus eliminating the amount of data that can travel through your subnet. Only traffic that is destined for elsewhere will exit the subnet. If you organize subnets around workgroups, you will have the opportunity to better your network organization. Some of the benefits of subnetting follow:

◆ Subnetting will help you isolate traffic within your network. This may actually be a security benefit, because traffic from a department won't be reaching other parts of your organization, helping you tighten security and privacy of information. In R&D departments, you can ensure that experimental software or hardware doesn't hose your entire network.

◆ If you manage a large network, using subnets may allow you to delegate network administration and IP management to smaller departments within your organization. Problems within each network segment will then affect only that portion of the network. If these network segments have their own system administrator, you won't have to deal with problems that arise within them.

◆ Subnetting can also help you isolate independent departments within your organizational structure without losing the overall control of your large network. This can have several benefits. Each department could handle its own internal network, but coordination of the corporate network could still go through a central control, thus ensuring that the left hand knows what the right hand is doing.

BUILDING A SUBNET

Building a subnet is not too tricky. However, there are a couple of things that you will need to understand: the math behind network masks and the reserved IPs that you cannot use for a machine.

The main thing you must decide is the number of segments you want to create. Subnetting works by specifying a different network mask from the default. The network mask specifies how many bits of the IP address belong to the network portion of the address. However many bits are left can be used for the host portion of the address. Table 12.4 lists the default network mask for each address class.

TABLE 12.4. DEFAULT NETWORK MASKS.

Address Class	Default Mask
A	255.0.0.0
B	128.0-191.255
C	192.0.0-223.255.255

Some of the octets represent network numbers, others represent host numbers. Each octet represents a function of the network mask. A *mask* is simply a binary number that specifies which bits belong to the network and which bits belong to the host portion. Bits that are "on" (represented by 1) will be used for network address.

For example, if you have an IP, such as 204.95.222.100, and the mask for this IP is 255.255.255.0, you can determine that the host portion can use all bits in the last octet; that amounts to 256 unique values ranging from 0–255. I find it easier to work with masks in binary:

```
204.95.222.100:  11001100.01011111.11011110.01100100
255.255.255.0:   11111111.11111111.11111111.00000000
```

In the next example the mask was set to 255.255.255.128:

```
204.95.222.100:   11001100.01011111.11011110.01100100
255.255.255.128:  11111111.11111111.11111111.10000000
```

This mask yields an extra bit for the network address (shown in bold). This means that you can have two subnets, and the host portion can use 7 bits, or 127 unique addresses, for each of the subnets.

CACHING PROXY SERVERS: REDUCING THE BANDWIDTH YOU CONSUME

Caching proxy servers can be a powerful tool in your arsenal to increase the performance of your internal Web traffic. While originally developed as a way of allowing access to the Web through a firewall, proxy servers can also be used to reduce the traffic your organization generates to popular Web sites.

Versions of Apache, beginning with 1.1, include a caching proxy server module that enables Apache to function as a caching proxy server.

WHAT IS A PROXY SERVER?

A proxy server is a Web server that sits between a local client and an external Web server. It acts as an intermediary to the client and fetches information from other Web servers. Instead of a client connecting to a server on the Internet directly, it establishes a connection with a proxy server in the user's local network. The proxy server then retrieves the resources requested and serves them to the client as if the resources were its own.

Besides negotiating a transaction for a client, proxy servers usually cache data they receive from other servers. Over time this cache will grow rich in pages from the most popular destinations on the Internet, allowing subsequent requests to be served from the local proxy.

Instead of each request consuming your WAN bandwidth, subsequent requests to the same URL are served from the cache, locally and at LAN speeds. This virtually eliminates the bulk of the traffic to previously contacted sites and improves access times dramatically. This functionality has the effect of freeing bandwidth that would have been used to download duplicate information for other purposes, such as to serve your company's pages to outside users.

If your connection to the Internet is not very fast, a catching proxy server can help you enhance your access to some of the most frequented sites on the Internet. Obviously, performance enhancements you obtain from a cache will depend on the richness of the cache, the surfing patterns of your users, and the amount of disk resources that you are willing to dedicate for this purpose.

Overall, dedicating a caching server in your organization may provide many potential benefits to warrant its deployment. Setup of a proxy is not complicated and requires very little administrative time.

CONTENT TUNING

So far, most of the issues I have talked about revolve around the software and hardware behind the server, but it is worth mentioning that there is one more way you can optimize performance.

The less bandwidth that your content requires for transmission, the more quickly transfers will occur. Organizing and breaking your documents into smaller pieces will help tremendously. For example, if you have a DS-1 line, you are capable of transmitting about 200KB per second. If your line were to support 50 users per second at optimal speed, your average reply should not exceed 4KB. Although requiring that each of your pages be 4KB in size is a very unreasonable request, it can help you to understand how many users your line can realistically support. The smaller your line, the smaller your reply content should be.

I have seen many Web pages that take quite a few seconds to download. Pages and images that are carefully designed can help provide the feel of a very fast site. Many designers who develop graphics for Web pages don't know how to prepare graphics that maximize the intent of the work while minimizing image size.

GRAPHICS

If you are using Graphical Interchange Format (GIF) files, you should be aware of Netscape's color cube. Netscape's color cube only supports 6×6×6 combinations of colors, or 216 colors. Any color that doesn't fall in the cube will be dithered. The Netscape color palette includes the values 00, 33, 66, 99, CC, and FF for each of the RGB channels. Some programs, such as Adobe's Photoshop, allow you to specify a custom color lookup table (CLUT) when converting images to GIF format. If you map and dither to this CLUT, what you see on your screen is what everyone else will see, too.

Also, be aware that Netscape has only four grays plus black and white, which can be very limiting. If you have artwork that is grayscale (no color), convert it to grayscale and then back to RGB format. This will set any pixels that dithered to a grayish tone but still will contain some color information to a true grayscale. You can then convert your artwork to GIF and map the grays to those that fall within the cube.

For a very interesting resource, visit http://www.adobe.com. This site has information on color reduction techniques that are very effective. They also have a CLUT available that you can use in Photoshop, which contains the Netscape palette.

Also visit the home of the Bandwidth Conservation Society at http://www.infohiway.com/faster/index.html. Their site contains a lot of information on how to get the most out of your images without requiring huge file transfers.

Another great tool that I use all the time is DeBabelizer. DeBabelizer is a powerful graphics program by Equilibrium (http://www.equilibrium.com) that can translate between many image formats. More importantly, it has a great color dithering algorithm that will reduce colors (reduce the file size) while maintaining an equally pleasing image. In most instances the results are amazing, and the reductions are significant. Color reductions by this software render equally well on all graphically capable browsers, eliminating color discrepancy issues.

Tip

Photographic images are usually smaller, and they dither better when saved in Joint Picture Experts Group (JPEG) format. Be aware that some old browsers don't support inline JPEG files.

CLIENT-SIDE IMAGE MAPS

Client-side image maps embed the map file right into the HTML document sent to the client. On selection, the browser does the hit detection and requests the appropriate document, instead of passing down the coordinates where the user clicked back to the server.

Client-side image maps will help remove a load from the server. However, their operation is not reliable on all browsers yet, and it's only supported by Netscape and Microsoft Internet Explorer. Netscape seems to dislike polygonal areas, while Microsoft Internet Explorer seems to work just fine.

SUMMARY

This chapter covers a great number of topics. Tuning your system for efficiency as you can see covers every possible area. There's so much an administrator can do that it is impossible to cover it all in one chapter. Your best strategy is to determine where the bottlenecks are and what can be done to address them. Many of the solutions will involve money. To make your action list work, you may want to assign a price to all possible solutions. That usually helps you to narrow your choices.

A great resource for tuning your server is Adrian Cockroft's Q&A article. It is available at http://www.sun.com:80/sunworldonline/swol-03-1996/swol-03-perf.html.

CHAPTER 13

Web Accounting

Soon after a Web site is up and running, you will get many requests for Web traffic statistics. Log administration, in terms of providing accounting information, ("Web accounting"), will be one of the primary services you'll be involved with after your Web site is up and running.

The importance and relevance of any Web accounting information depends on what you are going to do with it. If you are not going to do anything with this information, then don't even enable it!

However, Web accounting allows you to create a database of information that you can use in many aspects of your Web site administration. Even when deciding to implement a browser-specific feature, you may be interested in knowing how many visitors will be able to take advantage of the new feature. Logging provides the answers to this question and others, including the following:

◆ Who is visiting your Web site?

◆ How many visitors are there and where are they from?

◆ When do international users visit your Web site?

◆ Which Web sites refer visitors to your Web site?

◆ What are the most popular areas of your Web site?

◆ Which browsers do your visitors use?

◆ What are your Web site's peak load times?

◆ Is your Web site working properly?

All this information can be very useful to you as an administrator of the site and to the people responsible for the content. This accounting information can provide immediate feedback as to how your site is being accepted by the Internet community. If the service is useful, you will want to know which sections are more attractive to visitors and which areas need improvement. This information gives you the opportunity to modify and tweak your site to make it more responsive to your visitors' needs.

Sites that thrive on traffic will also be very interested in the traffic patterns because the cost of advertising could be rated according to the access patterns for a page. Instead of having a flat rate, you could develop a random ad banner. Ads could be targeted to match the profile of your visitors. The type of ad that appears can be dependent on factors such as the time of day, where the visitor is coming from, and so on. The possibilities are many. Chapter 5, "CGI (Common Gateway Interface) Programming," develops a program that you can use for implementing random banners.

Over time, your traffic information will grow to provide sufficient statistical information that depicts interesting patterns such as the resources most frequently requested, the peak times and days for server access, and the way that people travel from page to page.

As an administrator, your main interests will probably be centered around the overall traffic generated in terms of transfer rates. How much is requested will impact the overall performance of your server and network. The monitoring of the error logs should also be important. The error logs will provide you with information about broken links, security violation attempts, and problems related to your CGI programs. If you decide to log, you'll also have to deal with the physical management of the log files. They grow, and they grow fast!

Monitoring logs is an important task because it provides you with vital information and also acts as an indicator of the proper operation of your site.

Monitoring your site's traffic can be accomplished with many tools. Some of which are already built into your system. This chapter explores different ways that you can sift through the information and summarizes the results into useful information.

APACHE STANDARD ACCESS LOGS (COMMON LOGFILE FORMAT)

The Apache server provides several logging modules that will help you keep track of many things. The standard logging module, called `mod_log_common`, is built into Apache by default. This module logs requests using the Common Logfile Format (CLF).

Starting with Apache 1.2, the default logging module will be via `mod_log_config`, a fully configurable module. `mod_log_config` is explained in the "The `mod_log_config` Module" section later in this chapter.

Apache 1.2

The CLF is used by all major Web servers, including Apache. This is a good thing, because it means that you'll be able to run several log analysis tools that are both freely and commercially available for this purpose.

The CLF lists each request on a separate line. A line is composed of several fields separated by spaces. Fields for which information could not be obtained contain a dash character (-). Each log entry uses the following format:

```
host ident authuser date request status bytes
```

FIELDS AVAILABLE IN THE CLF

Here's a list of the data each field contains:

host   The *host* field contains the fully qualified domain name or IP, if the name was not available, of the machine that made the request.

Tip

> From a performance standpoint, you should not force your server to perform a reverse Domain Name System (DNS) lookup of the client. Some of the logging tools I'll describe can perform this reverse lookup at the time you create your reports. Apache 1.1.1 ships with a little support utility, called logresolve, which will obtain this information from the IP address stored in the log.

ident   If IdentityCheck is enabled and the client machine was running an identity daemon, the *ident* field will contain the name of the user that made the request. You should never trust this information, unless you know that the host is trusted. Otherwise, understand that this information can be spoofed and is not trustworthy. Don't bother enabling it!

authuser   If the request required authentication, the *authuser* field will contain the login of the user who made the request.

date   The *date* field contains the date and time of the request, including the offset from Greenwich Mean Time. The date format used is *day/month/year:hour:minute:second timezone*

request   The *request* field is set to the actual request received from the client. It is enclosed in double quotes (").

status   This field contains the three-digit HTTP status code returned to the client. Apache can return any of the following HTTP response codes:

200: OK
302: Found
304: Not Modified
400: Bad Request
401: Unauthorized
403: Forbidden
404: Not Found
500: Server Error
503: Out Of Resources (Service Unavailable)
501: Not Implemented
502: Bad Gateway

The HTTP standard defines many other codes, so this list is likely to grow as new features are implemented in Apache.

bytes   The size of the transfer in bytes returned to the client, not counting any header information.

ENABLING LOGGING

To enable logging using the standard log format, use the `TransferLog` directive. This directive allows you to specify the filename to receive the logging information. Instead of a file, you can also specify a program to receive the information on its Standard Input stream (`stdin`).

The syntax of the `TransferLog` directive is as follows:

Syntax: `TransferLog [filename] | [¦program]`
Default: `TransferLog logs/transfer_log`

filename is the name of a file relative of `ServerRoot`. If for some reason you don't want to log, specify `/dev/null` as the access log file.

¦program is the pipe symbol (`¦`) followed by a path to a program capable of receiving the log information on `stdin`.

As with any program started by the server, the program is run with the User ID (UID) and Group ID (GID) of the user that started the httpd daemon. If the user starting the program is root, be sure that the `User` directive demotes the server privileges to those of an unprivileged user such as `nobody`. Also, make sure the program is secure.

Here's a sample from an `accesslog` file generated by Apache for `http://www.PlanetEarthInc.COM`, a site hosted at accessLINK:

```
sundmz1.bloomberg.com - - [20/Jul/1996:09:56:03 -0500]
➡"GET /two.gif HTTP/1.0" 200 2563
sundmz1.bloomberg.com - - [20/Jul/1996:09:56:03 -0500]
➡"GET /three.gif HTTP/1.0" 200 4078
sundmz1.bloomberg.com - - [20/Jul/1996:09:56:03 -0500]
➡"GET /four.gif HTTP/1.0" 200 4090
pn3-ppp-109.primary.net - - [20/Jul/1996:09:57:29 -0500]
➡"GET / HTTP/1.0" 200 5441
pn3-ppp-109.primary.net - - [20/Jul/1996:09:57:36 -0500]
➡"GET /images/ultimate.gif HTTP/1.0" 200 7897
pn3-ppp-109.primary.net - - [20/Jul/1996:09:57:38 -0500]
➡"GET /sponsors/banner-bin/emusic2.gif HTTP/1.0" 200 8977
pn3-ppp-109.primary.net - - [20/Jul/1996:09:57:44 -0500]
➡"GET /images/hero.gif HTTP/1.0" 200 16098
128.58.101.231 - - [20/Jul/1996:09:59:19 -0500] "GET / HTTP/1.0" 200 5441
128.58.101.231 - - [20/Jul/1996:09:59:23 -0500] "GET / HTTP/1.0" 200 5441
slip-2-28.slip.shore.net - - [20/Jul/1996:10:03:44 -0500]
➡"GET / HTTP/1.0" 200 5439
slip-2-28.slip.shore.net - - [20/Jul/1996:10:04:07 -0500]
```

```
➥"GET /sponsors/banner-bin/books.gif HTTP/1.0" 200 5726
slip-2-28.slip.shore.net - - [20/Jul/1996:10:04:09 -0500]
➥"GET /images/ultimate.gif HTTP/1.0" 200 7897
slip-2-28.slip.shore.net - - [20/Jul/1996:10:04:16 -0500]
➥"GET /images/hero.gif HTTP/1.0" 200 16098
slip-12-16.ots.utexas.edu - - [20/Jul/1996:10:09:38 -0500]
➥"GET / HTTP/1.0" 200 5441
slip-12-16.ots.utexas.edu - - [20/Jul/1996:10:09:50 -0500]
➥"GET /anim.class HTTP/1.0" 200 12744
slip-12-16.ots.utexas.edu - - [20/Jul/1996:10:10:00 -0500]
➥"GET /one.gif HTTP/1.0" 404 -
slip-12-16.ots.utexas.edu - - [20/Jul/1996:10:10:01 -0500]
➥"GET /two.gif HTTP/1.0" 200 2563
slip-12-16.ots.utexas.edu - - [20/Jul/1996:10:10:05 -0500]
➥"GET /three.gif HTTP/1.0" 200 4078
slip-12-16.ots.utexas.edu - - [20/Jul/1996:10:10:09 -0500]
➥"GET /four.gif HTTP/1.0" 200 4090
slip-12-16.ots.utexas.edu - - [20/Jul/1996:10:10:12 -0500]
➥"GET /five.gif HTTP/1.0" 200 3343
slip-12-16.ots.utexas.edu - - [20/Jul/1996:10:10:15 -0500]
➥"GET /six.gif HTTP/1.0" 200 2122
slip-12-16.ots.utexas.edu - - [20/Jul/1996:10:10:18 -0500]
➥"GET /seven.gif HTTP/1.0" 200 2244
slip-12-16.ots.utexas.edu - - [20/Jul/1996:10:11:06 -0500]
➥"GET /eight.gif HTTP/1.0" 200 2334
www-j8.proxy.aol.com - - [20/Jul/1996:10:31:50 -0500]
➥"GET / HTTP/1.0" 200 5443
www-j8.proxy.aol.com - - [20/Jul/1996:10:31:57 -0500]
➥"GET /images/ultimate.gif HTTP/1.0" 200 7897
www-j8.proxy.aol.com - - [20/Jul/1996:10:31:57 -0500]
➥"GET /images/hero.gif HTTP/1.0" 200 16098
www-j8.proxy.aol.com - - [20/Jul/1996:10:31:57 -0500]
➥"GET /sponsors/banner-bin/ktravel.gif HTTP/1.0" 200 1500
sage.wt.com.au - - [20/Jul/1996:10:43:05 -0500] "GET / HTTP/1.0" 200 5441
```

By simple inspection of this log excerpt, you can see that most requests are answered successfully. Only one entry is suspicious:

```
slip-12-16.ots.utexas.edu - - [20/Jul/1996:10:10:00 -0500]
➥"GET /one.gif HTTP/1.0" 404 -
```

It has a response code 404 - "Not Found." The person maintaining this site should check to see if this error is repeated elsewhere because one of his pages could be referencing a broken link.

In addition to the standard mod_log_common logging module, Apache provides a log that is fully customizable. This log module is still considered experimental as of release 1.1, but according to some sources, it will be the preferred and default logging module for Apache 1.2. Even in its "experimental" state (actually it is just as reliable as the other one), its flexible log format may provide you with more useful logging capabilities and may give you the opportunity to reduce several logs into a single one.

Additional Logging Modules

While the default logging agent, `mod_log_common`, will be more than adequate for most needs, other logging modules may be useful to you. As of version 1.1.1, Apache included the following modules which added logging capability:

- `mod_cookies`
- `mod_log_agent` (NCSA 1.4 Compatibility)
- `mod_log_referer` (NCSA 1.4 Compatibility)
- `mod_log_config`

Of these four modules, the most important ones are `mod_log_config` and `mod_cookies`. `mod_log_config` is a configurable module that provides much more flexibility when logging information. `mod_cookies` also provides a log, but more importantly it enables the automatic generation of cookies from within Apache (these cookies should not be confused with Netscape persistent cookies. For information on Netscape persistent cookies, refer to Chapter 7, "Third-Party Modules").

Cookies are a unique identifier that get handed down by the server when a browser makes an initial connection. Because this identifier is guaranteed to be unique, you can use it to follow a user navigating through your Web site.

The `mod_log_agent` and `mod_log_referer` are compatibility modules for users of the NCSA 1.4 Web server that are migrating to Apache. `mod_log_agent` logs the client (browser) that was used to access the resource. `mod_log_referer` logs the Web site the user is coming from. This last piece of information is useful to help you determine where users are coming from and where your site is referenced. The `referer` module is also useful for tracking stale links that refer to resources that have since moved or have been removed from your site. `mod_log_config` allows logging of the same information provided by `mod_log_agent` and `mod_log_referer` except that instead of logging into several different files, the information can be consolidated into one log. `mod_log_config` will help you reduce the complexity of log analysis scripts you develop, while at the same time produce logging information that is compatible with CLF.

Apache 1.2 will introduce new logging capabilities, including the ability to redirect errors from your CGI to a logfile (an enhanced user-tracking, cookie-based log module) and the ability to have multiple configurable log files.

The `mod_log_config` Module

The `mod_log_config` module is not built into Apache by default. In order to use any of its directives, you need to reconfigure Apache to include this module, comment out the standard `mod_log_common` from the list, and recompile the server.

This module allows the logging of server requests using a user-specified format. It is considered experimental; however, in my experience it works great. As previously mentioned, this will be the default logging module for Apache 1.2 and beyond. `mod_log_config` implements the `TransferLog` directive (same as the common log module) and an additional directive, `LogFormat`. Because both the `mod_log_common` and `mod_log_config` implement the `TransferLog` directive, I would consider it wise to only compile one or the other into Apache. Otherwise, your results may be unexpected.

The log format is flexible; you can specify it with the `LogFormat` directive. The argument to the `LogFormat` is a string, which can include literal characters copied into the log files and percent sign (`%`) directives like the following:

`%h`	Remote host.
`%l`	Remote logname (from `identd`, if supplied).
`%u`	Remote user (from `auth`; may be bogus if return status (`%s`) is 401).
`%t`	Time of the request using the time format used by the Common Log Format.
`%r`	First line of request.
`%s`	Status. For requests that got internally redirected, this is the status of the original request; `%>s` for the last.
`%b`	Bytes sent.
`%{Header}i`	The contents of *Header*: header line(s) in the request sent to the client.
`%{Header}o`	The contents of *Header*: header line(s) in the reply.

One of the better features this module produces is conditional logging. Conditional logging can include the information depending on an HTTP response code. You can specify the conditions for inclusion of a particular field by specifying the HTTP status code between the `%` and letter code for the field. You may specify more than one HTTP status code by separating them with a comma (`,`). In addition, you can specify to log any of the environment variables, such as the `User-Agent` or the `Referer`, received by the server by specifying its name between braces (`{variable}`). Here are a few examples:

```
%400,500{User-agent}i
```

The preceding example logs `User-agent` headers only on `Bad Request` or `Not Implemented` errors.

You can also specify that a field be logged. If a certain HTTP code is not returned by adding an exclamation symbol (`!`) in front of the code, you want to check for

```
%!200,304,302{Referer}i
```

This example logs the Referer header information on all requests not returning a normal return code. When a condition is not met, the field is null. As with the common log format, a null field is indicated by a dash (-) character.

Virtual hosts can have their own LogFormat and/or TransferLog. If no LogFormat is specified, it is inherited from the main server process. If the virtual hosts don't have their own TransferLog, entries are written to the main server's log. To differentiate between virtual hosts writing to a common log file, you can prepend a label to the log format string:

```
<VirtualHost xxx.com>
LogFormat "xxx formatstring"
...
</VirtualHost>
<VirtualHost yyy.com>
LogFormat "yyy formatstring"
...
</VirtualHost>
```

LogFormat

The format of the log is specified as a string of characters:

> Syntax: LogFormat *string*
> Default: LogFormat "%h %l %u %t \"%r\" %s %b" (same as the CLF)

You are free to specify the fields in any order you want. But for compatibility with the CLF, you may want to observe the order of the standard elements (as in the CLF specification):

host ident authuser date request status bytes

I like the following format, which provides a lot of useful information:

```
"%h %l %u %t \"%r\" %s %b %{Cookie}i %{User-agent}i  %400,401,403,404{Referer}i"
```

In order to enable the Cookie header, I compiled in the mod_cookies. I also disabled the CookieLog by pointing it to /dev/null. There is no need to have a separate Cookie log when you can include this information in the main log.

To enable logging, you need to use the TransferLog directive:

> Syntax: TransferLog [*filename*] | [¦*program*]
> Default: TransferLog logs/transfer_log

filename is the name of a file relative of ServerRoot.

¦*program* is the pipe symbol (¦) followed by a path to a program capable of receiving the log information on stdin.

As with any program started by the server, the program is run with the UID and GID of the user that started the httpd daemon. If the user starting the program is root, be sure that the User directive demotes the server privileges to those of an unprivileged user such as nobody. Also, make sure the program is secure.

THE ERROR LOG

In addition to the transfer (or access) logs, you'll want to keep a close watch on the error log. The location of the error is defined with the ErrorLog directive, which defaults to logs/error_log. The format of this log is rather simple, it lists the date and time of the error, along with a message. Usually you'll want to look for messages that report a failed access because that could mean that there is a broken link somewhere.

If you are debugging CGI, you will want to be aware that information sent by a CGI to the standard error stream (stderr) is logged to the error log file, which makes the contents of this file invaluable while debugging your CGI.

Apache 1.2 introduces the ScriptLog directive, which will send all stderr messages to the log file specified with it. However, at the time of this writing, I could not obtain additional information to fully document this directive. Please check the Apache site for the latest information on Apache 1.2.

If you want to keep a watch on any of your log files as the entries are added, you can use the UNIX tail command. The tail command delivers the last part of a file. tail has an option that allows it to remain listening in for new text to be appended to a file. You can specify this functionality by specifying the -f switch:

```
tail -f /usr/local/etc/httpd/logs/error_log
```

This will display any error entries as they happen. You can also use this command on the transfer log and have up-to-the-second information regarding any activity on your Web server. (For an even better activity report, take a look at Chapter 11, "Basic System Administration," for information on the Status module.)

SEARCHING AND GATHERING

Now that you have your logs accumulating data, you may want to be able to quickly search them. UNIX comes with a wide range of tools that can easily search a large file for a pattern. Our examples use our richer log files. I used a CLF-file format that had extra information at the end. I used the mod_log_config module and specified a log format of

```
LogFormat "%h %l %u %t \"%r\" %s %b %{Cookie}i %{User-agent}i
➡%400,401,403,404{Referer}i"
```

This log format adds the `Cookie` header (a number) associated with each request. It also logs the browser the visitor was using and the `Referer` header information if the request was bad.

This format allows you to pack a lot of useful information into a single log file while still remaining compatible with most, if not all, of the standard logging tools available. (The order of the first seven fields is the same as the CLF.)

COUNTING THE UNIQUE NUMBER OF VISITORS

If you are interested in counting the number of visitors and you are logging the cookie information as in the example log format, it becomes a matter of just counting the number of unique cookies in your log file. On entering the site, each visitor is assigned a unique cookie by Apache. A cookie looks like the following:

```
Apache=#################
```

Each # character represents a number. Counting users becomes a matter of counting unique cookies. The following series of commands retrieves this information:

```
awk '{print $11}' logfile ¦ sort ¦ uniq ¦ wc -l
```

The `awk` command prints the eleventh field in the file. Fields in the `logfile` are separated by spaces, so each space creates a field. Output containing only the cookies' numbers is piped to sort, which will sort all the cookies in numerical order. The sorted output is piped to `uniq`, which removes duplicate lines. Finally, the thinned out list is sent to `wc`, which counts the number of lines in the result. This number matches the number of unique visitors that came to your site. For more information on these commands, please consult your UNIX documentation.

USING grep TO DETERMINE THE ORIGIN OF THE USER

Another tool that is very useful for extracting information from your logs is the `grep` program.

By issuing the simple command, `grep ibm.com access_log`, you can see all the requests that originated from the `ibm.com` domain. If you just wanted a count of the accesses that came from the `ibm.com` domain, issue a `-c` flag to the command:

```
grep -c ibm.com access_log
```

Daily Statistics

If you wanted to command a quick count of all the hits that your site sustained on a certain date, say on July 19, 1996, type the following:

```
grep -c 19/Jul/1996 access_log
```

To count all hits that your site sustained on July 19, 1996, between 3:00 p.m. and 3:59 p.m. (15:00 hours; UNIX time is expressed in the 24-hour format), type the following:

```
grep -c "19/Jul/1996:15" access_log
```

Home Page Statistics

To count all accesses to your home page, type the following:

```
grep -c "GET / " access_log
```

or

```
grep -c "GET /index.html " access_log
```

or

```
grep -c "~/username" accesslog
```

The sum of these two searches is the number of total accesses to your home page, assuming that your home page is at the `root` directory and it is named `index.html`. For private home pages, you should use the third option. Just replace `username` with the login of the user.

Searching the Error Log

You should frequently check your error logs. Of special interest are the messages `user not found` or `password mismatch`. If you get many repeated lines with these errors, someone may be trying to break into your site.

Tools for Summarizing Information

While the command line is invaluable for creating on-demand reports that search for something very specific, there are many tools available that create nice reports that summarize most everything you want to know about your site's traffic. Many of these tools are free, and they all answer, in varying degrees of effectiveness, the following basic questions:

◆ Who is visiting your site?

◆ How many visitors are there and where are they from?

◆ What are the most popular areas of your site?

◆ What are your site's peak load times?

Your choice will depend on what type of output you like. These tools are available in two types: graphical and text. You can find free, shareware, and expensive versions of these tools. Shop closely, and look on the Net for the latest on these tools. A good place to search is

```
http://www.yahoo.com/Computers_and_Internet/World_Wide_Web/HTTP/Servers/Log_
➥Analysis_Tools/
```

The higher-end tools, such as net.Analysis from net.Genesis (`http://www.netgen.com`), cost anywhere from $295–$2,995. They provide a number of features that may be interesting to very high-traffic sites.

In the inexpensive range (less than $100), there are many nice tools with tons of options available. My favorite tools are described in the following sections.

ACCESSWATCH

AccessWatch by Dave Maher, `http://netpressence.com/accesswatch/`, is a graphically appealing log analyzer. It provides information about today's Web access. The software is implemented as a Perl script, so it is portable to environments that run Perl. This software is free for the U.S. Government, noncommercial home use, and academic use. Any other use has a license of $40/year. Figures 13.1–13.5 show examples of AccessWatch reports.

Figure 13.1. AccessWatch daily access and predictions report.

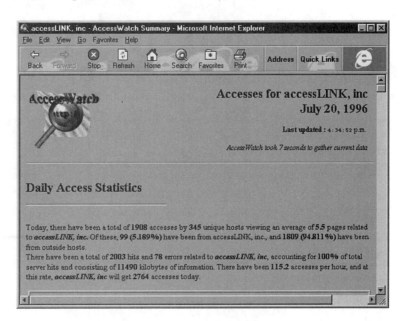

Figure 13.2.
AccessWatch
summary report.

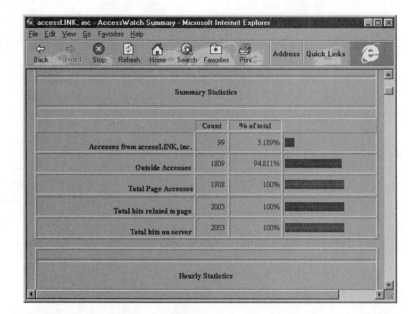

Figure 13.3.
AccessWatch
hourly access
report.

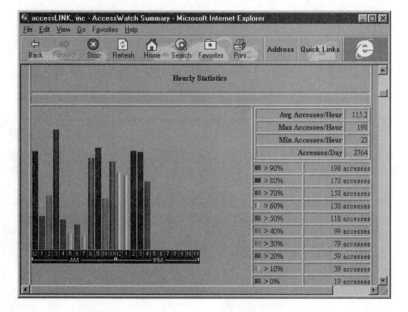

Figure 13.4.
AccessWatch page
access report.

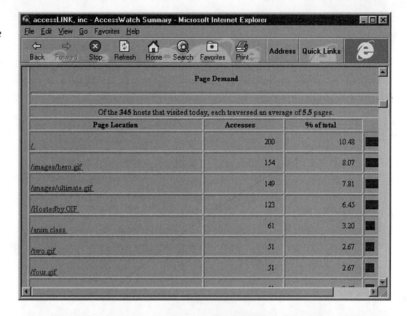

Figure 13.5.
AccessWatch
domain access
report.

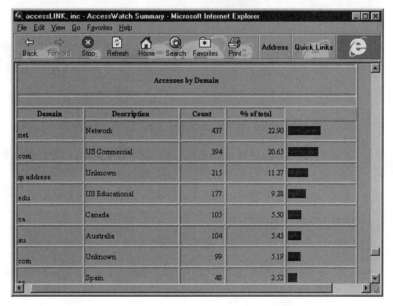

WUSAGE

Wusage by Thomas Boutell, `http://www.boutell.com`, is a powerful and appealing log analyzer that is distributed in binary form. There are versions for various types of UNIX and Windows programs. Wusage provides all the configuration commands you could possibly want. As a bonus, it comes with a friendly utility for configuring the program. It utilizes Boutell's GD Graphical Interchange Format (GIF) library to generate a variety of attractive charts. Its number-one feature is that it lets you create reports based on a pattern, be it a filename or a site. It can also analyze multiple log files at once. The license price varies depending on the number of copies you purchase and the intended use. Single user licenses are $25 for educational and nonprofit institutions. All others are $75. Various Wusage reports are shown in Figures 13.6–13.10.

Figure 13.6.
Wusage daily
access report.

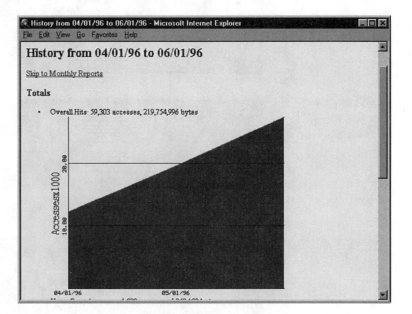

Figure 13.7.
Wusage monthly
access report.

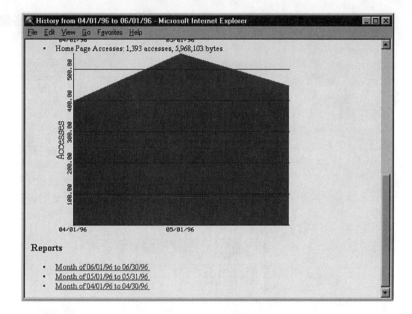

Figure 13.8.
Wusage hourly
graph report.

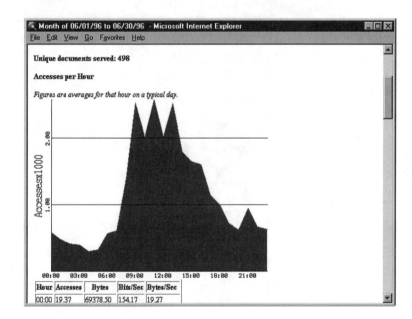

Figure 13.9.
Wusage domain
access report.

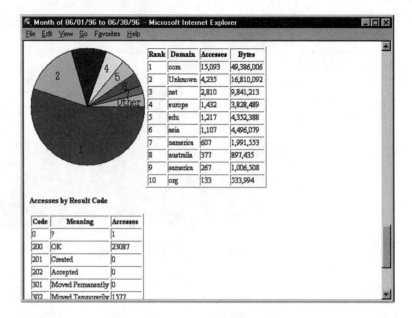

Figure 13.10.
Wusage Top 10
document
requests.

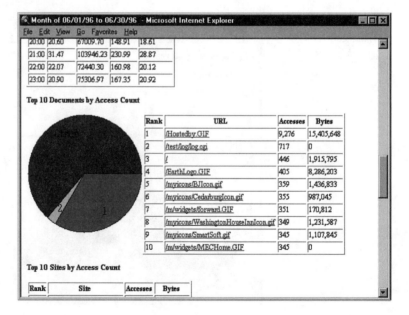

ANALOG

Analog by Stephen Turner with the Statistical Laboratory, University of Cambridge (`http://www.statslab.cam.ac.uk/~sret1/analog`), is highly configurable and is fully HTML 2.0 compliant. It does have some graphics options, but I like the text reports, as shown in Figures 13.11–13.14. They are very comprehensive. Analog runs under UNIX, Macintosh, and DOS.

wwwstat

Another popular utility is wwwstat (`http://www.ics.uci.edu/WebSoft/wwwstat/`). This utility, when coupled with gwstat (`ftp://dis/cs.umass.edu/pub/gwstat.tar.gz`), produces nice graphic reports. However, the graphic system only works under the X11 (The X Windowing System). I also had trouble with it processing my 40MB log file on a very fast PA-RISC server, something that leads me to believe that there was a compatibility problem on my side. The other software packages previously mentioned quickly processed the 40MB log file in a minute or so without any problems.

Figure 13.11. Analog's summary report.

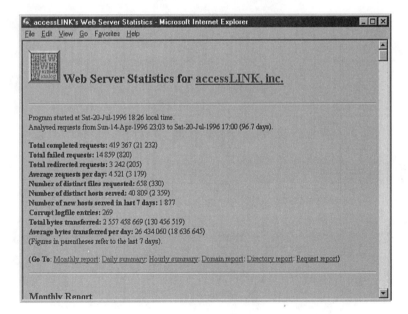

Figure 13.12.
Analog's monthly
report and
partially showing
the daily report.

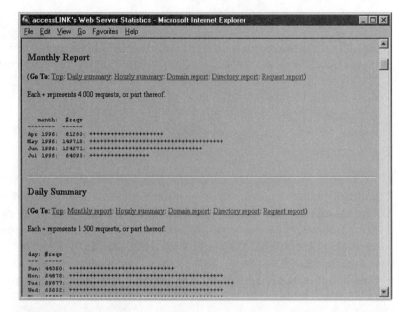

Figure 13.13.
Analog's hourly
summary report.

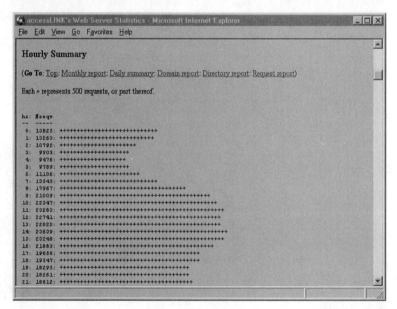

Figure 13.14.
Analog's domain
report.

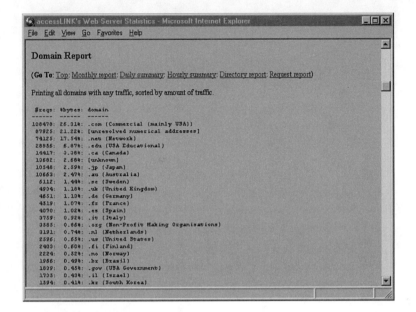

SUMMARY

Logging information provides you with interesting statistical information about visitors to your site. By carefully analyzing this data, you may be able to catch a glimpse of a trend. This information can be invaluable in terms of determining what visitors like to see in your site as well as pointing out the content you should enhance. Responding to these perceived needs will help you build a better site—one that is useful to your visitors and one that will attract more of them.

Using software tools to graph Web accounting information is better than looking at raw numbers. "A picture is worth a thousand words," and in this case, it will help you understand your site's traffic statistics better. Many of these reporting tools summarize information by time periods and access groups, which lets you see your information in several different ways. By associating this data with press releases and other media-dissemination information, you can gage customer interest in your products or services. Your traffic is your feedback.

- Secure Web Servers

- Access Control and
  User Authentication

- Web Server Security
  Issues

Security: Options and Procedures

CHAPTER 14

Secure Web Servers

With the increase in the use of the Internet as a vehicle for commercial transactions, there are more reasons now than ever to protect sensitive information from reaching unintended eyes. A whole slew of secure client/server applications are appearing every day. Also making an inroad is the *digital signature* technology, which helps certify that messages you received were indeed sent by the sender. Both of these technologies are rooted in the same core of public-key encryption, which is currently the only feasible way of implementing security over an insecure network such as the Internet. The scope of this technology is to ensure that any form of communication that may contain sensitive information is protected while in transit and to assure the receiver that the message was really sent by the sender.

In the case of Web server technology, this is accomplished with a server that implements encryption at the communication level. The current crop of products implementing security are based on the Secure Socket Layer (SSL) protocol specification developed by Netscape Communications for use with their server and browser products. For details on the SSL protocol, visit `http://home.netscape.com/newsref/std`.

Of the many reasons to use a secure HTTP server, the two most important ones are information privacy and data integrity. If you put sensitive information on your server, you may want to protect your information from being captured or modified by unscrupulous people while in transit. The SSL technology ensures this.

Note

> An SSL server is not secure in terms of prohibiting access to un-authorized users. All versions of the Apache server, SSL or plain, provide you with tools and configuration directives to help you control access to your site. The SSL technology only *secures* or makes it really difficult to spy or modify the transmission of the information from the server to the destination—the communication channel. Servers that contain highly sensitive information and *should* be secure don't belong on the Internet. The SSL technology is only designed to permit the safe transfer of sensitive data through an unsecured network such as the Internet; this technology is not designed to keep people out of your system.

Two variants of the Apache server, Apache-SSL and Stronghold (Apache-SSL-US), are available. They both provide 128-bit symmetric-key encryption that is fully compatible with the Netscape's SSL protocol. These servers are fully compatible with browsers that understand this protocol. Currently, this includes browser offerings from Netscape, Microsoft, and others.

Because of the technology involved, which flavor of the Apache software you'll be able to *legally* use will depend on where you live. There are two issues that affect most products that implement encryption technology, including SSL technologies:

1. The U.S. law regarding exportation of encryption technology (cryptography)
2. The Public Key Partners patent on Rivest-Shamir-Adleman (RSA) public-key cryptography

U.S. Law Regarding Exportation and Importation of Cryptography

Exportation of cryptographic technology is highly restricted and regulated by the U.S. State Department under the International Trade in Arms Regulation. This regulation classifies cryptographic devices, including software, as munitions (as in armament and ammunition).

Ultimately, any export license request for cryptographic technology is passed down for approval to the National Security Agency (NSA). The NSA has jurisdiction over the exportation of cryptographic technology issues because its mandate as an agency is to listen and decode all foreign communications of interest to the security of the United States. Encryption technology can obviously create problems for this agency when they are trying to go about their business. Naturally, from their point of view, they need a policy to eliminate sources of grief where they can. This means putting restrictions on the exportation of U.S. products that implement encryption technology.

In other words, the intention of the law is to reduce or prevent the possibility of some subversive country utilizing a U.S.-developed encryption technology that is too strong and time consuming for the NSA to break. This type of technology could make it difficult to decode information that may adversely affect the security of the United States.

The problem with this law is complex. The NSA will approve (and has done so in the past) exportation of cryptographic technologies that it is able to crack or have some sort of backdoor available for this purpose. Rumor has it that they have all the toys and best minds in the business dedicated to this purpose alone.

From a technology provider's point of view, the problem is that the intention of any cryptographic technology is to make it very difficult to read encrypted data. Even if it was feasible to crack through brute force, the resources needed for this task would approach government budgets. Even then it should take some time to crack. The result is that many encryption products don't make a debut outside of the United States because an international version may have to compromise its security to get the export license or the hassles involved in exporting it are too great. Developers of encryption technology are angry because this policy limits their ability to reach a world market. In a world-information system such as the Internet, it becomes very difficult to police and enforce this type of law.

THE PUBLIC KEY PARTNERS PATENT ON RSA (PUBLIC-KEY CRYPTOGRAPHY)

The second issue regarding use of Apache-SSL, Apache-SSL-US, and other encryption technologies has to do with the patent on public key encryption systems.

The traditional problem with encryption is that in order for the recipient to decode encrypted material, she would need to know the key used by the sender to encrypt it; the sender uses a key (like a password) to encrypt a message. The receiver must use the same key to decrypt it. Because the keys need to be the same, for both encryption and decryption, the problem with this technology (secret-key cryptography) lies in the transmission of the key. Exchange of the key information needs to transpire without anyone else learning it.

This makes the data vulnerable because even though the encrypted data could be easily and securely transmitted over open communication lines, the key portion could not. If anyone else got a hold of your key, be it by looking at your e-mail or listening in on your phone lines, he could decode the information. The more times you transmit and reuse the key, the more vulnerable the key becomes.

To eliminate the problem of key transmission, public-key cryptography was developed. This system uses two keys: a private key and a public key. The private key, as its name suggests, is kept private by its owner. This key is used for decoding information, it is never sent to anyone (see the following note). The public key on the other hand can be freely disseminated and can be publicly posted because it can be used only to encrypt messages destined to its owner.

When you wish to send a message to someone, you would use his public key to encrypt your message. Only the recipient, with his private key, would be able to decipher that message.

Note

A second benefit of public-key cryptography is that it can be used to create *digital signatures*. Digital signatures are great because they provide digital proof of the sender of the message. If you send a message to me, a value is computed using your private key and the message itself. That value can then be attached to a message. When I

> receive the message, I can compute another value by using the public key and the message itself. If your digital signature has a mathematical relation to the computed value, then I know that the message was unaltered, and that it was encoded by you. The only way to forge a message is to get a hold of your private key.

RSA, the algorithm that implements public-key encryption, is patented under U.S. Patent 4,405,829, which was issued on August 20, 1983 (this patent expires in the year 2000). The patent is held by Public Key Partners (PKP) of Sunnyvale, California. RSA is licensed under a royalty-based licensing policy, which works as follows:

1. If you develop a product and license the RSA technology, any one who purchases the product has a right to use the RSA technology within the product you developed. The U.S. government can use RSA without a license because it was invented in 1977 by Ron Rivest, Adi Shamir, and Leonard Adleman at Massachusetts Institute of Technology with partial government funding.

2. PKP allows free noncommercial use of RSA with written permission, for personal, educational, and intellectual reasons. RSA Laboratories has even made available a collection of cryptographic routines in source form that include the RSA algorithm, which can be used, improved, and redistributed noncommercially.

3. RSA is not patented outside of North America.

TWO VERSIONS OF APACHE-SSL

As mentioned earlier, there are currently two versions of the Apache server to implement SSL encryption technology. The SSL technology uses a public-key encryption system to encode the transmission.

APACHE-SSL

Apache-SSL is a set of patches developed in the United Kingdom by Ben Laurie (ben@algroup.co.uk) that incorporate SSL functionality to Apache. In addition to his patches available from http://www.algroup.co.uk/Apache-SSL, you'll need to obtain the sources to Apache and the SSLeay library to build Apache-SSL. The product is free for both commercial and noncommercial use. It supports 128-bit encryption, client authentication, and all the other features of Apache.

Apache-SSL uses the SSLeay, an implementation of the Netscape's SSL, the software encryption protocol behind Netscape's products. SSLeay was developed by Eric Young as a library that can provide SSL security to any TCP application. This implementation was programmed using only the publicly available protocols and supports DES, RSA, RC4, and IDEA encryption algorithms. You can obtain the SSLeay library from `http://www.psy.uq.oz.au/~ftp/Crypto/`. However, its use is only legal outside of the United States and Canada because of the patent issues with RSA and RC4.

STRONGHOLD (APACHE-SSL-US)

Stronghold, developed by Community ConneXion (`http://www.us.apache-ssl.com`), also uses the SSLeay SSL implementation. However, it licenses the RSAREF libraries from RSA Data Security Inc., which provide SSL configuration documentation. Stronghold also provides Certificate of Authority tools. Stronghold is free for noncommercial use. Commercial users must pay a licensing fee of $495.00. Customers upgrading from a competing SSL Web server from Netscape have a special discount price of $295.00.

Some of the technical differences between Apache-SSL and Stronghold are the licensing of the RSA technology, availability of the CA, additional software tools, and availability of support. Apache-SSL's SSL implementation doesn't license the RSA technology; Stronghold does. Because Stronghold licenses the RSAREF libraries, it is an approved product. So VeriSign, an offshoot of RSA, will issue a Certificate Authority (CA) for Stronghold, although in the future they may also do it for Apache-SSL. Stronghold also provides additional tools useful for creating new certificates and managing existing ones. Lastly and most importantly, you can think of Stronghold as shrink-wrap. Commercial licenses of Stronghold (paid versions) are entitled to technical support. The Stronghold software is also much easier to install because it comes as a complete package, not just as a set of patches. Stronghold is currently compatible with 16 platforms including SunOS, Sparc, Solaris, X86 Solaris, AIX, BSDI, Linux (ELF & a.out), FreeBSD, IRIX, UnixWare, Ultrix, DG/UX, HP-UX, OSF/1, and NeXTSTEP.

SO WHICH SECURE VERSION OF APACHE CAN YOU LEGALLY USE?

As I mentioned earlier, which version of Apache you are allowed to use depends on where you live. If you live in the United States or Canada, you must use Stronghold (Apache-SSL-US). This version of Apache uses the same SSLeay libraries as Apache-SSL, but it licenses the RSA libraries. By licensing the RSA libraries,

Community ConneXions eliminated the patent issues associated with the RSA public-key encryption implemented by the SSLeay libraries.

To add another twist, by legalizing Stronghold in the United States by incorporating the RSA libraries, exportation of Stronghold now falls under the regulations of the U.S. State Department under the International Trade in Arms Regulation, making its use possible only in the United States and Canada. Stronghold is not licensed to be exported outside of the United States under the current law.

If you live outside of the United States and Canada, then the United States patent on the public-key cryptographic system doesn't apply to you. Apache-SSL, with its own implementation of the RSA algorithm that doesn't incorporate any code from the RSAREF toolkit, can be used legally anywhere but in the United States and Canada. In those two countries it violates U.S. patent law. To be certain, you may also want to become aware of other local restrictions and regulations regarding the use of cryptographic technology before you implement a server that uses this technology.

INSTALLING APACHE-SSL

For users outside of the U.S. and Canada, Apache-SSL is distributed in patch form (note the version of the patches). The patches can be obtained from `http://www.algroup.co.uk/Apache-SSL`. You'll also need the SSLeay libraries, available in source form from `http://www.psy.uq.oz.au/~ftp/Crypto`; pick the latest version. You'll also need to verify that you have a matching version of the Apache server from `http://www.apache.org`.

As of this writing, the patches were for Apache version 1.1.1. The files you'll need are

> Apache source: `apache_1.1.1.tar.gz`
> SSLeay library: `SSLeay-0.6.3.tar.gz`
> SSL patches: `apache_1.1.1+1.3.ssl.tar.gz`

You should move all the distribution files to a directory. You can use `Apache Server` as a temporary holder. Here's how the patches are unpacked and applied. Note that `apache_1.1.1+1.3.ssl.tar.gz` is unpacked in the Apache 1.1.1 distribution directory. Doing this will install additional files for the patch program as well as create some files unique to the SSL distribution. The SSL patches are applied with the `patch` utility. If your system does not have `patch`, I have included a copy on the CD-ROM. Otherwise, you can download the latest version from `ftp://prep.ai.mit.edu/systems/gnu/patch-2.1.tar.gz`.

Before compiling SSLeay, read the INSTALL document. Then edit Makefile.ssl to match your system configuration. If your perl binary is in /usr/local/bin/perl and you don't mind installing the libraries and other programs in /usr/local/ssl, all you may need to do is set up your compiler options. When you are done, run the Configure program. Here's a listing of the commands you'll need to apply:

```
% mkdir ApacheServer
% mv apache_1.1.1  ApacheServer
% mv SSLeay-0.6.3.tar.gz  ApacheServer
% cd ApacheServer
% gzcat apache_1.1.1.tar.gz ¦ tar -xf -
% cd apache_1.1.1
% gzcat ../apache_1.1.1+1.3.ssl.tar.gz ¦ tar -xf -
% patch < SSLpatch
% cd ..
% gzcat SSLeay-0.6.3.tar.gz ¦ tar -xf -
% cd SSLeay-0.6.3
% ./Configure os-compiler
```

Replace os-compiler with the name of your system. To see a list of available configurations, run Configure, but don't provide an argument. Run by issuing make at the command prompt:

```
% make
```

After a while the libraries and tools will be built. To install them in their proper places, execute as root: make install.

After the libraries compile properly, you'll need to edit the Apache src/Configuration file. For an idea of a basic configuration, see Chapter 2, "Installing and Configuring the Apache Server." The SSL patch installed a few more directives in this file, which you need to set values for. The ones you'll want to look for are SSL_BASE.

I set SSL_BASE=../../SSLeay-0.6.1 to the location of our SSLeay-0.6.1 distribution. You should be able to do a make and the binary httpsd will be built. Move the httpsd binary to the apache_1.1.1 directory:

```
% mv httpsd ../
```

At this point your software is properly installed. The next step is configuring the software and generating a CA so that you can use the software.

CONFIGURING APACHE-SSL

Before you configure Apache-SSL you'll need to generate a Certificate Request. A test certificate can be generated simply by issuing a make certificate in the apache-sll/src directory:

```
control1 > make certificate
../../SSLeay-0.6.1/apps/ssleay req  -config ../../SSLeay-0.6.1/apps/ssleay.conf  -
↪new -x509 -nodes -out ../SSLconf/conf/httpsd.pem  -keyout ../SSLconf/conf/
```

```
➥httpsd.pem;  ln -s ../SSLconf/conf/httpsd.pem ../SSLconf/conf/`../
➥../SSLeay-0.6.1/apps/ssleay  x509 -noout -hash < ../SSLconf/conf/httpsd.pem`.0
Generating a 512 bit private key
..+++++
..................+++++
writing new private key to '../SSLconf/conf/httpsd.pem'
```

Next, you'll be prompted to enter information about yourself and your company. Follow the directions:

```
You are about to be asked to enter information that will be incorperated
into your certificate request.
What you are about to enter is what is called a Distinguished Name or a DN.
There are quite a few fields but you can leave some blank
For some fields there will be a default value,
If you enter '.', the field will be left blank.
-----
Country Name (2 letter code) [AU]:DO
State or Province Name (full name) [Queensland]:Distrito Nacional
Locality Name (eg, city) []:Santo Domingo
Organization Name (eg, company) [Mincom Pty Ltd]:CXA
Organizational Unit Name (eg, section) [MTR]:""
Common Name (eg, YOUR name) []:
Email Address []:webmaster@CXA.DO
```

Next, you'll need to edit the `SSLconf/conf/httpd.conf` file. This file contains many of the same configuration directives as `conf/httpd.conf`, but it also includes directives for specifying the location of the certificate and other things. The directives you need to set are fully documented.

INSTALLING AND CONFIGURING STRONGHOLD

Stronghold comes as a `prebuilt` binary, and it is by far the easiest Apache server to install. Community ConneXion has made a very nice interactive shell script that installs and configures both servers (the distribution includes both the non-SSL version of Apache (httpd) and Stronghold (httpsd). A future version, currently under development, will implement both the secure and plain servers in one server process.

To start the installation process, type the following:

```
# ./Install.sh
```

The program will show you a list of the available prebuilt binaries (if your distribution contains more than one). Enter the name of the operating system matching your platform like this:

```
Available platforms:

Pick your platform > NS
```

Next, it will ask you where to store the SSL security utilities. Enter a different pathname if you want Stronghold stored elsewhere.

```
Where do you want to install SSLeay? [/usr/local/ssl]
Testing permissions...done
Installing SSLeay...done
```

The installation script will then ask for the name of the directory where Stronghold will store Apache and other files necessary for the operation of the Web server.

```
Where would you like to locate the ServerRoot? [/usr/local/apache]
```

Next, it will request a directory for the normal logs (nonsecure transactions).

```
Where would you like to locate the non-SSL logs? [/usr/local/apache/logs]
```

and for the secure transaction logs:

```
Where would you like to locate the SSL logs? [/usr/local/apache/ssl_logs]
```

Next, the script will configure some of the server runtime configuration directives. First, it will request the server name. If the server will use an alias such as www.company.com, enter that name here:

```
What's the name of your server? [www.company.com]
```

Next, it will ask you for the e-mail address for the administrator responsible for this site. This address gets returned to the client in case of an error:

```
What is the email address of the server admin? [webmaster@company.com]
```

Next, it will ask you for the TCP port address for the plain (non-SSL) server. The standard HTTP port is 80:

```
What port do you want to run the plain server on? [80]
```

Now, it will ask you for the TCP port address for the SSL server. The standard SSL port is 443:

```
What port do you want to run the SSL server on? [443]
```

The following setting will control the User ID (UID) that the children server processes will run as. It should be set to a UID with minimal privileges, such as nobody:

```
What user should the server run as? [nobody]
```

Warning

Never set the UID the server runs as to root!

The final setting will control the Group ID (GID) that the children server processes will run as. It should be set to a UID with minimal privileges, such as nogroup:

```
What group should the server run as? [nogroup]
Installing Stronghold...done
Configuring Stronghold...done
```

At this point the basic software is configured. The installation program will add the /usr/local/ssl path to your environment. This will allow you to use the installed utilities without having to type their complete pathnames. You should follow the instructions printed by the program and add them to your .cshrc, .login, or .profile files. The instructions printed are

```
Now you must add SSLTOP=/usr/local/ssl to your environment.
Also add /usr/local/ssl/bin to your PATH.

Edit your .cshrc, .login, or .profile appropriately:

csh:
> setenv SSLTOP /usr/local/ssl
> setenv PATH /usr/local/ssl/bin:/etc:/usr/etc:/usr/ucb:/bin:/usr/bin:/usr/
➥local/bin:/usr/sybase/bin:/.

sh:
$ SSLTOP=/usr/local/ssl
$ PATH=/usr/local/ssl/bin:/etc:/usr/etc:/usr/ucb:/bin:/usr/bin:/usr/local/bin:/
➥usr/sybase/bin
$ export SSLTOP PATHHit return when ready:
```

You now need to generate the public/private encryption key pair. If you don't have an existing key, type B and follow the instructions:

```
Now you need to install a key/cert pair.
A) Convert an existing Netscape Commerce key/cert pair
B) Generate a new key/cert pair
Choose [A/B] B
The key will be called www.key.
The certificate will be called www.cert.
They will be stored in /usr/local/ssl

Hit return:
********* READ ME *************
You are now generating a new key and key request. The key request will be
sent to the CA of your choice and the keyfile will reside
/usr/local/ssl/private/www.key.

If you have already sent off a key request for this server before, make
sure you aren't overwriting your old key which is awaiting a corresponding
certificate from your CA.

If they key generation fails, move the file
/usr/local/ssl/private/www.key to a backup location and try again.
********* READ ME *************

Hit return:
Choose the size of your key. The smaller the key you choose the faster your
server response will be, but you'll have less security. Keys of less than 512
bits are trivially cracked, while for high security applications you
probably don't want a key of less than 1024 bits. Choosing an appropriate
keysize is your responsibility.
```

```
How many bits of key (384 minimum, 1024 maximum): 1024
Now we will generate some random data, using the truerand library
developed by Matt Blaze, Jim Reeds, and Jack Lacy at AT&T.
This may take some time.
Generating 2048 bits of randomness....................................................

Now we generate more random data, from keystrokes

We need to generate 2048 random bits.  This is done by measuring the
time intervals between your keystrokes.  Please enter some random text
on your keyboard until you hear the beep:
    0 * -Enough, thank you.
Finally, choose some files with random bits, to complete our random
number seed generation. You might want to put in logfiles, utmp, wtmp,
etc.

Once the key is generated you will be asked to enter a PEM pass phrase.
This is the pass phrase used to encrypt the key on the disk.

                    --- DO NOT LOSE THIS PASS PHRASE ---

Enter colon-separated list of files: /usr/adm/messages
Now we are generating the key. This may also take some time. Be patient.
The passphrase you enter here is very important. Do not lose it.
22320 semi-random bytes loaded
Generating RSA private key, 1024 bit long modulus
.+++++
......................................................+++++
e is 65537 (0x10001)
```

Next, you'll enter the permission phrase (your private password). Characters entered here are not echoed. Do NOT forget your permission phrase! Enter the following:

```
Enter PEM pass phrase:
Verifying password Enter PEM pass phrase:
Key generated
```

If you would like to send your Certificate Signing Request (CSR) to a CA, type y, otherwise type n. If you type y, the CSR will be sent to the CA. This process costs $290.00 from VeriSign. The session to prepare the Certificate Signing Request looks like this:

```
Would you like to send a Certificate Request to a CA? [Y/n] n
Not generating CSR
Now we will create a self-signed certificate for use until the CA of your
choice signs your certificate. You will have to use this cert until
your CA responds with the actual signed certificate.

Enter PEM pass phrase:
You are about to be asked to enter information that will be incorporated
into your certificate request.
What you are about to enter is what is called a Distinguished Name or a DN.
There are quite a few fields but you can leave some blank
For some fields there will be a default value,
If you enter '.', the field will be left blank.
-----
```

```
Country Name (2 letter code) [US]:
State or Province Name (full name) [California]:Somestate
Locality Name (city, town, etc.) [Springfield]:Somecity
Organization Name (company) [Random Corporation]:company, com.
Organizational Unit Name (division) [Secure Services Division]:
Common Name (webserver FQDN) [www.random.com]:www.company.com
--COMPLETE--
Your key has been generated and a test certificate has been installed
--COMPLETE--
Starting the server...
helium: Jul 22 23:41:19 1996 UTC - Aug 21 23:41:19 1996 UTC
WARNING: Certificate expires in 29 day(s)
```

Before the SSL server starts, you'll be asked to enter the permission phrase. This is done because the server is trying to access an encrypted file. The prompt will look like the following:

```
Enter PEM pass phrase:
```

Congratulations! Your secure server is now running. To access it you'll need an SSL-compliant browser. Secure servers are accessed by specifying an extra *s* following http (http secure), such as `https://www.company.com` URL. The visual differences between a secure and nonsecure site are shown in Figures 14.1 and 14.2.

To start and stop the server, use the scripts created by the installation program, `start` and `stop`.

In the case of Netscape, accessing the secure site causes the browser to show warnings because it doesn't know who certified this site. If the Certificate Request that you prepared earlier was approved by one of the authorities, such as VeriSign, the browser will not show these warnings.

Note

As of the second beta, Microsoft Internet Explorer (MIE) will not allow you to access a secure site when the CA was unknown to the software. Netscape Navigator had this same sort of behavior in its 1.*x* release. You'd think Microsoft would think about this possibility!

GENERATING A KEY PAIR AND CSR FOR STRONGHOLD

In addition to generating a key pair when doing the initial installation, you can use the `genkey` program to generate additional keys. Why do you need the key pair? The server generates a private and public key pair. The public key is used to encrypt transmissions to the server. The server's private key is used to decrypt the transmissions. Only the private key can be used to decrypt an encrypted message. It is kept in the server while the public key is sent to the client.

Blue bar

Figure 14.1.
The installed SSL
server looks like
this when viewed
by Netscape. Note
the bar under the
address area and
the icon on the
lower left corner
(on the computer
the bars are
rendered in blue).

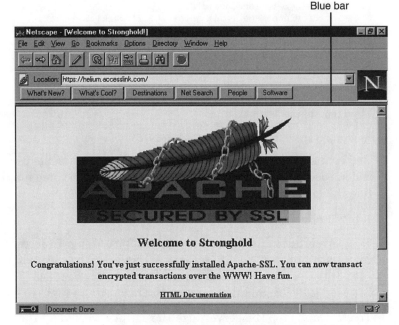

Figure 14.2.
A plain server
looks like this
when viewed by
Netscape. Note
the bar under the
address area is
missing, and the
key icon is
broken.

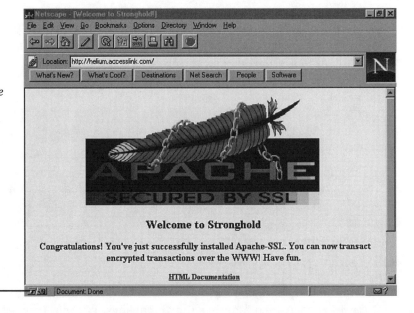

Broken key

In addition to the private/public key pair, genkey generates a CSR for sending to a CA—an entity that acts as a notary public, authenticating that the holder of a certificate is indeed the entity listed in the certificate itself. The certificate contains your server's public key, an expiration date, information about your organization, and the digital signature of the issuer.

When a server starts up a secure connection, it transmits the certificate to the client. The client decodes it by revealing your public key, an expiration date, information about your organization, and the digital signature of the issuer it displays to the user. The client then authenticates that the certificate has not been altered, and that it is signed by a CA it knows. This allows the client to generate a symmetric key that it can use to communicate with the server.

The `genkey` program allows you to generate the key pair and e-mail it to a CA, typically VeriSign. The certification process costs $290 and takes a few days. To complete the certification process, VeriSign will request more information about you or your organization before they issue the CA for your server. For more information, please visit `http://www.verisign.com`.

Once you receive your certificate, you must install it using the `getca` program. Remember to save a copy of this certificate in a safe place. Root install it with the following commands:

```
# getca hostname < certificate
```

`hostname` is your fully qualified hostname. `certificate` is the path to the certificate. Don't keep copies of your certificate laying around!

HOW MANY CERTIFICATES DO YOU NEED?

Most of the time you will only need to get one certificate. You will need to get an additional certificate if you are

- ◆ Using a different hostname or physical machine
- ◆ Using a different key pair
- ◆ Using a different brand of Web server

However, there may be creative ways of reducing your costs. Using Apache virtual hosts (described in Chapter 4, "Virtual Hosts"), you could implement a common site in your organization that handles all secure transactions for the various divisions in your organization, such as a point of sale system. All you need to do is create a link from your HTML to the secure URL when you need to transfer information via a secure environment. The secure server will then handle all secure transactions for all the other sites. Just remember to leave the "Organization Unit" field blank during configuration so that you don't confuse visitors. You may want to consider that while the most popular browsers support SSL, some may not, and you may want to offer a nonsecure transaction choice.

STRONGHOLD UTILITIES

The SSL distribution also includes a number of program utilities to help you manage your certificates and passwords.

`change_pass`	Sets the passphrase used to encrypt the server's private key. The private key should be kept encrypted to avoid any problems if someone obtains it. However, an encrypted private key will require providing a passphrase every time the server is started.
`decrypt_key`	This utility decrypts the private key to enable the server to start without requesting a passphrase. Having an unencrypted private key may jeopardize your key if someone is able to obtain it.
`gencert`	This tool is used to generate a test certificate. It also allows you to use private certificate authorities such as yourself (you authorize your own CA). Third-party tools are available to help you implement a more complex CA. For information, visit `http://www.xcert.com`.
`genkey`	This utility generates a private/public key pair and a CSR that you can send to a CA, such as VeriSign, for processing.
`getca`	This utility installs a certificate provided by a CA such as VeriSign.
`getreq`	This utility generates a CSR based on an existing private key located in `$SSLTOP/private/hostname.private`.
`makeca`	This utility sets up a self-signed CA for Stronghold.
`renewal`	This utility submits a certificate renewal request to your CA.

SSL-CONFIGURATION DIRECTIVES

Apache SSL extensions are incorporated into Apache via `ssl_module`. This module provides a number of configuration directives that you can use to control where the server will find configuration files, logs, and certificates among other things. Most of these configuration files are written to an `httpd.conf` file that resides in the `ssl_conf` directory if you are using Stronghold, or in `SSLconf/conf/` directory for Apache-SSL installations.

These directives can be used in a `<VirtualHost>` section. However, note that browsers, such as Netscape Navigator 2.x or better, check the URL against the hostname on the server certificate. This requires that you provide a different certificate for each virtual host you house.

BanCipher

Syntax: BanCipher *cipher*

Scope: Server configuration, directory, virtual host

This directive limits the use of ciphers that do not meet your security requirements for a particular directory:

```
<Directory path>
BanCipher cypher
</Directory>
```

RequireCipher

Syntax: RequireCipher *cipher*

Scope: Server configuration, directory, virtual host

This directive is typically used inside a <Directory> section to require a specific cipher for the specified directory:

```
<Directory path>
RequireCipher cipher
</Directory>
```

cipher can be any of the following cipher types:

Cipher Type	Description
NULL-MD5	No encryption, MD5 hash
RC4-MD5	Export-controlled, RC4-compatible cipher; MD5 hash
EXP-RC4-MD5	8-cent–secure, RC4-compatible cipher; MD5 hash
RC2-CBC-MD5	Export-controlled, RC2-compatible cipher in CBC mode; MD5 hash
EXP-RC2-CBC-MD5	Export-crippled, RC2-compatible in CBC mode; MD5 hash
IDEA-CBC-MD5	IDEA cipher in CBC mode, MD5 hash
DES-CBC-MD5	DES in CBC, MD5 hash
DES-CBC-SHA	DES in CBC, SHA hash
DES-CBC3-MD5	3DES in CBC, MD5 hash
DES-CBC3-SHA	3DES in CBC, SHA hash
DES-CFB-M1	DES in CFB

SSLCACertificateFile

Syntax: SSLCACertificateFile *filepath*

Scope: Server configuration, virtual host

The SSLCACertificateFile directive specifies the trusted CA root client certificate file instead of a certificate directory like the following SSLCACertificatePath directive.

SSLCACertificatePath

Syntax: SSLCACertificatePath *path*
Scope: Server configuration, virtual host

The SSLCACertificatePath directive specifies a path where trusted CA root certificates can be found. Root certificates for client certification should be stored here.

SSLErrorFile

Syntax: SSLErrorFile *filename*
Default: SSLErrorFile *SSLLogFile*
Scope: Server configuration, virtual host

The SSLErrorFile directive specifies a file where error messages and SSL-diagnostic output are sent. If omitted, these messages are logged to the file specified with the SSLLogFile directive.

SSLFakeBasicAuth

Syntax: SSLFakeBasicAuth
Scope: Server configuration, virtual host

If set, this option will translate client X509 in usernames that can be used for authentication.

SSLLogFile

Syntax: SSLLogFile *filename*
Scope: Server configuration, virtual host

The SSLErrorFile directive specifies a file where all SSL connections to the server are logged. It stores cipher and client authentication data.

SSLRequireCiphers

Syntax: SSLRequireCiphers *cipher:cipher:cipher...*
Scope: S erver configuration

This is a colon (:)-delimited list of cipher types permitted for all SSL transmission in order of preference.

SSLRoot

Syntax: SSLRoot *path*
Default: SSLRoot /usr/local/ssl
Scope: Server configuration, virtual host

The SSLRoot directive specifies where the SSL directory tree lives. *path* is prepended to all SSL file directives (except for the logging directives) that don't specify an absolute path.

SSLVerifyClient

Syntax: SSLVerifyClient [0] | [1] | [2]
Default: SSLVerifyClient 0
Scope: Server configuration, virtual host

This directive sets the X.509 Client Authentication option:

Option	Value
0	No certification is required.
1	X.509 certificate is optional.
2	X.509 certificate is required.

Client authentication can be an effective way of restricting access to your Web site.

SSLVerifyDepth

Syntax: SSLVerifyDepth *n*
Default: SSLVerifyDepth 0
Scope: Server configuration, virtual host

This directive controls the depth that the server will follow when verifying client certificates. The server will progressively search the CA chain until it reaches a decisive authority or reaches *n*.

SUMMARY

Secure transactions are the foundation for the commercialization of the Web. Currently there are a lot people looking at what's new, but not many people are using the Internet to purchase things. Most buyers have been frightened by the media into thinking that shopping the Internet could lead to someone using your credit card to make fraudulent charges. While this is possible, the real issue here is privacy and assurance that the person or company you are communicating with is indeed who she says she is. In the electronic age, the need for this technology is undeniable.

The Internet makes it possible to put bits of information about yourself together that are much more descriptive about you as a person. If you are using the Web to connect to another system, it is trivial for me to figure out what machine you are connecting from because this information is sent with every request you make. Some browsers, such as Internet Explorer, send additional information, such as the computer processor you are running and the color capabilities of your monitor. If you happen to be running some version of UNIX that allows fingering of your machine, there's a good chance of figuring out your name and address. With your name, it's easy to find your telephone number and everything you may have posted to Usenet. From that your hobbies and interests can be determined. With your address, it's easy to get a map of how to get to you or find where junk mail can be sent. All it takes is a few seconds. As more and more information about us floats out there, the scarier it becomes.

Encryption may solve one of the problems—how to avoid thugs from looking up your credit card number or some other important information. However, it doesn't do anything about other information that can easily be extracted from just pointing a Web browser to some URL.

- Host-Based Access Control (Domain-Level Access Control)

- User Authentication Control

- Group Authentication

CHAPTER 15

Access Control and User Authentication

User authentication and access control allow you to restrict access to your Web server's document tree. If you are building a site that will be accessible to the world and you don't need to restrict access to your materials, you may want to skip this chapter.

Servers with sensitive information should be behind a firewall or should use encryption technology that protects your materials from unauthorized viewing. Directly connecting to the Internet with a server that has sensitive information is asking for trouble.

Apache provides several methods you can use to restrict unauthorized access to your documents. These access control and user authentication extensions are implemented in the form of modules. Modules extend the functionality of Apache by adding new functionality that is not part of the Apache core itself. Modules provide additional directives that allow you to control the behavior of the server much the same way you control other aspects of the server's configuration.

As with any resource that needs to be secured, security factors depend on many issues. If the information you are publishing is of a highly sensitive nature, you should consider an alternative publishing medium. You may want to consider using a secure server, such as Apache-SSL or Stronghold. Both of these servers are based on the Apache source, but they add Secure Socket Layer (SSL) technology, which encrypts transactions between the server and the client when accessed with a compatible browser. Information on SSL servers is covered in Chapter 14, "Secure Web Servers."

The topics in this chapter offer an extremely basic measure of security, if you can call it that. User authentication and access control put a basic barrier between the user accessing your data and your server. If your data is sensitive, don't place your trust in any piece of software unless you understand the potential risks that could create a hole in your security scheme. Once again, do not place highly sensitive information on a publicly accessible server!

Apache provides a simple authentication scheme by which a user can prove his identity to the server: *Basic authentication*. While the mechanisms used to verify the authentication information are reliable, you should be aware that Basic authentication is not secure. It assumes that your network connection to the server is trustworthy—an assumption that is questionable once you access your server from outside your local network. Be aware when you transmit a password that unless you are using a secure server, the password transaction is not encrypted in any way by the client browser. It is encoded using a similar process to the UNIX uuencode program, which ensures its integrity during transmission. However, this method of encoding doesn't provide any encryption or other means of securing the data. Anyone with some technical ability who intercepts the request could decode the password information and use it to access your restricted materials. You should also be aware that when you authenticate, this process is repeated for every document you request (your password and User ID are sent with every page request, thus your password is sent not once, but many times).

Apache 1.1 adds a new form of authentication called *Digest authentication,* which uses RSA MD5 encryption technology. The use of Digest authentication requires a supporting Web browser. Be aware that unless you are using a secure server to access your documents, the information that you transmit is still sent in world-readable form.

Apache 1.1

Now you understand that not one single measure of security is enough or infallible; that passwords can be compromised by someone decoding or intercepting them; and that your networking wires can be tapped, or someone with access to a Domain Name System (DNS) server could make any machine masquerade as if it were in your network. The tools Apache provides can help you build a basic barrier to discourage and stop most unauthorized users from accessing your information.

Apache provides two methods you can use to control access to the documents you make available on the Web:

◆ Host-based or domain-level access control

◆ User authentication

You can enable access control and user authentication on a serverwide basis or on a per-directory basis by using the appropriate access control file (ACF):

◆ Serverwide access is controlled by settings on the global ACF, `conf/access.conf`.

◆ Per-directory access control can also be configured on the global ACF by using `<Directory>` sections or by using per-directory ACFs or `.htaccess` files. The use of per-directory ACFs may be restricted or not allowed by the global access control file.

Technical Note

A section is a special type of directive that follows an SGML-type syntax: `<directive option...>...</directive>`. Apache implements a few sections: `<VirtualHost>`, `<Directory>`, `<Limit>`, and new to 1.1, `<Location>`. The `<Location>` directive allows you to implement access control on a URL basis.

Access control on a per-file basis is not available to Apache versions prior to 1.1. If you need to restrict access to a file, you will need to create a directory for that file and restrict access to the directory instead.

Apache 1.1

Apache
1.2

> Apache 1.1 introduces the `<Location>` section, which allows you to restrict access based on a uniform resource locator (URL) or file address.
>
> Apache 1.2 will introduce a new section directive, `<File>`, which is similar in functionality to the `<Location>` section.

In general, per-directory ACFs are not a good idea for a site that needs tight security because some of the directives can override settings you specified on your global ACF. However, if for administration reasons you want to relegate access control management to the owners of the materials, per-directory access control files are the only way to go.

The name of the per-directory ACF is set by the `AccessFileName` directive. This directive is typically found in `conf/srm.conf`. The default value for `AccessFileName` is

```
AccessFileName .htaccess
```

Note that the period in the filename will make the file invisible to most users, unless they use the `-a` flag to `ls` (the program used for listing directories). Access control directives are usually found inside a `<Limit>` section. A `<Limit>` section contains control directives enclosed by a `<Limit>...</Limit>` tag pair:

```
<Limit method method ...>
ControlDirective
...
</Limit>
```

method refers to any HTTP valid access method (GET, POST, HEAD, and so on). Apache only enables GET, POST, and HEAD. The HEAD method returns an HTTP header describing the document, not the document itself. Other potentially dangerous methods are not implemented in Apache: PUT, DELETE, LINK, and UNLINK. So you should not have to worry about those. However, always read the documentation and be aware of HTTP methods that may compromise your security.

The enclosed directives only apply to the directory tree listed in a `<Directory>` section if the `<Limit>` section is in the global ACF. If they are found on a per-directory ACF, then all directories under that tree will share the requirements listed. If they are found outside a `<Directory>` section on the global ACF, then the requirement applies globally to all directories, even to documents outside your `DocumentRoot` pointed to by an `Alias` directive. (For more information, please refer to Chapter 10, "Apache Modules."

HOST-BASED ACCESS CONTROL (DOMAIN-LEVEL ACCESS CONTROL)

Host-based access control grants or denies access depending on the Internet Protocol (IP) address of the machine that generated the request. This system is the least intrusive to legitimate users because access is granted on the basis of the machine address. Machines matching a description are allowed or denied access to the document tree without requesting further information from the client.

Host-based access control is provided by the `mod_access` module. The `mod_access` module is compiled into Apache by default, so the directives it provides can be used without the need for additional configuration.

The `mod_access` module provides three directives to help you control access to your site:

- `order`
- `allow from`
- `deny from`

THE order DIRECTIVE

The `order` directive defines the order in which the `allow` and `deny` directives are evaluated within the `<Limit>` or `<Directory>` section. The syntax for the `order` directive is

```
order [deny,allow] | [allow,deny] | [mutual-failure]
```

The possible options are

`deny,allow`	Evaluates the `deny` directive first and then grants exceptions based on the `allow` directive.
`allow,deny`	Evaluates the `allow` directive first and then grants exceptions based on the `deny` directive.
`mutual-failure`	Evaluates so that only hosts that appear in the `allow` list and do not appear on the `deny` list are granted access.

THE allow DIRECTIVE

The `allow` directive lists hosts that are allowed access to the directory. `allow` has the following syntax:

```
allow from host host...
```

host can be specified by [all] | [*fully qualified host name*] | [*partial domain name*] | [*IP address*] | [*partial IP address*].

THE deny DIRECTIVE

The deny directive lists hosts that are denied access to the directory. deny has the following syntax:

deny from *host host...*

host can be specified by [all] | [*fully qualified host name*] | [*partial domain name*] | [*IP address*] | [*partial IP address*].

HOST-BASED ACCESS CONTROL EXAMPLES

To limit access control to your server's DocumentRoot to hosts in your domain (assuming that your document root is htdocs), you would have an entry in your conf/access.conf file that looks like this:

```
<Directory /usr/local/etc/httpd/htdocs>
<Limit GET POST>
order deny,allow
deny from all
allow from yourdomain.dom
</Limit>
</Directory>
```

If you were limiting access to a directory inside your DocumentRoot (using .htaccess), you would specify this:

```
<Limit GET POST>
order deny,allow
deny from all
allow from yourdomain.dom
</Limit>
```

As described in the syntax, you can also specify hosts by IP or partial IP address. Using an IP address to list hosts may be more secure than by name. The following is a more complex example. To only allow access to hosts in the *your.domain* domain and the marketing subnet of the friendly.com domain and to all hosts from network 204.95.160 (in this case, this is a C-class address so there are 254 possible hosts), the <Limit> section would look like this:

```
<Limit GET POST>
order deny,allow
deny from all
allow from yourdomain.dom marketing.friendly.com 204.95.160
</Limit>
```

USER AUTHENTICATION CONTROL

User authentication allows you to control access to the document tree on an individual user basis by utilizing user and passwords lists to provide the necessary authentication. When a user accesses a restricted portion of the site, the server requires him to log in by specifying a username and a password. If the user supplies the proper information, access is granted for him to roam across the site without additional login requests. (Although the user does not enter a password, the username and password get re-sent by the browser with each new request to the protected realm.) See Figure 15.1 for an example of a login panel and Figure 15.2 for an example of a rejected login.

Figure 15.1.
A login panel.
The message You need a password to access this page *was added by the* AuthName *directive.*

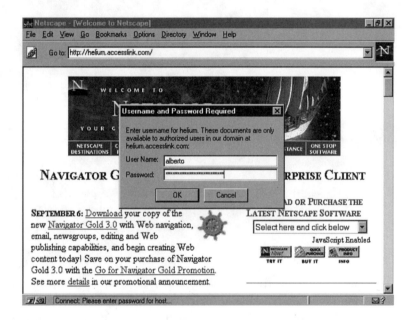

User authentication based on access control provides more selective security because access permission is validated on a per-user basis. Apache requires login and a password validation before granting access to a restricted portion of your site. It is important to note that there is no correlation between the UNIX password file (/etc/passwd) and the server's password files; it is not necessary for a user to have an account on your system to be able to access protected materials on your Web server. Also, it goes without saying that security is only as good as the passwords and the secrecy used to guard them.

15

ACCESS CONTROL AND USER AUTHENTICATION

Figure 15.2.
A rejected login.
This is the
message Apache
displays if the
client doesn't
provide the
correct auth-
entication
information.

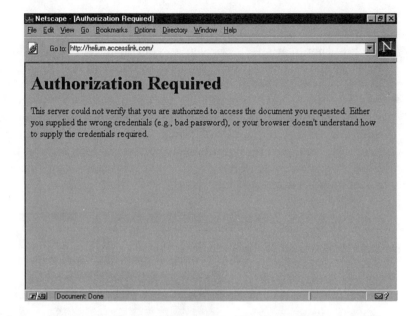

Warning

Because passwords are transmitted as encoded text, there are no safeguards preventing someone from intercepting a request and decoding the password. The security of your information really depends on the trustworthiness of the networks used to access your server—a condition that is nonexistent when your server is accessed from the Internet.

To provide user authentication you will need to create and maintain password files. You can have many different password files within your site; however, you may find it easier to create a single password file and create a group file to further refine permissions. By also using a group file, you can establish access restrictions based on the user's group memberships.

Currently, user authentication is provided by the following modules:

◆ mod_auth—Authentication using flat-file databases.

◆ mod_auth_dbm—Authentication using DBM (hashed database) files.

◆ mod_auth_db—Authentication using the Berkeley Software Distribution (BSD) UNIX DB files (BSD's hashed database format). This module is included in Apache 1.1. Users of Apache 1.0.*x* can find the module on the Apache site under third-party contributions.

The previous modules provide the following directives:

Module	User Authentication Directive
mod_auth	AuthUserFile *file*
mod_auth_dbm	AuthDBMUserFile *dbmfile*
mod_auth_db	AuthDBUserFile *dbfile*

The only difference between the modules, besides the small change in the naming of the directive, is the database format used to store the user and password information. The modules providing DBM and DB support offer incredible perfor- mance enhancements over the flat files used by mod_auth. DBM and DB formats are hashed tables. A *hashed table* orders all entries with a unique index, otherwise known as a *key*, which is generated from the username and a value. In order to look up a password, the hashing algorithm computes the key for the user and retrieves the password. In contrast, the flat file version (mod_auth) needs to read every user in the file, and when it finds a match, it retrieves it. This process becomes very inefficient and slow as soon as there are more than a few hundred users in the database.

The DBM version of the module was originally developed for HotWired (http:// www.hotwired.com), which has over 150,000 users.

REQUESTING A PASSWORD

To request authentication for your document tree to users within your network, just modify your access.conf configuration file to have an entry like this:

```
<Directory /usr/local/etc/httpd/htdocs>
  AllowOverride None
  AuthUserFile /usr/local/etc/httpd/passwords/passwordfile
# Group authentication is disabled by pointing it to /dev/null
  AuthGroupFile /dev/null
  AuthName These documents are only available to authorized users in our domain
  ➥name
  AuthType Basic
  <Limit Get>
    require valid-user
    order deny,allow
    deny from all
    allow from domain
  </Limit>
</Directory>
```

The order, deny, and allow directives limit who will get a login panel. If you want users to be able to use your server from outside your network, just omit these directives. Otherwise, just replace *domain* with the domain name for your organization, or better yet, specify your domain by using an IP address notation.

The previous example defines the location of the database using the `AuthUserFile` and `AuthGroupFile` directives provided by the `mod_access` module. If you wish to use the DBM or DB supporting modules, just replace the authentication configuration directives with the equivalent version provided by the module you wish to use.

Next, you'll need to create the password directory on your `httpd` tree:

```
# mkdir /usr/local/etc/httpd/passwords
```

Make sure the `/usr/local/etc/httpd/passwords` directory is readable by the user or group your server runs under. If the server cannot access the file, no one will be able to get in.

The tools you use to manage the password file depend on the type of authentication you use. If you are using flat files, you'll use the `htpasswd` program. If you are using database files, you'll use the `dbmmanage` script.

MANAGING FLAT-FILE PASSWORD FILES WITH `htpasswd`

To add users to your password file, you'll need to use the `htpasswd` program. The source code for this program is included in the support directory (`/usr/local/etc/httpd/support`), but it is not compiled by default. You'll need to edit the `CC=` directive in the makefile in that directory to match the name of your compiler. And then issue a `make`. After a few seconds, the binary `htpasswd` and other utilities will be built. Once `htpassword` is built, you can create a password file. The `htpasswd` program has the following syntax:

```
htpasswd [-c] passwordfile username
```

The `-c` flag creates the password file *passwordfile*. Here's a sample session:

```
# cd /usr/local/etc/httpd
# support/htpasswd -c passwords/passwordfile user
Adding password for user.
New password:
Re-type new password:
```

The passwords won't be displayed on the terminal as you type, so as a security measure, `htpasswd` will ask for the password twice. If the username you entered exists, `htpasswd` will ask you for the new password.

You can create as many password files as you like. However, you'll have to use different filenames to reference them.

Warning

Do not put a password file in the directory you are trying to protect. The best place for a password file is outside of your server's document root.

Managing DBM and DB Password Databases with dbmmanage

If you have more than a few visitors, you will need to authenticate; you'll want to use DBM or DB password databases. Password lookups using hashed databases are much more efficient. To manage DBM password files, you'll use the dbmmanage script. dbmmanage is a Perl script, so you'll need to have Perl installed. Perl is an interpreted programming language that is widely used for CGI program development. The Perl program is located in the support directory. You may have to edit the location of the Perl binary on the first line of the script to match the location of your copy. You'll also need to set the execute bit on the script so that your shell will execute it. The syntax of the dbmmanage program is

```
dbmmanage dbmfile [adduser] [add] [delete] [view] username password group
```

The name of your DBM database is *dbmfile*; if it doesn't exist, it will be created for you. Note that DBM databases may be implemented as two files: *dbmfile*.pag and *dbmfile*.dir. DBM files are not user readable. They contain binary information. Don't try to edit them by hand or alter their contents with anything besides the dbmmanage tool. The hashed database routine needs them both to operate correctly.

Technical Note

When I refer to *dbmfile* I am talking about the base name of the file without the .pag or .dir extensions! The DBM code used to access the files automatically references whichever of these files it needs to work with. All your references to DBM files should just specify the base name of the file, excluding any suffixes.

The adduser option to dbmmanage encrypts the *password* field. You can specify as many groups as you like. Just separate them with a comma (,) without any surrounding whitespace. Adduser is the option you'll use for adding users to your database. Here's an example:

```
# support/dbmmanage passwords/password adduser user1 pw group1,group2
User user1 added with password pw:group1,group2, encrypted to XXZx5yHFQJRp.:
➥group1,group2
```

```
# support/dbmmanage passwords/password adduser user2 pw group2
User user2 added with password pw:group2, encrypted to XXZx5yHFQJRp.:group2
```

The add option adds a key/value pair. You can use this to add descriptions or notes to your DBM file. Just make sure your key value doesn't overwrite a username. Also, if your value has more than one word, quote the contents:

```
# dbmmanage dbmfile add key "This is a multiword value"
```

The delete option deletes an entry matching *key*:

```
# dbmmanage dbmfile delete key
```

The view option displays all entries in dbmfile:

```
# support/dbmmanage passwords/password view
user1 = XXZx5yHFQJRp.:group1,group2
user2 = XXZx5yHFQJRp.:group2
```

Group Authentication

Besides authenticating users on an individual basis, you can group users. This grouping process is similar to the grouping concept used for permissions under UNIX. Grouping users is a convenient method for providing a finer degree of access control. It allows you to manage many users as a single entity.

If you request membership to a particular group as a requirement to access materials, then users not only need to provide a valid login and password, but they also need to be members of the specific group in order to gain access.

To enable group authentication to your document root, you'll need to edit your AuthGroupFile directive to point to a valid group file. As in the previous section, the directive you use to specify the location of your group file will vary depending on the module you use to provide the authentication. AuthGroupFile is available on the base release because the module mod_auth is compiled by default into Apache. The other variants, AuthDBMGroupFile and AuthDBGroupFile, are available if you reconfigure and recompile Apache to include mod_auth_dbm or mod_auth_db, respectively. Here's a sample configuration:

```
<Directory /usr/local/etc/httpd/htdocs>
  AllowOverride None
  AuthUserFile /usr/local/etc/httpd/passwords/passwordfile
  AuthGroupFile /usr/local/etc/httpd/passwords/groupfile
  AuthName These documents are only available to authorized users in our domain
  ↪name
  AuthType Basic
  <Limit Get>
    require group group1 group2 ...
    order deny,allow
    deny from all
    allow from domain
```

```
   </Limit>
</Directory>
```

The only changes made to the previous section were to the `AuthGroupFile` directive. Previously, I disabled group authentication by pointing it to `/dev/null` as the group file. I also modified the `require` directive. Earlier I was allowing any valid users in the password file. Now I am requiring that, besides being in the password file, the user belong to either *group1* or *group2*.

As previously, both the directive and the file used for group authentication depend on the module you are using:

Module	*Group Authentication Directive*
mod_auth	AuthGroupFile *groupfile*
mod_auth_dbm	AuthDBMGroupFile *dbmgroupfile*
mod_auth_db	AuthDBGroupFile *dbgroupfile*

To create a group file for use with the `mod_auth` module (`AuthGroupFile` directive), you'll need a text editor.

The format of the file is simple:

```
groupname: user1 user2 user3 ...
```

groupname is the name for the group followed by a colon (`:`), and then followed by a list of usernames that appear in the password file separated by spaces. Different groups are separated by a new line (`\n`) character:

```
group1: user1 user2 user3
group2: user2 user3
```

You'll need to restart `httpd` for your changes to take effect.

If you are using `mod_auth_dbm` or `mod_auth_db`, the group management process is a little easier. `dbmmanage` allows you to specify group memberships right on the password file.

Using the `adduser` option to `dbmmanage`, you can assign group memberships at the same time you add a user. You can specify as many groups as you like for each user. Just separate them with a comma (`,`) without any surrounding whitespace:

```
# support/dbmmanage passwords/password adduser user1 pw group1,group2
User user1 added with password pw:group1,group2, encrypted to XXZx5yHFQJRp.:
➥group1,group2
# support/dbmmanage passwords/password adduser user2 pw group2
User user2 added with password pw:group2, encrypted to XXZx5yHFQJRp.:group2
```

Then all you need to do is reference the same password file for group information:

```
AllowOverride None
 AuthDBMUserFile /usr/local/etc/httpd/passwords/passwordfile
 AuthDBMGroupFile /usr/local/etc/httpd/passwords/passwordfile
 AuthName These documents are only available to authorized users in our domain
 ➥name
```

```
AuthType Basic
<Limit Get>
  require group group1 group2 …
  order deny,allow
  deny from all
  allow from domain
</Limit>
```

In case it was not obvious, the examples have been using two or more forms of authentication at the same time. Using domain-level access plus user and group authentication methods provide additional levels of security because users need to meet several criteria before gaining access: They need to access the material from a specified domain, and then they need to have a valid login and password. Finally, their login name must belong to a group.

SUMMARY

As mentioned earlier, the access control and authentication methods provided by Apache can help to make your server relatively safe; however, no single mode of protection is bulletproof. If you can trust your DNS, then access control is a safe method for restricting access.

Passwords are transmitted in clear text form and encoded to ensure that they arrive intact. However, this encoding does not provide an encryption layer, so any user along the network could intercept a request to your server and decode the password. Finally, even if you trusted that no one will listen for passwords, remember that transactions on plain vanilla versions of Apache are not encrypted. Your materials are sent in world-readable form.

Beginning with Apache 1.1, some new authentication modules and methods are available. One of them, mod_auth_msql, allows you to store authentication information on a relational database (mSQL). For more information on how to use the mod_auth_msql directives, please refer to Chapter 10.

CHAPTER 16

Web Server
Security Issues

Throughout this book I have not discussed the security implications of running a Web server mainly because I wanted to focus all this vital information into a single chapter. My thinking is that by putting all security information together, it would be much easier for you to read and reference. While other chapters may have made a reference to security, they didn't address it. This chapter does.

More than likely after you read this information, you'll be worrying about a few things. That's good. You *should* worry. While at times I may sound paranoid, take it with a grain of salt. The level of security you implement should reflect the level of security that you need. Creating a secure network is a very extensive topic, and one that changes constantly. This chapter will focus closely on the issues that affect a Web server; general network security is touched on but not really addressed.

WHY SECURITY?

Connecting a computer to the Internet is a very exciting event. It opens up a world of information and communication. By setting up a Web server, you have plugged into that world and transformed yourself into an information provider. The only trouble is that by doing so you have just exposed your network to a series of potential security problems. These dangers are packaged in many forms, including the following:

◆ Unauthorized use of your computing resources

◆ Denial of service attacks

◆ Information theft

◆ Vandalism

While any of these issues should warrant terror from you, knowing what they do will help you prepare to face these possibly adverse situations.

Warning

> Before you go any further, you should think of dedicating a system to serving Web pages. This system should be a bare bones machine; it should have no user accounts and contain minimal software. It also should not be directly on your local area network (LAN). If you haven't set up a firewall yet, do it. A firewall will isolate your network from the Internet—a smart thing to do.

UNAUTHORIZED USE OF COMPUTING RESOURCES

Many of the attacks on a network have obtaining illicit use of your systems as their goal. These attackers will try to seize control of your system using its resources for whatever they see fit. While on the surface this seems like the least harmful of problems, these attackers can create serious problems that could even affect your reputation. For one, your systems could become the home base from which to launch attacks onto other networks. They could turn your computers into illegal software distribution depots by distributing copies of copyrighted or pornographic material right from your systems!

DENIAL OF SERVICE ATTACKS

Denial of service attacks are designed to keep you from using your own computing resources. Some of the attacks can capitalize on known vulnerabilities of your operating system, such as flooding your system with so much e-mail that it cannot keep up with other legitimate requests. Intruders can also shut down your equipment, affecting services that are available to other users of your network. Sometimes this sort of attack is part of a well-orchestrated attack towards another system. By making a trusted system unavailable, an attacker could make another computer masquerade as your trusted host and gain access to a different machine.

INFORMATION THEFT

Information theft may be a serious problem if you store sensitive information on your systems. Even if you don't, the information gathered could be used to gain further access to your system or personal information that should be kept private. Confidential information, be it your secret formula for lemonade or your banking records, should not be anyone's business but your own.

VANDALS

This is probably the most annoying of all attacks. A vandal will attempt to destroy information that you keep on your computer. Your best survival technique is simple. Have a backup of your data! Why would someone do this? Usually it's a personal attack by a disgruntled employee or someone else that somehow thinks he has a score to settle.

HOW DO THEY GET IN?

People who break into computers do it by exploiting some sort of software weakness. Usually, this is a bug in some program or a library. Many years back, `sendmail`, the mailer agent that delivers mail on most UNIX machines, was the target for one of these types of attacks. The `sendmail` worm exploited known bugs, and while it created no damage to data, the worm managed to consume all the resources of the effected computer. The `sendmail` worm managed to invade thousands of computers in just a few hours.

16

If you see what I am getting at, most security problems are rooted in software bugs. This is why it is extremely important that your software is kept up-to-date. Systems that are running old software are more likely to be broken into because they contain bugs and problems that are known.

Unlike PCs and Macintoshes, UNIX systems offer a wide range of services. For example, if you tried to FTP into a Mac or a PC, you would not be able to do it unless the user installed a program that supported this protocol. Under UNIX, this and many other client/server programs are already installed and waiting for a connection. For a list of what is running on your system, check your /etc/inetd.conf file.

Even if you don't know anything about plumbing, you can easily understand that the more complicated the plumbing, the easier it is to clog a drain. Software is not any different. The more complicated a program is, the more likely that it has bugs. Web servers are complicated programs, and your UNIX box is full of many complex programs, including shells and interpreters.

Thankfully, Apache doesn't have any known security problems. A basic configuration setting is fairly secure because it doesn't permit the execution of CGI programs or Server Side Includes (SSI). If you forget for a minute about all the other potential problems outside of your Web server, you will find that the source of security problems on a Web server is usually caused by you, the administrator. Here's a list of the possible holes you can open:

◆ Insecure CGI programs *you* write or insecure programs others write that get placed into your server.

◆ Permissive and promiscuous security policies *you* set; this allows other users or uninvited guests to override your security policies. This refers to permitting the use of per-directory access files (.htaccess).

◆ Additional server features that *you* enable. Unless you know what those third-party modules do and how they have been coded, it is difficult to see if any of them will cause you grief. The best defense is to run a minimal server: one that supplies the absolute minimum level of facilities that do what you need. This approach has the added benefit of making your server lighter in weight, which translates into a faster and more responsive server.

You should be able to tell I am emphasizing (and maybe putting my foot in my mouth) that Apache, from a software standpoint, is fairly secure. No known bugs have severe security implications in the current version, and if one was discovered, the Apache team would be quick to rectify the situation. Always run the latest and greatest software to avoid problems.

From a Web server standpoint, the main focus of your worries should focus on CGI and SSI because these two powerful features usually process user data. If you trust that the input data is good, you are in for something.

My first recommendation is that you should carefully evaluate any CGIs you have written. Your CGIs should be coded defensively because unexpected input will cause problems. This simply means that the information your CGI takes in should not be trusted and must be qualified before it is passed to another program for execution.

Data sent by a visitor via a form should be digested carefully. Just because input is generated by a form that you coded doesn't mean that the visitor didn't alter your form in an attempt to crash your program. Perhaps she returned different values or more data than what you expected. Her intent is to capitalize on a weakness, such as overflowing your CGI. Perhaps a path specification is different from what you would normally expect.

What your CGI can receive could be anything. Maybe through her e-mail address there's an attempt at getting your computer to do something else. Unless you are ready to cope with that possibility, you are creating a huge security risk.

AVOIDING BAD INPUT

Here's what you should keep in mind regarding filenames:

- Filenames you code are OK.
- Filenames sent by a form or coded by others are not.
- Restrict the files that others can supply to you. Perhaps have your program only access files that you explicitly permit.
- Your CGI programs should be able to gracefully handle a missing temporary file. Perhaps your CGI programs should be able to determine if the file they are opening is the one they thought it was.
- Filenaming. Keep it simple: Only allow filenames that use letters and numbers. Any other character is suspicious. Spaces or other whitespace in a filename can introduce problems. This also means that under UNIX, you really don't want files that start with periods (.), semicolons (;), or dashes (-). Files that include any of the shell metacharacters should not be permitted. Metacharacters are characters like * or ?, which have a special meaning to a shell.
- File permissions. Perhaps temporary files should not be world readable or writable because this allows users from within your organization to read information that they perhaps should not. This is the one reason to have your server run as a special user such as httpd, so that you can assign a reasonable umask. The umask (the user mask) is used to set the default file

permission. The easiest way to calculate a umask is to subtract the permissions from it.

> ## *Note*
>
> If you want your files to be readable and writable by you and no one else, you need to set your file mode to 700 (I added 400+200+100 from the following table). To create a umask that responds to this file mode, subtract 700 from 777. This leaves you with a umask of 77. Typically, you specify umasks with a 0 for the owner bit because you want to be able to have execute permissions on directories and executables you create, thus you would specify a 077 umask value.
>
> Permissions under UNIX take the following bits, which you can add or subtract to arrive at the permissions you want:
>
> | Bit Mode | Significance |
> | --- | --- |
> | 4000 | Set User ID on execution |
> | 2000 | Set Group ID on execution |
> | 1000 | Set sticky bit* |
> | 0400 | Read by owner |
> | 0200 | Write by owner |
> | 0100 | Execute (search in directory) by owner |
> | 0040 | Read by group |
> | 0020 | Write by group |
> | 0010 | Execute (search in a directory) by group |
> | 0004 | Read by others |
> | 0002 | Write by others |
> | 0001 | Execute by others |
>
> *When set, unprivileged users cannot delete or rename files of other users in that directory.

SECURING YOUR CGI

The main problem with CGIs is passing user variables when executing an exec() or system() call. These variables, if not carefully watched, could contain shell meta-characters that would cause the shell to do something other than what was intended.

Suppose you have a simple script that uses the UNIX utility grep to search the contents of a phone database. The user enters a first or last name, and the script returns any matching items. The script does most of its work like this (please note that Perl has much better, built-in ways of doing this). Here's the script:

```
system("grep $pattern database");
```

The pattern variable is set from a form input by the user. Now see what would happen if the user entered a line like the following:

```
"-v ffffffff /etc/passwd ¦mail someAddress"
```

This effectively would send your /etc/passwd file via e-mail to someAddress. The -v argument to grep tells it to include all lines that don't match. Our matching pattern ffffffff more than likely won't match anyone.

The real solution to this type of problem is to do several things. One easy way of dealing with this problem is by making a call to system a little differently:

```
system("/bin/grep", $pattern, "database");
```

By doing this, you have eliminated calling a shell. This effectively eliminated the calling of a shell, which would have interpreted the pipe and done something you didn't want. Alternatively, you could have escaped each special shell character before passing it to the grep call, as this line of Perl shows:

```
$pattern =~ s/[^\w]/\\\&/g;
system("grep \"$pattern\" database");
```

Perl has built-in checks for shell metacharacters and other expressions that could spell trouble. To enable this feature, just start your Perl scripts with #!/usr/local/bin/perl -T.

This will enable Perl's taint checks. Data from outside the program (environment variables, standard input stream, or program arguments) cannot use eval(), exec(), system(), or piped open() calls. Any program variable that obtains a value from one of these sources also becomes tainted and cannot be used either. In order for you to use a tainted variable, you'll need to *untaint* it. Untainting requires that you perform a pattern matching on the tainted variable that extracts matched substrings. To untaint an e-mail address, use the following code:

```
$email=~/([\w-.]+\@[\w-.]+)/;
```

Server Parsed HTML Security Issues

Server Parsed HTML (SPML), also known as Server Side Includes (SSI), provides a convenient way of performing server-side processing on an HTML file before it is sent to the client. This allows for the opportunity to introduce some dynamic features without having to program a CGI to provide the functionality.

SPML documents are processed by the server before they are sent to the client. Documents with a MIME type text/x-server-parsed-html or text/x-server-parsed-html3 are parsed. The resulting HTML is given a MIME type `text/html` and is sent back to the client.

SPML can include information such as the current time, can execute a program, or can include a document, just by adding some special SPML commands to your HTML page. When the HTML page is properly identified to the server as containing SPML tokens, the server parses the file and sends the results to the client requesting it. While this seems rather innocuous, it isn't. SSIs are parsed like a script and can be a source of grief.

File inclusion is not usually a problem, as long as users are not including sensitive files such as `/etc/passwd`. One condition to watch for is SSI that are built from data provided by a user over the Web. Suppose that you created a bulletin board SSI that would include items added by external users via a CGI. If your CGI was not smart enough to check for what it is being handed, it is possible for a user to add something nasty such as a line like `<!--#cmd cmd="/bin/rm -rf />`. This, as you guessed, would attempt to remove all files in your disk. Obviously, the example is intended as an illustration.

SECURITY AND PERMISSIONS

Exercising security on your Web site means enforcing policies. If you happen to allow per-directory access files, in a way you have relinquished some control over the implementation of that policy. From an administrative point of view, it is much better to manage one global access file (`conf/access.conf`) with many different entries than a minimal global configuration file plus hundreds of per-directory access files.

Per-directory access files also have the terrible side effect of slowing down your server considerably because, once enabled, your server will scan each directory in the path to a request. If found, it then needs to figure out what options to apply and in what order. This takes time.

THE Options DIRECTIVE

Permissions are specified in `<Directory>` sections in the global access control file or on a per-directory basis with `.htaccess` files. The `Options` directive specifies what server options are enabled for that particular server domain. Here are some of the options:

All	Enables all options *except* MultiViews.
ExecCGI	Enables the execution of CGI programs.
FollowSymLinks	Enables the traversing of symbolic links.
Includes	Enables the use of SSI.

IncludesNOEXEC	Enables the use of SSI with the following restrictions: The #exec and #include commands are disabled.
Indexes	Enables the return of a server-generated directory listing for requests where there is no DirectoryIndex file (index.html).
MultiViews	Enables content negotiation based on document language. See the LanguagePriority directive in Chapter 10, "Apache Modules."
SymLinksIfOwnerMatch	The traversing of symbolic links is allowed if the target file or directory is owned by the same user as the link. This setting offers better security than the FollowSymLinks option.

The following is a list of the security issues raised by the Options directive. Relevance to your particular application depends on what type of site you manage.

ExecCGI

On my site, the option to run CGIs on a directory other than cgi-bin doesn't pose many security risks because I control all CGI programs on the server. However, if you have a mélange of users, permitting execution of CGIs from anywhere may be too permissive and is a way of asking for trouble.

FollowSymLinks

The FollowSymLinks option is another option to worry about. If a user is able to create a link to a directory from inside your Web document tree, she's just created an alternative way of navigating into the rest of your filesystem. You can consider this option as an easy way to publish your entire disk to the world. The SynLinksIfOwnerMatch option tries to mitigate this option a bit. However, both these options are very dangerous if your ship is not a tight one.

Includes

Includes enables the execution of SSI in the directory. This option can be tamed down by specifying the IncludesNOEXEC option, which disables file inclusion (so your users cannot do a <!----#include virtual=/etc/passwd -->) or executes programs from within an include statement.

Indexes

This feature can be corrupted easily. If you recall the discussion about `FollowSynLinks`, automatic indexes go hand-in-hand with it. When the user travels to a directory that doesn't contain a user-generated index file, one gets generated by the server if you have automatic indexing enabled. This basically provides a nice listing of your files and provides a nice interface with which to retrieve them.

Access Control

Apache provides you with several methods of authenticating users before you grant them access to your materials. Third-party modules provide support for an even greater number. You can authenticate using cookies, SQL databases, flat files, and so on. You can also control access to your machine based on the IP of the host requesting the documents. Neither of these methods provides a good measure of security by itself; however, together they are much more robust.

There are a few issues that should be mentioned before you rely on any of these methods.

Filtering by Address

Although looking at a machine's address to determine if it is a friendly computer is better than not doing it, any host can be spoofed. Some evildoers on the Net can configure their computers to pretend to be someone you know. Usually this is done by making a real host unavailable and then making the Domain Name System (DNS) provide the wrong information. For your security, you may want to enable `-DMAXIMUM_DNS` while compiling the server software (under Apache 1.1 there's a new directive `HostnameLookups` that does the same thing as a runtime directive). This will solicit a little more work on your computer because DNS information will need to be verified more closely. Typically, the server will do a reverse lookup on the IP address of a client to get its name. Setting up the `HostnameLookups` will force one more test. After the name is received, the server will query DNS for its IP address. If they both match, things are cool. Otherwise, the access fails.

Login and Passwords

One problem with login and password verification over the Web is that an evildoer can have a ball at trying to crack a password. On many UNIX systems, if you tried this at a user account, the system would eventually disable access to the account, making it more difficult to break in. On the Web, you could try a few hundred passwords in a few seconds (with a little software) without anyone noticing it. Obviously, this doesn't present much danger, with the exception of obtaining access to private information, until you consider that most users use one password for most services.

BASIC AUTHENTICATION

Basic authentication is basic in that information exchanged between the browser and the server is not encrypted in any way. This method only encodes, not encrypts, the authentication session. Anyone that can intercept your authentication session can decode it and use the information to access your materials. The browser sends in authentication information with each request to the protected realm, which means that your login and password are sent not once, but several times through the wire.

To resolve this problem, a new method has been introduced: Digest authentication. Unlike Basic, Digest encodes and encrypts (trivially) the password in a way that it is valid only for the requested resource. If someone captured the authentication information and was able to decode it, that password would be useful to retrieve that one resource only. Access to each page requires a new password, which the browser generates. This makes the entire process a bit more secure.

If you want to have truly secure access to your server and you don't want to send passwords in the clear, the only current viable solution is to use an SSL server, such as Stronghold or Apache SSL. Chapter 14, "Secure Web Servers," goes into great detail about these products. An SSL server ensures that information sent between the browser and the server is kept confidential. So even if someone is spying on the line, it is very difficult to recover the original information. Secure transactions also ensure that the data you receive originated from a trusted point.

PROTECTING UNIX

One way of reducing the likelihood of a problem is to reduce the number of sources to potential problems. One way of dealing with this is to reduce the number of software systems that could be subverted in an unexpected way, meaning your server should be as light as possible in the software department.

- ◆ Your host should house the minimum number of users possible.
- ◆ Your host should house the necessary Internet services (see your `/etc/inetd.conf` file for services you are currently running). Remove services that are not needed.
- ◆ Your host should be running the latest stable versions of the server programs, including `sendmail`, `httpd`, `ftp`, and so on.
- ◆ The logfiles in your host should be checked often.

16

ADDITIONAL SOURCES OF SECURITY INFORMATION

If you don't do much about security, the least you could do is frequently read the newsgroup `comp.security.announce`. This Usenet group contains posts for the Computer Emergency Response Team (CERT), which lists security holes as they are found. The CERT home page (see Figure 16.1) can be found at `http://www.cert.org`.

Figure 16.1. The CERT Coordination Center's home page.

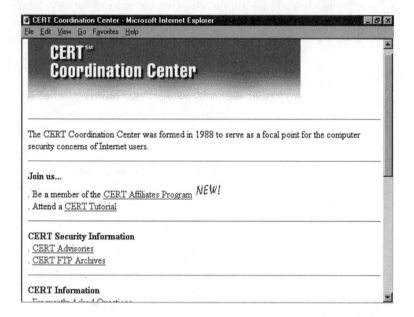

In addition to CERT advisories, you may want to check Internet Security Systems, Inc.'s home page (see Figure 16.2). It is located at `http://www.iss.net`. Its Web site has a nice mailing list and a vulnerability database for a variety of programs where security problems are grouped. Naturally, there's one for Apache too.

There are many excellent books available that will provide more detail than you'll probably ever need. Here's a few:

UNIX Security for the Organization, by Richard Bryant, Sams Publishing.

Internet Firewalls and Network Security, by Karanjit Siyan, Ph.D., and Chris Hare, New Riders Publishing.

Building Internet Firewalls, by D. Brent Chapman and Elizabeth D. Zwicky, O'Reilly & Associates, Inc.

Practical UNIX Security, by Simson Garfinkel and Gene Spafford, O'Reilly & Associates, Inc.

Figure 16.2.
Internet Security
Systems, Inc.'s
home page.

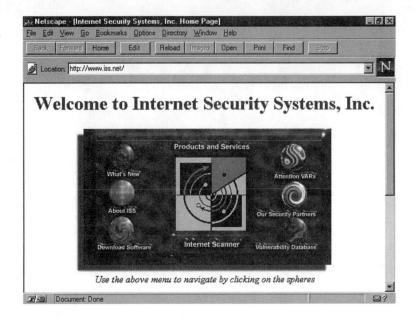

SUMMARY

The issues in this chapter only begin to address a few of the many configuration issues that may affect the security of your site. Security is a very complex issue. Because of UNIX and the networking necessary to make a Web server work, your task is a complicated one. I hope some of the warnings will point you in the right direction. And yes, while some of the examples are extreme, they were meant to catch your attention. The truth is you really cannot be sure of what can be done. Expect the unexpected, and prepare for disaster. This way, should you be unfortunate and have a security breach, you'll be prepared to deal with it from a practical, as well as an emotional, point of view.

Document any security problems you may find. If you think something is not right, document it. If you shut down your system, the intruder will know she's been had, and it will be very difficult for you to track her. On the other hand, if you wait and document, you may have a better chance of catching her and finding out her true identity.

- Un-CGI Version 1.7
  Documentation

- Managing Virtual
  Domains with
  `sendmail` V8

- FastCGI

- HTML Reference
  Guide

- DNS and BIND
  Primer

PART VI

Other References

- Introduction

- Installation

- Usage

- Other Features

- Frequently Asked
  Questions

APPENDIX A

Un-CGI Version 1.7
Documentation

Note

The Un-CGI documentation was reprinted, with minor alterations, with kind permission from its author, Steven Grimm. The most recent version of this software and its documentation are available via the Web at http://www.hyperion.com/~koreth/uncig.html.

INTRODUCTION

This is Un-CGI, a frontend for processing queries and forms from the Web on UNIX systems. You can get it via anonymous File Transfer Protocol (FTP) from ftp.hyperion.com or, depending on your browser, by following this link:

http://www.hyperion.com/~koreth/uncgi.html

If you wanted to process a form without this program, you would have to either write or dig up routines to translate the values of the form's fields from URL encoding to whichever your program required. This was a hassle in C and a real pain in the shell, and you had to do things differently for GET and POST queries.

This is where uncgi comes in. It decodes all the form fields and sticks them into environment variables for easy peruse by a shell script, a C program, a Perl script, or whatever you like. Then it executes whichever program you specify. (Actually, Un-CGI is something of a misnomer because the weird URL syntax is from the HTML forms specification, not from CGI itself.)

INSTALLATION

Let's assume that you have at least a passing familiarity with compiling and installing programs from the Internet. You know how to unpack a compressed tarfile and use make, and are familiar with the operation of your HTTP server. If you don't, you're probably not the right person to install Un-CGI; ask your system administrator to set it up for you.

To install, edit the makefile. Change the following settings:

CC	The name of your system's C compiler—typically cc or gcc.
SCRIPT_DIR	The directory where you want Un-CGI to look for your programs. This doesn't have to be the same as your server's CGI directory. Note that you cannot use a tilde (~) here to signify a home directory; you have to use the entire path, beginning with /.
DESTDIR	The directory where you want the Un-CGI executable to be installed. If your server has a cgi-bin directory, it is generally what you'll need to put here because the server needs to know

how to run Un-CGI as a CGI program. Often that can only happen for programs that are located in the server's cgi-bin directory.

Note that you cannot just make a directory called cgi-bin in your account and expect Un-CGI to be run from it. The HTTP server needs to be configured to know where to look for executable programs. If you don't manage the HTTP server on your system, you probably cannot install Un-CGI in the right place. (On some servers, you can put CGI programs anywhere if you give them a certain file extension; talk to your system administrator to find out if this is the case on your system. If so, see the next item.)

EXTENSION   If your server allows CGI programs to be run from anywhere as long as they have a particular filename extension (typically .cgi), you should set this to that extension, including the period (.). In that case, you can set DESTDIR to point into any directory that the server has access to (for example, your public_html directory).

You don't need to follow any particular naming rules for the programs you're going to ask Un-CGI to run. As long as they're in the SCRIPT_DIR directory, you can name them any way you see fit.

Once you're done editing the makefile, run make install and your system will build and install Un-CGI into the directory you specified as DESTDIR. If you get an error message like make: Command not found or cc: Command not found, talk to your system administrator. There's no way of magically knowing where your system happens to put its compiler tools.

Make sure the file permissions on the Un-CGI binary (and the directory it's in) are set so that the HTTP server can execute it. On most systems the HTTP server runs as user nobody or www. You may want to make Un-CGI a setuid program if you want to manipulate private files with your back-end scripts because they will ordinarily be run under the same User ID as the HTTP server. Consult your system administrator to find out your site's policy on setuid programs; they are frowned upon in some places.

USAGE

An example is the easiest way to demonstrate Un-CGI's use. Suppose you have the following in an HTML file:

```
<form method=POST action="/cgi-bin/uncgi/myscript">
What's your name?
```

```
<input type=text size=30 name=name>
<p>
Type some comments.
<br>
<textarea name=_comments rows=10 cols=60></textarea>
What problem are you having? <select name=problem multiple>
<option> Sleeplessness
<option> Unruly goat
<option> Limousine overcrowding
</select>
<p>
<input type=submit value="  Send 'em in!  ">
</form>
```

When the user selects the Send 'em in! button, the HTTP server will run Un-CGI. Un-CGI will set three environment variables—WWW_name, WWW_comments, and WWW_problem—to the values of the name, comments, and problem fields in the form, respectively. It will then execute myscript in the SCRIPT_DIR directory.

All the usual CGI environment variables (PATH_INFO, QUERY_STRING, and so on) are available to the script or program you tell Un-CGI to run. A couple of them (PATH_INFO and PATH_TRANSLATED) are tweaked by Un-CGI to the values they would have if your program were being executed directly by the server. PATH_INFO is, in case you haven't read up on CGI, set to all the path elements after the script name in your URL (if there is any). This is an easy way to specify additional parameters to your script without resorting to hidden fields.

myscript might be as simple as this:

```
#!/bin/sh
echo 'Content-type: text/html'
echo ''
mail webmaster <<__EOF__
$WWW_name is having $WWW_problem problems and said:
$WWW_comments
__EOF__
cat /my/home/directory/htmlfiles/thanks.html
```

With Un-CGI, that's all you need to write a script to send your mail from a form and print a prewritten file as a response. It's the same whether you want to use GET or POST queries.

If you're using Perl, $ENV{"WWW_xyz"} will look up the value of the xyz form field.

If more than one problem is selected in the previous example, the values will all be placed in WWW_comments and separated by hash marks (#). You can use the library function strtok() to separate and replace the hash marks with newlines using tr. Type the following:

```
echo $WWW_problem | tr '#' \\012 | while read value; do
echo $value 'selected.'
done
```

A useful learning tool is to point your form at a script that just prints the contents of the environment. On most systems there is a program to do that, called either env or printenv. You can write a little script that runs it:

```
#!/bin/sh
echo 'Content-type: text/plain'
echo ''
env
```

This script will print all the CGI environment variables set by the server.

SPECIAL PROCESSING

You eagle-eyed readers may have noticed that the text area in the previous example had an underscore (_) at the beginning of its name. When Un-CGI sees a form field whose name begins with an underscore, it strips whitespace from the beginning and end of the value and makes sure that all the end-of-line characters in the value are UNIX-style newlines (as opposed to DOS-style CR-LF pairs or Macintosh-style CRs, both of which are sent by some browsers). This makes processing text easier because your program doesn't have to worry about the browser's end-of-line conventions. Note that if a form field is named _xyz, you still get an environment variable called WWW_xyz. The extra underscore doesn't show up in the environment variable name.

Un-CGI also modifies variable names containing periods. The major source of which is <input type=image>. Shell scripts have trouble coping with periods in environment variable names, so Un-CGI converts periods to underscores. This is only done to variable names; periods in values will remain untouched.

OTHER FEATURES

If you compile with -DNO_MAIN, you can use Un-CGI as a library function in a C program of your own. Just call uncgi() at the start of your program.

Un-CGI will handle hybrid GET/POST requests. Specify a method of POST in the form, and add a GET-style query string to the action An example of this is as follows:

```
<from method=POST action="/cgi-bin/uncgi/myscript?form id=feedback">
```

When your script is run, WWW_form_id will be set to feedback. This will only work if your HTTP server supports it (NCSA's does, for now anyway).

Un-CGI is freeware. If you want to include it in a commercial product, please send me mail. I'll probably just ask you to include a pointer to this page with your product. If you want to pay me for Un-CGI, send me a picture postcard to help decorate my wall! My address is

Steven Grimm
Hyperion
173 Sherland Ave.
Mountain View, CA 94043

FREQUENTLY ASKED QUESTIONS

As with any kind of program, many questions arise regarding its use. What follows is a compilation of the most frequently asked questions about Un-CGI.

I GET AN ERROR ABOUT `sys_errlist` WHEN I COMPILE

Some UNIX variants' standard-include files contain a declaration for the list of system error codes, and some don't. For the latter, I need to include the declaration in `uncgi.c`. If you get an error about a previous declaration of `sys_errlist`, edit `uncgi.c` and remove the line:

```
extern char *sys_errlist[];
```

Then recompile and everything should work.

WHERE DO I PUT EVERYTHING?

Short answer: Look in the makefile.

Long answer: When you edit Un-CGI's makefile, you'll see two macro definitions relating to paths. The first, SCRIPT_DIR, tells Un-CGI where to look for your scripts or programs. It must be set to the name of an existing directory; you can set it to any directory you like.

Sometimes it is set to the location of your server's cgi-bin directory, although that's not necessary. The second, DESTDIR, tells the makefile where to install Un-CGI. It must point to your server's cgi-bin directory, if your server has one.

Note that you can't just create a directory called cgi-bin in your account and expect it to work. The server has configuration files that tell it where to look for scripts and programs. Talk to your system administrator if you aren't the person in charge of the server on your machine.

An additional makefile setting, EXTENSION, should be of help if your server allows you to put CGI programs anywhere on the system. Again, consult your system administrator to see if this is the case.

WHY DOES UN-CGI TELL ME IT CAN'T RUN MY SCRIPT?

First, make sure your script is in the right place; see the preceding section. Second, make sure your script can be executed by the server. Remember, Un-CGI is run by the server, which is probably using a system user ID, not your User ID. You need to set the permissions on your script so that it can be run by any user. Usually, you can say "`chmod 755 scriptname`" (replacing `scriptname` with the name of your script) to set the permissions properly.

If you're still having trouble, edit the makefile, uncomment the DEBUG_PATH line, and rebuild. This will instruct Un-CGI to include the full path to where it thinks your script should be in its error message.

WHAT DO I DO IN MY FORMS?

The `<form>` tag has two attributes, METHOD and ACTION. METHOD must be set to either GET or POST. Un-CGI will handle either one, but POST is preferred if you have text area fields or are expecting a lot of information from the client. Note that the attribute name (METHOD) can be upper or lowercase, but the value must be all caps.

ACTION should have the following components:

◆ The alias for your server's `cgi-bin` directory (usually just `/cgi-bin/`).

◆ `uncgi/` to tell the server which program to execute.

◆ The name of your script as it appears in the directory where you told Un-CGI to find your scripts and programs (the CGI_BIN macro in the makefile). Example: `myscript`.

◆ Optionally, a forward slash followed by additional parameters—often the path to another file you want your script to print. This path information will be available to your script in the PATH_INFO and PATH_TRANSLATED environment variables. The latter contains the full path to the document, including the path to the server root directory. Note that you can't use tilde (~) notation. Example: `/form_output/acknowledge.html`.

So, if you wanted to tell Un-CGI to run `sendmemail` with no additional parameters, you'd put `sendmemail` in the directory you specified as the value of CGI_BIN in Un-CGI's makefile, and use the following tag to begin your form:

```
<form method=POST action="/cgi-bin/uncgi/sendmemail">
```

I GET AN ERROR 403 WHEN I SUBMIT MY FORM

The usual cause of this is that your server requires a special filename extension on CGI programs. (Most often it's .cgi.) You need to give Un-CGI a name that will identify it as a CGI program to the Web server. There is nothing special about Un-CGI from the Web server's point of view; it's just another program that gets run like any other, and your installation of it has to obey the same rules as other programs.

I GET AN ERROR CODE 500 FROM THE SERVER

This usually means your script isn't specifying a content type to the server. The first thing your script needs to output is Content-type: text/html followed by a blank line. Note that the blank line following the header is not optional, and it has to be completely empty—no whitespace. (See Chapter 5, "CGI (Common Gateway Interface) Programming," for more information.) If you're writing a shell script, for instance, you'll need the following:

```
echo Content-type: text/html
echo ""
```

The empty quotes on the second line are necessary; otherwise, echo won't print anything, not even a blank line. Of course, if your script is outputting something other than HTML, adjust the content type accordingly.

MY SCRIPT DOESN'T SEE THE FORM VARIABLES

There are a few common causes for this:

◆ Make sure you're actually running Un-CGI. If you install Un-CGI but your form's ACTION attribute still points to something like /cgi-bin/myscript, Un-CGI isn't being executed by the Web server when the user submits the form. See the previous example forms.

◆ Environment variables are case sensitive, which means that if you have a field in your form named revision, Un-CGI will create an environment variable named WWW_revision, not WWW_REVISION or WWW_Revision.

◆ Most shells restrict the characters you can use in variable names. In particular, spaces and punctuation are usually illegal. Underscores and numbers are fine.

THE BROWSER JUST SITS THERE WHEN I SUBMIT MY FORM

The most common cause of hangs like that is from trying to convert an old CGI-compliant program or script to run under Un-CGI. Your script is detecting that the form was submitted with the POST method and is trying to read form results from the browser. Unfortunately, by the time your script is run, Un-CGI has already read the results, so your program sits there waiting forever for bytes that have already been consumed.

Remove the part of your code that reads a query from the standard input. It'll generally be located somewhere around the word POST, which is easy to search for. Replace it with code that fills your program's internal variables via getenv() calls (assuming that your program is in C) on the WWW_ variables defined by Un-CGI.

HOW DO I PARSE CHECK BOX RESULTS?

Un-CGI puts hash marks (#) between check box selections if there are several of them. How you parse depends entirely on which language you're using. In C, use strtok(). In Python, use string.splitfields(). In Perl, use split(). In Bourne shell, use something like the following:

```
echo $WWW_whatever ¦ tr \# \\012 ¦ while read result;
  do echo User picked $result
done
```

DO I NEED TO MAKE A DIRECTORY CALLED uncgi?

No. You're probably assuming that because your form has an ACTION like /cgi-bin/uncgi/xyz, there must be an uncgi directory under cgi-bin. That's not how it works.

The parts of a URL between the slashes are not directory names. They are symbols that tell the server where to find a particular document. In most cases, the server will look for a directory with the same name as the symbol in question. If there is one, go in that directory and proceed to the next symbol. However, that isn't always what happens. If the server sees that a particular symbol matches the name of a program, it will typically run that program and pass the rest of the URL to the program as an argument. And that's exactly what's happening here.

There's no uncgi directory. You can think of /cgi-bin/uncgi/xyz as /cgi-bin/uncgi xyz if that helps. (Strictly speaking, it's not accurate, but that's the concept.) Un-CGI sees the xyz argument and looks in its SCRIPT_BIN directory to find a program by that name.

If you're still not sure what all this means, just try it out and see what happens!

DOES UN-CGI STRIP OUT SPECIAL SHELL CHARACTERS THAT MIGHT CAUSE SECURITY PROBLEMS?

No, it doesn't for the simple reason that Un-CGI isn't tied to any one shell or any shell at all, for that matter. Un-CGI sits in front of C programs just as easily as Bourne shell scripts, Perl scripts, or Python scripts. (All of which, incidentally, are used in conjunction with Un-CGI at Hyperion.)

In most of those languages, there *aren't* any special characters that are inherently security problems, so having Un-CGI strip characters that cause problems for a particular shell would just end up pointlessly mangling the input to other kinds of scripts and programs. People using shells with different special characters would still have to specially handle them anyway.

On most unices, you can use the `tr -d` command to strip out characters that your shell processes. For example, to strip out dollar signs from a Bourne shell variable, you would type:

```
WWW_puppycount="`echo $WWW_puppy ¦ tr -d \$`"
```

SUMMARY

Un-CGI can be a key piece of software when you are developing quick shell-based CGIs to handle output from forms. However, you should keep in mind that Un-CGI doesn't perform any sort of security checks on the submitted values it processes. For more information on security issues that you should address on your CGI, please refer to Chapter 16, "Web Server Security Issues."

- Managing Several
  Domains

APPENDIX B

Managing Virtual Domains with sendmail V8

The technique described in this chapter will help you map e-mail addresses to a system mailbox. While in most installations you won't have to worry about this because UNIX will handle this for you, more complex installations that make use of virtual domains will probably require you to provide some sort of e-mail address support.

An Internet e-mail address can be divided into two components: the username and the domain name (`user@domain.dom`).

The `user` portion usually matches the login name of a local user. It can also be an alias to a different user or a distribution list for many other users in the system. As you may be aware, you cannot create two identical login names on the same machine under UNIX. It would also be unwise to create an alias that matched an existing user's login name. If you did create such an inconsistency, the results will be unexpected and more than likely not be what you want. Mail addressed to the user will end up delivered to someone else.

While under typical installation, this is never a problem. When it comes to dealing with virtual domain names and virtual Web sites, it's likely you will run into a problem. Someone responsible for handling e-mail for one of your virtual domains will want you to provide the ability to redirect mail written to `user@his.domain` to be mapped to his e-mail account on your system or forwarded elsewhere. For addresses such as `webmaster@domain`.com, you can easily see the problem. `sendmail`, by default, doesn't make a distinction between e-mail accounts destined to different domains. To `sendmail`, if the domain in question is not forwarded elsewhere, it must belong to the user addressed in the envelope, regardless of the domain name.

The following article is reprinted and enhanced from a posting made on November 10, 1995, to `comp.mail.sendmail` by Johan Svensson (`<johan@jos.net>`). He granted his kind permission for the inclusion of this article. It describes how to handle this situation by allowing each domain to have standard e-mail addresses, which are forwarded to the appropriate user based on the domain name information.

MANAGING SEVERAL DOMAINS

If you want to provide e-mail to several domains and be able to use identical usernames across different domains such as in

```
user@a.dom.ain        mb1@dom.ain
user@b.dom.ain        mb2@dom.ain
user@c.dom.ain        mb@outer.space
```

you'll need a way to map the full e-mail address to use an external database. You will also need to do some minor ruleset rewriting in the `sendmail.cf`. Many Internet Service Providers have asked for a general solution to this problem, and here's the solution.

This process involves two major steps:

1. Create a database to map from an e-mail address to a mailbox.
2. Modify a `sendmail` ruleset so that it uses the e-mail to mailbox database to figure out where to deliver the e-mail.

BUILDING THE DATABASE

The database is compiled out of an American Standard Code of Information Interchange (ASCII) file that has the following structure (the incoming e-mail address and the destination mailbox, which can be in a totally different system or machine):

```
user@a.dom.ain      mb1@dom.ain
user@b.dom.ain      mb2@dom.ain
user@c.dom.ain      mb@outer.space
```

The left column contains the e-mail address of a particular user, and the right column contains the corresponding mailbox. If you maintain several domains, you may want to create several databases (one per domain) and *cat* them together (using the UNIX `cat` program) prior to compilation. This may make it easier to maintain domain aliases for a domain in the future because maps for each domain are saved on their own file.

The following example may closely match your needs. Some of the destination addresses are forwarded to other domains for resolution (`webmaster@client2.se`). Others will be remapped to other addresses that will require reprocessing and derefencing the address several times before arriving at the final mailing address (`webmaster@client1.se`):

```
webmaster@josnet.se        wm.list@eowyn.josnet.se
webmaster@client1.se       joe@client1.se
webmaster@client2.se       anne@another.provider.se
webmaster@client3.se       joe@client3.se
joe@client1.se             c1_joe@mail.josnet.se
joe@client3.se             joeuser
```

Note that you need to write the complete e-mail address in the left column. The right column entry can be a local address (for example, `johan` if that account exists) or a complete e-mail address on another system (or a domain the server recognizes as local).

After you build the ASCII representation of the database, you'll need to compile it into a more efficient lookup table using the `makemap` utility that came with your `sendmail` distribution (if your system supports `hash`, `dbm`, or `btree`, you can use those commands instead). Your command will look something like the following:

```
makemap hash mbt.db <mbt
```

The resulting hashed database in this example is called `mbt.db`. The input ASCII database is called `mbt`.

CONFIGURING `sendmail` TO USE THE MAILBOX DATABASE

In `/etc/sendmail.cf`, add the following line right after the DM entry. You'll need to replace *method* with the type of database it is (use hash for makemap files, dbm -o for dbm files, or btree for a btree-generated databases):

```
Kmbt method /etc/sendmail/mbt.db
```

EDITING THE RULESETS

Edit the ruleset 98 section (S98) and add the following inside the ruleset. Which modifications you make will depend on the version of sendmail you are using.

For sendmail versions prior to 8.7.1, add the following:

```
R$+ < @ $+ . >        $: $1 < @ $2 > .
R$+ < @ $+ > $*       $: $(mbt $1@$2 $: $1 < @ $2 > $3 $)
R$+ < @ $+ > $*       $: $(mbt $2 $: $1 < @ $2 > $3 $)
R$+ < @ $+ > .        $: $1 < @ $2 . >
```

For sendmail versions later than 8.7.1, add this instead:

```
R$+< $+. >            $1< $2 >
R$+< $+ >             $: < > $(mbt $1$2 $)
R< > $+ @ $*          $: < $1 > $(mbt * @ $2 $)
R< > $*               $: $>3 $1
```

RESTARTING `sendmail`

Finally, restart sendmail to see your changes. You must do this in order to reread the configuration file and test with sendmail -bv or sendmail -bt.

SUMMARY

This technique will make it easier for you to support multiple info and webmaster mailboxes for the various domains you host. Because the various mapping are external to the sendmail configuration file, adding and deleting entries are much easier to maintain than would otherwise be possible.

APPENDIX C

FastCGI

FastCGI is a high-performance replacement to the CGI standard. It provides a significant improvement in performance over the existing CGI interface. In its current implementation, FastCGI provides many desirable enhancements that make it a very attractive and competitive alternative to proprietary technologies for developing Web-based applications. Under many circumstances, it will be a better choice to implement FastCGI than to develop a custom server module using Apache's proprietary server Application Programmer's Interface (API).

Note

FastCGI is available from `http://www.fastcgi.com`. (See Figure C.1.) The site is the official resource to all FastCGI information. It has complete documentation and whitepapers on FastCGI. Also nice is a mailing list—a threaded archive that is available through the Web.

*Figure C.1.
The FastCGI
home page.*

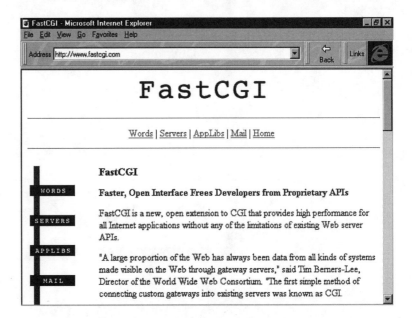

FastCGI is a proposed open standard; this means that it is not currently widely accepted, but it has received a warm welcome by many significant people on the Internet who are responsible for setting the standards. More than likely, this welcome will turn into acceptance on both free and commercial Web server offerings, which will help it in becoming "blessed" from a standard point of view.

FastCGI is appealing not only because of its performance enhancements but because the effort required to migrate existing code is very small. As a bonus, software developed under this proposed standard has a high degree of portability. These portability issues help a great deal toward setting it as a viable candidate to become a standard, especially on installations that have committed extensive resources to CGI development.

FastCGI is not a development environment in terms of having to learn yet another programming language. In a very simplistic description, FastCGI is a CGI program that uses additional libraries, so it does require that you learn an API. The basic API is tiny, though; one call is all you need to migrate many of your current programs.

FastCGI Features

The main features of FastCGI are as follows:

◆ A huge increase in performance. FastCGI programs continue to live between requests, making their responsiveness faster and reducing delays due to forking and program initialization.

◆ Programming language-independent implementation. Like CGI, you can develop your FastCGI application with a variety of languages. Currently there are programming libraries for Perl, C/C++, Tcl, and Java. Porting existing code to FastCGI is easy, allowing you to migrate your existing code base easily without having to redo what you have done.

◆ FastCGI processes are isolated from the Web server core. Much like CGI, FastCGI applications offer greater security and reliability than a similar functionality developed as a module using a server API.

◆ Server technology separation. There are FastCGI modules for various servers, including Apache, NCSA, and the Open Market Secure WebServer. For any other server that supports CGIs, the `cgi-fcgi program`, included in the FastCGI distribution, implements the FastCGI environment.

◆ Distributed computing support. FastCGI applications can execute on a different host from the Web server. This allows you to offload FastCGI execution to other application servers, permitting your Web server to handle an increased load. FastCGI programs can run on any host that can be reached over TCP/IP.

◆ The concept of *roles*. Traditional CGI programs fall into the responder role; they respond to some action initiated by a browser and send back some HTML. FastCGI programs can also perform other roles, such as acting as a filter or as part of some authentication scheme. This allows for providing extra functionality that would usually be relegated to a server module. The currently available FastCGI module for Apache does not include support for roles other than responder, but this may change in the future.

C

FastCGI

PERFORMANCE ENHANCEMENT

The increase in performance alone would be a good enough reason to migrate CGIs to FastCGI, especially on loaded servers. This increase in performance is achieved primarily because FastCGI processes are persistent. Forking under UNIX is very expensive, and FastCGI addresses this issue by reusing processes. This saves on the initialization time and can also provide enhancements when data calculated by one call to the program can be reused in another transaction.

Unlike CGIs, which are forked every time there's a request for the functionality, FastCGI processes are reused. After a request is fulfilled, the process remains, waiting for additional requests.

Programs that rely on an interpreter such as Perl or Tcl can gain a great deal from this technology because the command interpreter will compile the program once, not once per call. The time required to do all this pre-run initialization is eliminated. On the program side, this can yield to enhancements such as establishing a connection with a database or some other process because the connection needs to happen only once. Add to this the load to launch the interpreter program, and the savings are significant.

What sort of performance gains can you obtain? According to information posted on the FastCGI Web site, Open Market's tests show the following:

Request	Client, Server, and Application Processing Time
Static File	21ms + 0.19ms/KB
FastCGI	22ms + 0.28ms/KB
CGI	59ms + 0.37ms/KB

Add to this the cumulative time that it takes for an application to establish a TCP/IP connection to, say, a database. Under CGI, a process will have to initialize each time it is run. FastCGI can yield a performance increase of four times the speed of the same program used as CGI. In load terms, this could mean that your server could potentially handle four times your current CGI load. However, the level of enhancement will depend on the source of the bottleneck. If your database server is the current source of the problem, FastCGI cannot do much about that except reduce the number of connections that the database server will need to perform, perhaps giving it more time to process data instead.

FASTCGI API

The FastCGI API has a handful of calls:

◆ FCGI_Accept is used to implement the server connectivity and control the running of the FastCGI program.

◆ `FCGI_Finish` gives you control after the FastCGI program has executed, but before running the next request.

◆ `FCGI_SetExitStatus` is used to set the exit status of the request. Most CGI programs don't return a meaningful exit status, so this call is seldom used.

◆ `FCGI_StartFileterData` enables you to implement a special type of FastCGI application, called a *filter*. Currently the Apache implementation of the FastCGI module doesn't support roles, of which the filter type is a member, but this likely will change in the near future. Filters allow you to implement programs that will convert one data format to another on-the-fly (for example, TIFF to GIF).

Data is read and written through the standard input, output, and error streams. FastCGI also provides macros that map files and streams to native calls supported by your operating system.

Like CGI, you can create FastCGI applications in almost any language. However, you are currently limited to the ports of the library. Currently available are Perl, C/C++, Tcl, Java, and very soon Python, which should be available by the time you read this. Also in the works is a multithreaded C/C++ library that has not been released, but should be available as part of the 1.6 release. The multithreaded library enables a single application process to handle concurrent requests, which will allow you to implement things like HTTP-based chat applications.

Even though FastCGI is not universal, most developers should find themselves at home in one of the programming languages previously mentioned. As soon as FastCGI gains more acceptance, there will be additional libraries implemented. Developers are encouraged to port the FastCGI libraries to their programming language of choice, ensuring that the openness of the extension is more widely supported. The success of FastCGI will depend on getting many vendors and programmers to support it. Given its current feature set, it should have no trouble reaching this goal.

The design of FastCGI also wins big on the learning curve because unlike server APIs, you are still programming a CGI, so you can leverage what you already know. The only issues that you will need to address have to do with reorganizing your application so that the initialization code, which is done once, is kept separate from the application body. FastCGI applications are long-lived; they are kept alive between transactions. This also means that memory needs to be managed because unlike CGIs, which have a short life span, FastCGI processes may execute for undetermined amounts of time.

Data sent to a FastCGI application by the server is accessed through special streams that provide complete binary compatibility with the CGI standard. This also allows a FastCGI program to run as a regular CGI program. A FastCGI program can determine, at runtime, if it is being run as CGI or as FastCGI and behave accordingly.

This translates into an environment that allows you to migrate FastCGI programs down, should you ever need to. This provides server independence because the same binary can be run on two servers—say Apache and Netscape—under the same operating system without even needing to be rebuilt or requiring programming modifications, even if the server couldn't support FastCGI. This feature alone is very interesting from a legacy and recycling standpoint. Also, all servers support FastCGI. The FastCGI Developer's Kit comes with a program called cgi-fcgi that allows you to run FastCGI responder applications. The cgi-fcgi program enables any Web server that supports CGI to run FastCGI.

FastCGI applications communicate with Apache using a single full-duplex connection. Through this connection, the server transmits the environment variables and stdin to the FastCGI application; stdout and stderr streams from the application are sent back to the server.

WHAT A FASTCGI APPLICATION LOOKS LIKE

A modified version of my HelloWorld.c looks like this:

```
#include "fcgi_stdio.h"
#include <stdio.h>
int main (void)
{
  int timesVisited = 0;
  while(FCGI_Accept() >=0)
  {
    printf ("Content-type: text/html\r\n\r\n");
    printf("<HTML>");
    printf("<HEAD><TITLE>Hello World!</TITLE></HEAD>");
    printf("<BODY><H1>Hello, this is a FastCGI program!</H1>");
    printf("<BIG><P>I can tell that you are visiting from %s.</P>");
    printf("<p>This page has been accessed: %d times</P></BIG></BODY>",
    ➥getenv("REMOTE_HOST"), ++timesVisited);
    printf("</HTML>");
  }
}
```

This version makes use of the fact that the application is persistent and will maintain a count of the times the program is run (until the program dies).

As you can see from this example, FastCGI applications follow this sequence:

1. **Initialization**. Persistent connections or data that should be available from request to request are initialized in this section. Initialization is done only once. The initial environment for FastCGI applications is set through the AppClass directive, which is added by the FastCGI module.

2. **The Response Loop**. This loop is started by the `FCGI_Accept()` routine, implemented in the FastCGI library. A call to this routine blocks program execution until the program receives a client request. When it receives one, the routine unblocks, sets up an environment for the program, and runs one loop through the body. This routine is also responsible for determining the context under which the program is running (FastCGI or CGI) and sets the environment accordingly.

3. **Body**. This portion of the program gets executed by each request. This is the meat of your program. Each request will have its own environment variables, just as in a regular CGI.

4. **End of Response**. A subsequent call to `FCGI_Accept` informs the server that the program has completed a request and is ready for another. `FCGI_Accept` once more blocks execution until the next request.

This process is repeated until the FastCGI application is killed by the system administrator or the Web server. If the process were to die, the FastCGI module or `cgi-fcgi` program in the Web server is responsible for making a FastCGI process available to handle the request. This means that if it dies, the server will fork another process to replace the original.

FastCGI and C

FastCGI implements two libraries: `fcgi_stdio` and `fcgiapp`. Both of these libraries are provided for building C applications utilizing the FastCGI toolkit.

The `fcgi_stdio` library implements `stdio`-compatible functionality and can be used for developing or porting existing C CGI applications. This library provides full binary compatibility between FastCGI and CGI programs.

`fcgiapp` provides additional functionality to FastCGI applications at the expense of losing the CGI compatibility. There's also an increase in the knowledge required to develop the application.

FastCGI with Perl and Tcl

You can run Perl- and Tcl-interpreted programs under FastCGI. In order to run them, you'll have to compile a special version of the interpreter that has been modified to work with FastCGI. You will not, however, need to maintain both a regular and a special version of the interpreter. The special version will work as expected when used under a normal context. Future versions of Perl and Tcl will incorporate changes that will make it possible to use unmodified versions of the program with FastCGI.

C

FastCGI

Patches for both Perl and Tcl are available. Some prebuilt binaries are also available at `http://www.fastcgi.com`.

INSTALLING AND CONFIGURING FASTCGI

To build and run FastCGI applications, you'll need to have two different pieces of software: the FastCGI module for Apache and the FastCGI Developer's Kit.

Both the toolkit and the Apache module are included in the CD-ROM that accompanies this book; however, you should make sure that they are still current. At the time of this writing, the Apache module was still based on a beta version of 1.1. The latest and greatest versions of the module and developer's kit are available at the FastCGI Web sites: `http://www.fastcgi.com/servers` and `http://www.fastcgi.com/applibs`, respectively. The version of the toolkit included on the CD-ROM is 1.5.

INCORPORATING FASTCGI FUNCTIONALITY INTO APACHE

To add the FastCGI module to Apache is simple. Copy `apache-fastcgi/src/mod_fastcgi.c` to the Apache source directory (`/usr/local/etc/httpd/src`). Then you need to add an entry for the module in Apache's `src/Configuration` file. Add the following line at the end of the `Module` listings:

```
Module fastcgi_module mod_fastcgi.o
```

You'll need to run Apache's configuration program, `src/Configure`, and rebuild the Apache server by issuing a `make` command while focused on the Apache `src` directory.

While Apache builds, you can add the following configuration directives to your server's `conf/srm.conf` configuration file:

```
AddType application/x-httpd-fcgi .fcgi
Alias /fcgi-bin/ /usr/local/etc/httpd/fcgi-bin
# AppClass
```

Create the `fcgi-bin` directory, while in `/usr/local/etc/httpd`:

```
% mkdir fcgi-bin
```

As you may be able to guess by now, FastCGI applications should be run from a directory other than the `cgi-bin` directory.

After Apache builds, issue the following commands:

```
% cd /usr/local/etc/httpd
% mv httpd httpd.prev
% mv src/httpd .
% strip httpd
% kill -HUP `cat /usr/local/etc/httpd/logs/httpd.pid`
```

This will restart the server and force rereading of the new configuration directives you just added. Watch for any error messages. If you get an error, more than likely one of the directives you added is incorrect.

If the restart of the server proceeded without problems, congratulations—your server is now ready to run FastCGI programs.

cgi-fcgi

An alternative way of implementing FastCGI on Apache, or any other server, is to use the cgi-fcgi program. cgi-fcgi is a standard CGI program that uses TCP/IP sockets to communicate with FastCGI applications. cgi-fcgi takes the pathname or host/port name as a parameter and connects to the FastCGI application listening on that TCP port. cgi-fcgi then forwards the environment variables and stdin to the FastCGI application and returns to the server the stdout and stderr streams. When the FastCGI application ends the connection, cgi-fcgi flushes and exits.

Although this is not as efficient as a module embedded into the server because the cgi-fcgi program gets forked with every request, it is much better than not having it. For example, if your Perl FastCGI program takes 1 second to compile and 2 seconds to connect to a database, you'll still have significant savings over forking Perl and recompiling the program with each request. cgi-fcgi is a tiny program when compared to Perl and many other programs.

BUILDING THE FASTCGI DEVELOPER'S KIT

To build the developer's kit, you'll need to configure it. The folks at Open Market have provided a nice script that automates the configuration process to run it. Just type ./configure while focused inside the fcgi-devel-kit directory. After a few moments you should be able to type make and have the libraries built. You will need this kit to build FastCGI-savvy interpreters or C programs.

After you build the kit, you may be interested in installing the library libfcgi/libfcgi.a to some useful place such as /usr/local/lib. Remember to do a ranlib on the library after you move it to refresh it. While you're at it, you may want to copy the include directory to /usr/local/include/fcgi. That way it will be easier for you to reference it while building your own programs.

After the kit is built, you may want to try your luck at building the sample HelloWorld.c program listed earlier. Note that you may need to change the location of the fcgi_stdio.h header file to reflect its new location.

To build the FastCGI program, issue the following commands:

```
cc -o Hello.fcgi -lfcgi HelloWorld.c
```

Put the resulting `Hello.fcgi` on your `fcgi-bin` directory. Before you can access it, you'll need to add an `AppClass` entry into your `srm.conf`:

```
AppClass /usr/local/etc/httpd/fcgi-bin/Hello.fcgi
```

and restart the server with

```
% kill -HUP `cat /usr/local/etc/httpd/logs/httpd.pid`
```

The `AppClass` directive takes care of starting and maintaining the FastCGI application. At this point you should be able to access it by pointing your browser to `http://localhost/fcgi-bin/Hello.fcgi`.

You should get a similar result to those displayed in Figure C.2.

Figure C.2.
The FastCGI
version of Hello
World!. *Notice*
that it keeps state.
My version is
fancier than the
HelloWorld
listing.

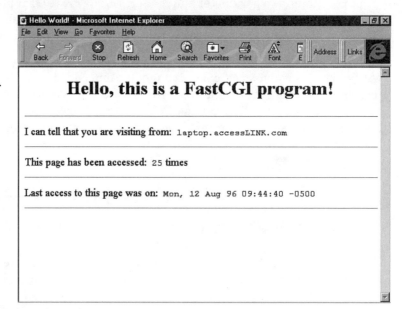

MAKING PERL FLY

You will notice an even bigger improvement on Perl CGIs. This is because FastCGI will keep the Perl program running; the interpreter won't have to fork, exec, compile, and execute for each request. A good thing.

Before you can incorporate FastCGI into your Perl programs, you have to build a special version of Perl. The FastCGI Developer's Kit contains the patches you'll need to build a version of Perl that supports FastCGI. After you build this version, there's no need to keep your old Perl around. A FastCGI-savvy Perl binary will work just fine with regular Perl scripts.

Future versions of Perl may have support for FastCGI right out of the box. Currently there's an active discussion on the perl5-porters mailing list regarding the issues that need to change in Perl's implementation to support FastCGI as a true Perl module—that is, requiring no recompiling. The Tcl7.5 FastCGI module, when it makes its debut, won't require a rebuild of Tcl. The new Python module also doesn't need a rebuild.

At the time of this writing, the patches available for FastCGI were for version 5.002 of Perl. By the time you read this, they will be updated to the current Perl version, 5.003.

The patch process is simple; you just replace a few files in the standard Perl distribution with files provided in the kit. Here's the process:

1. Put the unarchived Perl and fcgi-devel-kit on a directory side by side and issue the following commands:

```
% cd perl5.002
% mv perl.c perl.c.dist
% mv proto.h proto.h.dist
% mv Configure Configure.dist
% cp -r ../fcgi-devel-kit/perl-5/perl5.002/*
% cp -r ../fcgi-devel-kit/perl-5/common/*
```

2. Set the environment variable FCGIDIR to the absolute path of the fcgi-devel-kit. In my case, the distribution was in the /tmp/fcgiPerl directory. This variable will tell the configuration program where to find things:

```
setenv FCGIDIR /tmp/fcgiPerl/fcgi-devel-kit
```

3. If you don't use gcc, set the environment variable CC to the name of your compiler:

```
setenv CC cc
```

4. If you want to install the Perl distribution somewhere other than /usr/local/bin, define the environment variable PERL_PREFIX. I kept the default setting.

5. Execute the fcgi-configure script:

```
% ./fcgi-configure
```

The fcgi-configure script is a wrapper that automatically sets some of the configure variables without requiring user input. If this fails, you'll have to run the Configure command in the Perl directory. You may want to take a look at the documentation that came with the FastCGI Developer's Kit for any tips to solve the problem.

6. Do a make to build the software:

```
% make
```

C

FastCGI

If it all goes smoothly, you can finish the installation with a make install, which will install Perl to the location specified. That's it for the install! Make sure your scripts reference the correct version of Perl.

PERL FASTCGI PROGRAMS

The modified version of my HelloWorld.c looks like this:

```perl
#!/usr/local/bin/perl
use strict;
use FCGI;
my($timesVisited) = 0;
while(FCGI::accept() >=0){
  print "Content-type: text/plain\n\n";
  print <<STOP;
  <HTML>
  <HEAD>
  <TITLE>Hello World!</TITLE>
  </HEAD>
  <BODY>
  <H1>Hello, this is a FastCGI program!</H1>
  <P>I can tell that you are visiting from $ENV{REMOTE_HOST}</P>
  <P>This page has been accessed: ++$timesVisited</P>
  </BODY>
  </HTML>
  STOP
}
```

As you can see, this is pretty much the same organization as the C program. The one gotcha with Perl is that if the initial environment to a FastCGI Perl application is empty when the first call to FCGI::accept returns, the environment will still be empty. The easiest workaround is to add an environment with the AppClass -initial-env directive. See the section titled, "The AppClass Directive," for more detailed information.

THE mod_fastcgi MODULE

The FastCGI module provides Apache compatibility to FastCGI applications. This module is not part of the standard Apache release, so you'll have obtain a copy from http://www.fastcgi.com. A copy of the latest version at the time this was written, August 1996, is included on the CD-ROM.

This module processes any file with a MIME-type application/x-httpd-fcgi. Because the ScriptAlias directive may have higher priority over AddType, FastCGI applications should not reside on the cgi-bin directory; if they do, they may be processed by the mod_cgi module regardless of the extension given. This means that the application/x-httpd-fcgi MIME type is given to files that do *not* reside in the ScriptAlias directory and that have a name using the extension defined by the AddType application/x-httpd-cfgi directive. Typically this will be .fcgi. The reason for this is that Apache assigns priority to the directives based on the order of compilation in the modules.

The AppClass Directive

Syntax: AppClass *executablePath* [-processes *p*] [-listen-queue-Depth *q*]
            [-restart-delay *secs*] [-priority *N*] [-initial-env *key=value*]

Default: AppClass *executablePath* [-processes 1] [-listen-queue-Depth 5]
            [-restart-delay 5] [-priority *sameAsHTTP*]

Context: srm.conf

Module: mod_fastcgi

The AppClass directive, provided by mod_fastcgi, is responsible for starting up one or more FastCGI application processes using the executable specified by *executablePath*.

When a request for the file specified by *executablePath* is received, the request is handled by the mod_fastcgi module, which connects the request to the appropriate process belonging to the proper AppClass.

In addition to starting the process, the server will ensure that a process for handling a particular AppClass will be available. Should a process exit because of an error or some other condition, the server will launch another process capable of handling the requests.

AppClass has several other options:

processes	Specifies the number of FastCGI processes that the server will spawn. Default value for this setting is 1.
listen-queue-depth	Sets the depth of the listen queue that is shared by the processes. The *listen queue* stores additional requests that may be received while the FastCGI application is processing another. Requests will queue until they reach the limit imposed by listen-queue-depth. Additional requests beyond the size of the queue are responded with an error to the client. Default value is 5.
restart-delay	Specifies the number of seconds the server will wait before restarting a dead FastCGI process. The server won't restart a process more often than the time specified by this flag. The default value is 5 seconds.
priority	This flag specifies the execution priority of the FastCGI process. The default priority is inherited from the parent httpd server process.

C

FastCGI

initial-env   This flag enables you to specify the initial environment sent to a FastCGI program when the program initializes. You can specify multiple initial-env flags, one per *key=value* pair. If not specified, the initial environment is empty. It would be very useful to provide the FastCGI application with information during its initialization phase.

EXAMPLE

If you wanted to start the HelloWorld.fcgi program, you would need to type this:

```
AppClass /usr/local/etc/httpd/fcgi-bin/HelloWorld.fcgi -processes 2
```

For a Perl program, to circumvent the environment problem, you would have to type this:

```
AppClass /usr/local/etc/httpd/fcgi-bin/HelloWorld.fcgi -processes 2 -initial-
➥env: DB_PATH_NAME=/proj/accts/db2
```

SUMMARY

Although FastCGI is not the sole alternative for high performance CGI alternatives, the features and price cannot be beat. It's especially interesting that existing code can be ported easily without a real learning curve. This alone makes it very attractive for programmers who have a backlog and don't have much time to spend experimenting with new tools, yet need to implement a high-performance CGI solution. FastCGI is a great choice—the learning-and-setup curve is hours, not days like other environments.

- HTML Formatting
  Tag Structure

- HTML Document
  Structure

APPENDIX D

HTML Reference Guide

Hypertext Markup Language (HTML) is the most important component of the Web. It is responsible for providing the "formatting" to the pages you see every day on the Web.

HTML does not provide the formatting control you would expect, simply because different browsers render HTML in different ways. The task has been to abuse and creatively use tags to provide a desired look to a page. Creative types will find that HTML is fairly limited in what it can do; however, it is amazing to see the level of quality that can be brought out given the current control. The markup language is rapidly evolving to allow for more page-oriented layout, while keeping with the device-independent intent of HTML. Designers will always find a way of getting their intentions across.

Early in the Web, there was a lot of concern with being compatible with low resolution browsers such as Lynx—a text-only browser. Lynx has been used for a long time as a way of testing HTML for universal compatibility. This meant that you could not rely in the nonstandard HTML tags for your formatting or on graphic items alone for navigation. This interest—while still kept active by many people—is quickly dying out. I know of many Web service providers that will implement sites with a compatibility set to Netscape or Microsoft Internet Explorer. I believe that there's room for everybody, but the implementation specifications should really be set by the owner of the site and the intended target audience. This is due mostly to the evolution of the Web and supporting technologies. Personal bandwidth has increased very quickly, with 28.8Kbps modems becoming the low end, and faster technologies enabling higher bandwidth than it was thought possible over standard copper wires a few years ago. With the advent of inexpensive high bandwidth, visitors will demand more complex sites that offer a variety of multimedia presentation systems.

While many people will disagree, the reality of the Web is that much of the interest is based on the graphic appeal of a Web site. For once the graphical user interface (GUI) provided by a particular page is appealing, letting the visual types have more fun. Although Lynx does provide a serviceable interface to information you need while behind a terminal, the use of graphical browsers such as Netscape and Internet Explorer is where the technology is going.

This means that the basic design target has been changed to accommodate the features implemented by these browsers, perhaps at the expense of losing usability on the lower-end browsers. However, this has always been the argument in computers. Before GUI applications were popular, the issues were why did you need a mouse. Now that GUIs are the standard, many people find it dreadful to downgrade to a command prompt, although it may be very helpful sometimes. The Web is not TV; it is interactive. A great deal of its power comes from the its multimedia capabilities and its ability to give a feeling of being there. This can only be accomplished with graphic-capable browsers.

So to what standard should you develop your pages? It really depends on who is your target audience. If your message is too important *not* have it seen by some users, yet you want an enhanced site, the solution is simple: You'll need to prepare two or three versions of your pages that can be used with different levels of richness. This way you won't limit or stifle the more advanced browsers. You'll be able to provide features that will make it easier for people visiting your site to navigate through it. If their browser doesn't provide the proper support, then you'll have a scaled down version of your Web site that provides the information more plainly.

This doesn't mean the site is less capable; it just means that you are giving your users options. This also gives you the opportunity to provide different bandwidth versions of your site, which will allow people with the bigger intakes to enjoy more complex pages. Bandwidth conservation should still be a priority. A site should be designed to use the least amount of bandwidth possible given the design intent. This allows your material to zip through. Your users will love it, and your server will be able to serve more users.

With that thought in mind, here's an HTML reference manual. This appendix is not intended as an HTML style guide. It assumes that you have a basic understanding of HTML. Most of the options you see will only work with Netscape or Microsoft Internet Explorer. At the current time of this writing, Microsoft just released (Aug. 13, 1996) Internet Explorer 3.0. Netscape, following suit, also will unleash their new Navigator. As I see it now, the competition is red hot. Both products have their advantages, and they offer an almost 99 percent feature match. I like them both equally well. However, I think in terms of the future, Netscape will have to be much further ahead to justify its price. Explorer is free and will ship with every new PC, giving it the price and distribution advantage.

HTML FORMATTING TAG STRUCTURE

HTML is a markup language, which means that text is marked up with tags to produce the desired results. You can create HTML with any good text editor. However, there are many editors specially made for editing and marking up HTML. HTML is fairly easy to learn. HTML markup tags surround text or other items that they affect. Tags are a formatting directive enclosed in angle brackets (< and >). Most tags have an opening and a closing tag. Opening tags are just the name of the directive. Closing tags prefix a forward slash (/) to the name of the directive. If the closing tag is optional, it is better to close them anyway in most cases. This will make your HTML style more consistent and readable, and will reduce problems associated with a missing close tag. Here's the basic syntax of any HTML tag:

```
<tag>some object</tag>
```

Some tags may contain additional options. For example, the <P> tag, which defines a new paragraph, allows some simple formatting in some browsers. These options are specified as <P ALIGN=center>...</P>. This simply says that the paragraph should align center. The closing tag never takes any arguments.

Formatting tags can be nested with other tags to produce compound results. However, the nesting order is important. Some tags don't like to be nested. Each tag described in this appendix will include an *elements allowed within* and an *element is allowed inside* table. The first lists all the HTML elements that can nest inside the currently described element. The second lists all the HTML elements that can contain the currently described element.

HTML DOCUMENT STRUCTURE

HTML documents have a very precise structure; they have a head and a body. In addition, HTML 3.2 requires that the first line of any HTML document you write contains the following line:

```
<!DOCTYPE HTML PUBLIC "-//W3C//DTD HTML 3.2//EN">
```

This specifies the version of HTML that you are using among other things. The basic structure for an HTML document is

```
<!DOCTYPE HTML PUBLIC "-//W3C//DTD HTML 3.2//EN">
<HTML>
<HEAD>
infomation about your document
</HEAD>
<BODY>
content, what users see
</BODY>
</HTML>
```

The first thing you do is set the document type. Then that the document contains HTML markup. The HTML surrounds your document's content. Notice that HTML contains the HEAD and BODY sections.

The HEAD element of an HTML document contains information about the document itself. This information is only usable by the browser and other programs. For example, browsers render the title of your document based on a TITLE element inside the HEAD section.

The BODY element contains your content—information you want displayed to your users. This is what you see on your browser.

The simplest HTML page you could write that does something useful is HelloWorld.html. This is what such a page would look like in HTML:

```
<!DOCTYPE HTML PUBLIC "-//W3C//DTD HTML 3.2//EN">
<HTML>
```

```
<HEAD>
<TITLE>Hello World in HTML </TITLE>
</HEAD>
<BODY>
<P>Hello World!</P>
</BODY>
</HTML>
```

This example does a couple of things: It sets up the basic structure of the document and uses the TITLE element in the HEAD section. The TITLE element titles the document, and the browser uses this information to put a title in the windows title bar.

In the BODY section, our small sample starts a paragraph with the <P> tag, and then prints the words Hello World!. It finishes the paragraph with the optional close paragraph tag, </P>. There are many more elements that will help you control the organization and formatting of your document, but they all basically work in the same form.

The list of elements that follows describes most, if not all, the elements as of HTML 3.2 that are implemented in the two most popular graphic browsers (Netscape and Internet Explorer). In the interest of saving space, all the figures will show the HTML element's use with Internet Explorer 3.0.

A (ANCHOR)

The A element defines a hyperlink anchor that references a resource. The referenced resource, or destination, can be located in the current document or in a different uniform resource locator (URL) altogether. The A element is the fundamental building element of the Web. It allows you to easily jump from one document to another.

The basic syntax of the A element specifies an anchor address or Uniform Resource Identifier (URI). The URI is optionally followed by a pound symbol (#) and a token called a *fragment identifier*, which specifies a particular location within the referenced resource (a bookmark).

The HREF attribute sets the target to be a URI or a local reference within the same document. Local references are specified by prefixing a token with a # symbol. Destinations or *fragment* identifiers are specified by using another <A> tag with the NAME attribute.

Activating a local reference will jump the browser to the location of the reference be it by scrolling the current document or by loading the referenced URL. Anchors are represented graphically by underlined text, but this visual clue is user controlled and can be turned off in most browsers. The A element requires a closing tag. A elements cannot nest. See Figure D.1 for an example of the A element.

Figure D.1.
The A element.

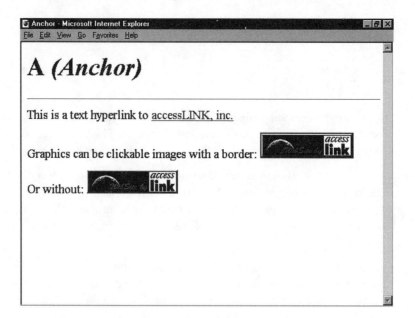

Syntax:

```
<A HREF=url NAME=#token REL=relation REV=relation
TARGET=window-name TITLE=title>...</A>
```

The A element has the following options:

Option	Description
HREF=*url*	Specifies a destination address. Resources are specified in URL format or as *#name* for a reference within the current document.
NAME=*name*	Defines a named anchor for use as a hyperlink destination.
REL=*relation*	Defines a relationship of the HREF (source) to the anchor (destination), which is authorized and recognized by the source document.
REV=*relation*	Defines a relationship anchor (destination) to the HREF (source), which is desired and claimed by the destination, but needs to be verified by the source.
TITLE=*title*	Informational token, used to describe the HREF
TARGET=*window*	Netscape 2.0 extension that defines the window name for use by the retrieved hyperlink. If the named window is not yet open, Navigator will open a new window and assign this name to it.

The A element is allowed within these elements:

> APPLET, B, BIG, BR, CITE, CODE, DFN, EM, FONT, I, IMG, INPUT, KBD, MAP, SAMP, SCRIPT, SELECT, SMALL, STRIKE, STRONG, SUB, SUP, TEXTAREA, TT, U, and VAR

The element is allowed inside the following:

> ADDRESS, B, BIG, BLOCKQUOTE, BODY, CAPTION, CENTER, CITE, CODE, DD, DFN, DIV, DT, EM, FONT, FORM, H1...H6, I, KBD, LI, P, PRE, SAMP, SMALL, STRIKE, STRONG, SUB, SUP, TD, TEXTFLOW, TH, TT, U, and VAR

EXAMPLE OF A

```
<A NAME="accesslink">This is a text hyperlink to <A HREF="http://
www.accesslink.com">accessLINK, inc.</A>
<P>
Graphics can be clickable images with a border:
<A HREF="#accesslink"><IMG SRC="websiteby.gif" ALT="Web Site By AccessLink"></A>
<P>
Or without: <A HREF="http://www.accesslink.com"><IMG SRC="websiteby.gif" BOR-
DER=0></A>
```

ADDRESS

The ADDRESS element is used to render multiline contact information (such as a name, address, and signature). This element acts much like a paragraph; it automatically puts breaks before and after itself. The ADDRESS element requires a closing tag.

Figure D.2.
The ADDRESS
element.

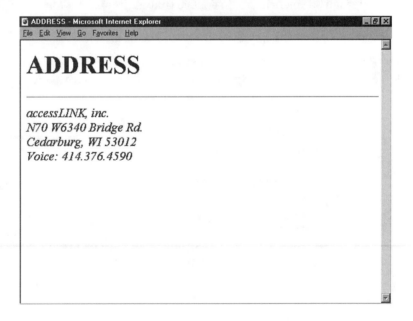

D

Syntax: <ADDRESS>...</ADDRESS>

The ADDRESS element is allowed within these elements:

A, APPLET, B, BIG, BR, CITE, CODE, DFN, EM, FONT, I, IMG, INPUT, KBD, MAP, SAMP, SCRIPT, SELECT, SMALL, STRIKE, STRONG, SUB, SUP, TEXTAREA, TT, U, and VAR

The element is allowed inside the following:

BLOCKQUOTE, BODY, CENTER, DIV, FROM, TD, and TH

EXAMPLE OF ADDRESS

```
<ADDRESS>
accessLINK, inc. <BR>
N70 W6340 Bridge Rd.<BR>
Cedarburg, WI  53012 <BR>
Voice: 414.376.4590
</ADDRESS>
```

APPLET

The APPLET element specifies the Java application to load and execute for Java-enabled browsers. This element allows you to embed a Java applet right into HTML documents. Java applets are usually used to dynamically provide additional functionality to a browser, often in the form of an animation or some other adornment. However, Java applets can also be used to provide client-side processing, such as verification, to ensure that all items on a form have been completed by the visitor prior to sending it back to the server. The content of the APPLET element is displayed if the applet cannot be executed.

Parameters can be passed to an applet by using the PARAM element inside the APPLET element. You can specify multiple PARAM elements to provide multiple parameters to the applet. The APPLET element requires a closing tag.

Syntax: <APPLET ALIGN=*alignment* ALT=*text* CODEBASE=*url* CODE=*appletFile*
                  HEIGHT=*n* HSPACE=*n* NAME=*appletInstance* VSPACE=*n* HSPACE=*n*
                  WIDTH=*n*>...</APPLET>

Options for APPLET include the following:

Option	Description
ALIGN=*alignment*	Specifies the alignment in the applet window. The various legal options are TOP, MIDDLE, BOTTOM, LEFT, and RIGHT.
ALT=*text*	Sets the alternate text displayed when the applet cannot be loaded.

CODE=*appletFile*	Specifies the Java class to load and execute.
CODEBASE=*url*	Specifies the base URL of the applet—the directory where the applet is located.
HEIGHT=*n*	Sets the initial suggested height of the applet window in pixels.
HSPACE=*n*	Sets the horizontal space (in pixels) reserved for a gutter around the applet.
NAME=*appletInstance*	Name of the applet instance. This name allows multiple applets on the same page to communicate.
VSPACE=*n*	Sets the vertical space (in pixels) reserved for a gutter around the applet specified in pixels.
WIDTH=*n*	Sets the initial suggested width of the applet window in pixels.

The APPLET element is allowed within these elements:

PARAM and TEXTFLOW

The element is allowed inside the following:

A, ADDRESS, B, BIG, BLOCKQUOTE, BODY, CAPTION, CENTER, CITE, CODE, DD, DFN, DIV, DT, EM, FONT, FORM, H1...H6, I, KBD, LI, P, PRE, SAMP, SMALL, STRIKE, STRONG, SUB, SU, TD, TEXTFLOW, TH, TT, U, and VAR

Figure D.3.
The LED applet.

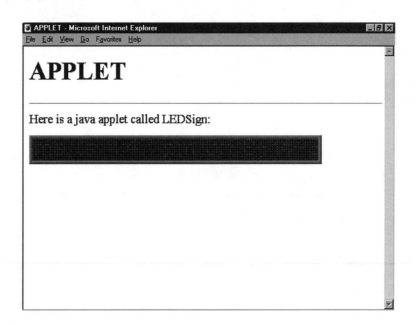

EXAMPLE OF APPLET

```
...
<applet codebase="../LED" code="LED.class" width=500 height=48 align=center>
<param name="script" value="../scripts/Demo.led">
<param name="border" value="2">
<param name="bordercolor" value="100,130,130">
<param name="spacewidth" value="3">
<param name="wth" value="122">
<param name="ht" value="9">
<param name="font" value="../fonts/default.font">
<param name="ledsize" value="3">
<hr>
If you were using a Java-enabled browser,
you would see an animated scrolling text sign that looks like this:
<BR>
<IMG SRC="LEDSign.gif">
<hr>
</applet>
...
```

AREA

The AREA element is used to implement client-side image maps. The various elements allow you to define regions in an image that, when activated, will hyperlink the resource identified by the HREF attribute. When multiple AREA elements in the same MAP overlap, the first encountered takes precedence. This can be useful to define complex areas.

The AREA element is allowed within a MAP element only. The AREA closing tag is optional.

Syntax:
```
<AREA SHAPE=shape COORDS=coords HREF=url|NOHREF
[TARGET=window]>
```

Options for AREA include the following:

Option	Description	
ALT=text	Sets the alternate text displayed if the browser doesn't accept images.	
COORDS=coords	A comma-separated list of coordinates. Format is dependent on the shape used.	
	RECT: x,y,w,h	Upper-left corner x,y with a width and height w,h.
	CIRCLE: x,y,r	Circle centered at x,y with radius r.
	POLY: $x1,y1,x2,y2...xi,yi$	Ordered coordinate pairs that define a closed polygon.

HREF=*url*	Specifies the hypertext destination of the specified area.
NOHREF	Specifies an area that has no action.
SHAPE=*shape*	Specifies the shape of the area. Possible values are

RECT	Rectangle
CIRCLE	Circle
POLY	Polygon

TARGET=*window*	Specifies that the target be loaded into the specified window. Possible values for window are

window	Specifies to load the link into the named window.
blank	Creates the frame in a new unnamed window.
self	Loads the frame in the parent window.
parent	Loads in the parent window.
top	Loads in the top window.

The AREA element is allowed within the following element:

MAP

The element is allowed inside the following:

None. The AREA element is not a container.

EXAMPLE OF AREA

Note that the USEMAP option requires a # sign (just like a local HREF) before the name of the fragment containing the map coordinates:

```
<AREA SHAPE=RECT COORDS="56,7,106,86" HREF="#b" ALT=b>
<AREA SHAPE=CIRCLE COORDS="219,63,23" HREF="#e" ALT=e>
```

B (BOLD)

The B element provides emphasis by rendering its contents in boldface. The B element requires a closing tag.

Syntax: `<B>...</B>`

The B element is allowed within these elements:

A, APPLET, B, BIG, BR, CITE, CODE, DFN, EM, FONT, I, IMG, INPUT, KBD, MAP, SAMP, SCRIPT, SELECT, SMALL, STRIKE, STRONG, SUB, SUP, TEXTAREA, TT, U, and VAR

B is allowed inside the following:

> A, ADDRESS, B, BIG, BLOCKQUOTE, BODY, CAPTION, CENTER, CITE, CODE, DD, DFN, DIV, DT, EM,
> FONT, FORM, H1...H6, I, KBD, LI, PRE, SAMP, SMALL, STRIKE, STRONG, SUB, SUP, TD,
> TEXTFLOW, TH, TT, U, and VAR

EXAMPLE OF B

```
<B>Bold</B> can be used on normal text.<BR>
<PRE>
You can also use <B>Bold</B> on preformatted text.
</PRE>
<BR>
You can even use <B>Bold</B> and <I>Italics</I> <B><I>together</I></B>!<BR>
```

Figure D.4.
The B element.

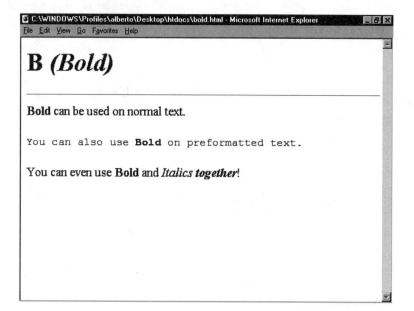

BASE

The BASE element provides an absolute URL from which to interpret any relative URL links specified in the document. This allows the original document to be moved, while preserving all relative links. The default base address is the URL used to access the document; however, when the document is moved or copied elsewhere, the default base URL is not correct. The BASE element is very useful in ensuring that hyperlinks don't break when a page is moved or is mirrored by an user.

This element is only allowed within a HEAD element.

Syntax: `<BASE HREF=url [TARGET=window]>`

Options include the following:

Option	Description
HREF	Specifies the base URL
TARGET	Netscape 2.0 extension that allows to define a named target window for each hyperlink in the document that doesn't set an explicit TARGET attribute

The BASE element is allowed within these elements:

Not applicable. Element is not a container.

The element is allowed inside the following:

HEAD

EXAMPLE OF BASE

```
<BASE HREF="http://www.somewhere.com/files/">
<BASE HREF="http://www.somewhere.com/files/ TARGET=_blank>
```

BASEFONT

The BASEFONT element alters the base font that is used as a default for any nonspecifically formatted text.

Figure D.5.
The BASEFONT
element.

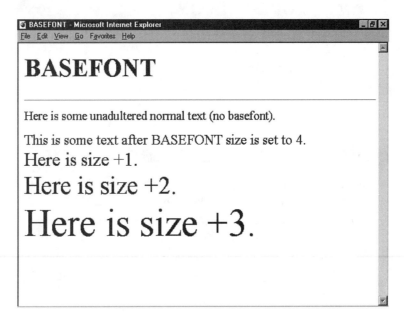

Syntax: `<BASEFONT COLOR=color NAME=name SIZE=n>`

Options include the following:

COLOR=color   Specifies the color of the base font. Colors are specified using hexadecimal notation for each component in the RGB channel in the following format: `#RRGGBB`, or by specifying one of the Microsoft Internet Explorer predefined colors: Aqua, Black, Blue, Fuchsia, Gray, Green, Lime, Maroon, Navy, Olive, Purple, Red, Silver, Teal, Yellow, or White.

NAME=name   Specifies the name of the font.

SIZE=n   Specifies the size of the base font to be one of seven predefined sizes. The default size is 3, and the largest is 7. You can specify sizes relative to BASEFONT using the FONT element. n can range in size from 1 to 7, inclusive.

The BASEFONT element is allowed within these elements:

None. BASEFONT is not a container element.

BASEFONT is allowed inside the following:

A, ADDRESS, B, BLOCKQUOTE, BODY, CITE, CODE, DD, DT, EM, FORM, H1, H2, H3, H4, H5, H6, I, KBD, LI, P, PRE, SAMP, STRONG, TT, and VAR

EXAMPLE OF BASEFONT

```
Here is some unadultered normal text (no basefont).
<P>
<BASEFONT SIZE=4>
This is some text after BASEFONT size is set to 4.
<BR>
<FONT SIZE=+1>Here is size +1.</FONT><BR>
<FONT SIZE=+2>Here is size +2.</FONT><BR>
<FONT SIZE=+3>Here is size +3.</FONT><BR>
```

BGSOUND (Background Sound)

The BGSOUND element is a Microsoft Internet Explorer 2.0 extension which defines the audio file to be played as a background to the document.

Syntax: `<BGSOUND SRC=url LOOP=n>`

Options for BSOUND include the following:

SRC=url   Specifies the URL of the audio file to play.

LOOP=*n* ¦ INFINITE   Specifies the number of times the source sound will play while the document is displayed. The default is to play once, but you can also specify infinite for unlimited playback. There's no way of disabling the audio, except for turning off the volume or traveling to another page.

The BGSOUND element is allowed within these elements:

None. BGSOUND is not a container element.

The element is allowed inside the following:

A, ADDRESS, B, BLOCKQUOTE, BODY, CAPTION, CENTER, CITE, CODE, COMMENT, DD, DFN, DT, EM, ENTITY, FONT, FORM, H1...H6, HEAD, I, KBD, LI, MARQUEE, P, SAMP, STRIKE, STRONG, TD, TH, TT, U, and VAR

EXAMPLE OF BGSOUND

```
<BGSOUND SRC="/sounds/my.mid" LOOP=INFINITE>
```

BIG

The BIG element specifies that the enclosed text be rendered one size larger than the current font. The BIG element requires a closing tag.

Figure D.6.
The BIG element.

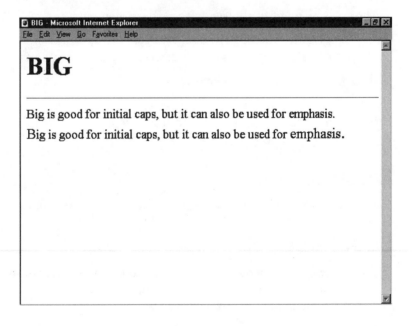

Syntax: `<BIG>...</BIG>`

The BIG element is allowed within these elements:

A, APPLET, B, BIG, BR, CITE, CODE, DFN, EM, FONT, I, IMG, INPUT, KBD, MAP, SAMP, SCRIPT, SELECT, SMALL, STRIKE, STRONG, SUB, SUP, TEXTAREA, TT, U, and VAR

BIG is allowed inside the following:

A, ADDRESS, B, BIG, BLOCKQUOTE, BODY, CAPTION, CENTER, CITE, CODE, DD, DFN, DIF, DT, EM, FONT, FORM, H1...H6, I, KBD, LI, P, SAMP, SMALL, STRIKE, STRONG, SUB, SUP, TD, TEXTFLOW, TH, TT, U, and VAR

EXAMPLE OF BIG

```
...
Big is good for initial caps, but it can also be used for emphasis.
<BR><BIG>B</BIG>ig is good for initial caps, but it can also be used for
<BIG>emphasis</BIG>.
...
```

BLINK

The BLINK element specifies that the enclosed text be rendered using a blinking font. BLINK is a Netscape only extension. The BLINK element requires a closing tag.

Syntax: `<BLINK>...</BLINK>`

The BLINK element is allowed within these elements:

A, APPLET, B, BIG, BR, CITE, CODE, DFN, EM, FONT, I, IMG, INPUT, KBD, MAP, SAMP, SCRIPT, SELECT, SMALL, STRIKE, STRONG, SUB, SUP, TEXTAREA, TT, U, and VAR

BLINK is allowed inside the following:

A, ADDRESS, B, BIG, BLOCKQUOTE, BODY, CAPTION, CENTER, CITE, CODE, DD, DFN, DIF, DT, EM, FONT, FORM, H1...H6, I, KBD, LI, P, SAMP, SMALL, STRIKE, STRONG, SUB, SUP, TD, TEXTFLOW, TH, TT, U, and VAR

EXAMPLE OF BLINK

```
<P>This is normal text. <BLINK>Hello, this text blinks!</BLINK>
```

BLOCKQUOTE

The BLOCKQUOTE element specifies that the enclosed text represents a blockquote. Blockquotes are rendered by indenting both the left and right margins. The BLOCKQUOTE element requires a closing tag.

Figure D.7.
The BLOCKQUOTE
element.

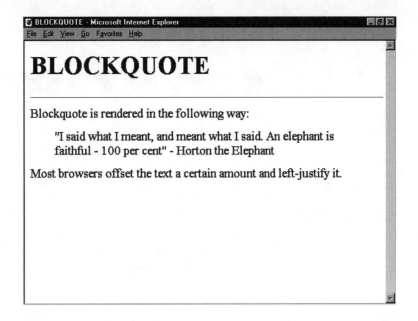

Syntax: `<BLOCKQUOTE>...</BLOCKQUOTE>`

The BLOCKQUOTE element is allowed within these elements:

A, ADDRESS, APPLET, B, BIG, BLOCKQUOTE, BR, CENTER, CITE, CODE, DFN, DIR, DIV, DL, EM, FONT, FORM, H1...H6, HR, I, IMG, INPUT, ISINDEX, KBD, LISTING, MAP, MENU, OL, P, PRE, SAMP, SCRIPT, SELECT, SMALL, STRIKE, STRONG, SUB, SUP, TABLE, TEXTAREA, TT, U, UL, VAR, and XMP.

BLOCKQUOTE is allowed inside the following:

BLOCKQUOTE, BODY, CENTER, DD, DIV, FORM, LI, TD, and TH

EXAMPLE OF BLOCKQUOTE

```
...
<BLOCKQUOTE>
"I said what I meant, and meant what I said.  An elephant is faithful - 100 per
cent"
- Horton the Elephant
</BLOCKQUOTE>
...
```

BODY

The BODY element contains the content of a document. It specifies the beginning and end of the document body. This contrasts with the HEAD of a document, which contains information about the document. All displayable elements should be included within the BODY section. The opening and closing of the BODY element is inferred, so it is optional. However, it is considered good style to open and close it.

Figure D.8.
Some changes to
the standard BODY
settings.

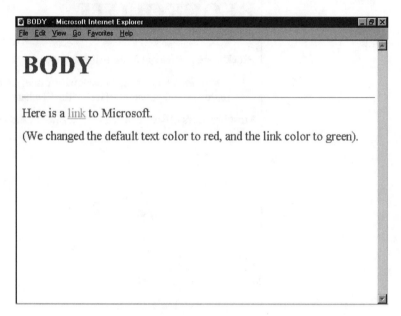

Syntax: <BODY ALINK=*color* BAGROUND=*url* BGCOLOR=*color* BGPROPERTIES=FIXED
LEFTMARGIN=*n* LINK=*color* TEXT=*color* TOPMARGIN=*n* VLINK=*color*>...</
BODY>

The options available for BODY include the following:

ALINK=*color*   Specifies the color of the active link. Colors are specified in the HEX, 00-FF for each component of the RGB channel in the #RRGGBB format.

BACKGROUND=*url*   Specifies an image to be used as the background.

BGCOLOR=*color*   Specifies the background color of the document. Colors are specified in the HEX, 00-FF for each component of the RGB channel in the #RRGGBB format, or by specifying one of the Microsoft Internet Explorer predefined colors: Aqua, Black, Blue, Fuchsia, Gray, Green, Lime, Maroon, Navy, Olive, Purple, Red, Silver, Teal, Yellow, or White.

BGPROPERTIES=FIXED   Specifies that the BACKGROUND image be used as a watermark. The image is not replicated and remains stationary in the center of the window.

LEFTMARGIN=*n*	Sets the margin for the left of the page. When set to zero, the left margin is set on the left edge of the window.
LINK=*color*	Specifies the color of a normal link. Colors are specified in the HEX, 00-FF for each component of the RGB channel in the #RRGGBB format.
TEXT=*color*	Specifies the color of normal text. Colors are specified in the HEX, 00-FF for each component of the RGB channel in the #RRGGBB format.
TOPMARGIN=*n*	Sets the margin for the top of the page. When set to zero, the top margin is set on the top edge of the window.
VLINK=color	Specifies the color of a visited or viewed link. Colors are specified in the HEX, 00-FF for each component of the RGB channel in the #RRGGBB format.

The BODY element is allowed within these elements:

A, ADDRESS, APPLET, B, BIG, BLOCKQUOTE, BR, CENTER, CITE, DFN, DIR, DIV, DL, EM, FONT, FORM, H1...H6, I, IMG, INPUT, ISINDEX, KBD, LISTING, MAP, MENU, OL, P, PRE, SAMP, SCRIPT, SELECT, SMAL, STRIKE, STRONG, SUB, SUP, TABLE, TEXTAREA, TT, U, UL, VAR, and XMP

The element is allowed inside the following:

HTML

EXAMPLE OF BODY

```
<BODY BGCOLOR="#FFFFFF" TEXT="#FF3333" LINK="00FF00" VLINK="#00FF00"
ALINK="#00FF00">
<H1>BODY</H1>
<HR>
Here is a <A HREF="http://www.microsoft.com">link</A> to Microsoft.
<P>(We changed the default text color to red, and the link color to green).
</BODY>
```

BR (BREAK)

The BR element inserts a line break and continues the rendering of objects that follow in the next line.

Figure D.9.
The BR element.

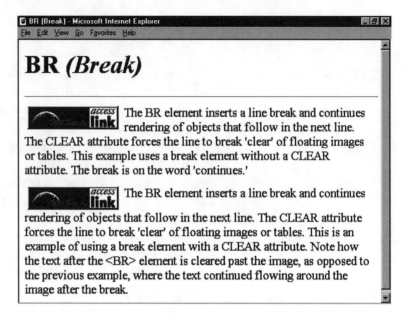

Syntax: `<BR CLEAR=align-type>`

Options include the following:

CLEAR
> The CLEAR attribute forces the line to break clear of floating images or tables. Possible values for the CLEAR attribute are

> LEFT   Move down until the left margin is clear.

> ALL   Move down until all margins are clear.

> RIGHT   Move down until the right margin is clear.

> NONE   Do not clear the margins.

The BR element is allowed within these elements:

Not applicable.

BR is allowed inside the following:

A, ADDRESS, B, BIG, BLOCKQUOTE, BODY, CAPTION, CENTER, CITE, CODE, DD, DFN, DIV, DT, EM, FONT, FORM, H1...H6, I, KBD, LI, P, PRE, SAMP, SMALL, STRIKE, STRONG, SUB, SUP, TD, TEXTFLOW, TH, TT, U, and VAR

EXAMPLE OF BR

```
<IMG SRC="websiteby.gif" ALT="Web Site By AccessLink" ALIGN=LEFT HSPACE=5>
The BR element inserts a line break and continues<BR> rendering of objects
that follow in the next line. The CLEAR attribute forces the line to break
'clear' of floating images or tables. This example uses a break element
without a CLEAR attribute. The break is on the word 'continues.'
<P>
<IMG SRC="websiteby.gif" ALT="Web Site By AccessLink" ALIGN=LEFT HSPACE=5>
The BR element inserts a line break and continues <BR CLEAR=ALL> rendering
of objects that follow in the next line. The CLEAR attribute forces the line
to break 'clear' of floating images or tables. This is an example of using
a break element with a CLEAR attribute. Note how the text after the andlt;BRandgt;
element is cleared past the image, as opposed to the previous example,
where the text continued flowing around the image after the break.
```

CAPTION

The CAPTION element is used to label a table. The ALIGN attribute specifies the alignment of the caption. The CAPTION element requires a closing tag.

Figure D.10.
The CAPTION
element.

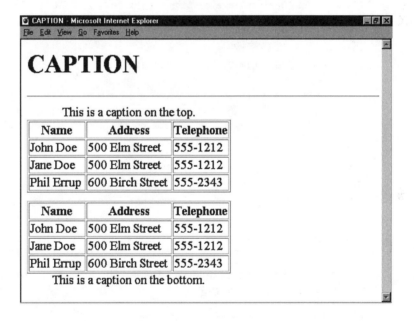

Syntax: `<CAPTION ALIGN=align-type>...</CAPTION>`

Options for CAPTION include the following:

ALIGN   The ALIGN attribute specifies what edge to place the caption relative of.

LEFT   Places captions on the left.

RIGHT   Places captions on the right.

TOP   Places caption at the top.

BOTTOM   Places captions at the bottom of the image. This is the default setting.

The CAPTION element is allowed within these elements:

A, APPLET, B, BIG, BR, CITE, CODE, DFN, EM, FONT, I, IMG, INPUT, KBD, SAMP, SCRIPT, SELECT, SMALL, STRIKE, STRONG, SUB, SUP, TEXTAREA, TT, U, and VAR

CAPTION is allowed inside the following:

TABLE

EXAMPLE OF CAPTION

```
...
<CAPTION ALIGN=TOP>This is a caption on the top.</CAPTION>
<TR>
<TH>Name</TH> <TH>Address</TH> <TH>Telephone</TH>
</TR>
<TR>
<TD>John Doe <TD>500 Elm Street <TD>555-1212
</TR>
</TABLE>
<P>
<TABLE BORDER=1>
<CAPTION ALIGN=BOTTOM>This is a caption on the bottom.</CAPTION>
<TR>
<TH>Name</TH> <TH>Address</TH> <TH>Telephone</TH>
</TR>
<TR>
</TR>
</TABLE>
...
```

CENTER

The CENTER element centers objects between the left and right margins. The CENTER element requires a closing tag.

Syntax: `<CENTER>...</CENTER>`

Figure D.11.
The CENTER
element.

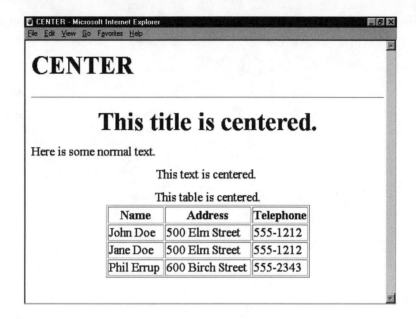

The CENTER element is allowed within these elements:

A, ADDRESS, APPLET, B, BIG, BLOCKQUOTE, BR, CENTER, CITE, CODE, DFN, DIR, DIV, DL, EM, FONT, FORM, H1...H6, HR, I, IMG, INPUT, ISINDEX, KBD, LISTING, MAP, MENU, OL, P, PRE, SAMP, SCRIPT, SELECT, SMALL, STRIKE, STRONG, SUB, SUP, TABLE, TEXTAREA, TT, U, UL, VAR, and XMP.

CENTER is allowed inside the following:

BLOCKQUOTE, BODY, CENTER, DD, DIV, FORM, LI, TD, and TH

EXAMPLE OF CENTER

```
<CENTER>
<P>
This text is centered.
</CENTER>
```

CITE

The CITE element renders its contents—a reference to a book, paper, or other published materials—as a citation. The CITE element requires a closing tag.

Figure D.12.
The CITE element.

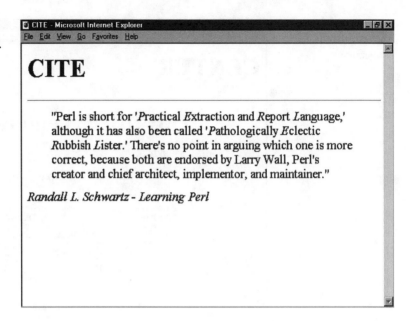

Syntax: `<CITE>...</CITE>`

The CITE element is allowed within these elements:

A, APPLET, B, BIG, BR, CITE, CODE, DFN, EM, FONT, I, IMG, INPUT, KBD, MAP, SAMP, SCRIPT, SELECT, SMALL, STRIKE, STRONG, SUB, SUP, TEXTAREA, TT, U, and VAR

CITE is allowed inside the following:

A, ADDRESS, B, BIG, BLOCKQUOTE, BODY, CAPTION, CENTER, CITE, CODE, DD, DFN, DIV, DT, EM, FONT, FORM, H1...H6, I, KBD, LI, P, PRE, SAMP, SMALL, STRIKE, STRONG, SUB, SUP, TD, TEXTFLOW, TH, TT, U, and VAR

EXAMPLE OF CITE

```
<CITE>Randall L. Schwartz - Learning Perl </CITE>
```

CODE

The CODE element renders its contents as computer code. It is intended for short words or phrases. Multiline listings should use the PRE element instead. CODE is usually rendered in a monospaced font. The CODE element requires a closing tag.

Figure D.13.
The CODE element.

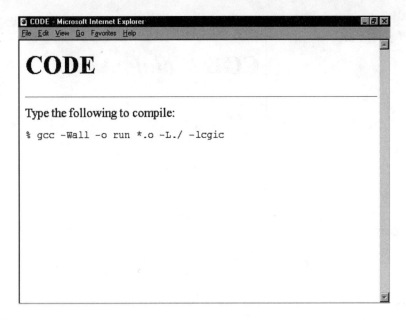

Syntax: `<CODE>...</CODE>`

The CODE element is allowed within these elements:

A, APPLET, B, BIG, BR, CITE, CODE, DFN, EM, FONT, I, IMG, INPUT, KBD, MAP, SAMP, SCRIPT, SELECT, SMALL, STRIKE, STRONG, SUB, SUP, TEXTAREA, TT, U, and VAR

The element is allowed inside the following:

A, ADDRESS, B, BIG, BLOCKQUOTE, BODY, CAPTION, CENTER, CITE, CODE, DD, DFN, DIV, DT, EM, FONT, FORM, H1...H6, I, KBD, LI, P, PRE, SAMP, SMALL, STRIKE, STRONG, SUB, SUP, TD, TEXTFLOW, TH, TT, U, and VAR

EXAMPLE OF CODE

```
<CODE>
% gcc -Wall -o run *.o -L./ -lcgic
</CODE>
```

COL (COLUMN PROPERTIES)

The COL element sets the properties of one or more columns on a table. It is used together with the COLGROUP element to set the properties of columns within a group. The end tag is not required.

Figure D.14.
The COL *element.*

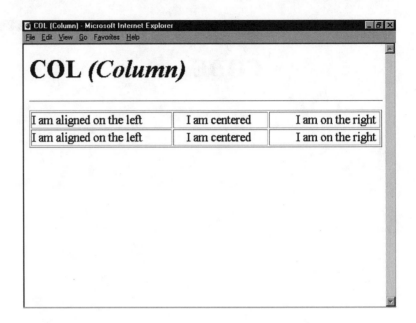

Syntax: `<COL ALIGN=align-type SPAN=n>`

Options include the following:

ALIGN=*align-type*   Specifies the alignment of text in the column. Legal values are

CENTER   Centers text in the column.

LEFT   Text is left aligned in the column.

RIGHT   Text is right aligned in the column.

SPAN=*n*   Specifies the number of consecutive columns that this property affects.

The COL element is allowed within these elements:

Not applicable.

The element is allowed inside the following:

COLGROUP

EXAMPLE OF COL

```
...
<TABLE WIDTH=600 BORDER=1>
<COLGROUP>
<COL ALIGN=LEFT>
```

```
<COL ALIGN=CENTER>
<COL ALIGN=RIGHT>
<TBODY>
<TR>
<TD>I am aligned on the left
<TD>I am centered
<TD>I am on the right
</TR>
<TR>
<TD>I am aligned on the left
<TD>I am centered
<TD>I am on the right
</TR>
</TABLE>
...
```

COLGROUP (COLUMN GROUP)

The COLGROUP element sets properties for one or more columns. A closing tag is not required.

Figure D.15.
The COLGROUP
element.

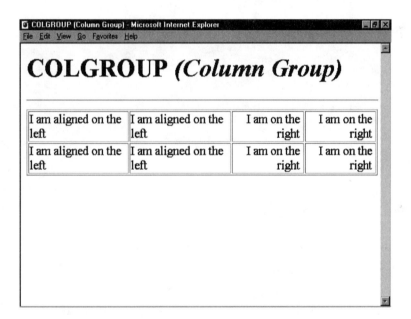

Syntax: `<COLGROUP ALIGN=align-type SPAN=n>`

Options include the following:

ALIGN=*align-type*   Specifies the alignment of text in the column. Legal values are

CENTER   Centers text in the column.

LEFT	Text is left aligned in the column.
RIGHT	Text is right aligned in the column.
SPAN=n	Specifies the number of consecutive columns that this property affects.

The COLGROUP element is allowed within these elements:

Not applicable.

The element is allowed inside the following:

TABLE

EXAMPLE OF COLGROUP

```
...
<TABLE BORDER=1 WIDTH=600>
<COLGROUP ALIGN=LEFT SPAN=2>
<COLGROUP ALIGN=RIGHT SPAN=2>
<TBODY>
<TR>
<TD>I am aligned on the left
<TD>I am aligned on the left
<TD>I am on the right
<TD>I am on the right
</TR>
<TR>
<TD>I am aligned on the left
<TD>I am aligned on the left
<TD>I am on the right
<TD>I am on the right
</TR>
</TABLE>
...
```

COMMENT

This element defines a comment. The text it contains is ignored unless it contains HTML code.

Syntax: <COMMENT>...</COMMENT>

The COMMENT element is allowed within these elements:

Any valid HTML; however, that makes for an oxymoron!

The element is allowed inside the following:

Anywhere.

EXAMPLE OF COMMENT

```
<COMMENT>This is a comment</COMMENT>
```

If you really need comments, you may want to use SGML-style comments, which are supported by all browsers. SGML comments follow this syntax: `<!-- comment -->`. Any text inside the comment brackets won't print, and it can handle multiple lines of text between the tags:

```
<!-- some comment
More comments
-->
```

DD (DEFINITION)

The DD (definition) element is used to provide a definition for a DT (definition term) within a DL (definition list) element. The closing tag is optional.

Figure D.16.
The DD element.

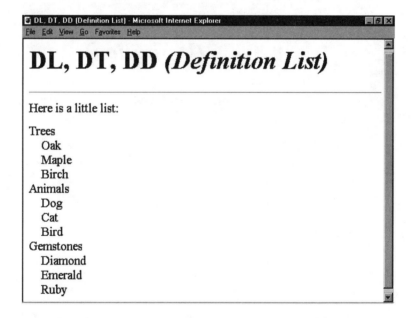

Syntax: `<DD>...</DD>`

The DD element is allowed within these elements:

A, APPLET, B, BIG, BLOCKQUOTE, BR, CENTER, CITE, CODE, DFN, DIR, DIV, DL, EM, FONT, FORM, HR, I, IMG, INPUT, ISINDEX, KBD, LISTING, MAP, MENU, OL, P, PRE, SAMP, SCRIPT, SELECT, SMALL, STRIKE, STRONG, SUB, SUP, TABLE, TEXTAREA, TT, U, UL, VAR, and XMP

The element is allowed inside the following:

```
DL
```

EXAMPLE OF DD

```
<DL>
<DT>Tree<DD>Vegetable
<DT>Dog<DD>Animal
<DT>Diamond<DD>Expensive mineral
</DL>
```

DFN (DEFINITION)

The DFN element renders its content as a definition. The DFN closing element is required.

Figure D.17.
The DFN element.

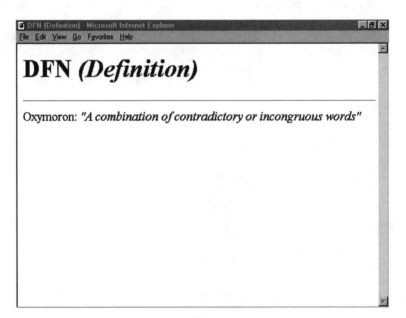

Syntax: `<DFN>...</DFN>`

The DFN element is allowed within these elements:

A, APPLET, B, BIG, BR, CITE, CODE, DFN, EM, FONT, I, IMG, INPUT, KBD, MAP, SAMP, SCRIPT, SELECT, SMALL, STRIKE, STRONG, SUB, SUP, TEXTAREA, TT, U, and VAR

The element is allowed inside the following:

> A, ADDRESS, B, BIG, BLOCKQUOTE, BODY, CAPTION, CENTER, CITE, CODE, DD, DFN, DIV, DT, EM,
> FONT, FORM, H1...H6, I, KBD, LI, P, PRE, SAMP, SMALL, STRIKE, STRONG, SUB, SUP, TD,
> TEXTFLOW, TH, TT, U, and VAR

Example of DFN

```
<P>Oxymoron: <DFN>"A combination of contradictory or incongruous words"</DFN>
```

DIR (Directory)

The DIR element specifies a directory list of items, each starting with a LI element and none containing more than 20 characters. The list should display in columns (current third generation browsers don't). An ending tag is required.

Figure D.18.
The DIR element.

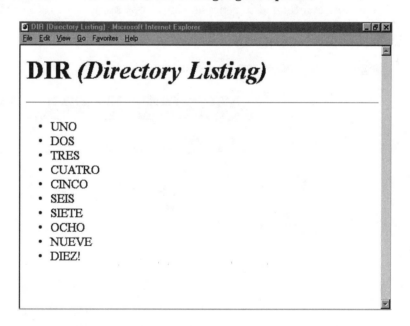

Syntax: `<DIR><LI>...<LI>...<LI>......</DIR>`

The DIR element is allowed within this element:

> LI

The element is allowed inside the following:

> BLOCKQUOTE, BODY, CENTER, DD, DIB, FORM, LI, TD, and TH

EXAMPLE OF DIR

```
<DIR>
<LI>UNO
<LI>DOS
<LI>TRES
<LI>CUATRO
<LI>CINCO
<LI>SEIS
<LI>SIETE
<LI>OCHO
<LI>NUEVE
<LI>DIEZ!
</DIR>
```

DIV (DIVISION)

The DIV element is used to create divisions or groupings of related elements. The DIV element is intended to represent different kinds of containers (such as a chapter, section, abstract, or appendix) when used with the CLASS attribute. DIV allows the enclosed group of elements to be given a distinctive style. The closing tag is required.

Syntax: `<DIV ALIGN=align-type CLASS=container-type>...</DIV>`

Figure D.19.
The DIV element.

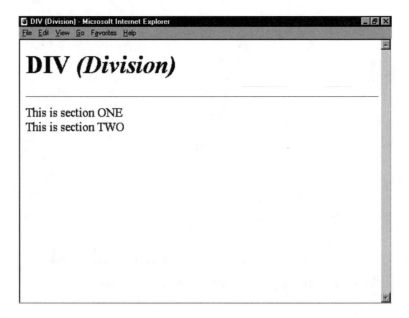

Options include the following:

ALIGN=*align-type* Specifies the horizontal alignment of text. *align-type* can be

    LEFT Text is placed flush to the left margin. This is the default value.

    CENTER Text is placed center between the margins.

    RIGHT Text is placed flush to the right margin.

CLASS=*container-type* Specifies the type of container.

    container-type can be set to different kinds of containers, such as a chapter, section, abstract, or appendix.

The DIV element is allowed within these elements:

A, ADDRESS, APPLET, B, BIG, BLOCKQUOTE, BR, CENTER, CITE, CODE, DFN, DIR, DIV, DL, EM, FONT, FORM, H1, H2, H3, H4, H5, H6, HR, I, IMG, INPUT, ISINDEX, KBD, LISTING, MAP, MENU, OL, P, PRE, SAMP, SCRIPT, SELECT, SMALL, STRIKE, STRONG, SUB, SUP, TABLE, TEXTAREA, TT, U, UL, VAR, and XMP

The element is allowed inside the following:

BLOCKQUOTE, BODY, CENTER, DD, DIV, FORM, LI, TD, and TH

EXAMPLE OF DIV

```
<DIV>This is section ONE</DIV>
<DIV>This is section TWO</DIV>
```

DL (DEFINITION LIST)

The DL element defines a definition list. A definition list is used to build two-column lists for terms and their corresponding definitions. The closing tag is required.

Syntax: `<DL><DT>...<DD>...</DL>`

Options include the following:

COMPACT This setting suggests that items in the list are rendered in a compact way, by using a smaller font size or by reducing the vertical spacing between items in the list whenever possible.

The DL element is allowed within these elements:

DD and DT

The element is allowed inside the following:

BLOCKQUOTE, BODY, CENTER, DD, DIV, FORM, LI, TD, and TH

EXAMPLE OF DL

```
<DL>
<DT>Tree<DD>Vegetable
<DT>Dog<DD>Animal
<DT>Diamond<DD>Expensive mineral
</DL>
```

DT (DEFINITION TERM)

The DT element specifies a term within a definition list (DL) element. The closing tag is optional.

Syntax: <DT>...</DT>

The DT element is allowed within these elements:

A, APPLET, B, BIG, BR, CITE, CODE, DFN, EM, FONT, I, IMG, INPUT, KBD, MAP, SAMP, SCRIPT, SELECT, SMALL, STRIKE, STRONG, SUB, SUP, TEXTAREA, TT, U, and VAR

The element is allowed inside the following:

DL

EXAMPLE OF DT

```
<DL>
<DT>Tree<DD>Vegetable
<DT>Dog<DD>Animal
<DT>Diamond<DD>Expensive mineral
</DL>
```

EM (EMPHASIS)

The EM is used for text that should be rendered with emphasis; usually it is rendered in italics. The EM element doesn't have any attributes.

Syntax: <EM>...</EM>

The EM element is allowed within these elements:

A, APPLET, B, BIG, BR, CITE, CODE, DFN, EM, FONT, I, IMG, INPUT, KBD, MAP, SAMP, SCRIPT, SELECT, SMALL, STRIKE, STRONG, SUB, SUP, TEXTAREA, TT, U, and VAR

The element is allowed inside the following:

A, ADDRESS, B, BIG, BLOCKQUOTE, BODY, CAPTION, CENTER, CITE, CODE, DD, DFN, DIV, DT, EM, FONT, FORM, H1, H2, H3, H4, H5, H6, I, KBD, LI, P, PRE, SAMP, SMALL, STRIKE, STRONG, SUB, SUP, TD, TEXTFLOW, TH, TT, U, and VAR

Figure D.20.
The EM *element.*

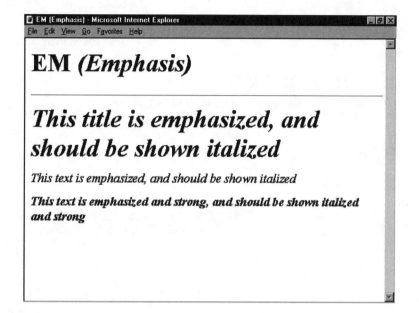

EXAMPLE OF EM

```
<H1><EM>This title is emphasized, and should be shown italized</EM></H1>
<EM>This text is emphasized, and should be shown italized</EM>
<P>
<STRONG><EM>This text is emphasized and strong,
and should be shown italized and strong</EM></STRONG>
```

EMBED

The EMBED element allows the insertion of arbitrary objects directly into an HTML page. Embedded objects obtain support via plug-ins and allow arbitrary attributes that plug-ins support. You should consider using the OBJECT element.

Syntax:
```
<EMBED HEIGHT=n NAME=name OPTIONAL PARAM="value"
PALETTE="option" SRC=url WIDTH=n>
```

Options for EMBED include the following:

HEIGHT=*n*   Sets the height of the object in pixels.

NAME=*name*   Sets the name of the object.

OPTIONAL PARAM=*value*	Sets parameters sent to the object. You can have as many of these as you need.
PALETTE=*foreground¦background*	Sets the color palette for the foreground and background.
SRC=*url*	Sets the URL of any data to be inputted into the object.
WIDTH=*n*	Specifies the width of the object in pixels.

EXAMPLE OF EM

```
<EMBED WIDTH=300 HEIGHT=180 SRC="foo.wrl">
</EMBED>
```

FONT

The FONT element changes the font size and color.

Figure D.21.
The FONT element.

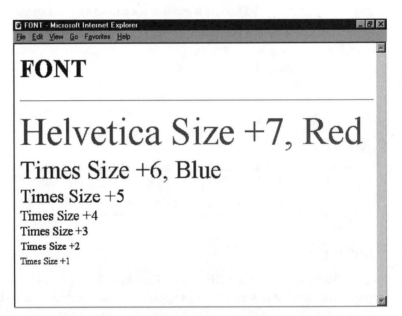

Syntax: `<FONT COLOR=color FACE=name SIZE=n>`

Options for FONT include the following:

COLOR=*color*	Specifies the color of the font. Colors are specified in the HEX, 00-FF for each component of the RGB channel in the following format: #RRGGBB

FACE=*name*	Sets the font. A list of comma-separated fonts can be provided. The system will search for the first available match. If none are available, the default font is used.
SIZE=*n*	Specifies the size of the font. Font size ranges from 1–7 inclusive, with 7 being the largest. Prefixing *n* with a + or - sign specifies a relative font size based on the base font (usually set to 3).

The FONT element is allowed within these elements:

A, APPLET, B, BIG, BR, CITE, CODE, DFN, EM, FONT, I, IMG, INPUT, KBD, MAP, SAMP, SCRIPT, SELECT, SMALL, STRIKE, STRONG, SUB, SUP, TEXTAREA, TT, U, and VAR

The element is allowed inside the following:

A, ADDRESS, B, BIG, BLOCKQUOTE, BODY, CAPTION, CENTER, CITE, CODE, DD, DFN, DIV, DT, EM, FONT, FORM, H1, H2, H3, H4, H5, H6, I, KBD, LI, P, SAMP, SMALL, STRIKE, STRONG, SUB, SUP, TD, TEXTFLOW, TH, TT, U, and VAR

EXAMPLE OF FONT

```
<FONT SIZE=7 FACE="Helvetica" COLOR=RED> Helvetica Size +7, Red</FONT>
<BR>
<FONT SIZE=6 FACE="Times" COLOR=BLUE> Times Size +6, Blue </FONT>
<BR>
<FONT SIZE=5 FACE="Times"> Times Size +5</FONT>
<BR>
<FONT SIZE=4 FACE="Times"> Times Size +4</FONT>
<BR>
<FONT SIZE=3 FACE="Times"> Times Size +3</FONT>
<BR>
<FONT SIZE=2 FACE="Times"> Times Size +2</FONT>
<BR>
<FONT SIZE=1 FACE="Times"> Times Size +1</FONT>
```

FORM

The FORM element is used to create fill-out forms. The browser will permit the user to enter data into the fields provided and will send the entered data to the CGI program specified in the URL by the ACTION option. Closing tags are required.

Syntax:
```
<FORM ACTION=url ENCTYPE="application/x-www-form-urlencoded"
METHOD=GET¦POST TARGET=window>...</FORM>
```

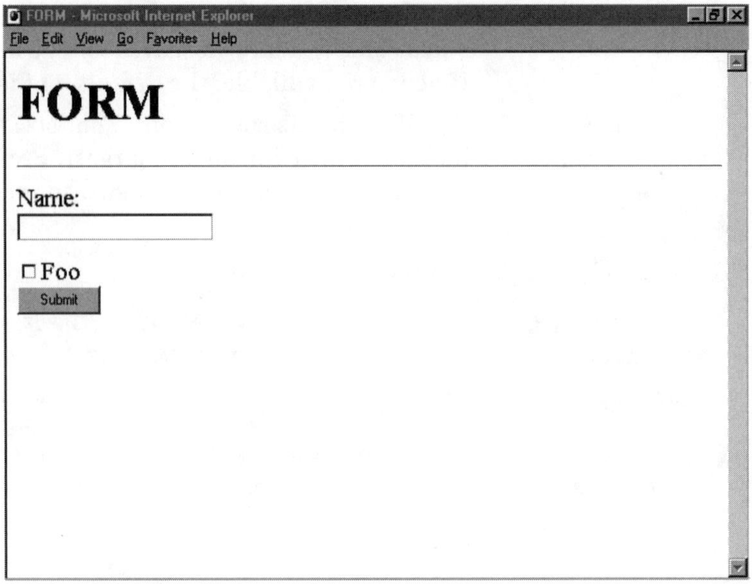

Figure D.22.
The FORM element.

Options for FORM include the following:

ACTION	A URL that specifies the location to submit the contents.
ENCTYPE	MIME-content type for encoding (*application/x-www-form-urlencoded*).
METHOD	Specifies variations in the protocol to send form contents.

	GET	Information is passed via an environment variable.
	POST	Information is passed via the programs stdin.

TARGET=*window*	Specifies that the target is loaded into the specified window. Possible values for window are

	window	Specifies to load the link into the named window.
	blank	Creates the frame in a new unnamed window.
	self	Loads the frame in the parent window.
	parent	Loads in the parent window.
	top	Loads in the top window.

The FORM element is allowed within these elements:

A, ADDRESS, APPLET, B, BIG, BLOCKQUOTE, BR, CENTER, CITE, CODE, DFN, DIR, DIV, DL, EM, FONT, H1, H2, H3, H4, H5, H6, HR, I, IMG, INPUT, ISINDEX, KBD, LISTING, MAP, MENU, OL, P, PRE, SAMP, SCRIPT, SELECT, SMALL, STRIKE, STRONG, SUB, SUP, TABLE, TEXTAREA, TT, U, UL, VAR, and XMP

The element is allowed inside the following:

BLOCKQUOTE, BODY, CENTER, DD, DIV, LI, TD, and TH

EXAMPLE OF FORM

```
...
<FORM ACTION="http://localhost/cgi-bin/printenv" METHOD="GET">
<INPUT TYPE="text" NAME="name" SIZE=30>
<P>
<INPUT TYPE=checkbox NAME=foo>  Foo
<BR>
<INPUT TYPE="submit" VALUE="Submit">
</FORM>
...
```

FRAME

The FRAME element defines a frame in a FRAMESET. The SRC attribute value is the URL of the document to be displayed inside the frame. If the SRC attribute is not specified, leave the frame blank.

Figure D.23. The FRAME element.

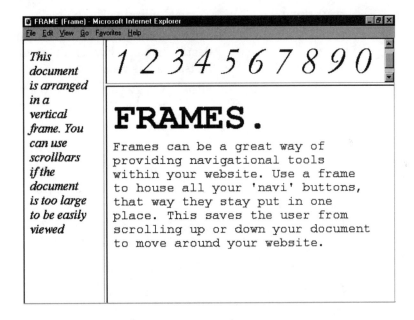

Syntax: `<FRAME ALIGN=align-type FRAMEBORDER=0¦1 MARGINHEIGHT=n`
`MARGINWIDTH=n NAME=name SCROLLING=YES¦NO SRC=url>`

Options for FRAME include the following:

ALIGN=*align-type* Specifies the alignment of the frame with respect to the surrounding text. Possible values are

TOP Places the top of the image at the text baseline.

MIDDLE Centers the image on the text baseline.

BOTTOM Places the bottom of the image at the text baseline.

LEFT Image is aligned flush with the left margin.

RIGHT Image is flush with the right margin.

FRAMEBORDER=*0¦1* Draws a tridimensional border. If 1, the default draws it. If 0, it doesn't display a border.

SCROLLING=*YES¦NO* This attribute specifies whether a scrollbar will be provided for the frame. This attribute accepts three values: YES, NO, or AUTO. AUTO is the default value.

MARGINWIDTH=*n* Horizontal margin size in pixels.

MARGINHEIGHT=*n* Vertical margin size in pixels.

NAME=*name* The *name* attribute specifies a name for using as the destination of a hyperlink (similar to the A element). Netscape has reserved the following values for NAME:

blank Creates the frame in a new unnamed window

self Loads the frame in the parent window.

parent Loads in the parent window.

top Loads in the top window.

NORESIZE NORESIZE prevents the user from resizing the frame.

SRC=*url* This specifies the URL for the document that will be displayed inside the frame. If this value is not defined, the frame is left blank.

The FRAME element is allowed within these elements:

None. FRAME element is not a container.

The element is allowed inside the following:

FRAMESET

EXAMPLE OF FRAME

```
<FRAME SRC="frame2.html">
<FRAME SRC="frame3.html">
```

FRAMESET

The FRAMESET element takes the place of the BODY element. It hosts the FRAME, FRAMESET, and NOFRAME elements. FRAMESET is used in HTML documents whose purpose is to define the layout of a FRAME-based document—one that includes additional HTML documents into specified areas of a window. FRAMESETs are specified as a list of comma-separated values.

Syntax: `<FRAMESET COLS=n FRAMEBORDER=1¦0 FRAMESPACING=n ROWS=n>`

Options for FRAMESET include the following:

ROWS=n
: Specifies the height of the FRAMESET.
Values are specified as integers with optional subfix modifiers:
A % specifies a percentage of the window size. Legal values are between 1–100.
A * specifies a multiplier of the width height.
A plain number (no subfix) specifies the size in pixels. This is the default setting.
A single * with no number specifies whatever is left of the window.

COLS=n
: Specifies the width of the FRAMESET.
Values are specified as integers with optional subfix modifiers:
A % specifies a percentage of the window size. Legal values are between 1–100.
A * specifies a multiplier of the width height.
A plain number (no subfix) specifies the size in pixels. This is the default setting.
A single * with no number specifies whatever is left of the window.

FRAMEBORDER=0¦1
: Draws a tridimensional border. If 1, the default draws it. If 0, displays no border.

FRAMESPACING=n
: Adds additional spacing (specified in pixels) between frames.

EXAMPLE OF FRAMESET

```
<FRAMESET ROWS=100%>
<NOFRAMES>
<BODY>
You don't have frames!
</BODY>
```

```
</NOFRAMES>
<FRAMESET COLS=25%,75%>
<FRAME SRC="frame1.html">
<FRAMESET ROWS=25%,75%>
<FRAME SRC="frame2.html">
<FRAME SRC="frame3.html">
</FRAMESET>
</FRAMESET>
</FRAMESET>
```

H*n* (HEADING)

The heading elements H1–H6 specify the size of a header in varying levels. The biggest header is H1, the smallest is H6, and all the others are in descending order between those two.

Figure D.24.
H1 *through* H6 *as rendered by Microsoft Internet Explorer.*

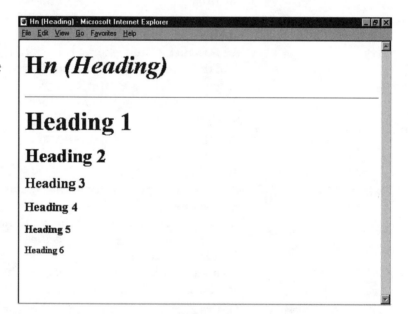

Syntax: `<Hn>...</Hn>`

Options for H*n* include the following:

n	Is the heading size. Possible values are 1-6 with 1 being the largest heading size.
ALIGN=*align-type*	This attribute specifies the horizontal alignment of the header. Possible values are
	LEFT Header is set flush with the left margin.

CENTER   Header is centered.

RIGHT   Header is set flush with the right margin.

The Hn element is allowed within these elements:

A, APPLET, B, BIG, BR, CITE, CODE, DFN, EM, FONT, I, IMG, INPUT, KBD, MAP, SAMP, SCRIPT, SELECT, SMALL, STRIKE, STRONG, SUB, SUP, TEXTAREA, TT, U, and VAR

The element is allowed inside the following:

BLOCKQUOTE, BODY, CENTER, DD, DIV, LI, TD, and TH

EXAMPLE OF Hn

```
<H1>Heading 1</H1>
<H2>Heading 2</H2>
<H3>Heading 3</H3>
<H4>Heading 4</H4>
<H5>Heading 5</H5>
<H6>Heading 6</H6>
```

HEAD

The HEAD element of an HTML document contains information about the document itself. None of the elements that legally belong on the HEADER section are displayed for the user. All displayed elements should appear in the BODY section. In addition to the following elements that are allowed within the HEAD, you can also use META tags. META tags provide additional information that is useful to indexing robots or to caching proxy servers.

The HEAD element is allowed within these elements:

BASE, ISINDEX, and TITLE

The element is allowed inside the following:

HTML

EXAMPLE OF HEAD

```
<HEAD>
<TITLE="This is my document">
<META NAME="created" CONTENT="AUG, 12 Mon 1996 22:46:36 CST">
<META HTTP-EQUIV="Content-Language" CONTENT="en-us">
<META HTTP-EQUIV="Last-Modified" CONTENT="AUG, 12 Mon 1996 22:46:36 CST">
<BASE HREF="http://www.someaddress.com/ TARGET=_blank>
</HEAD>
```

HR (HORIZONTAL RULE)

The HR element is used for drawing horizontal rules or lines. Horizontal rules can be used to visually divide sections.

Figure D.25.
The HR element.

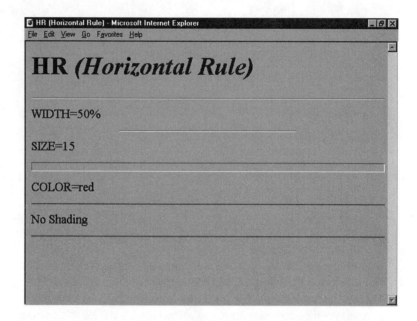

Syntax: `<HR ALIGN=align-type COLOR=color NOSHADE SIZE=n WIDTH=n>`

Options include the following:

ALIGN=align-type	Specifies alignment of the rule. Allowed values are
	LEFT Rule is aligned to the left margin.
	CENTER Rule is centered.
	RIGHT Rule is aligned to the right margin.
COLOR=color	Specifies the color of the base font. Colors are specified using hexadecimal notation for each component in the RGB channel in the following format: #RRGGBB, or by specifying one of the Microsoft Internet Explorer predefined colors: Aqua, Black, Blue, Fuchsia, Gray, Green, Lime, Maroon, Navy, Olive, Purple, Red, Silver, Teal, Yellow, or White.
NOSHADE	Specifies that no shading should be used on the rule and that it should be displayed as a plain line.

SIZE	The thickness of the rule in pixels.
WIDTH	The width of a rule. Allowed values are

number	Width in pixels.
percentage (*number%*)	Specifies width of the rule as a percentage of the width of the window.

The HR element is allowed within these elements:

Not applicable.

The element is allowed inside the following:

BLOCKQUOTE, BODY, CENTER, DD, DIV, FORM, LI, TD, and TH

EXAMPLE OF HR

```
WIDTH=50%<HR WIDTH=50%>
SIZE=15<HR SIZE=15>
COLOR=red<HR COLOR="#FF0000">
No Shading<HR NOSHADE>
```

HTML

The HTML element encloses an entire HTML document; they are the outermost elements and should not be nested inside any other element. While their specification is not required, it is considered good practice to do it.

Syntax: <HTML>...</HTML>

The HTML element is allowed within these elements:

BODY and HEAD

The element is allowed inside the following:

Not applicable.

EXAMPLE

```
<HTML>
<HEAD>
<TITLE>This is HTML</TITLE>
</HEAD>
<BODY>
<H1>This is HTML</H1>
</BODY>
</HTML>
```

I (ITALICS)

The I element specifies that its contents are rendered in italics.

Figure D.26.
The I element.

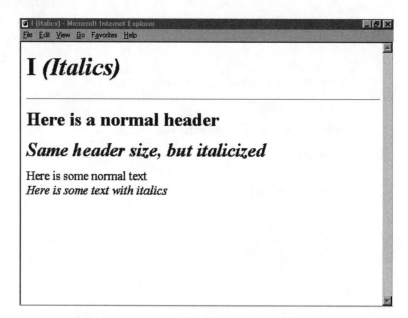

Syntax: `<I>...</I>`

The I element is allowed within these elements:

A, APPLET, B, BIG, BR, CITE, CODE, DFN, EM, FONT, I, IMG, INPUT, KBD, MAP, SAMP, SCRIPT, SELECT, SMALL, STRIKE, STRONG, SUB, SUP, TEXTAREA, TT, U, and VAR

The element is allowed inside the following:

A, ADDRESS, B, BIG, BLOCKQUOTE, BODY, CAPTION, CENTER, CITE, CODE, DD, DFN, DIV, DT, EM, FONT, FORM, H1...H6, I, KBD, LI, P, PRE, SAMP, SMALL, STRIKE, STRONG, SUB, SUP, TD, TEXTFLOW, TH, TT, U, and VAR

EXAMPLE OF I

```
<H2>Here is a normal header</H2>
<H2><I>Same header size, but italicized</I></H2>
Here is some normal text<BR>
<I>Here is some text with italics</I><BR>
```

IMG (IMAGE)

The IMG element is used to insert inline graphics into an HTML document. The closing tag is optional.

Syntax: `<IMG ALIGN=align-type ALT=text BORDER=n CONTROLS DYNSRC=url HEIGHT=n HSPACE=n ISMAP LOOP=n SRC=address START=start-event USEMAP=map-name VSPACE=n WIDTH=n>`

Figure D.27.
The IMG element.

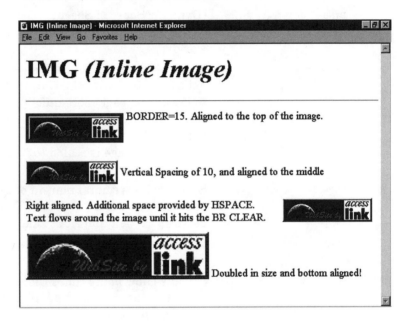

Options include the following:

ALIGN=*align-type*

Specifies the vertical alignment of the image with respect to the text line, possible values are

TOP	Places the top of the image at the text baseline.
MIDDLE	Centers the image on the text baseline.
BOTTOM	Places the bottom of the image at the text baseline.
LEFT	The image is aligned flush with the left margin and text flows around it.
RIGHT	The image is flush with the right margin and text flows around it.

ALT=*text*	Specifies a description that will be displayed on nongraphical browsers or when pictures are turned off.
BORDER=*n*	Specifies a border to be displayed around the image in pixels if the image is a hyperlink.
CONTROLS	If the image is a video clip, a set of controls is displayed under the clip.
DYNSRC=*url*	(Dynamic Source); Specifies the address of the video clip or Virtual Reality Modeling Language (VRML) world.
HEIGHT=*n*	Specifies the height of the image in pixels. This value, together with the width, allows the browser to layout the page more quickly because it can reserve space for the image beforehand. If you specify a different size than the actual size of the image, the image is scaled to fit into the specified dimension.
HSPACE=*n*	Specifies a horizontal margin or gutter that gets added to the picture in pixels. The *n* amount is split between the left and right sides of the image.
ISMAP	Is used to identify the image as a server-side image map.
LOOP=*n*	Specifies how many times the video clip will loop when the page is activated. If set to INFINITE or -1, the clip will loop forever.
SRC	Specifies the URI of the image to be inserted.
START=*start-event*	Starts playing the file specified by DYNSRC. *start-event* can be one of the following:

	FILEOPEN	Starts playing as soon as the file is downloaded (default setting).
	MOUSEOVER	Starts playing when the user moves the mouse over the animation.

USEMAP=*map*	Specifies that the image is a client-side image map and specifies that *map* should be used for defining the hotspots. Maps are defined using the MAP element.
VSPACE	Specifies a vertical margin or gutter in pixels around the image. It's split between the top and bottom sides of the image.

WIDTH

Specifies the width of the image in pixels. This value, together with the height, allows the browser to lay out the page more quickly because it can reserve space for the image beforehand. If you specify a different size than the actual size of the image, the image is scaled to fit into the specified dimension.

The IMG element is allowed within these elements:

Not applicable.

The element is allowed inside the following:

A, ADDRESS, B, BIG, BLOCKQUOTE, BODY, CAPTION, CENTER, CITE, CODE, DD, DFN, DIV, DT, EM, FONT, FORM, H1...H6, I, KBD, LI, P, SAMP, SMALL, STRIKE, STRONG, SUB, SUP, TD, TEXTFLOW, TH, TT, U, and VAR

EXAMPLE OF IMG

```
<A HREF="http://localhost"><IMG SRC="websiteby.gif" WIDTH=156 HEIGHT=39
ALT="WBAL" BORDER=15 ALIGN=TOP></A> BORDER=15
Aligned to the top of the image.<BR CLEAR=ALL>
<P>
<IMG SRC="websiteby.gif" WIDTH=156 HEIGHT=39 ALT="WBAL" VSPACE=10 ALIGN=
[ic:ccc]MIDDLE>
Vertical Spacing of 10, and aligned to the middle <BR CLEAR=ALL>
<P>
<IMG SRC="websiteby.gif" WIDTH=156 HSPACE=10 HEIGHT=39 ALT="WBAL" ALIGN=RIGHT>
Right aligned. Additional space provided by HSPACE.
Text flows around the image until it hits the BR CLEAR.<BR CLEAR=ALL>
<P>
<IMG SRC="websiteby.gif" WIDTH=312 HEIGHT=78 ALT="WBAL" ALIGN=BOTTOM>
Doubled in size and bottom aligned!<BR CLEAR=ALL>
```

INPUT

INPUT specifies a form control that the user can use to return values to a program on the server.

Syntax:

```
<FORM ALIGN=align-type [CHECKED] MAXLENGTH=n NAME=name SIZE=n
SRC=url TYPE=type VALUE=value>
```

D

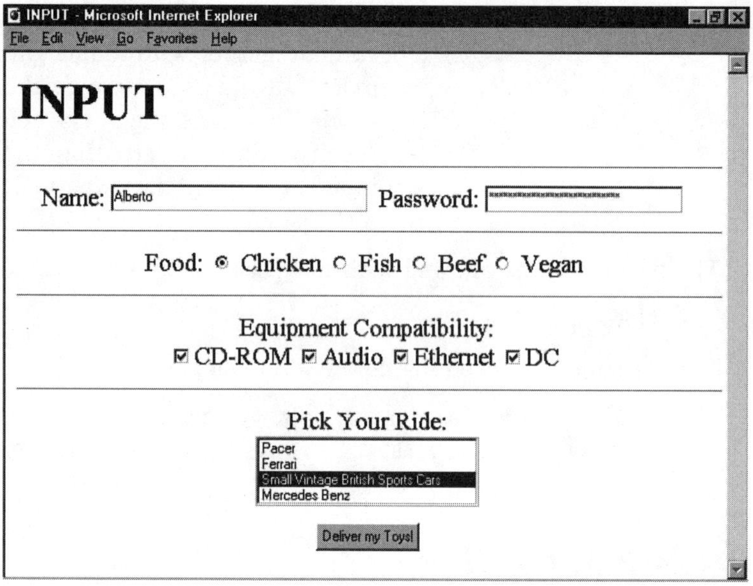

Figure D.28.
The INPUT
element.

Options for INPUT include the following:

ALIGN=*align-type*	Used when the TYPE is set to image. It specifies how the following line of text will be aligned with the image. Valid alignment types are

TOP	Text is aligned with the top of the image.
MIDDLE	Text is aligned with the center of the image.
BOTTOM	Text is aligned with the bottom of the image.

CHECKED	Sets a check box or radio control to selected setting when the form is initially loaded.
MAXLENGTH=*n*	Specifies the maximum number of characters that the input field will accept.
NAME=*name*	Sets the name of the control.
SIZE=*size*	Specifies the size of the control in characters.
SRC=*url*	Specifies the URL for an image type control.
TYPE=*type*	Specifies the type of control to use. It can be any of the following:

CHECKBOX	A simple control that allows ON or OFF relationships. The default setting is set to YES.

HIDDEN	The input field is hidden from the user; however, the contents of the field are returned to the server. Hidden fields can be used for passing values between your CGI and the browser without having them displayed in the browser window.
IMAGE	Sets the input field to be a graphic that when clicked submits the form. The coordinates where the user clicked are returned to the server with the upper-left corner of the image being the origin. Coordinates are returned as two values matching the name of the field with the coordinate designator .x or .y appended to it.
PASSWORD	Specifies a text field where the user can enter a password or other information that should not be echoed back in the form.
RADIO	A radio button allows the user to select one of several options. Each radio button part of a group should be named the same. Only the selected button will return a value, which should be explicitly set using the VALUE option.
RESET	A button that when activated will reset the contents of the form to their default settings. You can specify a different name for the RESET button using the VALUE option.
SUBMIT	A button that when activated will submit the contents of the form. You can rename the button with the VALUE option. If the NAME option is set, the SUBMIT button will contribute the value set in NAME to the submitted data.
TEXT	A single line text entry field. This is the default control type.

VALUE=*value*   Sets the default value for text or numerical controls.

The INPUT element is allowed within these elements:

Not applicable.

The element is allowed inside the following:

A, ADDRESS, B, BIG, BLOCKQUOTE, BODY, CAPTION, CENTER, CITE, CODE, DD, DFN, DIV, DT, EM, FONT, FORM, H1, H2, H3, H4, H5, H6, I, KBD, LI, P, PRE, SAMP, SMALL, STRIKE, STRONG, SUB, SUP, TD, TEXTFLOW, TH, TT, U, and VAR

EXAMPLE OF INPUT

```
<FORM ACTION="http://www.accesslink.com/cgi-bin/envvar" METHOD="GET">
Name: <INPUT TYPE="text" NAME="name" SIZE=40>
Password: <INPUT TYPE="password" NAME="passwd" SIZE=30>
<HR>
Food:
<INPUT TYPE=radio NAME="food" VALUE="chicken"> Chicken
<INPUT TYPE=radio NAME="food" VALUE="fish"> Fish
<INPUT TYPE=radio NAME="food" VALUE="beef"> Beef
<INPUT TYPE=radio NAME="food" VALUE="vegies"> Vegan
<HR>
Equipment Compatibility:<BR>
<INPUT TYPE=checkbox NAME=equip VALUE="cd-rom">CD-ROM
<INPUT TYPE=checkbox NAME=equip VALUE="audio">Audio
<INPUT TYPE=checkbox NAME=equip VALUE="networking">Ethernet
<INPUT TYPE=checkbox NAME=equip VALUE="battery">DC
<HR>
Pick Your Ride:<BR>
<SELECT NAME="car" MULTIPLE>
<OPTION SELECTED VALUE="pacer"> Pacer
<OPTION VALUE="ferrari"> Ferrari
<OPTION VALUE="small convertible"> Small Vintage British Sports Cars
<OPTION VALUE="luxurious german sendan"> Mercedes Benz
</SELECT>
<P>
<INPUT TYPE="submit" VALUE="Deliver my Toys!">
</FORM>
```

ISINDEX

The ISINDEX element is a precursor of the FORM element. It informs the browser that the document is searchable. This element automatically generates an input field for the user.

Syntax: `<ISINDEX ACTION=url PROMPT=prompt>`

Options include the following:

ACTION=*url*   Specifies the URL of the CGI program that will handle the entered information.

PROMPT=*prompt*   Specifies the text placed next to the input field. The default message is You can search this index. Type the keyword(s) you want to search for:.

The ISINDEX element is allowed within these elements:

Not applicable.

The element is allowed inside the following:

BLOCKQUOTE, BODY, CENTER, DD, DIV, FORM, HEAD, LI, TD, and TH

Figure D.29.
The ISINDEX
element.

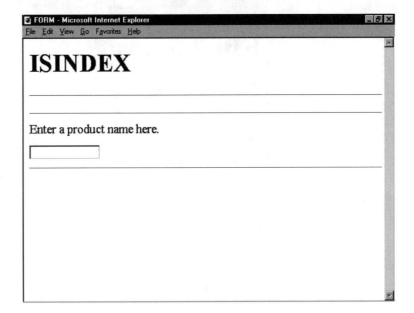

EXAMPLE OF ISINDEX

```
<ISINDEX ACTION="http://www.somesite.com/seach" PROMPT="Enter a product name
here.">
```

KBD

The KBD element renders text to represent text that the user should enter at the keyboard. Generally this is represented using a monospaced bold font. Closing tags for this element are required.

Syntax: `<KBD>...</KBD>`

The KBD element is allowed within these elements:

A, APPLET, B, BIG, BR, CITE, CODE, DFN, EM, FONT, I, IMG, INPUT, KBD, MAP, SAMP, SCRIPT, SELECT, SMALL, STRIKE, STRONG, SUB, SUP, TEXTAREA, TT, U, and VAR

The element is allowed inside the following:

A, ADDRESS, B, BIG, BLOCKQUOTE, BODY, CAPTION, CENTER, CITE, CODE, DD, DFN, DIV, DT, EM, FONT, FORM, H1-H6, I, KBD, LI, P, PRE, SAMP, SMALL, STRIKE, STRONG, SUB, SUP, TD, TEXTFLOW, TH, TT, U, and VAR

Figure D.30.
The KBD *element.*

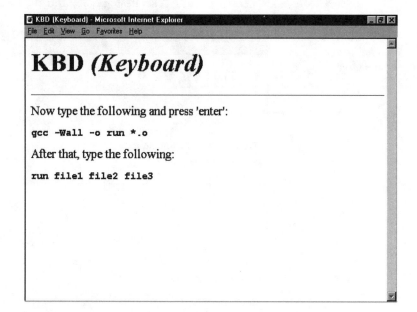

EXAMPLE OF KBD

```
<KBD>
gcc -Wall -o run *.o
</KBD>
<P>
After that, type the following:
<P>
<KBD>
run file1 file2 file3
</KBD>
```

LI (LIST)

The LI element is used to specify an element in a list under a DIR, MENU, OL, or UL element. The closing tag is optional and seldom used.

Syntax: `<LI TYPE=order-type VALUE=n>...</LI>`

*Figure D.31.
The LI element as
rendered by
Microsoft
Explorer.*

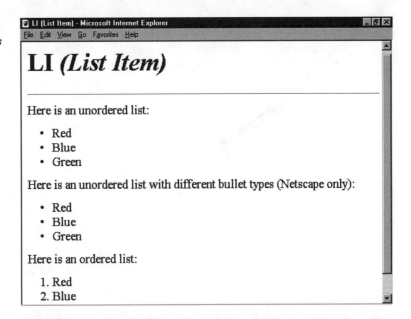

*Figure D.32.
The LI element as
rendered by
Navigator.*

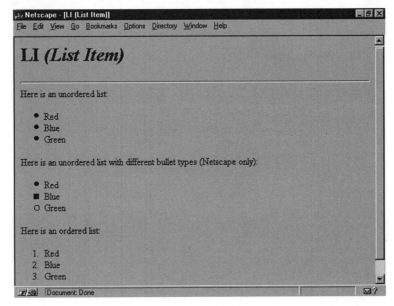

Options include the following:

TYPE=*order-type*	Specifies the type of bullet to be used in the list. Valid values are

DISK	A standard solid bullet.
SQUARE	Square bullets
CIRCLE	Unfilled circles
1	Bullets with numbers
a	Bullets with lowercase letters
A	Bullets with uppercase letters
i	Bullets with small Roman numerals
I	Bullets with large Roman numerals

VALUE=*n*	Specifies the number for the first item on the list. It is specified as a number and converted as needed.

The LI element is allowed within these elements:

A, APPLET, B, BIG, BLOCKQUOTE, BR, CENTER, CITE, CODE, DFN, DIR, DIV, DL, EM, FONT, FORM, HR, I, IMG, INPUT, ISINDEX, KBD, LISTING, MAP, MENU, OL, P, PRE, SAMP, SCRIPT, SELECT, SMALL, STRIKE, STRONG, SUB, SUP, TABLE, TEXTAREA, TT, U, UL, VAR, and XMP

The element is allowed inside the following:

DIR, MENU, OL, and UL

EXAMPLE OF LI

```
Here is an unordered list:
<UL>
<LI>Red
<LI>Blue
<LI>Green
</UL>
Here is an unordered list with different bullet types (Netscape only):
<UL>
<LI TYPE=DISK>Red
<LI TYPE=SQUARE>Blue
<LI TYPE=CIRCLE>Green
</UL>
Here is an ordered list:
<OL COMPACT>
<LI>Red
<LI>Blue
<LI>Green
</OL>
```

LINK

The LINK element is used to define a relationship between the current document and another object or document. Multiple LINK relationships can exist in a single document. This element is not widely used, and many browsers don't support it yet. However, it provides useful information because it relates documents to authoritative sources responsible for the contents. You may use more than one LINK element.

Syntax: `<LINK HREF=URL ID=ID REL=rel REV=rev TITLE=cdata>`

Options include the following:

HREF	The URL of the object being linked to.
ID	The SGML ID attribute.
REL	Defines a relationship where the target recognizes, authorizes, or verifies. (Not usually implemented.)
REV	Defines a relationship where the source desires and expects a claimed relationship. However, this relationship needs to be verified with the target (not usually implemented).
TITLE	Used to label a link, perhaps with the title of the document.

The LINK element is allowed within these elements:

The LINK element is an empty container. As such it doesn't have any content.

The element is allowed inside the following:

HEAD

EXAMPLE OF LINK

```
<LINK HREF="http://www.someplace.com/products.html">
```

LISTING

The LISTING element renders text literally. It does not reinterpret whitespace so multiline entries are rendered as they are in the source text with the same line breaks and multiple spaces. LISTING is usually rendered in a monospaced font. The LISTING element was a precursor to the PRE element. This element is available for backward compatibility purposes. Open and close tags are required.

Figure D.33.
The LISTING
element.

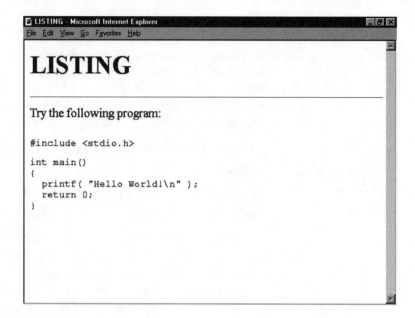

Syntax: `<LISTING>...</LISTING>`

The LISTING element is allowed within these elements:

Not applicable.

The element is allowed inside the following:

BLOCKQUOTE, BODY, CENTER, DD, DIV, FORM, LI, TD, and TH

EXAMPLE OF LISTING

```
Try the following program:
<P>
<LISTING>
#include <stdio.h>

int main()
{
printf( "Hello World!\n" );
return 0;
}

</LISTING>
```

MAP

The MAP element is used to define a client-side image map. A client-side image map specifies a set of regions on an image that can be used as hyperlinks by clicking them.

The advantage of client-side image maps is that they take map processing loads from the server, as well as activate additional visual cues on the user's browser regarding "hot spots" in the images. The closing tag is required.

Syntax: `<MAP NAME="#name">...</MAP>`

The following is an option:

NAME   Specifies the NAME used to reference the map in the IMG attribute USEMAP option. Note the pound sign (#) before the name.

The MAP element is allowed within this element:

AREA

The element is allowed inside the following:

A, ADDRESS, B, BIG, BLOCKQUOTE, BODY, CAPTION, CENTER, CITE, CODE, DD, DFN, DIV, DT, EM, FONT, FORM, H1, H2, H3, H4, H5, H6, I, KBD, LI, P, PRE, SAMP, SMALL, STRIKE, STRONG, SUB, SUP, TD, TEXTFLOW, TH, TT, U, and VAR

EXAMPLE OF MAP

Note that USEMAP option requires a # sign (just like a local HREF) before the name of the fragment containing the map coordinates. An example is as follows:

```
<MAP NAME=map>
<AREA SHAPE=RECT COORDS="56,7,106,86" HREF="#b" ALT=b>
<AREA SHAPE=CIRCLE COORDS="219,63,23" HREF="#e" ALT=e>
</MAP>
<IMG SRC=letters.GIF ALT=letters USEMAP=#map>
<A NAME=b>
<P> You clicked on B!</A>
<A NAME=e>
<P> You clicked on E!</A>
```

MARQUEE

The MARQUEE element defines an area where scrolling text will be displayed. This is a Microsoft Internet Explorer 2.0 extension. The MARQUEE element provides many options to control the behavior of the MARQUEE and provides an interesting way of adding text animation without increasing download requirements.

Syntax: `<MARQUEE ALIGN=align-type BEHAVIOR=type BGCOLOR=color`
`DIRECTION=direction HEIGHT=n HSPACE=n LOOP=n SCROLLAMOUNT=n`
`SCROLLDELAY=n VSPACE=n WIDTH=n>...</MARQUEE>`

Figure D.34.
The MARQUEE
element.

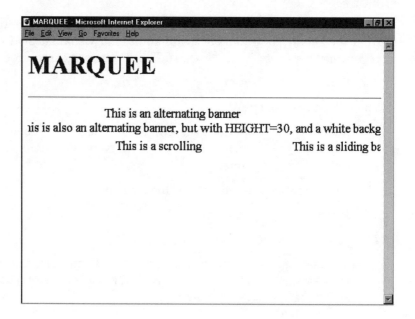

Options include the following:

ALIGN=*align-type*   Specifies the alignment of the text surrounding the marquee. Legal values for *align-type* are

TOP   Aligns the surrounding text with the top of the marquee.

MIDDLE   Aligns the surrounding text with the middle of the marquee.

BOTTOM   Aligns the surrounding text with the bottom of the marquee.

BEHAVIOR=*type*   Specifies how the text scrolls. Type can be one of the following values:

SCROLL   Scrolls text starting on one side and disappearing on the other, reappears again on the starting side.

SLIDE   Starts on one side and stops scrolling as soon as the text touches the opposite margin.

ALTERNATE   Bounces back and forth between margins.

BGCOLOR=*color*	Specifies the background color of the document. Colors are specified in the HEX, 00-FF for each component of the RGB channel in the #RRGGBB format. or by specifying one of the Microsoft Internet Explorer predefined colors: Aqua, Black, Blue, Fuchsia, Gray, Green, Lime, Maroon, Navy, Olive, Purple, Red, Silver, Teal, Yellow, or White.
DIRECTION=*direction*	DIRECTION specifies the direction of travel that the text will follow. Possible values are LEFT or RIGHT. The default value is LEFT (text starts scrolling from the right).
HEIGHT=*n*	Specifies the height of the marquee. HEIGHT can be specified as pixels or as a percentage of the screen size when suffixed with a % character.
HSPACE=*n*	Specifies the horizontal gutter to separate surrounding elements from the marquee.
LOOP=*n*	Specifies the number of iterations that the marquee will loop. A setting of -1 or INFINITE will loop the text while the page remains on the screen.
SCROLLAMOUNT=*n*	Specifies the number of pixels the text will scroll at a time.
SCROLLDELAY=*n*	Specifies the number of milliseconds between successive draws of the marquee.
VSPACE=*n*	Specifies the vertical gutter that separates surrounding elements from the marquee.
WIDTH=*n*	Specifies the width of the marquee. WIDTH can be specified as pixels or as a percentage of the screen size when suffixed with a % character.

The MARQUEE element is allowed within these elements:

A, B, BGSOUND, BR, CITE, CODE, DFN, EM, ENTITY, FONT, I, IMG, KBD, MAP, MARQUEE, NOBR, SAMP, STRIKE, STRONG, TT, U, VAR, and WBR

The element is allowed inside the following:

A, ADDRESS, B, BLOCKQUOTE, BODY, CAPTION, CENTER, CITE, CODE, COMMENT, DD, DFN, DT, EM, ENTITY, FONT, FORM, H1...H6, I, KBD, LI, MARQUEE, P, SAMP, STRIKE, STRONG, TD, TH, TT, U, and VAR

D

EXAMPLE OF MARQUEE

```
<MARQUEE ALIGN=MIDDLE BEHAVIOR=ALTERNATE>
This is an alternating banner
</MARQUEE>
<MARQUEE ALIGN=MIDDLE BEHAVIOR=ALTERNATE BGCOLOR="#FFFFFF" HEIGHT=30
DIRECTION=LEFT>
This is also an alternating banner, but with HEIGHT=30, and a white background.
</MARQUEE>
<MARQUEE ALIGN=MIDDLE BEHAVIOR=SCROLL WIDTH=50%>
This is a scrolling banner, WIDTH=50%
</MARQUEE>
<MARQUEE ALIGN=MIDDLE BEHAVIOR=SLIDE WIDTH=50%>
This is a sliding banner, WIDTH=50%
</MARQUEE>
```

MENU

The MENU element defines an list of items. Each entry is started with a LI element.

Figure D.35.
The MENU *element.*

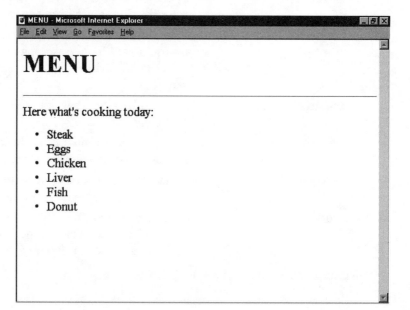

Syntax: <MENU>...</MENU>

Options include the following:

COMPACT   Specifies the items that should be rendered in a compact
                   form, usually by reducing the vertical space between list
                   items.

The MENU element is allowed within this element:

>   LI

The element is allowed inside the following:

>   BLOCKQUOTE, BODY, CENTER, DD, DIV, FORM, LI, TD, and TH

EXAMPLE OF MENU

```
<MENU>
<LI>Steak
<LI>Eggs
<LI>Chicken
<LI>Liver
<LI>Fish
<LI>Donut
</MENU>
```

META

The META element provides information about the HTML document to browsers and programs such as search engines or caching proxy servers. META information is placed in the HEAD section of a document.

Syntax: `<META HTTP-EQUIV=response CONTENT=description NAME=description URL=url>`

The options available for META include the following:

CONTENT=description	Sets the description to be associated with the given NAME or HTTP-EQUIV response header. It can be used with a URL= and a date/time specification to reload a document at a specified interval.
HTTP-EQUIV=response	Binds the META element to the HTTP response header. The server will include *response* as fields in the header information.
NAME=description	A description.
URL=url	The document's URL.

The META element is allowed within this element:

>   HEAD

The element is allowed inside the following:

>   Not applicable because it is not a container element.

EXAMPLE OF META

A typical use of the META element is to embed expiration date dates for documents. This will avoid any caching of a document past the specified date. In addition, you can use META tags to insert reply-to information (an e-mail address for the person responsible for the document). An interesting use is to specify an auto-refresh setting that will force the browser to reload the contents of the document every so often or to load an entirely different document, as with a client-pull. Another frequent use is to embed keywords that indexing robots will use to classify your document. Here are some examples (they can all coexist in the same document):

```
<META HTTP-EQUIV="Expires" CONTENT="Aug, 11 Mar 1996 12:00:00 -0600">
<META HTTP-EQUIV="Reply-to" CONTENT="info@yourcompany.com">
<META HTTP-EQUIV="REFRESH" CONTENT="10" URL="http://www.yourcompany.com/
timeIsUp.html">
<META NAME="keywords" CONTENT="This document describes the META tag which you can
only view for 10 seconds">
```

NOBR

The NOBR element turns off line breaking. The browser won't wrap text when the window is resized. This is originally a Netscape 1.x extension. Microsoft Internet Explorer supports this feature since version 3.0.

Figure D.36.
The NOBR element.

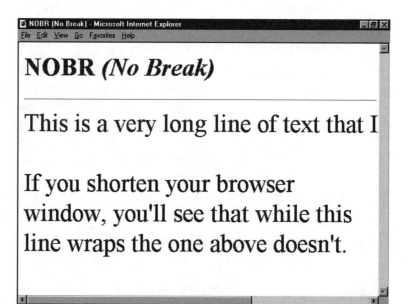

Syntax: <NOBR>...</NOBR>

The NOBR element is allowed within these elements:

A, B, BLOCKQUOTE, BR, CITE, CODE, DIR, DL, EM, FORM, I, IMG, ISINDEX, KBD, LISTING, MENU, OL, P, PRE, SAMP, STRONG, TT, UL, VAR, and XMP

The element is allowed inside the following:

A, ADDRESS, B, BLOCKQUOTE, BODY, CITE, CODE, DD, DT, EM, FORM, H1-H6, I, KBD, LI, P, PRE, SAMP, STRONG, TT, and VAR

EXAMPLE OF NOBR

```
<NOBR>This is a very long line of text that I don't it to be broken.</NOBR> <BR>
If you shorten your browser window, you'll see that while this line wraps the one
above doesn't
```

NOFRAMES

The NOFRAMES element contains HTML that gets displayed to browsers that don't have support for frames. By using the NOFRAMES element, you can create an entry page that is compatible with all browsers because you can present two different entrances to your frame content. Frame-aware browsers ignore this element.

This was originally a Netscape 2.0 extension that has since been adopted by Microsoft Internet Explorer 3.0.

Figure D.37.
The browser
renders the
content of the
NOFRAMES *element.*

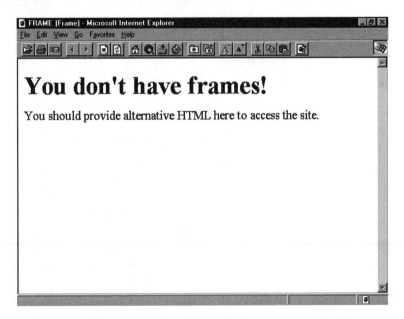

The NOFRAMES element is allowed within these elements:

A, ADDRESS, APPLET, B, BIG, BLINK, BLOCKQUOTE, BR, CENTER, CITE, CODE, DFN, DIR, DIV, DL, EM, FONT, FORM, H1, H2, H3, H4, H5, H6, HR, I, IMG, INPUT, ISINDEX, KBD, LISTING, MAP, MENU, OL, P, PRE, SAMP, SCRIPT, SELECT, SMALL, STRIKE, STRONG, SUB, SUP, TABLE, TEXTAREA, TT, U, UL, VAR, and XMP

The element is allowed inside the following:

FRAMESET

EXAMPLE OF NOFRAMES

```
<NOFRAMES>
<BODY>
<H1>You don't have frames!</H1>
You should provide alternative HTML here to access the site.
</BODY>
</NOFRAMES>
```

OBJECT

The OBJECT element inserts an object such as an image, document, applet, or control into an HTML document. It is intended to be a more general and flexible mechanism for handling multimedia elements.

Syntax: `<OBJECT ALIGN=align-type BORDER=n CLASSID=url CODEBASE=url CODTYPE=codetype DATA=url DECLARE HEIGHT=n HSPACE=n NAME=url SHAPES STANDBY=message TYPE=type USEMAP=utl VSPACE=n WIDTH=n>...</OBJECT>`

Options include the following:

ALIGN=align-type   Specifies the alignment for the object:

BASELINE	The bottom of the object aligns to the baseline of the surrounding text.
CENTER	The object is centered between the margins. Text following the object is placed on the next line.
LEFT	The object is left-margin aligned. Text wraps along the right edge of the object.
MIDDLE	The middle of the object is aligned with the baseline of the surrounding text.
RIGHT	The object is right-margin aligned. Text wraps along the left side of the object.

	TEXTBOTTOM	The bottom of the object aligns with the bottom of the text.
	TEXTMIDDLE	The middle of the object aligns with the middle of the text.
	TEXTTOP	The top of the object aligns with the top of the text.
BORDER=*n*		Specifies the width of the border displayed for objects that are hyperlinks.
CLASSID=*url*		Identifies the object implementation. The syntax for the URL depends on the object type.
CODEBASE=*url*		Identifies the codebase for the object. Syntax is object dependent.
CODETYPE=*codetype*		Specifies the Internet media type for code.
DATA=*url*		Specifies the source for the data. Syntax is object dependent.
DECLARE		Declares the object without creating it. Useful if you are creating a cross-reference or using the object as a parameter.
HEIGHT=*n*		Specifies the height of the object.
HSPACE=*n*		Specifies the horizontal gutter for the object.
NAME=*url*		Sets the name of the object when submitted as part of a form.
SHAPES		Specifies that the object has hyperlinks, as in a client-side image map for the object.
STANDBY=*message*		Sets the message that is displayed while the object is loaded.
TYPE=*type*		Specifies the Internet media type for the data.
USEMAP=*utl*		Specifies the image map to use with the object.
VSPACE=*n*		Specifies the vertical gutter.
WIDTH=*n*		Specifies the width of the object.

The element is allowed inside the following:

All elements that are legal inside a BODY element.

A, ADDRESS, B, BIG, BLOCKQUOTE, BODY, CAPTION, CENTER, CITE, CODE, DD, DFN, DIV, DT, EM, FONT, FORM, H1...H6, I, KBD, LI, P, PRE, SAMP, SMALL, STRIKE, STRONG, SUB, SUP, TD, TEXTFLOW, TH, TT, U, and VAR

D

OL (ORDERED LIST)

The OL element specifies an ordered list. An ordered list consists of a number of LI elements that are ordered numerically in some way. OL elements need to be properly closed.

Figure D.38.
The OL element.

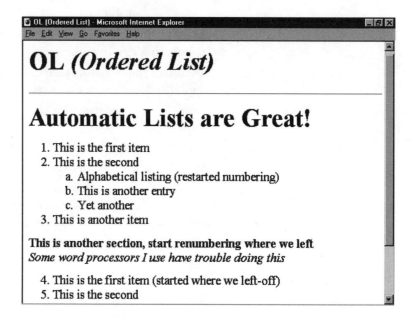

Syntax: `<OL COMPACT START=n TYPE=order-type>...</OL>`

Options include the following:

COMPACT	Specifies that the list should be rendered in compact form, perhaps by reducing the leading between entries.
START=n	Specifies the starting number for the list. Representation of this number will vary depending on the TYPE specified.
TYPE=order-type	TYPE specifies the numbering style for the list. Legal values include the following:

A   Use uppercase letters.

a   Use lowercase letters.

I   Use large Roman numerals.

i   Use small Roman numerals.

1   Use numbers.

The OL element is allowed within this element:

> LI

The element is allowed inside the following:

> BLOCKQUOTE, BODY, CENTER, DD, DIV, FORM, LI, TD, and TH

EXAMPLE OF OL

This example shows the use of the OL element. Note that it is very flexible in terms of what you need to do to start renumbering in the right spot.

```
<H1>Automatic Lists are Great!</H1>
<OL>
<LI> This is the first item
<LI> This is the second
<OL TYPE=a>
<LI>Alphabetical listing (restarted numbering)
<LI>This is another entry
<LI>Yet another
</OL>
<LI>This is another item
</OL>
<B> This is another section, start renumbering where we left </B><BR>
<I>Some wordprocessors I use have trouble doing this</I>
<OL START=4>
<LI> This is the first item (started where we left-off)
<LI> This is the second
<OL TYPE=a>
<LI>Alphabetical listing
<LI>This is another entry
<LI>Yet another
</OL>
<LI>This is another item
</OL>
```

OPTION

The OPTION element specifies one choice in a SELECT element, which in turn is part of the contents of a FORM element.

Syntax:	`<OPTION SELECTED VALUE=value>`

Options include the following:

SELECTED	Designates the default item. If the item doesn't exit, then the first element becomes the default.
VALUE	Specifies the value that will be returned to the server if this were chosen.

The OPTION element is allowed within these elements:

Not applicable. Element is not a container.

The element is allowed inside the following:

SELECT

EXAMPLE OF OPTION

```
<INPUT TYPE=radio NAME="food" SELECTED VALUE="chicken"> Chicken
```

P (PARAGRAPH)

The P element inserts a paragraph break and separates two blocks of text. Paragraph elements do not nest, so starting a new paragraph automatically implies closing the previous one. Many elements imply a text separation, such as headings, list elements, and blockquotes. A closing paragraph tag is not required, but is considered good style.

Figure D.39.
The P element.

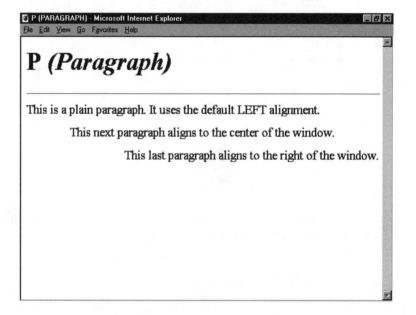

Syntax: `<P ALIGN=align-type>...</P>`

Options include the following:

ALIGN   The ALIGN options are Netscape extensions. Microsoft
                         Internet Explorer supports them, too. ALIGN sets the
                         alignment for the paragraph. Possible alignment
                         types are LEFT, CENTER, and RIGHT. The default setting
                         is LEFT.

The P element is allowed within these elements:

A, APPLET, B, BIG, BR, CITE, CODE, DFN, EM, FONT, I, IMG, INPUT, KBD, MAP, SAMP, SCRIPT,
SELECT, SMALL, STRIKE, STRONG, SUB, SUP, TEXTAREA, TT, U, and VAR

The element is allowed inside the following:

ADDRESS, BLOCKQUOTE, BODY, CENTER, DD, DIV, FORM, LI, TD, and TH

EXAMPLE OF P

```
<P>This is a plain paragraph. It uses the default LEFT alignment.</P>
<P ALIGN=CENTER>This next paragraph aligns to the center of the window.</P>
<P ALIGN=RIGHT>This last paragraph aligns to the right of the window.</P>
```

PARAM

The PARAM element is used to pass values to a given object, such as a Java applet.

Syntax: `<PARAM NAME=name VALUE=value VALUETYPE=type TYPE=type>`

Options include the following:

NAME=name   Identifies the name of the parameter or key that
                         VALUE will set.

VALUE=value   Specifies the value passed to the object.

VALUETYPE=type   On Microsoft Internet Explorer only, it specifies how
                         to interpret the value. The type can be any of the
                         following:

                         DATA   The value is data. This is the default value
                                 type.

                         REF   The value is an URL.

                         OBJECT The value is an URL of an object in the
                                 same document.

Type=type   On Microsoft Internet Explorer only, it specifies the
                         MIME-type of the object.

The PARAM element is allowed within these elements:

Not applicable. Element is not a container.

The element is allowed inside the following:

APPLET, (Microsoft Internet Explorer only: OBJECT)

EXAMPLE OF PARAM

```
<applet codebase="../LED" code="LED.class" width=500 height=48 align=center>
<param name="script" value="../scripts/Demo.led">
<param name="border" value="2">
<param name="bordercolor" value="100,130,130">
<param name="spacewidth" value="3">
<param name="wth" value="122">
<param name="ht" value="9">
<param name="font" value="../fonts/default.font">
<param name="ledsize" value="3">
</applet>
```

PLAINTEXT

The PLAINTEXT element renders text in a fixed font without processing elements until a closing PLAINTEXT tag is found. Text is rendered with a monospaced font.

Figure D.40.
The PLAINTEXT
element.

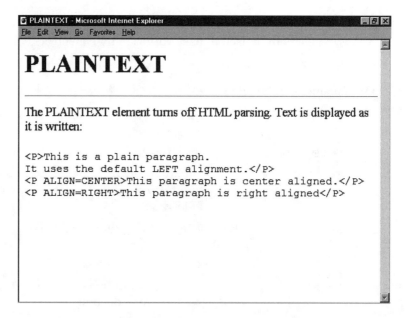

Syntax: `<PLAINTEXT>...</PLAINTEXT>`

The PLAINTEXT element is allowed within these elements:

Not applicable. Element disables HTML parsing.

The element is allowed inside the following:

Not applicable. Element disables HTML parsing.

EXAMPLE OF PLAINTEXT

```
<PLAINTEXT>
<P>This is a plain paragraph.
It uses the default LEFT alignment.</P>
<P ALIGN=CENTER>This paragraph is center aligned.</P>
<P ALIGN=RIGHT>This paragraph is right aligned</P>

</PLAINTEXT>
```

PRE (PREFORMATTED)

The PRE element renders text in a fixed font. It is useful for displaying ASCII art or any other type of formatting that relies on the spacing of the characters.

Figure D.41.
The PRE element.

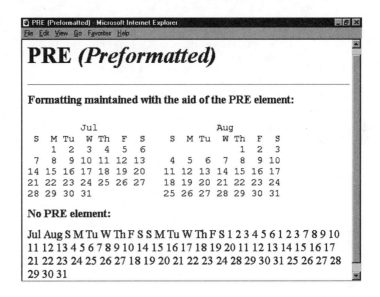

Syntax: `<PRE WIDTH=n>...</PRE>`

The following is an option:

WIDTH   The browser will try to render at least *n* characters.

The PRE element is allowed within these elements:

A, APPLET, B, BR, CITE, CODE, DFN, EM, I, INPUT, KBD, MAP, SAMP, SCRIPT, SELECT, STRIKE, STRONG, TEXTAREA, TT, U, and VAR

The element is allowed inside the following:

BLOCKQUOTE, BODY, CENTER, DD, DIV, FORM, LI, TD, and TH

EXAMPLE OF PRE

```
<!DOCTYPE html PUBLIC "-//Netscape Comm. Corp.//DTD HTML//EN">
<HTML>
<HEAD>
<TITLE>PRE Sample</TITLE>
</HEAD>
<BODY>
<B>Formatting maintained with the aid of the PRE element</B>
<PRE>
        Jul                 Aug                 Sep
  S  M Tu  W Th  F  S   S  M Tu  W Th  F  S   S  M Tu  W Th  F  S
     1  2  3  4  5  6            1  2  3   1  2  3  4  5  6  7
  7  8  9 10 11 12 13   4  5  6  7  8  9 10   8  9 10 11 12 13 14
 14 15 16 17 18 19 20  11 12 13 14 15 16 17  15 16 17 18 19 20 21
 21 22 23 24 25 26 27  18 19 20 21 22 23 24  22 23 24 25 26 27 28
 28 29 30 31           25 26 27 28 29 30 31  29 30
</PRE>
<B>No PRE element</B><BR>
        Jul                 Aug                 Sep
  S  M Tu  W Th  F  S   S  M Tu  W Th  F  S   S  M Tu  W Th  F  S<BR>
     1  2  3  4  5  6            1  2  3   1  2  3  4  5  6  7<BR>
  7  8  9 10 11 12 13   4  5  6  7  8  9 10   8  9 10 11 12 13 14<BR>
 14 15 16 17 18 19 20  11 12 13 14 15 16 17  15 16 17 18 19 20 21<BR>
 21 22 23 24 25 26 27  18 19 20 21 22 23 24  22 23 24 25 26 27 28<BR>
 28 29 30 31           25 26 27 28 29 30 31  29 30<BR>
</BODY>
</HTML>
```

S (STRIKETHROUGH)

The S element renders text in strikethrough type.

Syntax: `<S>...</S>`

The S element is allowed within these elements:

A, APPLET, B, BIG, BR, CITE, CODE, DFN, EM, FONT, I, IMG, INPUT, KBD, MAP, SAMP, SCRIPT, SELECT, SMALL, STRIKE, STRONG, SUB, SUP, TEXTAREA, TT, U, and VAR

The element is allowed inside the following:

A, ADDRESS, B, BIG, BLOCKQUOTE, BODY, CAPTION, CENTER, CITE, CODE, DD, DFN, DIV, DT, EM, FONT, FORM, H1, H2, H3, H4, H5, H6, I, KBD, LI, P, PRE, SAMP, SMALL, STRIKE, STRONG, SUB, SUP, TD, TEXTFLOW, TH, TT, U, and VAR

Figure D.42.
The S element.

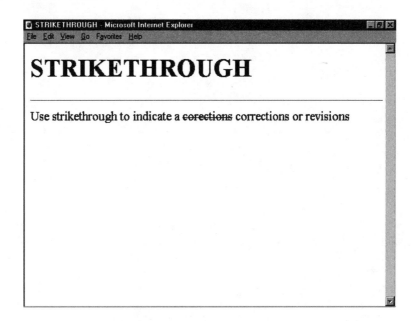

EXAMPLE OF S

```
Use strikethrough to indicate a <S>corections</S> corrections or revisions
```

SAMP

The SAMP element renders its context as sample text.

Syntax: <SAMP>...<SAMP>

The SAMP element is allowed within these elements:

A, APPLET, B, BIG, BR, CITE, CODE, DFN, EM, FONT, I, IMG, INPUT, KBD, MAP, SAMP, SCRIPT, SELECT, SMALL, STRIKE, STRONG, SUB, SUP, TEXTAREA, TT, U, and VAR

The element is allowed inside the following:

A, ADDRESS, B, BIG, BLOCKQUOTE, BODY, CAPTION, CENTER, CITE, CODE, DD, DFN, DIV, DT, EM, FONT, FORM, H1, H2, H3, H4, H5, H6, I, KBD, LI, P, PRE, SAMP, SMALL, STRIKE, STRONG, SUB, SUP, TD, TEXTFLOW, TH, TT, U, and VAR

Figure D.43.
The SAMP element.

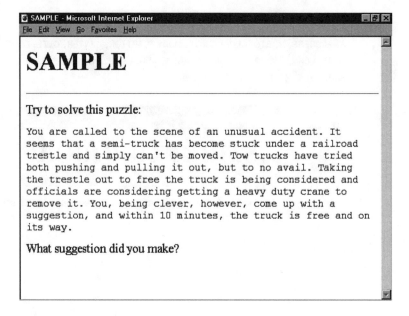

EXAMPLE OF SAMP

```
<P>
<SAMP>
You are called to the scene of an unusual accident.
It seems that a semi-truck has become stuck under
a railroad trestle and simply can't be moved.
Tow trucks have tried both pushing and pulling it out,
but to no avail.  Taking the trestle out to free the
truck is being considered and officials are considering
getting a heavy duty crane to remove it.
You, being clever, however, come up with a suggestion,
and within 10 minutes, the truck is free and on its way.
</SAMP>
<P>
What suggestion did you make?
```

SCRIPT

The SCRIPT element denotes the inclusion of a script that a script-enabled browser can execute. Scripts execute and instatiate objects in the order in which they appear in the HTML document.

Options include the following:

LANGUAGE=*scripting-language*	The language used for the script. Valid options are
VBScript	For Visual Basic Scripts
JavaScript	For JavaScripts

The SCRIPT element is allowed within these elements:

Not applicable.

The element is allowed inside the following:

A, ADDRESS, B, BIG, BLOCKQUOTE, BODY, CAPTION, CENTER, CITE, CODE, DD, DFN, DIV, DT, EM, FONT, FORM, H1, H2, H3, H4, H5, H6, HEAD, I, KBD, LI, P, PRE, SAMP, SMALL, STRIKE, STRONG, SUB, SUP, TD, TEXTFLOW, TH, TT, U, and VAR

EXAMPLE OF SCRIPT

```
<SCRIPT LANGUAGE="JavaScript">
</SCRIPT>
```

SELECT

The SELECT element creates a single or multiple choice MENU.

Syntax: `<SELECT MULTIPLE NAME=name SIZE=n>...</SELECT>`

Options include the following:

MULTIPLE	Enables multiple item selection.
NAME=name	Specifies the name of the list.
SIZE=n	Specifies the height of the list control.

The SELECT element is allowed within this element:

OPTION

The element is allowed inside the following:

A, ADDRESS, B, BIG, BLOCKQUOTE, BODY, CAPTION, CENTER, CITE, CODE, DD, DFN, IV, DT, EM, FONT, FORM, H1, H2, H3, H4, H5, H6, I, KBD, LI, P, PRE, SAMP, SMALL, TRIKE, STRONG, SUB, SUP, TD, TEXTFLOW, TH, TT, U, and VAR

EXAMPLE OF SELECT

```
Pick Your Ride:<BR>
<SELECT NAME="car" MULTIPLE>
<OPTION SELECTED VALUE="pacer"> Pacer
<OPTION VALUE="ferrari"> Ferrari
<OPTION VALUE="small convertible"> Small Vintage British Sports Cars
<OPTION VALUE="luxurious german sendan"> Mercedes Benz
</SELECT>
```

D

HTML REFERENCE GUIDE

SMALL

The SMALL element renders its contents one size smaller, if appropriate.

Figure D.44.
The SMALL
element.

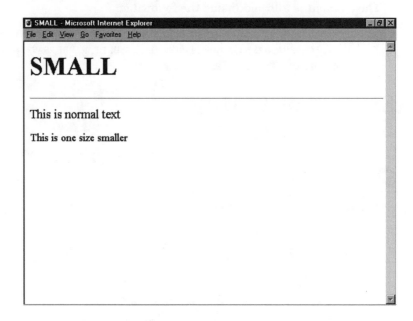

Syntax: <SMALL>...</SMALL>

The SMALL element is allowed within these elements:

A, APPLET, B, BIG, BR, CITE, CODE, DFN, EM, FONT, I, IMG, INPUT, KBD, MAP, SAMP, SCRIPT, SELECT, SMALL, STRIKE, STRONG, SUB, SUP, TEXTAREA, TT, U, and VAR

The element is allowed inside the following:

A, ADDRESS, B, BIG, BLOCKQUOTE, BODY, CAPTION, CENTER, CITE, CODE, DD, DFN, DIV, DT, EM, FONT, FORM, H1, H2, H3, H4, H5, H6, I, KBD, LI, P, PRE, SAMP, SMALL, STRIKE, STRONG, SUB, SUP, TD, TEXTFLOW, TH, TT, U, and VAR

EXAMPLE OF SMALL

```
<P>This is normal text
<P>
<SMALL>This is one size smaller</SMALL>
```

STRIKE

The STRIKE element renders text in strikethrough type. This element produces similar results to the previously mentioned s element.

Figure D.45.
The STRIKE
element.

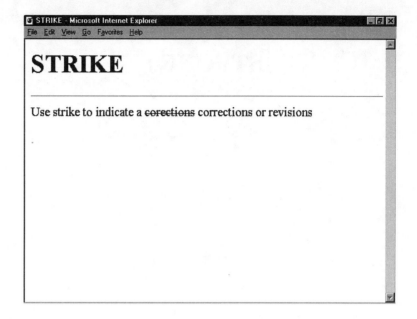

Syntax: `<STRIKE>...</STRIKE>`

The STRIKE element is allowed within these elements:

A, APPLET, B, BIG, BR, CITE, CODE, DFN, EM, FONT, I, IMG, INPUT, KBD, MAP, SAMP, SCRIPT, SELECT, SMALL, STRIKE, STRONG, SUB, SUP, TEXTAREA, TT, U, and VAR

The element is allowed inside the following:

A, ADDRESS, B, BIG, BLOCKQUOTE, BODY, CAPTION, CENTER, CITE, CODE, DD, DFN, DIV, DT, EM, FONT, FORM, H1, H2, H3, H4, H5, H6, I, KBD, LI, P, PRE, SAMP, SMALL, STRIKE, STRONG, SUB, SUP, TD, TEXTFLOW, TH, TT, U, and VAR

EXAMPLE OF STRIKE

```
Use strike to indicate a <STRIKE>corections</STRIKE> corrections or revisions
```

STRONG

The STRONG element emphasizes text, which is usually rendered in boldface. Its use may be more desirable than the B element for backwards compatibility.

Figure D.46.
The STRONG
element.

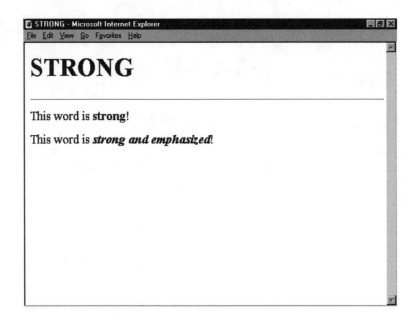

Syntax: `<STRONG>...</STRONG>`

The STRONG element is allowed within these elements:

A, APPLET, B, BIG, BR, CITE, CODE, DFN, EM, FONT, I, IMG, INPUT, KBD, MAP, SAMP, SCRIPT, SELECT, SMALL, STRIKE, STRONG, SUB, SUP, TEXTAREA, TT, U, and VAR

The element is allowed inside the following:

A, ADDRESS, B, BIG, BLOCKQUOTE, BODY, CAPTION, CENTER, CITE, CODE, DD, DFN, DIV, DT, EM, FONT, FORM, H1, H2, H3, H4, H5, H6, I, KBD, LI, P, PRE, SAMP, SMALL, STRIKE, STRONG, SUB, SUP, TD, TEXTFLOW, TH, TT, U, and VAR

EXAMPLE OF STRONG

```
<P>This word is <STRONG>strong</STRONG>!
<P>This word is <STRONG><EM>strong and emphasized</EM></STRONG>!
```

SUB

The SUB element renders text as subscript.

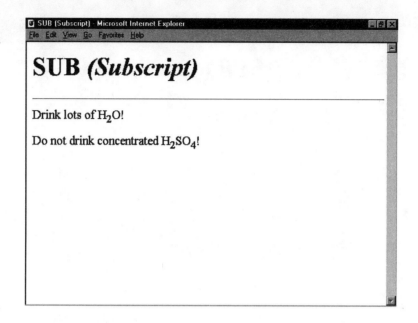

Figure D.47.
The SUB *element.*

Syntax: `<SUB>...</SUB>`

The SUB element is allowed within these elements:

A, APPLET, B, BIG, BR, CITE, CODE, DFN, EM, FONT, I, IMG, INPUT, KBD, MAP, SAMP, SCRIPT, SELECT, SMALL, STRIKE, STRONG, SUB, SUP, TEXTAREA, TT, U, and VAR

The element is allowed inside the following:

A, ADDRESS, B, BIG, BLOCKQUOTE, BODY, CAPTION, CENTER, CITE, CODE, DD, DFN, DIV, DT, EM, FONT, FORM, H1, H2, H3, H4, H5, H6, I, KBD, LI, P, PRE, SAMP, SMALL, STRIKE, STRONG, SUB, SUP, TD, TEXTFLOW, TH, TT, U, and VAR

EXAMPLE OF SUB

```
<P>Drink lots of H<SUB>2</SUB>O!
<P>Do not drink concentrated H<SUB>2</SUB>SO<SUB>4</SUB>!
```

SUP

The SUP element renders text as superscript.

Figure D.48.
The SUP *element.*

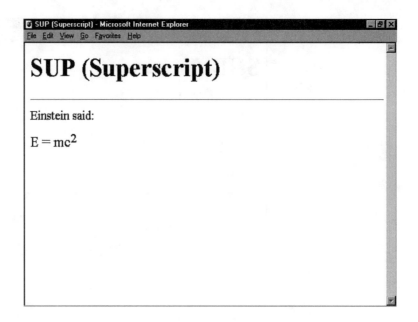

Syntax: ^{...}

The SUP element is allowed within these elements:

A, APPLET, B, BIG, BR, CITE, CODE, DFN, EM, FONT, I, IMG, INPUT, KBD, MAP, SAMP, SCRIPT, SELECT, SMALL, STRIKE, STRONG, SUB, SUP, TEXTAREA, TT, U, and VAR

The element is allowed inside the following:

A, ADDRESS, B, BIG, BLOCKQUOTE, BODY, CAPTION, CENTER, CITE, CODE, DD, DFN, DIV, DT, EM, FONT, FORM, H1, H2, H3, H4, H5, H6, I, KBD, LI, P, PRE, SAMP, SMALL, STRIKE, STRONG, SUB, SUP, TD, TEXTFLOW, TH, TT, U, and VAR

EXAMPLE OF SUP

E = mc²

TABLE

The TABLE element creates an empty table to which you can add rows and cells using the TR, TD, and TH elements.

*Figure D.49.
The TABLE
element.*

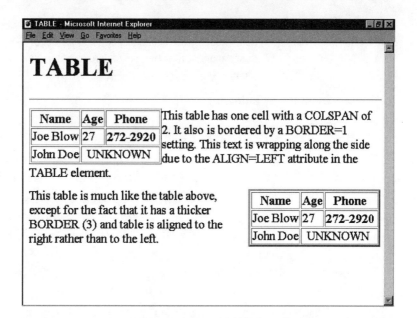

*Figure D.50.
Another TABLE
example. Note
that table cells
can have different
attributes under
Microsoft Internet
Explorer.*

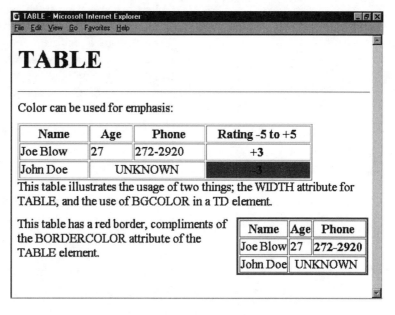

Syntax: `<TABLE ALIGN=`*align-type* `BACKGROUND=`*url* `BGCOLOR=`*color* `BORDER=`*n*
`BORDERCOLOR=`*color* `BORDERCOLORDARK=`*color*
`BORDERCOLORLIGHT=`*color* `CELLPADDING=`*n* `CELLSPACING=`*n* `COLS=`*n*
`FRAME=`*frame-type* `RULES=`*rules* `WIDTH=`*n*`>`...`</TABLE>`

Options include the following:

`ALIGN=`*align-type*	Specifies the alignment of the contents of the table. Align type can be

	`LEFT`	The table contents align to the left edge of the table. This is the default setting.
	`CENTER`	The table contents are aligned to the center edge of the table.
	`RIGHT`	The table contents align to the right edge of the table.

`BACKGROUND=`*url*	Specifies a background picture to be tiled in the table background.
`BGCOLOR=`*color*	Specifies the background color of the document. Colors are specified in the HEX, `00-FF` for each component of the RGB channel in the `#RRGGBB` format, or by specifying one of the Microsoft Internet Explorer predefined colors: Aqua, Black, Blue, Fuchsia, Gray, Green, Lime, Maroon, Navy, Olive, Purple, Red, Silver, Teal, Yellow, or White.
`BORDER=`*n*	Specifies the size, in pixels, of the table border. The default is zero.
`BORDERCOLOR=`*color*	Specifies the border color of the table. Colors are specified in the HEX, `00-FF` for each component of the RGB channel in the `#RRGGBB` format.
`BORDERCOLORDARK=`*color*	Specifies the dark color used for drawing tri-dimensional table borders. Colors are specified in the HEX, `00-FF` for each component of the RGB channel in the `#RRGGBB` format.
`BORDERCOLORLIGHT=`*color*	Specifies the light color used for drawing tri-dimensional table borders. Colors are specified in the HEX, `00-FF` for each component of the RGB channel in the `#RRGGBB` format.
`CELLPADDING=`*n*	Specifies the amount of space in pixels between the sides of a cell and its contents.
`CELLSPACING=`*n*	Specifies the amount of space in pixels between cells.

COLS=*n*	Specifies the number of columns in a table. This option can speed up the rendering of complex tables because the browser doesn't need to calculate various settings.
FRAME=*frame-type*	Specifies which sides of the frame are displayed. Possible values include

VOID	Removes all borders.
ABOVE	Displays a border on the top side of the table frame.
BELOW	Displays a border on the bottom side of the table frame.
HSIDES	Displays a border on the horizontal sides, that is top and bottom sides of the table frame.
LHS	Displays a border on the left side of the table frame.
RHS	Displays a border on the right side of the table frame
VSIDES	Displays a border on the vertical sides of the table frame, which is the left and right table frames.
BOX	Displays a border on all sides of the table frame.
BORDER	Displays a border on all sides of the table frame.

RULES=*rules*	Specifies the inner lines of the table frame. Possible values are

NONE	Doesn't display interior table lines.
GROUPS	Displays horizontal lines between all table sections or groups, such as the head, body, foot, and column groups (by use of the THEAD, TBODY, TFOOT, and COLGROUP elements, respectively).
ROWS	Displays horizontal lines between all table rows.
COLS	Displays vertical lines between table columns.
ALL	Displays all lines.

WIDTH=*n*   Sets the width of the table in pixels, or as a percentage of the window if *n* is specified with the % suffix.

The TABLE element is allowed within these elements:

CAPTION and TR

The element is allowed inside the following:

BLOCKQUOTE, BODY, CENTER, DD, DIV, FORM, LI, TD, and TH

EXAMPLE OF TABLE

```
<TABLE BORDER=1 ALIGN=LEFT>
<TR>
<TH>Name<TH>Age<TH>Phone
</TR>
<TR>
<TD>Joe Blow<TD>27<TH>272-2920
</TR>
<TR>
<TD>John Doe<TD COLSPAN=2 ALIGN=CENTER>UNKNOWN
</TR>
</TABLE>
This table has one cell with a COLSPAN of 2.  It also is bordered
by a BORDER=1 setting.  This text is wrapping along the side due to
the ALIGN=LEFT attribute in the TABLE element.
<BR CLEAR=ALL>
<P>
<TABLE BORDER=3 ALIGN=RIGHT >
<TR>
<TH>Name<TH>Age<TH>Phone
</TR>
<TR>
<TD>Joe Blow<TD>27<TH>272-2920
</TR>
<TR>
<TD>John Doe<TD COLSPAN=2 ALIGN=CENTER>UNKNOWN
</TR>
</TABLE>
This table is much like the table above, except for the fact
that it has a thicker BORDER (3) and table is aligned to the
right rather than to the left.
```

TBODY

TBODY defines the body of the table in contrast to the header or footer. The TBODY element is optional if the table doesn't have a header and a footer. A table can have multiple TBODY elements. The closing tag is optional.

Syntax: <TBODY>...</TBODY>

The TBODY element is allowed within this element:

TABLE

The element is allowed inside the following:

TR, TH, and TD

EXAMPLE OF TBODY

```
<TABLE>
<THEAD>
<TR>
    </TR>
<TBODY>
<TR>
    </TR>
</TBODY>
</TABLE>
```

TD

The TD element is used to define a table data cell.

Syntax: `<TD ALIGN=align-type BACKGROUND=url BGCOLOR=color BORDERCOLOR=color`
`BORDERCOLORDARK=color BORDERCOLORLIGHT=color COLSPAN=n`
`NOWRAP=NOWRAP ROWSPAN=n VALIGN=align-type>...</TD>`

Options include the following:

ALIGN=align-type	Specifies the alignment of the contents of the cell, align-type can be one of the following:
	LEFT The contents are left aligned.
	CENTER The contents are centered.
	RIGHT The contents are right aligned.
BACKGROUND=url	Specifies a background picture to be tiled in the cell background.
BGCOLOR=color	Specifies the background color of the document. Colors are specified in the HEX, 00-FF for each component of the RGB channel in the #RRGGBB format. or by specifying one of the Microsoft Internet Explorer predefined colors: Aqua, Black, Blue, Fuchsia, Gray, Green, Lime, Maroon, Navy, Olive, Purple, Red, Silver, Teal, Yellow, or White.

BORDERCOLOR=*color*	Specifies the border color of the cell. Colors are specified in the HEX, 00-FF for each component of the RGB channel in the #RRGGBB format.
BORDERCOLORDARK=*color*	Specifies the dark color used for drawing tri-dimensional cell borders. Colors are specified in the HEX, 00-FF for each component of the RGB channel in the #RRGGBB format.
BORDERCOLORLIGHT=*color*	Specifies the light color used for drawing tri-dimensional cell borders. Colors are specified in the HEX, 00-FF for each component of the RGB channel in the #RRGGBB format.
VALIGN=*align-type*	Specifies the vertical alignment of the objects inside the cell. *align-type* can be one of the following values:

TOP	Text is aligned with the top of the cell.
MIDDLE	Text is centered vertically with the middle of the cell. This is the default setting.
BOTTOM	Text is aligned with the cell's bottom.
BASELINE	Text in neighboring cells is aligned along a common baseline.

The TD element is allowed within these elements:

A, ADDRESS, APPLET, B, BIG, BLOCKQUOTE, BR, CENTER, CITE, CODE, DFN, DIR, DIV, DL, EM, FONT, FORM, H1...H6, HR, I, IMG, INPUT, ISINDEX, KBD, LISTING, MAP, MENU, OL, P, PRE, SAMP, SCRIPT, SELECT, SMALL, STRIKE, STRONG, SUB, SUP, TABLE, TEXTAREA, TT, U, UL, VAR, and XMP

The element is allowed inside the following:

TR

EXAMPLE OF TD

```
<TR>
<TD>John Doe<TD COLSPAN=2 ALIGN=CENTER>UNKNOWN
</TR>
```

TEXTAREA

The TEXTAREA creates a multiline text entry widget that can be used to enter and edit multiple lines of text.

Figure D.51.
The TEXTAREA
element.

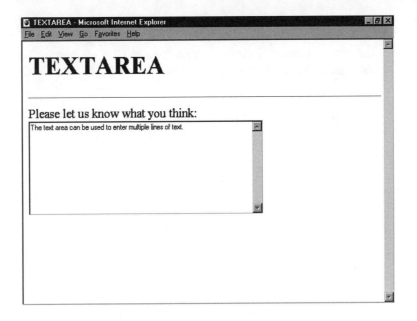

Syntax: `<TEXTAREA COLS=n NAME=name ROWS=n>`

Options include the following:

COLS=*n*   Sets the width of the text area in characters.

NAME=*name*   Sets the name of the text area. *name* is used to map the
                contents of the widget to a variable that is submitted when
                the form is sent.

ROWS=*n*   Sets the height of the text area in lines of text.

The TEXTAREA element is allowed within these elements:

Not applicable. The TEXTAREA element is not a container element.

The element is allowed inside the following:

A, ADDRESS, B, BIG, BLOCKQUOTE, BODY, CAPTION, CENTER, CITE, CODE, DD, DFN, DIV, DT, EM,
FONT, FORM, H1...H6, I, KBD, LI, P, PRE, SAMP, SMALL, STRIKE, STRONG, SUB, SUP, TD,
TEXTFLOW, TH, TT, U, and VAR

EXAMPLE OF TEXTAREA

`<TEXTAREA COLS=80 ROWS=10 NAME=textarea></TEXTAREA>`

TFOOT

The TFOOT element defines a table footer. This element is optional and is used to distinguish possible rows in the head and body of a table. Closing tag is optional.

Syntax: `<TFOOT>...</TFOOT>`

The TFOOT element is allowed within this element:

TR

The element is allowed inside the following:

TABLE

EXAMPLE OF TFOOT

```
<TABLE>
<THEAD>
<TR>
   </TR>
<TBODY>
<TR>
   </TR>
</TBODY>
<TFOOT>
<TR>
   </TR>
</TFOOT>
</TABLE>
```

TH (TABLE HEADING)

The TH element creates a row or column heading in a table. Elements in the table head are emphasized because they label the columns.

Syntax: `<TD ALIGN=align-type BACKGROUND=url BGCOLOR=color`
`BORDERCOLOR=color BORDERCOLORDARK=color`
`BORDERCOLORLIGHT=color COLSPAN=n NOWRAP=NOWRAP ROWSPAN=n`
`VALIGN=align-type>...</TD>`

The following are options for TH:

ALIGN=*align-type*   Specifies the alignment of the contents of the cell. *align-type* can be one of the following:

LEFT   The contents are left aligned.

CENTER   The contents are centered.

RIGHT   The contents are right aligned.

BACKGROUND=*url*   Specifies a background picture to be tiled in the cell background.

BGCOLOR=*color*	Specifies the background color of the document. Colors are specified in the HEX, 00-FF for each component of the RGB channel in the #RRGGBB format, or by specifying one of the Microsoft Internet Explorer predefined colors: Aqua, Black, Blue, Fuchsia, Gray, Green, Lime, Maroon, Navy, Olive, Purple, Red, Silver, Teal, Yellow, or White.
BORDERCOLOR=*color*	Specifies the border color of the cell. Colors are specified in the HEX, 00-FF for each component of the RGB channel in the #RRGGBB format.
BORDERCOLORDARK=*color*	Specifies the dark color used for drawing tridimensional cell borders. Colors are specified in the HEX, 00-FF for each component of the RGB channel in the #RRGGBB format.
BORDERCOLORLIGHT=*color*	Specifies the light color used for drawing tridimensional cell borders. Colors are specified in the HEX, 00-FF for each component of the RGB channel in the #RRGGBB format.
VALIGN=*align-type*	Specifies the vertical alignment of the objects inside the cell. *align-type* can be one of the following values:

TOP	Text is aligned with the top of the cell.
MIDDLE	Text is centered vertically with the middle of the cell. This is the default setting.
BOTTOM	Text is aligned with the cell's bottom.
BASELINE	Text in neighboring cells is aligned along a common baseline.

The TH element is allowed within these elements:

A, ADDRESS, APPLET, B, BIG, BLOCKQUOTE, BR, CENTER, CITE, CODE, DFN, DIR, DIV, DL, EM, FONT, FORM, H1...H6, HR, I, IMG, INPUT, ISINDEX, KBD, LISTING, MAP, MENU, OL, P, PRE, SAMP, SCRIPT, SELECT, SMALL, STRIKE, STRONG, SUB, SUP, TABLE, TEXTAREA, TT, U, UL, VAR, and XMP

The element is allowed inside the following:

TR

D

EXAMPLE OF TH

```
<TABLE BORDER=3 ALIGN=RIGHT >
<TR>
<TH>Name<TH>Age<TH>Phone
</TR>
</TABLE>
```

THEAD

The THEAD element defines a table header. This element is optional and only one is allowed per table. Its purpose is to give control of the rendering of the rows from those in the table body and table footer.

Syntax: `<THEAD>...</THEAD>`

The THEAD element is allowed within this element:

TR

The element is allowed inside the following:

TABLE

EXAMPLE OF THEAD

```
<TABLE>
<THEAD>
<TR>
    </TR>
<TBODY>
<TR>
    </TR>
</TBODY>
<TFOOT>
<TR>
    </TR>
</TFOOT>
</TABLE>
```

TITLE

The TITLE element specifies the title of the document. The title specified is usually displayed as the window title. This element is only valid within the HEAD element. A closing tag is required.

Syntax: `<TITLE>...</TITLE>`

The TITLE element is allowed within these elements:

Not applicable.

The element is allowed inside the following:

HEAD

EXAMPLE OF TITLE

```
<TITLE>This is the title of my document</TITLE>
```

TR

The TR element creates a row inside a table. The closing tag is optional.

Syntax: `<TR ALIGN=align-type BACKGROUND=url BGCOLOR=color`
               `BORDERCOLOR=color BORDERCOLORDARK=color`
               `BORDERCOLORLIGHT=color VALIGN=align-type>...</TR>`

Options include the following:

ALIGN=align-type	Specifies the alignment of the contents of the cell, align-type can include one of the following:
	LEFT The contents are left aligned.
	CENTER The contents are centered.
	RIGHT The contents are right aligned.
BACKGROUND=url	Specifies a background picture to be tiled in the cell background.
BGCOLOR=color	Specifies the background color of the document. Colors are specified in the HEX, 00-FF for each component of the RGB channel in the #RRGGBB format, or by specifying one of the Microsoft Internet Explorer predefined colors: Aqua, Black, Blue, Fuchsia, Gray, Green, Lime, Maroon, Navy, Olive, Purple, Red, Silver, Teal, Yellow, or White.
BORDERCOLOR=color	Specifies the border color of the cell. Colors are specified in the HEX, 00-FF for each component of the RGB channel in the #RRGGBB format.
BORDERCOLORDARK=color	Specifies the dark color used for drawing tri-dimensional cell borders. Colors are specified in the HEX, 00-FF for each component of the RGB channel in the #RRGGBB format.

BORDERCOLORLIGHT=*color*   Specifies the light color used for drawing tridimensional cell borders. Colors are specified in the HEX, 00-FF for each component of the RGB channel in the #RRGGBB format.

VALIGN=*align-type*   Specifies the vertical alignment of the objects inside the cell. *align-type* can be one of the following values:

TOP   Text is aligned with the top of the cell.

MIDDLE   Text is centered vertically with the middle of the cell. This is the default setting.

BOTTOM   Text is aligned with the cell's bottom.

BASELINE   Text in neighboring cells is aligned along a common baseline.

The TR element is allowed within these elements

TD and TH

The element is allowed inside the following:

TABLE

EXAMPLE OF TR

```
<TABLE>
<TR>
    </TR>
</TABLE>
```

TT (TELETYPE)

The TT element specifies that text should be rendered in a monospace font to simulate output from a teletype.

Syntax: <TT>...</TT>

The TT element is allowed within these elements:

A, APPLET, B, BIG, BR, CITE, CODE, DFN, EM, FONT, I, IMG, INPUT, KBD, MAP, SAMP, SCRIPT, SELECT, SMALL, STRIKE, STRONG, SUB, SUP, TEXTAREA, TT, U, and VAR

The element is allowed inside the following:

A, ADDRESS, B, BIG, BLOCKQUOTE, BODY, CAPTION, CENTER, CITE, CODE, DD, DFN, DIV, DT, EM, FONT, FORM, H1...H6, I, KBD, LI, P, PRE, SAMP, SMALL, STRIKE, STRONG, SUB, SUP, TD, TEXTFLOW, TH, TT, U, and VAR

Figure D.52.
The TT (teletype)
element.

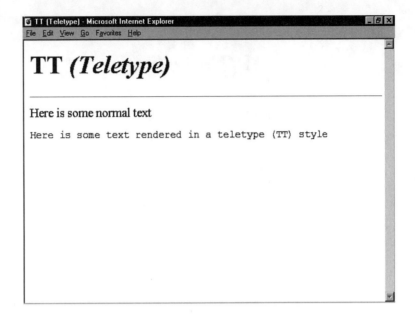

EXAMPLE OF TT

```
...
<TT>
Here is some text rendered in a teletype (TT) style
</TT>
...
```

U (UNDERLINE)

The U element renders emphasis on the text by underlining it.

Syntax: <U>...</U>

The U element is allowed within these elements:

A, APPLET, B, BIG, BR, CITE, CODE, DFN, EM, FONT, I, IMG, INPUT, KBD, MAP, SAMP, SCRIPT, SELECT, SMALL, STRIKE, STRONG, SUB, SUP, TEXTAREA, TT, U, and VAR

The element is allowed inside the following:

A, ADDRESS, B, BIG, BLOCKQUOTE, BODY, CAPTION, CENTER, CITE, CODE, DD, DFN, DIV, DT, EM, FONT, FORM, H1, H2, H3, H4, H5, H6, I, KBD, LI, P, PRE, SAMP, SMALL, STRIKE, STRONG, SUB, SUP, TD, TEXTFLOW, TH, TT, U, and VAR

Figure D.53.
The U *element.*

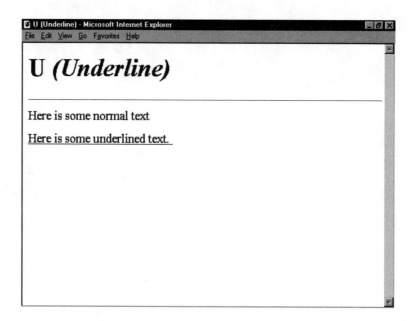

EXAMPLE OF U

```
<U>
Here is some underlined text.
</U>
```

UL (UNORDERED LIST)

The UL element renders lines of text as a bulleted list. Each element in the list is denoted by a LI element. Open and closing tags are required.

Syntax: `<UL COMPACT TYPE=bullet-type>...</UL>`

Options include the following:

COMPACT   This setting suggests that items in the list are rendered in a compact way, by using a smaller font size or by reducing the vertical spacing between items in the list whenever possible.

TYPE=*bullet-type*   Specifies the type of bullet to render. Possible options include

DISK   Renders a standard solid bullet.

SQUARE   Renders a square bullet.

CIRCLE   Renders a nonsolid solid bullet.

The UL element is allowed within this element:

LI

The element is allowed inside the following:

BLOCKQUOTE, BODY, CENTER, DD, DIV, FORM, LI, TD, and TH

VAR

The VAR element renders the enclosed text as a variable. Text is displayed in a small monospaced font. Open and close tags are required.

Figure D.54.
The VAR element.

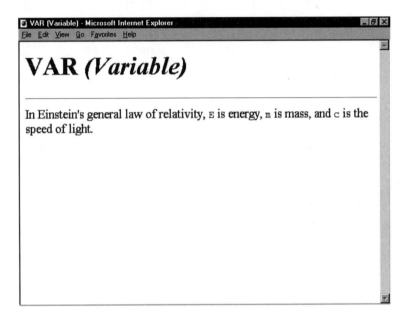

Syntax: <VAR>...</VAR>

The VAR element is allowed within these elements:

A, APPLET, B, BIG, BR, CITE, CODE, DFN, EM, FONT, I, IMG, INPUT, KBD, MAP, SAMP, SCRIPT, SELECT, SMALL, STRIKE, STRONG, SUB, SUP, TEXTAREA, TT, U, and VAR

The element is allowed inside the following:

A, ADDRESS, B, BIG, BLOCKQUOTE, BODY, CAPTION, CENTER, CITE, CODE, DD, DFN, DIV, DT, EM, FONT, FORM, H1, H2, H3, H4, H5, H6, I, KBD, LI, P, PRE, SAMP, SMALL, STRIKE, STRONG, SUB, SUP, TD, TEXTFLOW, TH, TT, U, and VAR

EXAMPLE OF VAR

```
In Einstein's general law of relativity, <VAR>E</VAR> is energy,
<VAR>m</VAR> is mass, and <VAR>c</VAR> is the speed of light.
```

WBR

This element inserts a soft line break in a block of NOBR text. A *soft line break* is used to break a line at a convenient place if necessary.

Syntax: `<WBR>`

The WBR element is allowed within these elements:

Not applicable. Element is not a container.

The element is allowed inside the following:

NOBR

EXAMPLE OF WBR

```
<NOBR>
<P>This is a very long line of text that I want to break here,
<WBR> because I want this line unbroken!
</NOBR>
```

XMP (EXAMPLE)

The XMP element renders text it encloses as an example. Usually, the text is rendered in a monospaced font.

Syntax: `<XMP>...</XMP>`

The XMP element is allowed within these elements:

Not applicable.

The element is allowed inside the following:

BLOCKQUOTE, BODY, CENTER, DD, DIV, FORM, LI, TD, and TH

Figure D.55.
The XMP element.

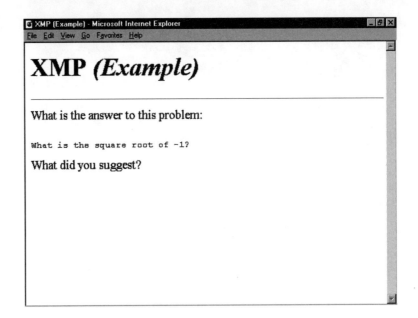

EXAMPLE OF XMP

```
<HTML>
<HEAD>
<TITLE>XMP (Example)</TITLE>
</HEAD>
<BODY>
<H1>XMP <EM>(Example)</EM></H1>
<HR>
What is the answer to this problem:
<P>
<XMP>
What is the square root of -1?
</XMP>
<P>
What did you suggest?
</BODY>
</HTML>
```

APPENDIX E

DNS and BIND Primer

The Internet is a vast collection of networks. Before a computer can talk to another, it needs an address. This address typically takes the form of a name because names are easier for people to remember. Computers, on the other hand, prefer numbers.

Without the Domain Name System (DNS), your computer would need to have a huge address book of names and addresses that included every computer on the Internet. If you wanted to send e-mail to a user at host.foo.com, the system would have to figure out that you wanted to talk to the machine at address 1.2.3.4 and do its thing.

This approach has several problems, including the following:

◆ Your address book would always have to be up-to-date. An old address book would not have entries that were recently added; or worse, if a host changed addresses, you would no longer be able to communicate with that host.

◆ Your address book would have to include every address for every system that you wanted to communicate with.

◆ No two hosts could share the same name.

What a mess! Believe it or not, this was the way that it was until 1984. A large host table (HOSTS.TXT) was maintained in one server at the Stanford Research Institute Network Information Center (the NIC). With more and more networks going online, it became almost impossible to keep the host list up-to-date. Before the list would be downloaded by all hosts, someone would have introduced a change that would require downloading yet another new list!

Vestiges of this address book are still used by your system to look up hosts in your local network— the /etc/hosts file.

DNS: THE DOMAIN NAME SYSTEM

A new system developed by Paul Mockapetris of USC's Information Sciences Institute was proposed as a replacement for HOSTS.TXT. Mockapetris's system addressed the network-load and consistency problems that the infamous HOSTS.TXT system had. Mockapetris's system boasted the following capabilities:

1. The elimination of the single repository for host information would eliminate network traffic problems caused by network administrators downloading an updated version of the HOSTS.TXT file.

2. It would also introduce a name-based domain system, where each domain would have its own internal context; thus allowing for hosts in different domains to have the same name.

3. And most importantly, it would allow for delegation of host information management. The responsibility for managing each network and each network's subdomain was handed to the local administrator for the zone in

question, which made the task of keeping information up-to-date much more manageable. Local host information could be made available globally through the client/server nature of the system, ensuring that each request was answered with reliable data from an authoritative source.

The original DNS system was described in the 1983 Request for Comment (RFC) documents 882 and 883. Both have been updated and superseded in 1987 by RFCs 1034 and 1035, and again in 1990 by RFCs 1101 and 1183, which implement the current specification of the DNS. In software, DNS is implemented on UNIX systems as the Berkeley Internet Name Domain (BIND) system. BIND is shipped in almost every UNIX box.

The current BIND release is composed of several programs including: `named`, `named-xfer`, `named.restart`, `named.reload`, `ndc`, `nslookup`, and the resolver libraries. The resolver libraries provide routines for programs to query DNS name servers, so you can design programs that make use of the DNS. Here's a list of the entire distribution and what each does:

`dig`	A domain information groper; a command line tool that can be used to gather information from a DNS server. It has zillions of options.
`dnsquery`	A program that uses the BIND resolver library calls to query name servers.
`host`	A program that does reverse DNS lookups. Instead of specifying a hostname to find its IP address, you supply the IP, and `host` returns the hostname.
`named-xfer`	A tool for doing zone transfers. Usually this program is called by other software. It can also be used to debug a zone transfer problem. But more than likely you won't use it at all.
`named`	The Internet domain name server daemon, and the focus of my attention in this appendix.
`named.reload`	A convenience program to restart the named daemon and force the server to reload and update its database files, if necessary. This program uses a hangup (SIGHUP) signal.
`named.restart`	A convenience program to restart the named daemon and to force the server to reload and update its database files, if necessary. This program kills the name server by using a kill (SIGKILL) signal and then starts a new server.
`ndc`	A cool program that allows you to send various signals to the named daemon. This command allows you to monitor the status of the server as well as to force database reloads. It has many other options.

WHAT IS DNS?

DNS is a distributed database. By distributed I mean that no single repository contains complete information regarding other domains. A program called *name server* is responsible for implementing the server portion of the equation. When a machine is configured to use DNS, client programs making calls to the `gethostbyname()` and `gethostbyaddr()` library routines use the *resolver* library. This library enables them to query a name server across a network instead of looking up information in the `/etc/host` file.

The structure of the Internet domain system is similar to that of the UNIX file system. There's a root domain and a series of directories called *top-level domains*. In turn, top-level domains are composed of other subdirectories or subdomains. Each domain or subdomain is separated by a dot (.). Each second-level domain can have up to 26 characters. Subdomain labels can have up to 63 characters in length. The root domain is null, meaning there's no label, and is usually represented by empty quotes (`""`). Unlike a file path, domain names are written and read from the bottom up:

```
host.subdomain.domain.topleveldomain
```

The `host` label is the name of the machine.

The `subdomain` label is a subdivision of a domain. Typically subdomains are used to create logical groupings of machines to match some internal organization criteria. Don't be surprised if you ever see more than one subdomain. As a matter of fact, subdomains are common under geographical domain designations.

The `domain` is the domain name of the organization, usually matching the organization's name, such as IBM, APPLE, and NEXT.

The `topleveldomain` is a classification of the domain.

TOP-LEVEL DOMAIN DESIGNATIONS IN THE UNITED STATES

In the United States, the top-level domains are graphically depicted in Figure E.1.

COM	Reserved for commercial organizations such as Digital Equipment Corporation (`digital.com`) or Hewlett-Packard Corporation (`hp.com`).
EDU	Used by educational organizations such as the University of Wisconsin (`uw.edu`).
GOV	Used by U.S. government organizations and agencies such as NASA (`nasa.gov`) or the Federal Bureau of Investigation (`fbi.gov`).

MIL	Reserved for use by the U.S. Armed Forces such as the Air Force (`af.mil`) or the Navy (`navy.mil`).
NET	Reserved for networking organizations and leased line providers such as Internet Connect (`inc.net`), a regional Internet service provider in Wisconsin.
ORG	Reserved for noncommercial organizations such as the popular Electronic Frontier Foundation (`eff.org`).
INT	International organizations such as NATO (`nato.int`).
ARPA	This is a historical domain that was used during transition from the host tables to the DNS. Organizations and networks originally found under this domain have since migrated to their appropriate locations on one of the previous subdomains.

Figure E.1.
The U.S. Top-Level Domains. Domains are shown in ovals. A machine is shown as a box.

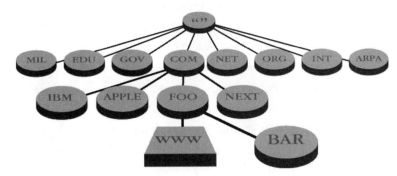

This statement is actually not the full truth. The original classifications originated before the Internet became an international entity. Given its incredible and unexpected success everywhere, additional classifications emerged—geographical designations.

GEOGRAPHICAL DOMAIN DESIGNATIONS

Geographical designations follow the ISO 3166 standard, which establishes a two-letter abbreviation for country names. The only inconsistency is Great Britain, which goes by UK instead of GB. The United States also has a geographical designation, US, which is not yet as widely used as the others. The U.S. geographical domain is supposed to accommodate U.S. state and local government agencies, schools, libraries, museums, and individuals.

Geographical domains are at the same hierarchical level as the standard U.S. domains and are properly registered with the NIC. However, administration of those domains is handled by different organizations in various countries.

The subdomains for the U.S. domain follow postal abbreviation's conventions for the states and territories. Each state can then further subdomain according to an individual city name, locale, plus the hostname.

In addition to the state subdomains, there are two other categories: FED for agencies of the federal government and DNI for Distributed National Institutes or organizations that span state, regional, and other organization boundaries that are national in scope.

Within each state's subdomain there are *locality* names. These can be cities, counties, or local names. The locality can be a CI for city or CO for county:

`hostname.CI.locality.state.US -> pear.CI.CEDARBURG.WI.US`

`hostname.CO.locality.state.US -> apple.CO.MILWAUKEE.WI.US`

A state subdomain groups the following subdomains:

K12	For public schools. Private schools add the PVT name, `schoolname.PVT.K12.state.US`
CC	For community colleges: `collegename.CC.state.US`
TEC	For technical colleges: `collegename.TEC.state.US`
LIB	For libraries: `library.LIB.state.US`
STATE	For state government agencies: `agency.STATE.state.US`
GEN	For General Independent Entity. For anything that doesn't fit in the other categories.

Figure E.2 diagrams the U.S. domain.

Figure E.2.
The U.S. domain.
Notice that other
countries and
standard U.S. top
level domains
share the same
level.

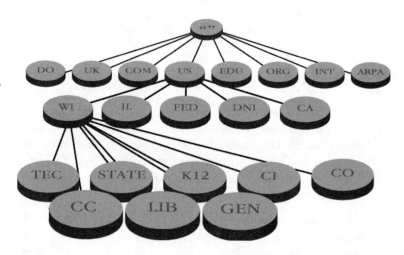

Table E.1 lists all the top-level domains known at the time of this writing. However, this may be outdated by now. This table is a reflection on the dynamics of our world: New countries are formed, and new countries join the Internet community.

TABLE E.1. GEOGRAPHICAL DOMAINS.

Domain	Country or Organization
AD	Andorra
AE	United Arab Emirates
AF	Afghanistan
AG	Antigua and Barbuda
AI	Anguilla
AL	Albania
AM	Armenia
AN	Netherlands Antilles
AO	Angola
AQ	Antarctica
AR	Argentina
AS	American Samoa
AT	Austria
AU	Australia
AW	Aruba
AZ	Azerbaijan
BA	Bosnia and Herzegovina
BB	Barbados
BD	Bangladesh
BE	Belgium
BF	Burkina Faso
BG	Bulgaria
BH	Bahrain
BI	Burundi
BJ	Benin
BM	Bermuda
BN	Brunei Darussalam
BO	Bolivia

continues

TABLE E.1. CONTINUED

Domain	Country or Organization
BR	Brazil
BS	Bahamas
BT	Bhutan
BV	Bouvet Island
BW	Botswana
BY	Belarus
BZ	Belize
CA	Canada
CC	Cocos (Keeling) Islands
CF	Central African Republic
CG	Congo
CH	Switzerland
CI	Cote D'Ivoire (Ivory Coast)
CK	Cook Islands
CL	Chile
CM	Cameroon
CN	China
CO	Colombia
CR	Costa Rica
CS	Czechoslovakia (former)
CU	Cuba
CV	Cape Verde
CX	Christmas Island
CY	Cyprus
CZ	Czech Republic
DE	Germany
DJ	Djibouti
DK	Denmark
DM	Dominica
DO	Dominican Republic
DZ	Algeria
EC	Ecuador

Domain	Country or Organization
EE	Estonia
EG	Egypt
EH	Western Sahara
ER	Eritrea
ES	Spain
ET	Ethiopia
FI	Finland
FJ	Fiji
FK	Falkland Islands (Malvinas)
FM	Micronesia
FO	Faroe Islands
FR	France
FX	France, Metropolitan
GA	Gabon
GD	Grenada
GE	Georgia
GF	French Guiana
GH	Ghana
GI	Gibraltar
GL	Greenland
GM	Gambia
GN	Guinea
GP	Guadeloupe
GQ	Equatorial Guinea
GR	Greece
GS	S. Georgia and S. Sandwich Isls.
GT	Guatemala
GU	Guam
GW	Guinea-Bissau
GY	Guyana
HK	Hong Kong
HM	Heard and McDonald Islands

continues

E

DNS AND BIND PRIMER

TABLE E.1. CONTINUED

Domain	Country or Organization
HN	Honduras
HR	Croatia (Hrvatska)
HT	Haiti
HU	Hungary
ID	Indonesia
IE	Ireland
IL	Israel
IN	India
IO	British Indian Ocean Territory
IQ	Iraq
IR	Iran
IS	Iceland
IT	Italy
JM	Jamaica
JO	Jordan
JP	Japan
KE	Kenya
KG	Kyrgyzstan
KH	Cambodia
KI	Kiribati
KM	Comoros
KN	Saint Kitts and Nevis
KP	Korea (North)
KR	Korea (South)
KW	Kuwait
KY	Cayman Islands
KZ	Kazakhstan
LA	Laos
LB	Lebanon
LC	Saint Lucia
LI	Liechtenstein
LK	Sri Lanka

Domain	Country or Organization
LR	Liberia
LS	Lesotho
LT	Lithuania
LU	Luxembourg
LV	Latvia
LY	Libya
MA	Morocco
MC	Monaco
MD	Moldova
MG	Madagascar
MH	Marshall Islands
MK	Macedonia
ML	Mali
MM	Myanmar
MN	Mongolia
MO	Macau
MP	Northern Mariana Islands
MQ	Martinique
MR	Mauritania
MS	Montserrat
MT	Malta
MU	Mauritius
MV	Maldives
MW	Malawi
MX	Mexico
MY	Malaysia
MZ	Mozambique
NA	Namibia
NC	New Caledonia
NE	Niger
NF	Norfolk Island
NG	Nigeria

E

DNS AND BIND PRIMER

continues

TABLE E.1. CONTINUED

Domain	Country or Organization
NI	Nicaragua
NL	Netherlands
NO	Norway
NP	Nepal
NR	Nauru
NT	Neutral Zone
NU	Niue
NZ	New Zealand (Aotearoa)
OM	Oman
PA	Panama
PE	Peru
PF	French Polynesia
PG	Papua New Guinea
PH	Philippines
PK	Pakistan
PL	Poland
PM	St. Pierre and Miquelon
PN	Pitcairn
PR	Puerto Rico
PT	Portugal
PW	Palau
PY	Paraguay
QA	Qatar
RE	Reunion
RO	Romania
RU	Russian Federation
RW	Rwanda
SA	Saudi Arabia
SB	Solomon Islands
SC	Seychelles
SD	Sudan
SE	Sweden

Domain	Country or Organization
SG	Singapore
SH	St. Helena
SI	Slovenia
SJ	Svalbard and Jan Mayen Islands
SK	Slovak Republic
SL	Sierra Leone
SM	San Marino
SN	Senegal
SO	Somalia
SR	Suriname
ST	Sao Tome and Principe
SU	USSR (former)
SV	El Salvador
SY	Syria
SZ	Swaziland
TC	Turks and Caicos Islands
TD	Chad
TF	French Southern Territories
TG	Togo
TH	Thailand
TJ	Tajikistan
TK	Tokelau
TM	Turkmenistan
TN	Tunisia
TO	Tonga
TP	East Timor
TR	Turkey
TT	Trinidad and Tobago
TV	Tuvalu
TW	Taiwan
TZ	Tanzania

E

DNS AND BIND PRIMER

continues

TABLE E.1. CONTINUED

Domain	Country or Organization
UA	Ukraine
UG	Uganda
UK	United Kingdom
UM	U.S. Minor Outlying Islands
US	United States
UY	Uruguay
UZ	Uzbekistan
VA	Vatican City State (Holy See)
VC	Saint Vincent and the Grenadines
VE	Venezuela
VG	Virgin Islands (British)
VI	Virgin Islands (U.S.)
VN	Vietnam
VU	Vanuatu
WF	Wallis and Futuna Islands
WS	Samoa
YE	Yemen
YT	Mayotte
YU	Yugoslavia
ZA	South Africa
ZM	Zambia
ZR	Zaire
ZW	Zimbabwe
COM	U.S. commercial
EDU	U.S. educational
GOV	U.S. government
INT	International
MIL	U.S. military
NET	Network
ORG	Nonprofit organization
ARPA	Old style Arpanet
NATO	NATO field

How named WORKS

named (pronounced name-d) is the BIND name server daemon. This software answers queries about hostnames and IP addresses. When named doesn't know the answer to a query, it asks other servers (typically in the top-level domains) that provide information on how to contact other name servers responsible for the domain in question. named caches this information in case there's a need to find another host near that domain. This allows it to ask a closer name server for the answer in future queries. This effectively skips the top-level name servers from the process and reduces the overall effort required to obtain the new address.

There are three types of name servers:

◆ Primary

◆ Secondary

◆ Caching-only

Name servers are distinguished by the source of their information and if the server providing the information is authoritative for the domain. Authoritative name servers provide information that is "guaranteed" to be correct. While nonauthoritative answers are usually correct, primary and secondary servers for a domain are the only servers authoritative for the information. Caching-only name servers are never authoritative, although they help speed up the process a great deal.

I should qualify the guaranteed qualifier I used in the last paragraph. It is possible for information provided by a secondary name server to be stale. Unless the system administrator manually updates the secondary servers, it is possible for secondary servers to distribute stale information until their *refresh period* expires. A refresh period forces secondary name servers to check for changes on the domain database file after the period of time specified by the administrator managing the domain is complete. Typically this period is no longer than six hours.

If you were wondering about the reliability of cached information, it will satisfy your curiosity to learn that DNS information is usually cached for a little while. Cached information exists only until the Time To Live (TTL) delay expires. The TTL for DNS-cached records is usually set to one day. You should also be aware that the top-level and sometimes second-level domain name servers never cache information. Otherwise, top-level information could be vulnerable to tainted information. Also, because of the amount of information they handle, their caches would quickly grow and bloat, which increases the computational load required to find an answer.

RUNNING YOUR OWN DOMAIN NAME SERVER

Before you proceed, you will need to register your domain name with the InterNIC if your domain falls into any of the ORG, NET, EDU, GOV, and COM domains. If you want to register a U.S. domain, go to http://www.isi.edu/in-notes/usdnr.

Registering your domain involves a few steps:

1. Figure out where in the domain hierarchy your organization falls.
2. Find a domain name that is not in use by another site in that domain hierarchy.
3. If you are not on the Internet yet, find someone who will host a temporary name server for you.
4. Fill out an application.
5. Wait for the application to be approved.

Registering your domain can be a great thing. It establishes your identity in the Internet and makes you available to the world. To search for names that have not been taken, you can visit http://rs.internic.net for searches involving ORG, NET, EDU, GOV, and COM domains. To search in the U.S. subdomain, visit http://www.isi.edu/in-notes/usdnr).

Choose the registration services link. Once on that page, choose the *Whois registration tool*. This page gives you a Web interface to the whois program. The whois program allows you to research domain name information among other things. If you find a match, your name is in use. Some things to keep in mind: domain names cannot be longer than 26 characters and can contain only letters, digits, and dashes.

Once you find a name that is not in use, you can go ahead and complete the World Wide Web application form. You will need to have the address for two name servers that supply information about your domain. The machines you list in the application will be queried for information about your domain, so you need to make sure that they are reachable or if your network is not up, that someone runs DNS for you temporarily. Usually your service provider can help with this. If the name servers are not found during the verification process, your application will be delayed.

Once you complete the online form, a copy of the application will be mailed to you. Please note that the application you filled online is not processed. To process the request you need to e-mail the form back to domreg@internic.net.

A small charge is associated with registering a domain name. New registrations cost $100, and the registration is good for two years. Subsequent renewals are $50/year. If you don't pay your registration fee, the top-level domain servers will forget about your domain, and no one will be able to reach you. That's power!

Once your domain is approved, you are ready to set up your own domain name server. Approvals can take anywhere from one day to three weeks depending on load and other things.

To run a domain name server, you will need to install BIND. The source for BIND can be found at `ftp://ftp.vix.com/pub/bind/release/bind.tar.gz` or from `http://www.isc.org/isc`. For your convenience, a copy has been included on the CD-ROM that accompanies this book.

Once you obtain the source, you should follow the compilation instructions in the package. The official release at the time I grabbed my copy was 4.9.3. As usual, running outdated software creates a source of security problems. If your system comes with an older version of the software, you really should upgrade. The installation steps are as follows:

1. FTP the source.

2. Unpack the source.

3. Change your directory to the BIND distribution directory.

4. Create a build directory by issuing a `make DST=build links`.

5. Cd to the build directory you just created.

6. Set the appropriate options, if any, in `conf/options.h`.

7. Configure the makefile for settings appropriate for your *machine/os*. This is easily done by removing the `#` from all the lines under the section that describes your operating system. If you have special locations where you want the binaries installed, set the `DEST` (for destination) variable to a path more palatable to you.

Tip

> To avoid confusion, keep the default paths and rename your distribution copies of `named` and `nslookup` that came with your system to `named.dist` and `nslookup.dist`, respectively. This way you can keep your original binaries in case you run into trouble and you need to revert to something known to work.

8. Type `make` to build everything.

If compilation fails, you may want to add `./bin` to your path. You can do this simply enough on a `csh` by issuing the following:

```
set path = (./bin $path)
```

After `make` builds everything, you will want to verify which files are going to be installed. Issue a `make -n install` to see where `make` wants to install everything. This will list all the commands that are going to be executed by the install target without actually running them. You should then backup or rename any remaining files that are going to be replaced with an `.orig` extension.

If you are running SunOS 4.1.x, NetBSD-1 or Solaris 2.x, you can integrate the new client-side resolver library into your system shared libraries. This will upgrade all dynamically linked programs to use the new libraries instead of the old ones. For more information, read the information included in the `shres` directory of the BIND release.

If the installation proceeded properly, BIND should now be installed in your system. Congratulations!

DNS CONFIGURATION FILES

The first step in setting up your DNS database is to convert your existing `/etc/hosts` file into its equivalent DNS format. To configure DNS you'll need to create a few databases and startup files. I placed everything in `/usr/local/named` with the exception of `/etc/named.boot`. `named`, which looks by default for its boot file in `/etc/named.boot`. To get things running, you'll need to create a few files (replace `DOMAIN` with your domain name, and `IP` with your network IP address):

   ◆ `/etc/named.boot`
   ◆ `/usr/local/named/db.DOMAIN`
   ◆ `/usr/local/named/db.IP`
   ◆ `/usr/local/named/db.127.0.0`

The `db` files: `db.DOMAIN` and `db.IP`, contain hostname-to-IP and IP-to-hostname translation tables, respectively. The basic components for these files are

   ◆ SOA Record
   ◆ NS Records
   ◆ Address and Alias Records
   ◆ PTR Records

While the structure of the `db` files is similar, there's one significant difference. I mentioned that the `db.DOMAIN` maps hosts to IP addresses. Data in DNS is indexed by name, including addresses. Mapping from an IP address to a hostname (the reverse) actually turns out to be a little more difficult. Given the current design, searching for a name would require searching the entire database until a match was found. Obviously, this would not be very efficient. To solve the problem, the designers of DNS created a special domain that uses IP addresses as names. This domain is called the `IN-ADDR.ARPA` domain.

REVERSE LOOKUPS: IP TO HOSTNAME, THE IN-ADDR.ARPA DOMAIN

The IN-ADDR.ARPA domain has four levels of subdomains. Each level represents one of the octets in a 32-bit IP address. Each level has 256 (from 0 to 255) subdomains, each named after each possible octet value.

The IN-ADDR.ARPA domain has enough room for every host on the Internet given the current 32-bit (four-octet) IP representation.

Remember the domain names are read from the bottom up, like *host.domain.dom*. Because of this, IN-ADDR.ARPA domains are represented with their IP addresses in reverse.

If your host IP address is 1.2.3.4, your host number is 4, and the IN-ADDR.ARPA name would be written as 4.3.2.1.IN-ADDR.ARPA.

This way the name server can group, organize, and retrieve IP-to-hostname queries as efficiently as the regular name-based queries.

Before you proceed, you may want to create your db.*DOMAIN* and db.*IP* files. I created mine in /usr/local/named and renamed *DOMAIN* and *IP* to the name of my domain and network IP, respectively (db.ACCESSLINK.COM and db.204.95.222).

SOA RECORD

A start of authority (SOA) resource record is the first entry in a db file. This record indicates that the name server is authoritative. An authoritative name server provides the most accurate and reliable information about a domain. A single SOA record is required at the beginning of each db.*DOMAIN* and db.*IP* file.

An SOA record looks like this:

```
domain.dom IN SOA hostname.domain.dom. root.domain.dom. {
1     ; Serial ID
10800    ; Record Refresh in seconds (3 hours)
3600    ; Retry after one hour (in seconds)
604800   ; Expire after one week (in seconds)
86400 )   ; Minimum TTL (Time to live) of one day
```

On your db.*DOMAIN* file, replace *domain.dom* with the name of your domain (for example, acme.com).

IN stands for Internet. There are other possible values, but for this example, and more likely for your needs, this will fit the bill.

Replace *hostname.domain.dom.* with the fully qualified domain name of the host where you are creating this data. Note that the trailing period needs to be there.

Replace `root.domain.dom.` with a valid e-mail address for the person managing your DNS. Replace the @ sign on the e-mail address with a period. Again, note that there's a trailing period after the address.

The serial id of the record is very important. Any time you update any of the database files, you must increment this number. If for some reason you forget to increment the serial id, the secondary name servers won't realize that you have modified the database and won't update their information. Secondary name servers use this number to determine if their copy of the `db` file is up-to-date. A good strategy is to put the current date in a format such as *YYYYMMDDR* where

> *YYYY* is the year: 1996.
>
> *MM* is the month: 06.
>
> *DD* is the day: 30.
>
> *R* is the number of the revision (in case you modify the file more than once on the same day): 1.
>
> The *refresh interval* tells the secondary server how often to check for updates on this file.
>
> The *retry interval* tells the secondary server how long to wait before trying to reach the primary server, if the initial attempt failed.

If the secondary server repeatedly fails to contact the primary after the *expire interval*, data on the database is going to be considered stale, and the secondary server will stop responding to requests for the domain.

The TTL value specifies how long resource records served from this file will remain in a caching server's cache. After the TTL expires, the server will have to requery your server for information about your domain.

NS RECORDS

Next, you need to specify the names of domain name servers in your domain. You do this by using name server (NS) resource records. They look like this:

```
"domain.dom IN NS hostname.domain.dom."
```

All domain name servers that you list here will be designated authoritative for the domain. Replace `domain.dom` and `hostname.domain.dom.` with the name of your domain (don't forget the period) and the fully qualified domain name of the domain name server. An example of this is as follows:

```
ACCESSLINK.COM IN NS ns1.ACCESSLINK.COM.
ACCESSLINK.COM IN NS ns2.ACCESSLINK.COM.
```

ADDRESS AND ALIAS RECORDS

Now you'll create name-to-address mappings. Resource records for Address and Alias Records look like this:

```
; Host Addresses
localhost   IN  A  127.0.0.1
router      IN  A  204.95.222.100
www         IN  A  204.95.222.200
hydrogen    IN  A  204.95.222.1
lithium     IN  A  204.95.222.3

; Aliases
mailhost    IN  CNAME hydrogen.ACCESSLINK.COM.
ns1         IN  CNAME hydrogen.ACCESSLINK.COM.
ns2         IN  CNAME  lithium.ACCESSLINK.COM.
ftp         IN  CNAME hydrogen.ACCESSLINK.COM.
```

THE db.IP FILE

The db.IP file stores an IP-to-name lookup table. The main difference between the two is that instead of listing regular IP addresses, it uses the funny IN-ADDR.ARPA notation.

Like the db.DOMAIN file, the db.IP file has an SOA Record. The only difference is that the name of the domain is specified as IN-ADDR.ARPA domain notation:

```
222.95.204.IN-ADDR.ARPA IN SOA hostname.domain.dom. root.domain.dom. {
1       ; Serial ID
10800    ; Record Refresh in seconds (3 hours)
3600     ; Retry after one hour (in seconds)
604800   ; Expire after one week (in seconds)
86400 )   ; Minimum TTL (Time to live) of one day
```

The db.IP file also lists NS resource records. These are also specified in IN-ADDR.ARPA domain notation:

```
1.222.95.204.IN-ADDR.ARPA.  IN NS ns1.ACCESSLINK.COM.
3.222.95.204.IN-ADDR.ARPA.  IN NS ns2.ACCESSLINK.COM.
```

In addition, the db.IP file also lists its reverse version of the Address Records (IN A entries, in your db.DOMAIN file). These are called PTR Records.

PTR RECORDS

The DNS resource records used for IP-to-name mappings are called Pointer (PTR) Records. There's one record for each IP address on your network. All IP addresses are specified using the IN-ADDR.ARPA domain notation:

```
1.222.95.204    IN PTR hydrogen.ACCESSLINK.COM.
3.222.95.204    IN PTR lithium.ACCESSLINK.COM.
100.222.95.204 IN PTR router.ACCESSLINK.COM.
200.222.95.204 IN PTR www.ACCESSLINK.COM.
```

THE LOOPBACK INTERFACE

In addition to the db.DOMAIN and db.IP files, the server will need a db.IP file for the loopback interface. This is a special IP address that hosts use to route traffic to themselves. The address of the loopback network is (almost always) 127.0.0.0, and the host number for the localhost is 127.0.0.1.

The file is pretty standard. If you copy your other db.IP file, you'll only need to delete all PTR records and insert a new PTR record pointing to the localhost, the last line in the following listing:

```
222.95.204.IN-ADDR.ARPA IN SOA hostname.domain.dom. root.ACCESSLINK.COM. {
1        ; Serial ID
10800    ; Record Refresh in seconds (3 hours)
3600     ; Retry after one hour (in seconds)
604800   ; Expire after one week (in seconds)
86400 )  ; Minimum TTL (Time to live) of one day

; Name Servers
;
1.222.95.204.IN-ADDR.ARPA.   IN NS ns1.ACCESSLINK.COM.
3.222.95.204.IN-ADDR.ARPA.   IN NS ns2.ACCESSLINK.COM.
;
; localhost
1.0.0.127.IN-ADDR.ARPA. IN PTR localhost.
```

THE named.root FILE

In addition to knowing all the gory details about your network, DNS needs to know how to contact the name servers for the root domain. Your BIND release should have included a copy of this file. If not, you can find a copy at

```
ftp://ftp.rs.internic.net/domain/named.root
```

This file is used only at startup. After named is able to contact the top-level name servers, it updates its internal information.

THE /etc/named.boot FILE

If you are following at the terminal, you have now developed and downloaded all the files you need to get named going. However, you need to create a configuration file that can tell named where to find all its files. If you have followed my example and created your files in /usr/local/named, your boot file will look like this:

```
directory /usr/local/named
primary domain.dom  db.DOMAIN
primary xxx.xxx.xxx.IN-ADDR.ARPA  db.IP
primary 0.0.127.IN-ADDR.ARPA db.127.0.0
cache . named.root
```

Here's how my boot file looks after I replace the placeholders with the naming convention described earlier:

```
directory /usr/local/named
primary ACCESSLINK.COM  db.ACCESSLINK
primary 222.95.204.IN-ADDR.ARPA  db.204.95.222
primary 0.0.127.IN-ADDR.ARPA db.127.0.0
cache . named.root
```

STARTING named

To start the name server as root on a terminal, type:

```
/etc/named.
```

If you located your boot file somewhere other than in the default `/etc/named.boot`, you can tell `named` where to look for it by using the `-b` flag, `/etc/named -b` *pathtobootfile*.

If there were any errors in your configuration files, `named` will log an error using `syslog`, and if the error is bad enough, it will quit. To see where `named` will log any errors, type in the following:

```
grep daemon /etc/syslog.conf
```

This will print the name of the file where `named` will log errors to. In my case, the result of this command is `/usr/adm/messages`; yours may be `/usr/var/messages` or something like that. Please note that by default `named` logs a `restart` message whenever it starts. It is very likely that if you made a typo or forgot to enter a field, `named` will complain by saying ...`Unknown type:`... or ...`unknown field 'foo'`.... Look for the offending line and compare it to the examples.

TESTING YOUR NAME SERVER

If `named` started correctly, then you can use `nslookup` to see if it is serving information correctly. If your machine was not on the Internet before, chances are that you have not set the domain name for it. On some systems this is done with the `hostname` command. Other systems use `domainname`. To check if your system has been set up, type `hostname` (or `domainname`) on a terminal.

If the domain name has not been set up, the superuser can set it up by giving the command an argument:

```
domainname domain.dom
```

Replace *domain.dom* with the name of your domain. You may want this to happen automatically at the system startup time. Just include the line `domainname domain.dom` on your `/etc/rc.local` or equivalent system startup file.

To see if it is all working correctly, type the following:

```
% nslookup lithium
Server: ns1.ACCESSLINK.COM
Address: 204.95.222.1


Name:    lithium.ACCESSLINK.COM
Address: 204.95.222.3
```

You may want to also see if you can use nslookup to find a machine out of your network:

```
% nslookup www.next.com
Server: ns1.ACCESSLINK.COM
Address: 204.95.222.1

Non-authoritative answer:
Name:    ftp.next.com
Address: 129.18.1.3
Aliases: www.next.com
```

A final test involves querying a remote name server to see if it can obtain your address. You can do this easily with nslookup by specifying the address of the remote name server after the host you are looking for:

```
% nslookup lithium.accesslink.com beta.inc.net
Server: ns1.inc.net
Address: 204.95.160.2


Name:    lithium.ACCESSLINK.COM
Address: 204.95.222.3
```

If it works, then you'll probably want named to be started up when you reboot the computer. You can accomplish this easily enough by putting an entry such as the following in your /etc/rc.local file:

```
if -f [/etc/named.boot]; then
  echo "starting named ..."
  /usr/etc/named
fi
```

The preceding script will check to see if your /etc/named.boot file exists in the /etc directory. If it does, name server is started.

Tip

If when you Telnet or FTP to other machines, you find that there's a long lag (10 seconds or so) between connecting and receiving a login prompt, more than likely your reverse DNS lookups are not working properly. It is possible that your ISP, to whom your IP addresses are registered, is not providing the proper information. Have them check their DNS information.

Congratulations, your primary name server is now running.

CONFIGURING A SECONDARY NAME SERVER

Configuring a secondary name server is a lot less work. You should strongly consider running a secondary name server on your site or have someone else run one for you. It is even better to have someone else run DNS for you at another site, and remember to add the address of that name server to your domain registration form. This will ensure that if your name servers go down, your network doesn't grid to a halt.

To build a secondary name server, follow these steps:

1. Install the software as you did for your primary name server.
2. Copy `/etc/named.boot` to the other computer's `/etc` directory.
3. Copy `/usr/local/named/named.root` and `db.127.0.0` to `/usr/local/named/` on the other computer.
4. Edit the file `/etc/named.boot` on your secondary server. Change all instances of primary to secondary, with the exception of the line referring to `db.127.0.0`. This name server is also primary for the loopback address; it is its own loopback address.

And that's it. To finish, copy the startup commands you put in your primary server's `rc.local` file.

On starting the secondary server, it will transfer a copy of all the databases to the `/usr/local/named` directory.

CONFIGURING HOSTS IN YOUR NETWORK TO USE THE NAME SERVER

Before any client in your network can use your name server, you'll need to create the `/etc/resolv.conf` file. This file contains a list of all the name servers in your network and the order in which they are queried. The basic format is as follows:

```
search domainname...
nameserver ipaddress
```

AccessLINK's looks like this:

```
seach accesslink.com
nameserver 204.95.222.1
nameserver 204.95.222.2
```

SUMMARY

Because the intention of this appendix was to provide you with a basic reference and to help you quickly set up DNS, the information is by no means complete. DNS is not particularly complicated. However, complex networks require complex DNS setups, and as should be expected, powerful software cannot be mastered in an appendix; DNS keeps the Internet running. This appendix gets your DNS running; it is not an absolute reference on the subject. For more information, I would suggest that you read the documentation included with your release of DNS. If you FTPed the package, it contains excellent documentation as well as a frequently asked questions (FAQ) list. As for printed information, the following might be helpful.

DNS and BIND, by Paul Albitz & Cricket Liu, is published by O'Reilly and Associates, Inc. It's a great book. However, some of the information is a little out-of-date.

For an excellent UNIX system administration book, the best this author has ever seen, check out *UNIX System Administration Handbook*, now in its second edition. While it is impossible to cover UNIX in one volume, it does an excellent job of explaining the art of UNIX system administration. It has more than enough detail to get you going. This book was written by Evi Nemeth, Garth Snyder, Scott Seebass, and Trent R. Hein. It is published by Prentice Hall.

A

Index

X–Y–Z

Netscape Server Survival Guide

—David Gulbransen Jr.

With the recent reduction in the price of its server technology, Netscape's marketability is increasing. Both current and migrating Netscape administrators alike will need the comprehensive coverage found in this book.

This book teaches the reader how to install, configure, and maintain a Netscape server. It also discusses third-party products, commonly used Netscape utilities, and offers an extensive troubleshooting guide. The CD-ROM contains software demonstrations, sample configuration files, and exotic logon scripts.

Price: $49.99 USA/$70.95 CDN   *User Level: Accomplished–Expert*
ISBN: 1-57521-111-4   *800 pages*

CGI Programming Unleashed

—Daniel Berlin, et al.

Readers learn to master CGI—a popular scripting language used to develop professional Web content. Unlike other titles on the subject, this book is devoted entirely to CGI and covers every aspect of this popular tool. Programmers will create end-user Internet applications that run programs on a Web server.

This book teaches CGI and HTML integration. The CD-ROM contains source code from the book and powerful utilities.

Price: $49.99 USA/$70.95 CDN   *User Level: Accomplished–Expert*
ISBN: 1-57521-151-3   *800 pages*

Client/Server Unleashed

—Neil Jenkins, et al.

This book leads the reader through the often confusing client/server world. It defines every aspect of the client/server architecture and gives an overview of all the products and tools. Readers will be conceptually lead through all the major steps in planning and implementing their client/server architecture.

This book guides the reader through planning projects and evaluating business considerations. It also covers migration from standard systems to client/server systems. The CD-ROM contains demonstrations of various products and a multimedia client/server product encyclopedia.

Price: $45.00 USA/$63.95 CDN   *User Level: Accomplished–Expert*
ISBN: 0-672-30726-X   *1,200 pages*

Netscape 3 Unleashed, Second Edition

—Dick Oliver

Readers learn how to fully exploit the new features of this latest version of Netscape—the most popular Web browser in use today. The book teaches how to install, configure, and use Netscape Navigator 3.0 and covers how to add interactivity to Web pages with Netscape. The CD-ROM includes Netscape Navigator™ 3, source code from the book, and powerful utilities.

Price: $49.99 USA/$70.95 CDN   *User Level: Accomplished–Expert*
ISBN: 1-57521-164-5   *1,000 pages*

Intranets Unleashed

—Sams.net Development Group

Intranets—internal Web sites that can be accessed within a company's firewalls—are quickly becoming the status quo in business. This book shows IS managers and personnel how to effectively set up and run large or small intranets. Everything from design to security is discussed. The CD-ROM contains source code and valuable utilities.

Price: $59.99 USA/$84.95 CDN   *User Level: Accomplished–Expert*
ISBN: 1-57521-115-7   *900 pages*

Perl 5 Unleashed

—Kamran Husain, et al.

Perl 5 Unleashed is for the programmer who wants to get the most out of Perl. This comprehensive book provides in-depth coverage on all Perl programming topics, including using Perl in Web pages. This is the reference Perl programmers will turn to for the best coverage of Perl. It includes coverage of these and other Perl topics: scalar values, lists and array variables, reading and writing files, subroutines, control structures, Internet scripting, system functions, debugging, and many more. It covers Version 5. The CD-ROM includes source code from the book, programming and administration tools, and libraries.

Price: $49.99 USA/$70.95 CDN   *User Level: Intermediate–Advanced*
ISBN: 0-672-30891-6   *800 pages*

HTML 3.2 & CGI Unleashed, Professional Reference Edition

—John December

Readers will learn the logistics of how to create compelling, information-rich Web pages that grab the readers' attention and keep users returning for more. This comprehensive professional instruction and reference guide for World Wide Web covers all aspects of the development processes, implementation, tools, and programming. The book covers the new HTML 3.2 specification, plus new topics like Java, JavaScript and ActiveX. The CD-ROM features coverage of planning, analysis, design, HTML implementation, and gateway programming.

Price: $59.99 USA/$84.95 CDN   *User Level: Accomplished–Expert*
ISBN: 1-57521-177-7   *900 pages*

Java Developer's Reference

—Mike Cohn, et al.

This is the information resource-packed development package for professional developers. It explains the components of the Java Development Kit (JDK) and the Java programming language. Everything needed to program Java is included within this comprehensive reference, making it the tool developers will turn to over and over again for timely, accurate information on Java and the JDK. The book includes tips and tricks for getting the most from Java and your Java programs. It also contains complete descriptions of all the package classes and their individual methods. The CD-ROM contains source code from the book and powerful utilities.

Price: $59.99 USA/$84.95 CDN   *User Level: Accomplished–Expert*
ISBN: 1-57521-129-7   *1,400 pages*

Add to Your Sams.net Library Today
with the Best Books for Internet Technologies

ISBN	Quantity	Description of Item	Unit Cost	Total Cost
1-57521-111-4		Netscape Server Survival Guide (Book/CD-ROM)	$49.99	
1-57521-151-3		CGI Programming Unleashed (Book/CD-ROM)	$49.99	
0-672-30726-X		Client/Server Unleashed (Book/CD-ROM)	$45.00	
1-57521-164-5		Netscape 3 Unleashed, Second Edition (Book/CD-ROM)	$49.99	
1-57521-115-7		Intranets Unleashed (Book/CD-ROM)	$59.99	
0-672-30891-6		Perl 5 Unleashed (Book/CD-ROM)	$49.99	
1-57521-177-7		HTML 3.2 & CGI Unleashed, Professional Reference Edition (Book/CD-ROM)	$59.99	
1-57521-129-7		Java Developer's Reference (Book/CD-ROM)	$59.99	
		Shipping and Handling: See information below.		
		TOTAL		

Shipping and Handling: $4.00 for the first book, and $1.75 for each additional book. If you need to have it NOW, we can ship product to you in 24 hours for an additional charge of approximately $18.00, and you will receive your item overnight or in two days. Overseas shipping and handling adds $2.00. Prices subject to change. Call between 9:00 a.m. and 5:00 p.m. EST for availability and pricing information on latest editions.

201 W. 103rd Street, Indianapolis, Indiana 46290

1-800-428-5331 — Orders   1-800-835-3202 — FAX   1-800-858-7674 — Customer Service

Book ISBN 1-57521-175-0